Career Re-Invention in the Post-Pandemic Era

Shalin Hai-Jew
Kansas State University, USA

A volume in the Advances in Business Strategy and Competitive Advantage (ABSCA) Book Series

IGI Global
PUBLISHER of TIMELY KNOWLEDGE

Published in the United States of America by
IGI Global
Business Science Reference (an imprint of IGI Global)
701 E. Chocolate Avenue
Hershey PA, USA 17033
Tel: 717-533-8845
Fax: 717-533-8661
E-mail: cust@igi-global.com
Web site: http://www.igi-global.com

Library of Congress Cataloging-in-Publication Data

Names: Hai-Jew, Shalin, editor.
Title: Career re-invention in the post pandemic era / Shalin Hai-Jew, editor.
Description: Hershey, PA : Business Science Reference, [2022] | Includes bibliographical references and index. | Summary: "This work explores the present moment with 470 million people around the world who are unemployed and / or under-employed (according to UN numbers) and who need to meet basic survival needs in a time of high disruption (in the middle of the COVID-19 pandemic) encouraging new thinking, exploring who they are and what they are capable of as they acquire new knowledge and skills"-- Provided by publisher.
Identifiers: LCCN 2021035367 (print) | LCCN 2021035368 (ebook) | ISBN 9781799886266 (hardcover) | ISBN 9781799886273 (paperback) | ISBN 9781799886280 (ebook)
Subjects: LCSH: Career changes. | Career development. | Vocational guidance. | Organizational change.
Classification: LCC HF5384 .C37 2022 (print) | LCC HF5384 (ebook) | DDC 650.14--dc23
LC record available at https://lccn.loc.gov/2021035367
LC ebook record available at https://lccn.loc.gov/2021035368

This book is published in the IGI Global book series Advances in Business Strategy and Competitive Advantage (ABSCA) (ISSN: 2327-3429; eISSN: 2327-3437)

British Cataloguing in Publication Data
A Cataloguing in Publication record for this book is available from the British Library.

Advances in Business Strategy and Competitive Advantage (ABSCA) Book Series

ISSN:2327-3429
EISSN:2327-3437

Editor-in-Chief: Patricia Ordóñez de Pablos Universidad de Oviedo, Spain

MISSION

Business entities are constantly seeking new ways through which to gain advantage over their competitors and strengthen their position within the business environment. With competition at an all-time high due to technological advancements allowing for competition on a global scale, firms continue to seek new ways through which to improve and strengthen their business processes, procedures, and profitability.

The **Advances in Business Strategy and Competitive Advantage (ABSCA) Book Series** is a timely series responding to the high demand for state-of-the-art research on how business strategies are created, implemented and re-designed to meet the demands of globalized competitive markets. With a focus on local and global challenges, business opportunities and the needs of society, the **ABSCA** encourages scientific discourse on doing business and managing information technologies for the creation of sustainable competitive advantage.

COVERAGE

- Globalization
- Ethics and Business Strategy
- Differentiation Strategy
- Co-operative Strategies
- Business Models
- Value Creation
- Entrepreneurship & Innovation
- Joint Ventures
- Outsourcing
- Innovation Strategy

IGI Global is currently accepting manuscripts for publication within this series. To submit a proposal for a volume in this series, please contact our Acquisition Editors at Acquisitions@igi-global.com or visit: http://www.igi-global.com/publish/.

The Advances in Business Strategy and Competitive Advantage (ABSCA) Book Series (ISSN 2327-3429) is published by IGI Global, 701 E. Chocolate Avenue, Hershey, PA 17033-1240, USA, www.igi-global.com. This series is composed of titles available for purchase individually; each title is edited to be contextually exclusive from any other title within the series. For pricing and ordering information please visit http://www.igi-global.com/book-series/advances-business-strategy-competitive-advantage/73672. Postmaster: Send all address changes to above address.

Titles in this Series

For a list of additional titles in this series, please visit:
www.igi-global.com/book-series/advances-business-strategy-competitive-advantage/73672

Cases on Digital Strategies and Management Issues in Modern Organizations
José Duarte Santos (Instituto Superior Politecnico, Spain)
Business Science Reference • © 2022 • 365pp • H/C (ISBN: 9781799816300) • US $195.00

Employee Share Ownership and Impacts on Organizational Value and Behavior
Sara Elouadi (Hassan II University, Casablanca, Morocco)
Business Science Reference • © 2022 • 255pp • H/C (ISBN: 9781799885573) • US $215.00

ICT as Innovator Between Tourism and Culture
Célia M.Q. Ramos (University of Algarve, Portugal) Silvia Quinteiro (University of Algarve, Portugal) and Alexandra R. Gonçalves (University of Algarve, Portugal)
Business Science Reference • © 2022 • 319pp • H/C (ISBN: 9781799881650) • US $215.00

Handbook of Research on Big Data, Green Growth, and Technology Disruption in Asian Companies and Societies
Patricia Ordóñez de Pablos (The University of Oviedo, Spain) Xi Zhang (Tianjin University, China) Mohammad Nabil Almunawar (Universiti Brunei Darussalam, Brunei) and José Emilio Labra Gayo (University of Oviedo, Spain)
Business Science Reference • © 2022 • 415pp • H/C (ISBN: 9781799885245) • US $295.00

Driving Factors for Venture Creation and Success in Agricultural Entrepreneurship
Mohd Yasir Arafat (Aligarh Muslim University, Aligarh, India) Imran Saleem (Aligarh Muslim University, Aligarh, India) Jabir Ali (Indian Institute of Management, Jammu, India) Adil Khan (O.P. Jindal University, Raigarh, India) and Hamad Hussain Balhareth (Saudi Electronic University, Saudi Arabia)
Business Science Reference • © 2022 • 356pp • H/C (ISBN: 9781668423493) • US $215.00

Handbook of Research on Emerging Business Models and the New World Economic Order
Jose Manuel Saiz-Alvarez (Catholic University of Avila, Spain, & Catholic University of Santiago de Guayaquil, Ecuador)
Business Science Reference • © 2022 • 454pp • H/C (ISBN: 9781799876892) • US $275.00

For an entire list of titles in this series, please visit:
www.igi-global.com/book-series/advances-business-strategy-competitive-advantage/73672

IGI Global
PUBLISHER of TIMELY KNOWLEDGE

701 East Chocolate Avenue, Hershey, PA 17033, USA
Tel: 717-533-8845 x100 • Fax: 717-533-8661
E-Mail: cust@igi-global.com • www.igi-global.com

Table of Contents

Section 2
A New Post-Pandemic Workplace

Section 3
Sector-Level Changes to Work Post-Pandemic

Detailed Table of Contents

the scaling down of big companies owing to the negative effects of the COVID-19 pandemic. Although much has been said and written on the role of entrepreneurship in economic development and growth, scant is known about its role in economic recovery from crises. Therefore, this chapter aims to investigate how entrepreneurship education can act as a catalyst for economic recovery in the post-COVID-19 pandemic era. It was observed that entrepreneurship plays a catalyst role in promoting economic recovery through producing enterprising graduates and promoting divergent thinking in solving wicked problems in the post-pandemic era. Nonetheless, it was also observed that the theoretical approach of teaching entrepreneurship was dominant at the expense of the practical approach due to limited resources. The outcomes of this study help practitioners and policymakers in making evidence-informed decisions.

The SARS-CoV-2/COVID-19 pandemic has been disruptive of various industries globally, due to the need for social distancing in the absence of effective vaccines and treatments in the first year and counting. As humanity has racked up losses, many people have been sidelined from the workforce, which was already under pressure with the incursions of high technology in the Fourth Industrial Revolution (4IR). To survive, people have had to raid savings, liquify whatever they have of value, and rely on family and friends and public charity to survive. Many have left bills unpaid, for rent, for auto loans, for credit card debt, and others. As the world slowly comes out of the pandemic, thanks to multiple effective vaccines (by BioNTech and Pfizer, Moderna, Johnson & Johnson, stateside), many are starting to reenter the job market, with varying outcomes. This work explores various career retooling paths in this moment based on content analysis of available formal and informal data. There is primary research from the Social Web.

The Covid-19 pandemic has led to a digital transformation in global higher education because universities were forced to close, and higher education students faced interrupted education processes. Currently, online learning in higher education is a new phenomenon, and the pandemic has highlighted the importance of digital skills for higher education students for both new distance teaching and learning methods and the new labor market. The longer universities remain closed, the more higher education students will lose their future, resulting in a permanent loss of digital skills for the post-pandemic world. Accordingly, this study presents the current

they were more satisfied than the older ones. It is concluded that despite the fact that all teachers expressed having adapted, the older ones encountered greater difficulties and, consequently, had to resort to a greater diversity of adaptation strategies.

While the most serious part of the pandemic was taking place, key economic variables were aggravated such as unemployment, cost of the basic food basket, precariousness of the basic salary, and distribution of wealth (Gini). The objective of this chapter is to analyze the emergence of bartering during the pandemic as an anti-crisis measure and an initiative of mutual support, which originates from the population in the central highlands of Ecuador (the Andes), an area with social, cultural, and economic importance for the country. To achieve this objective, a methodology with a quantitative approach was applied with descriptive scope and non-probabilistic sampling, consisting of direct observation, interviews, and surveys. The results obtained reveal that bartering is a collaborative commercial exchange practiced to minimize the economic effects caused by COVID-19 and to compensate for the inefficiency of an absent state.

The world as we knew it has changed forever as a result of the COVID-19 pandemic. Tourist service providers had to adjust their services to the mandatory changes imposed by authorities' regulations and consistently with the demand of service users. This chapter focuses on detecting those potentially lasting changes and mark the new parameters in the tourism sector. The qualitative research chosen consisted of in-depth interviews with hotel and restaurant managers in the tourism industry of the four provinces of Galicia (Northwest Spain). Based on the theoretical review, the first conclusion is that, although tourism has been affected many times, whether by

Preface

Long before SARS-CoV-2/COVID-19 emerged, humanity was already facing a challenging economic moment, with human jobs going to automation, artificial intelligence (AI), and machines for efficiencies, in a time of the Fourth Industrial Revolution (4IR). Given the context, what would a virulent-transmissible airborne pathogen do to global trade, global travel, wages, living costs, livelihoods, lifestyles, cultures, education, and other aspects? Would children be hobbled in their learning, and to what degree? How would various sectors of the economy be affected?

At the start of 2021, some 470 million people around the world were unemployed and / or under-employed, according to UN numbers. Many lacked the means to meet basic survival needs, in a time when countries that contributed aid historically were also under pressure. In the downward slope of the pandemic, large percentages of the world's population are without work, and many are still in isolation and social distancing for biosafety and health.

While people try to sort out issues at the macro- and meso-levels, people are responsible for their own well-being and so need to engage in new thinking, revisioning who they are and what they are capable of, and they need to acquire new knowledge, skills, and abilities (KSAs) to adapt. As noted in the call for chapters, this work aims to address the following questions:

- How are people thinking of the present moment and the near future in terms of their livelihoods?
- How are people surviving the present moment of sparsity and shortages and massive uncertainty?
- How are people retooling themselves to adapt to a new economy, whatever that might look like out the other side?

This work explores how people in their respective localities (developed and less developed spaces) are adapting for a new economy through new understandings of the world and concomitant re-conceptualizations of the self. There are the efforts at self-learning, retraining, apprenticeships, gig work, and higher education. There are intensifications of hobbyist skills. This work also explores how people are re-branding themselves for the new economy. There are applications of extreme measures for survival in a job-scarce zero-sum environment.

DIFFERENT MANIFESTATIONS OF A PANDEMIC

When a crisis like a global pandemic arrives, the crisis is not singular. This is especially true of the global scale crisis with an airborne pathogenic virus, SARS-CoV-2 / COVID-19 (severe acute respiratory syndrome coronavirus 2 / coronavirus disease 2019). As the world witnessed in 2020, the discovery of the airborne transmissibility of this virus slowed and then stopped human travel; it shut down borders. The pattern through 2021 has been the opening and closing of borders, and the starting up and shutting down of travel as well. The need for people to socially distance and mask up was hindered by access to effective masks. As larger swaths of human populations became ill and died and contact tracing failed in many countries, governments instituted mass lockdowns and restrictions on human movements domestically. (Many of the government lockdowns were preceded by slowdowns of humanity prior. In other words, people knew to go to ground without having government interventions to tell them to go to ground.)

Workplaces, including schools, stopped meeting in person where possible. Meanwhile, those deemed essential still had to go to work and bear many undue risks. These included healthcare workers, grocery workers, meat processors, law enforcement, the military, and so on. Governments that could afford it issued payments, so people could survive. They blocked evictions to prevent a homeless crisis in the West, and they also prevented foreclosures by requiring banks to extend mortgages. People lost jobs because businesses could no longer justify having employees when their customer-base disappeared. Under pressure, people's sense of social comity often broke down, and there were outbreaks of violence and social unrest (against injustices). Not only was humanity under biological survival pressure but financial.

Meanwhile, scientists, researchers, healthcare professionals, epidemiologists, drugmakers, and others applied their knowledge at breakneck pace but with high accuracy and high rigor to try to understand the mechanisms of the virus and ways to set up a credible bio-defense against its ravages. In the late fall of 2020, pharmaceutical companies released news of breakthroughs in their vaccine development. By early 2021, people started receiving vaccinations in the West.

Although there were some false starts with shutdowns and then reopenings throughout 2021 in various regions, the virus would return with mass infections and super-spreader events, and people would again go to ground. The vaccinations, though, gave people hope that perhaps they could return to in-person work and school and some level of normalcy. However, as if fall, the U.S. is yet in another wave of infections, based on the delta variant and the fact that many had chosen to remain unvaccinated due to a political narrative of freedom and other reasons. Children 12 and older can receive vaccinations but not those under 12, until research has been conducted as to the proper dosage and safety of the vaccines.

With the current opening, though, many have engaged in mass resignations. Government programs, protecting people against evictions and providing some funding for food and unemployment benefits, meant that some people had sufficient resources to not work. Others may have passive income. Some had savings to draw on. So why the resignations? The general thought is that the crisis helped people realize more what is important. For many who had lost jobs and were behind on rent or mortgage payments, restarting in a lower wage job would not really help with paying down the piles of debt. Shifting from a year or more of non-work for many of the long-term unemployed (those unemployed six months or longer) would be traumatizing work-wise and certainly in terms of adjusting to the presence of others. Certainly, most work landscapes have changed after a more than a year-and-a-half storm.

Many returned to workplaces to find that their social interactions were strained, and people were stressed, and trust was in very short supply. For many, typical interactions were typified by incivilities. People who tended towards exceeding politeness ended up raging, in some contexts. The "meatspace" and shared physical airspace were too much to handle.

The experiences in the U.S. were one thing. What happened around the world varied. Societies have been wounded, with social ties strained and often broken. How people survived and what they anticipated out the other side differed. Every context was strained. Where people might give each other the benefit of the doubt, many did not under the strain of new realities.

The book that emerged in the year or so of development is comprised of the following Table of Contents (TOC).

LIGHT OVERVIEWS OF THE RESPECTIVE CHAPTERS

Section 1: Retooling the Self for Post-Pandemic Work

This collection opens with "Retooling the Self for the Post-Pandemic Economy: Identity, Work, and Well-Being" (Ch. 1), by Maureen Ebben (University of Southern Maine) and Katie Drescher (Katie Drescher & Coaching & Consulting). This work explores the fundamental shifts caused by the severe global COVID-19 pandemic and considers how people need to remake themselves, their work, and their senses of well-being. This work provides insights on how to define personal values and to build personal resilience. This chapter is bolstered by real-world case studies.

The pandemic resulted in precipitous and extreme losses of productivity and resulting income, based on the need for people to social distance to protect human life. There ensued mass shutdowns and slowdowns. Mufaro Dzingirai and Rodgers Ndava, both of Midlands State University, in Zimbabwe, follows next with "Entrepreneurship Education as a Driver for Economic Recovery in the Post-Pandemic Age" (Ch. 2). These researchers suggest the importance of entrepreneurship education in the post-pandemic era, for both individual and societal survival and thriving. They highlight the importance of the social creation of entrepreneurs.

Shalin Hai-Jew, of Kansas State University, USA offers "Career Retooling in a Pandemic-Recovery Phase" (Ch. 3), which focuses on the individual ego-level struggles to come out of a pandemic that ended livelihoods and lives and left many with large debts and unpaid bills. She highlights some methods for retooling a career based on where individuals are in their lives and identities and interests.

Asli Gunay, University of Ankara, Turkey, notes the criticality of digital skills for the post-pandemic era, in "Equipping Higher Education Students With Digital Skills for the Post-Pandemic World" (Ch. 4). Virtuality, a main stable of work during the early years of the pandemic (2020 – 2021), is here to stay, given the acceleration to a neo-new world order.

Section 2: A New Post-Pandemic Workplace

The workplace has also changed. "Returning to the In-Person Workplace in a (Post?) Pandemic Context" (Ch. 5), by Shalin Hai-Jew, highlights some of these changes given that the pandemic is not obviously and cleanly over yet (and it is not clear if and when that day will arrive), and given the social losses from a year-and-a-half of non-social-interaction except virtually. This work explores how people share "airspace" and how they make room for each other (or not, in some cases).

Many parts of the human population were of especial importance during the pandemic. One study focuses on one such group—teachers in Argentina. Gabriela Vergara (National University of Rafaela) and Constanza Faracce Macia (University of Palermo) offer an original research work titled "Skills, Practices, and Emotions for Teaching in Times of Pandemic: An Analysis of Pre-School, Primary, and Secondary School Teachers (Argentina, 2020)" (Ch. 6). The well-being and continuing training of particular parts of a population may be hyper critical for the recovery of societies.

COVID-19 showed how human societies may be disrupted fundamentally, including in terms of government, economies, and commerce, and other mass-scale societal functions. Chapter 7, "Collaborative Trade Exchange and the Post-COVID Event: Bartering in the Andean Region of Ecuador" (Ch. 7), by Jessica Silvana

Matute-Petroche, Uriel Hitamar Castillo-Nazareno, and Luis Fernando Pazmino-Crespo, Universidad Católica de Santiago de Guayaquil, explores peoples turning to bartering to survive. This work shows the importance of having the skills and resources to create trade-able goods and the social connections to engage in informal trade with others. This work highlights societal mechanisms that enable such trade, such as barter fairs. It showcases the importance of agriculture as a core source of trade-able goods.

Section 3: Sector-Level Changes to Work Post Pandemic

Andrea Areán Magnou and Noella Araújo-Vila, both of Universidade de Vigo in Spain, address "Permanent Changes to the Tourism Industry: The Case of Galicia, Spain" (Ch. 8), given the fallout from the COVID-19 pandemic. They review the global literature on tourism impacts during the pandemic and note the sectors of tourism that were centrally affected and then those lesser affected. Then, they explore how Galicia, Spain, is faring tourism-wise and ways to ensure that it is back on the map for tourists post pandemic.

Tanzania is another area of focus. In "Innovations in Agriculture and Tourism for Tanzania's Workforce Beyond the COVID-19 Pandemic" (Ch. 9), by Nyanjige Mbembela Mayala and Ambrose Karoli Tesha, Mwenge Catholic University, Tanzania, this work focuses on the critical need for innovations in both agriculture and tourism, as critical sectors. They point to various technologies and practices that may benefit the sectors and their contribution to the economy and livelihoods.

In "Sustainable Career in Agile Environment: Cross-Sectorial Investigations" (Ch. 10), the team of Sheikh Mohammed Rafiul Huque, Mohammad Nazmul Islam, Tahira Farzana, and Tasnima Aziza, all of Jahangimagar University, Bangladesh, involves interview research of principals from a range of fields, to understand adaptivity in the current pandemic moment. A critical emergent theme is the need to be agile and adaptable in a pervasively pressure-filled period.

Section 4: Macro-Level Changes to Work Post Pandemic

The sheer breadth of the COVID-19 pandemic may be seen in the final chapter. "Career Reinvention through Entrepreneurial Mindset and Entrepreneurial Orientation in the Post-Pandemic Era: Multiple Cases From the Developed and Developing Countries" (Ch. 11) shows variant approaches to adapting to the pandemic. This work is by Lukman Raimi (Universiti Brunei Darussalam, School of Business and Economics) and Jainaba M.L. Kah (The Gambia, Office of the President).

CONCLUSION

In the moment, the core premise of this collection has its challenges. Will people re-invent, or will they merely hold tight to what is familiar and let the world pass them by? After all, high education is still disrupted. Many who would be students have been attracted by more menial jobs with higher wages than before. Many, especially women, have left the job market long-term, and many do not have any intention to return. Where this all goes is still in question.

Of some relief is the observation that the center, while shifted in the mass death of the pandemic, is somewhat holding. This is not to say that opportunists did not try to overtake the U.S. political system, among others.

Will the international community come together to support new economies, maybe green ones? 5G ones? Will the global order share resources to enable the protection of vast swaths of humanity? Will people come up with the "blue sky" visioning necessary to enable new economic advances? Will people be able to reinvent themselves and not fall into the false safety of prior lock-in? Will humanity be able to pivot to what works? What is achievable given the on-ground realities? If it is true that crisis brings out opportunities, this is a highly opportune moment for (traumatized) humanity to redefine and move forward.

November 2021

Shalin Hai-Jew
Kansas State University, USA

Acknowledgment

Thanks to the respective authors and teams who contributed to this book. Without their deep professionalism and knowledge, this book would not be. And it would not exist with the level of richness and insight, which may inform the future as the world recovers from the inordinate damage of SARS-CoV-2 / COVID-19.

Thanks to Katie McLoughlin of IGI Global for reaching out to other authors to round out this text. Your help has been critical in helping this text come together. Thanks to Tori Parks for being flexible about the cover, which is now more diverse and inclusive than the earlier design.

Thanks to IGI Global for supporting this work.

This is for R. Max, Lily, and Asher, who work as a loving team even in times of high difficulty as the years of the pandemic have been.

Section 1
Retooling the Self for Post-Pandemic Work

Chapter 1
Retooling the Self for the Post-Pandemic Economy: Identity, Work, and Well-Being

Maureen Ebben
https://orcid.org/0000-0001-8620-372X
University of Southern Maine, USA

Katie Drescher
Katie Drescher Coaching and Consulting, USA

ABSTRACT

This chapter addresses the self, work, and well-being through the explication of four heuristics and their associated tools and strategies to foster knowledge for the creation of a new identity in relation to work. These include 1) the values in action (VIA) inventory of strengths; 2) the positive emotion, engagement, relationships, meaning, and accomplishments model (PERMA); 3) the process of resilience-building; and 4) the process of values identification. The practical application of these frameworks is illustrated through five case studies gleaned from practitioner experiences in the applied field of leadership development, training, and well-being coaching. The case studies demonstrate how persons from a diverse range of occupations and career stages use the concepts and strategies discussed to grapple with new understandings of self and address the distinctive challenges of work in the post-pandemic era.

DOI: 10.4018/978-1-7998-8626-6.ch001

INTRODUCTION

In the wake of the COVID-19 pandemic much has shifted. While some people have been insulated from the worst personal and economic effects and others bore its full import, the impacts have been universally felt (Lund et al., 2021). Experiences of social isolation and loss of familiar ways of living and working have left many searching for ways to address these disruptions. One way forward is through new understandings of self, work, and well-being.

This chapter asserts that gaining increased well-being in relation to work entails self-reflection, going inward to think about how one relates to work. While individuals have limited control over the macro levels of social and economic life, there are steps one can take at the micro, individual level to gain agency and foster well-being. Who is the self in relation to work? How can one access knowledge about the self to gain new understandings about the self and work? How can that knowledge be used to retool and transform self-identity for work? Jimenez (2021) contends that the post-pandemic world of work requires a new "toolkit"—that is, new insights, perspectives, and understandings about the self in relation to work.

The loss of activities outside of work coupled with the social separation of COVID-19 quarantines, while disruptive, also slowed the frantic, frenetic pace of life. These circumstances created newfound time and space for self-reflection that many used for a self "reset" of work goals and practices, responding in constructive, meaningful, and effective ways to the potential latent in the quarantine moments of expanded time with the self. However, others were simply burned out, having endured chronic stress, exhaustion, cynicism, and inefficacy (Davis, 2021). This chapter offers concepts and strategies for people at any point--whether engaging in their own reset or languishing--to journey toward deep reflection about the self in relation to work.

The self in relation to work is addressed in two parts: conceptual and applied. The first half of this chapter explicates the conceptual frameworks of four (4) heuristics and their associated practical tools and strategies to foster self-knowledge for the creation of a new self-identity for work. These include

- VIA (Values in Action) Inventory of Strengths (Peterson et al., 2007),
- PERMA positive emotion, engagement, relationships, meaning, and accomplishments model (Seligman, 2018),
- Process of intentional resilience-building to reduce work burnout (Sellers et al., 2019),
- Process of values identification and goal setting to align a person's behaviors with their values (Jimenez, 2021).

The second half of the chapter illustrates these conceptual frameworks, tools, and strategies in practice through five case studies. The case studies are de-identified composites gleaned from the practitioner experiences of the co-author who has worked in the applied field of leadership development, training, and well-being coaching for nearly a decade. The case studies demonstrate how persons from a diverse range of occupations, industries, career stages, and work settings use the frameworks, tools, and strategies discussed to grapple with coming to a deeper understanding about their self-identity and address the distinctive challenges posed by the COVID-19 pandemic.

FRAMEWORKS FOR UNDERSTANDING THE SELF AND WELL-BEING IN RELATION TO WORK

Self-identity

What is the self? What is the self in relation to work? This chapter locates the notion of the self within Bronfenbrenner's (2009) ecological systems theory of self-identity. The theory posits that the self exists in relation to five dimensions of the social world. These are comprised of

- Microsystem which includes the self and persons with whom the self routinely interacts such as family members, co-workers, colleagues, classmates, peers, and community groups members;
- Mesosystem which is the site of communication between the microsystem and the exosystem;
- Exosystem which includes social contexts such as mass media and larger social institutions and communities such as social and legal services, friends, and neighbors;
- Macrosystem that denotes the attitudes and ideologies held by the culture in which an individual is situated, and
- Chronosystem that depicts time in a socio-historical context and refers to the patterning of environmental events and transitions over the life course of a person (Bronfenbrenner, 2009).

Each of these interrelated systems can be understood as concentric circles with the self nested at the center. The self is conceptualized as the individual person who possesses particular attributes such as ethnicity, gender, age, ability, and sex. It is important to note that placing the individual self at the center of this model is not meant to privilege the individual over, say, the natural world, but rather to signal that, as a theory of self-identity, the self occurs *in relation* to these other systems. Locating the self at the center of concentric rings points to the interconnections among these systems and the self. The self is part of each of these systems and these systems are part of the self.

Bronfenbrenner's theory of self-identity has been used as a conceptual framework and applied to analyses across a range of social circumstances, from educational settings (Gonzales, 2020) to leadership studies (Campbell et al., 2019). Here, we use Bronfenbrenner's concept of identity to situate the self in relation to work. We mark the site of the relationship of the self to work as one that occurs at the nexus of intersecting social contexts--what Bronfenbrenner refers to as the self embedded within the micro-, meso-, exo-, macro-, and chronosystems.

While social contexts, such as the COVID-19 pandemic, and other external circumstances shape one's conditions of work, this discussion goes further to also consider the self at a deeper level--the inner-self. The self is composed not only of relationships with others and the external world, but also of the self within. The inner-self is part of the self-identity that Bronfenbrenner postulates because the inner-self is always situated within the interrelated spheres of the micro-, meso-, exo-, macro-, and chronosystems. While ideas about the inner-self vary from culture to culture (Tafarodi et al., 2004), over time (Cary, 2000), and even questioned altogether (Patterson, 2006), in this chapter, the inner-self is understood as the fixed basis of one's subjectivity and autonomy in the world. The inner-self can be thought of as the "continuity of the intimately familiar *me* across time and place" (Tafarodi et al., 2004, p. 97). How can the inner-self be understood? In what ways can knowledge about the inner-self help to align self-identity in relation to work? In the next sections, four conceptual frameworks and their associated tools and strategies are advanced as ways to access and understand the self at this inner level. Insights gleaned about the inner-self, an aspect of self-identity, can be used to gain increased skills and abilities to foster relations to work that enable human flourishing.

VIA Inventory of Character Strengths

One way to access the inner-self is through the Values in Action (VIA) Inventory of Strengths. This conceptual framework and practical tool enable discovery of an individual's innate traits or "character strengths." Stemming from the collective work of 55 scholars who conducted a systematic review of research literature in psychology, philosophy, and theology, the VIA Inventory of Strengths identifies, classifies, and measures universally valued positive traits in human beings (Littman-Ovadia et al., 2021). Character strengths comprise an important aspect of the self as each person possesses a unique constellation or "signature" of attributes (Davis, 2021; Niemiec & McGrath, 2019). It is important to note that character strengths are different from talents and interests. They are "traits in the sense of individual differences with a temporal stability and generality; they are not necessarily based on immutable biogenetic characteristics" (Martinez-Mari et al., 2020, p. 2).

As a heuristic, the VIA Inventory of Strengths is composed of domains with associated character strengths. For example, the intellectual domain of wisdom and knowledge includes character strengths of creativity, curiosity, open-mindedness, love of learning, and perspective-taking. The domain of courage consists of traits like bravery, perseverance, honesty, and zest. Other domains include justice that is made up of character strengths of teamwork, fairness, and leadership. The domain of transcendence includes character strengths including the appreciation of beauty and excellence, gratitude, hope, humor, and spirituality, and the domain of temperance is made up of character strengths of forgiveness, humility, prudence, and self-regulation (Peterson & Seligman, 2004). Understood as "values in action" (Lavy & Benich-Weisman, 2021) and a tool for self-knowledge (McGrath, 2019), the VIA Inventory of Strengths, has been used by more than 13,000,000 people globally (Littman-Ovadia et al., 2021).

Research employing character strengths in organizational and workplace studies has examined how self-awareness of individual strengths can foster teamwork (Gander, Gaitzsch, & Ruch, 2021), and be a valuable resource in career coaching (Littman-Ovadia, Lazar-Butbul, & Benjamin, 2014). Research has also demonstrated a positive relationship between a person's understanding of their character strengths and use of them at work with life-work satisfaction (Gander, Hofmann, & Ruch, 2021). Knowing and using one's strengths intentionally contributes to well-being, strengthened relationships with others, and the increased ability to identify pathways through stressful situations toward the accomplishment of professional and personal goals (Huber et al., 2020; Niemiec & McGrath, 2019). In the context of COVID-19, Martinez-Marti et al. (2020) research on character strengths "provides original evidence showing that character strengths seem to promote resilience over time in adverse situations such as the pandemic" (np).

Positive Emotion, Engagement, Relationships, Meaning, and Accomplishments (PERMA)

While character strengths illuminate the self within, the positive emotion, engagement, relationships, meaning, and accomplishments model (PERMA) articulates the interactional dimensions of the self and well-being. PERMA is a conceptual framework and practical tool for gaining self-awareness and self-efficacy (Seligman, 2018). It recognizes the interconnection of vital human dynamics including emotions, intentional engagement, positive relationships, awareness of what is most important, and accomplishments. These dynamics operate together to create the conditions for the well-being of the self in relation to work as well as in life more broadly (Kun, Balogh, & Krasz, 2017). Well-being is understood as more than basic functioning and more than transitory happiness. Well-being is the flourishing of the self (Fredrickson et al., 2013) with flourishing understood as "the experience of life going well. Flourishing is synonymous with a high level of mental well-being, and epitomizes mental health" (Agenor, Conner, & Aroian, 2017, p. 915). It is a combination of feeling good and functioning effectively.

In the PERMA model, positive emotions are the first element. These include feelings like hope, interest, joy, love, compassion, pride, amusement, and gratitude and are important for well-being (Seligman, 2012). Taking the time to recognize, enjoy, and delight in positive emotions, large and small, as they arise in everyday life can contribute to flourishing. Experiences of positive emotions can even help to counteract the harmful psychological and physical effects associated with negative emotions, and can enhance resilience (Tugade & Fredrickson, 2004). Persons can increase their experiences with positive emotions by being more intentional about creating opportunities for positive emotions to occur through engaging in activities that they enjoy, spending time in the company of loved ones, and being mindful of all the good that one may encounter. Positive emotion is not to be confused with cheerfulness--which is an attribute unequally distributed across the human population with about one-third of people naturally possessing this characteristic (Seligman, 2012)—or, worse, "toxic positivity," a disingenuous and superficial affect. Rather, positive emotion is, for most people, a learned skill that is generative for the well-being of the self and others.

Second, is the concept of engagement, or the self in "flow" (Csikszentmihalyi & LeFevre, 1989). It refers to those moments of life when a person is fully absorbed or engrossed in an activity, living in the moment with little sense of the passage of time. Usually the experience of flow occurs when an activity reflects the right combination of challenge (to keep it interesting) with an appropriate level of mastery (so that a person is competent). Given that humans are social creatures, the third element, positive relationships, refers to feeling supported, loved, and valued by others and encompasses interactions with family, friends, and co-workers (Seligman, 2012). Building a network of support and care is a key in the PERMA model of well-being. Specific behaviors can help form supportive interpersonal bonds such as communicating good news and celebrating accomplishments (Siedlecki et al., 2014).

Meaning is the fourth element in the PERMA model. Meaning is the idea that a person feels they have purpose in life, that they are connected to ideas, goals, or organizations that are perceived to be important, and that their actions have an impact. Meaning can be related to work or personal life or both, and often stems from the values that a person holds (see Values discussion below). The fifth, and final, element is accomplishments which is the sense of achievement that, in turn, can foster self-fulfillment. Achievements gained through dedication, passion, hard work, and persistence relate to internal motivation. Accomplishments may be sought for external or internal rewards and, like meaning, are often related to one's values—as accomplishing something that a person does not deem to be important may not be gratifying.

The concepts of PERMA have been applied to the complex dynamics of work. This research focuses on understanding the self in its singular identity and in its relations to others, including the expression of positive emotions, forms of engagement with work in ways that bring meaning and enable flow, workplace relationships and interactions, and professional and career goals and accomplishments (Chia & Kern, 2020; Chia, Kern, & Neville, 2020). Through use of the PERMA model, essential dimensions of the self can be brought to an individual's awareness with the insights used to adapt the habits and practices of work in ways that may be more creative and affirming of the self. To the extent that each of the elements delineated in the PERMA model can be part of a person's work role, satisfaction with work may increase (Kern et al., 2014). Ongoing research in the vein of PERMA has furthered the model by making explicit the importance of the bodily materiality of the self as it exists within larger, social and economic circumstances with confirmation of the essential role of adequate sleep, proper nutrition, regular physical activity, along with the benefits of psychological and emotional optimism (Seligman, 2012).

Resilience

Next, resilience and its relationship to perceptions of work selves is considered. Resilience is the ability to bounce back from adverse circumstances. It involves maintaining a healthy degree of subjective well-being even in stressful situations (Sellers et al., 2019). Empirical evidence suggests a relationship between character strengths and resilience as "all character strength factors (except strengths of spirituality and gratitude), yielded significant positive correlations with resilience" (Martinez-Mari et al., 2020, p. 3). Knowledge, skills, and agency for finding purpose, reframing failure (e.g., understanding the outcomes of events in new ways), and persisting towards goals all foster resilience of the self (Reivich, Seligman, & McBride, 2011; Robertson-Kraft & Duckworth, 2014).

The concept of intentional resilience-building involves learning to deploy strategies to *respond* rather than *react* to stress or adversity and thereby enhance self-resilience. It is important to acknowledge that work stress or adverse conditions may be shaped by issues beyond the workplace such as larger political, economic, and social problems that are often beyond an individual's control (Davis, 2021). However, as persons develop proficiency in building resilience, they can gain skills for increased agency for aspects of work within their control.

A key aspect of resilience is the dynamic of shame. In response to setbacks, persons can often get stuck in the experience of shame, precluding the ability to move forward. Shame is the fear of social disconnection and is a universal human emotion (Brown, 2006). Shame resilience (e.g., bouncing back from the experience of shame) offers a way to move through the disappointments and failures that inevitably occur in work. There are four aspects of becoming more resilient to shame. These entail

1. acknowledging, identifying, and understanding when instances of shame occur;
2. recognizing the external factors that contributed to the experiences of shame;
3. connecting with other people for emotional support and empathy; and
4. communicating about the specific experiences and emotions related to shame with others rather than withdrawing (Brown, 2012).

To enact resilience to shame, connection rather than isolation is required. Brown's insights have been confirmed by subsequent research such as Arnink (2020) who "found a significant correlation between shame resilience and subjective well-being" (p. 1).

In Brown's Shame Resilience model, empathy is key to coping effectively with outcomes that do not go as planned. Empathy refers to the ability to understand the feelings of others. "Empathy and vulnerability can lead to feeling valued and seen by others. While shame isolates, empathy builds connection and compassion for others and for yourself" (Integrative Life Center, 2021, np). As a learned skill that can be intentionally leveraged, resilience has the capacity to transform the perception of a conversation, relationship, and career.

Values

Values are integral to the self, well-being, and work. Values are defined as what is most important to us (Lee & Kawachi, 2019). In the midst of the myriad challenges of the post-pandemic economy, actions can be driven by emotional responses to external situations. It may be easy to lose track of what is most valuable. Informed by Kegan's (1982) seminal theory of the adult development of consciousness, the current era is one in which individuals have shifted from an "authorship-modern" mindset (i.e., who we are) to a "reflective-postmodern" mindset (i.e., what do we stand for?). In Kegan's formulation, the identity of the self has expanded to include the examination of what an individual values. In the postmodern era, the self carries a greater consciousness seeking to answer the question: what does the self stand for? What the self stands for is expressed through a person's values.

Further, values are not about vague or lofty aspirations, but rather about conscious and intentional behaviors informed by particular goals. To live by one's values, one must first name them, and then develop concrete plans of action. Asking oneself simple yet profound questions like, "what matters most to me?" and taking time to reflect with deep thought and honesty is one way to identify values. Often values are influenced by a person's upbringing, what was learned in educational systems, social life, or cultural imperatives. Values are also reflected in the ways in which people live their lives such as how time and resources are spent. One might consider their values both in relation to their self and their work self. How can one live out their values at work? Gaining conscious awareness about values and identifying them helps one be more intentional about establishing behaviors that support important values.

In relation to work, the self-reflective process of values clarification can be used to examine the work role, to consider the person one is at work, and make adjustments to align the individual self with the work self. Defining an individual's values in relation to work, and setting goals to move closer to the desired work roles and career directions can bring greater meaning and reduce stress (Wrzesniewski & Dutton, 2001). A further part of the process of defining and understanding values includes the recognition that values evolve and change over time. For example, a changing value can be seen in the situation of a person who holds the value of financial independence and security in which, over time, this value has been met. As a result, it may be reasonable to work less or change jobs to another role that brings more joy. Values can shift as one's circumstances change.

The relationship among a person's values, their circumstances, and their behaviors is critical. Ideally, all should be in alignment. That is, a person's values acknowledge their circumstances and are supported by their behaviors. To bring one's values into alignment with one's behaviors, setting goals can be useful. For example, a person might say they value close family relationships. However, their behaviors demonstrate that they do not spend much time with their family members. If they seek to bring their behaviors into alignment with their stated values, then they might decide to establish a new goal to make dinner and eat at home together three times a week. Or, they might set the goal to connect with family members who live far away by planning regular weekly video calls. Another value and behavior misalignment may be present when a person values work relationships but possesses few skills for building relational connections. They could identify a mentor to offer professional perspectives and guidance beyond what they receive from their direct manager. A more experienced person who identifies a value of community and service but struggles to live out this value, especially at work, may take action by mentoring a person who is just starting out in their career, possibly helping them to land an internship and build a professional network. In the next section, these four frameworks are illustrated through the discussion of five case studies.

RETOOLING THE SELF THROUGH NEW UNDERSTANDING

The second half of the chapter illustrates these conceptual frameworks, tools, and strategies in practice through five case studies. The case study approach was utilized because it is appropriate "for realists whose goal is to describe and explain phenomena" (Lindgreen, Di Benedetto, & Beverland, 2020, p. A7). Depicting the practical application of the frameworks, the case studies bring forth details of individuals' experiences using the tools and strategies as they seek a deeper understanding about their self-identity to address work issues and challenges related to the COVID-19 pandemic and beyond.

The case studies come from the co-author's practitioner experience as a certified leadership coach and consultant working with multinational and governmental organizations in tech, finance, hospitality, and creative arts for over a decade. Gleaned from the co-author's thousands of hours of coaching with individuals of various ages, ethnicities, and genders from across a range of work roles, industries, and career stages, the five case studies are composed of de-identified composites in which all identifying information was changed to preserve anonymity.

The scenarios portray snapshots of pandemic circumstances and the processes involved with using the concepts and tools to clarify aspects of the self. In some instances, the outcomes of working with these concepts, tools, and strategies are clear. In other instances, the outcomes are in-process or just starting to emerge. As such, the case studies demonstrate the processual quality of these approaches in practice.

Case studies

Prachi

Prachi is a 48-year-old, Indian-American, female-identifying engineer with an MBA living in Silicon Valley, California, who manages 15 teams in the financial technology sector. At the start of the pandemic, her teams shifted to work from home. As a result, she faced myriad challenges coordinating with her teams as many lived in tiny San Francisco area apartments with a partner, spouse, or roommate and little space to accommodate two people conducting remote work. Although her team members were paying for the highest level of internet service available, many faced limited bandwidth that did not accommodate multiple video calls with cameras turned on. In addition, there were babies and young children competing for the attention of her team members as schools and daycares closed. Cats and dogs also sought to engage with their owners who were suddenly around all day. Some team members resolved their space constraints by turning their bathtub into a second workspace. Others worked in shifts, trading off with partners or spouses to share childcare duties and conserve bandwidth. These circumstances were chaotic and pressure-filled.

Prachi sought to support her team on a human level while needing to figure out how to accomplish work remotely. Company-financed budgets for home office equipment helped to an extent, but communication and task coordination that had been easily achieved through in-person interactions in the workplace, became difficult and even demoralizing when performed remotely during the pandemic. Not having team members with essential knowledge present during video conference meetings, and communication without cameras caused confusion that diminished the teams' ability to meet project deadlines.

Working with a combination of tools and strategies of VIA, PERMA, and values clarification, Prachi built resilience. Through the VIA inventory of strengths, Prachi identified that her primary character strengths included the appreciation of beauty and excellence, creativity, curiosity, honesty, and love of learning. Finding ways to use these strengths in her new virtual workplace started with leaning into honesty. Prachi created a twice-weekly, open-agenda meeting time for any team members interested in sharing triumphs and challenges as they adjusted to remote work. Prachi modeled empathy and vulnerability with her team by sharing her adjustment with having college-age children return home with opposite sleep-wake schedules. Opening up to her team about how her disrupted sleep led to irritability and strained relations with her kids helped Prachi feel less frustrated. It also led to her awareness that she was actually grateful that her children were safely at home, and that they could work out a sleep-wake schedule that was acceptable. Her team members similarly shared stories about the challenges they were facing and how they were coping.

For Prachi, the honest communication contributed to her sense of "flow" (i.e., ease of action, with the sense that the tasks of work or daily life are not burdensome, but interesting and even enjoyable), and improved trust and communication among her team members. Further, Prachi realized that positive relationships were one of her core values. She leaned into building stronger relational connections at home and at work through greater focus on listening rather than immediate results. These changes helped her teams and children feel more seen and heard, empowering them to creatively solve shared challenges.

As a result of this self-knowledge, Prachi is now more in flow than ever. Her listening has led to increased communication among her team members with more input and involvement for problem-solving. For example, team members decided to form sub-groups to work a split-shift, with half working in the late morning and half working in the evening, after kids' bedtimes so that they could focus, and have sufficient bandwidth for video meetings. Prachi's teams' productivity skyrocketed. She was promoted, and is working with newfound confidence empowering others to find solutions that work best for them. Prachi's self-identity was transformed from the perception that she needed to supply all the answers to understanding herself as a communication facilitator who fosters the generation of possibilities. Perhaps most significantly, her identity as a leader in her work role now occupies a smaller part of her overall identity. Family, friendships, and other aspects of life, such as curiosity about others and learning by listening, that got left behind when she was single-mindedly pursuing success at work are now central to her self-identity promoting work-life satisfaction.

Saul

Saul is a 41-year-old, Black, male-identifying aeronautical engineer. Saul is married, and has two children, ages 3 and 5. Born abroad and raised on military bases, he now lives in the Southern U.S. and reports feeling disconnected from the local culture.

Describing himself as an introvert's introvert, during the first coaching session, Saul asked, "Am I enough? I am very hard on myself." In addition to imposter-syndrome, (i.e., the sense that one is falsely competent), Saul had a goal of improving his interpersonal communication skills as he was expanding his reach at work into more people-leading roles. During the week following the first coaching session, Saul was going to be filling-in for his boss who would be away for training. Saul was experiencing stress and wondering if he could perform the demands of his boss's job, especially while caring for his young children as he worked from home.

Saul was interested in exploring his values as a place to start his coaching journey. "Being the best Dad I can be, adding value to the organization I work for, having fun, and taking responsibility for the choices I make" are the values that Saul reported as most important. He explored how responding to the opportunity to add value at work might relate to living in alignment with his values. His concerns over the possibility that his young children might be a hindrance dissipated as Saul developed a plan for how he would respond with vulnerability and humility if there were a conflict between his value to be the best Dad he can be and his goal to add value at work. The week went smoothly. His preparation for handling the potential conflict expanded his identity at work to encompass not only his sense of himself as an excellent technician, but also as a well-rounded parent with a young family. Moreover, what he had worried about turned out to be a gift that strengthened his relationship with his work team.

Motivated by the success of articulating and acting on his values, Saul was open to learning more about his strengths and took the VIA survey. His top character strengths were love, humility, gratitude, fairness, and perspective. Saul located his character strength of love in his experience of growing up in a close-knit family that moved frequently due to his father's military career. He consciously carries love with him in his interactions with his wife and children as well as his interactions with his family-of-origin. He identified his character strength of humility as stemming from his desire to be part of something bigger than himself, living by the credo of leaving the world in a better place than he found it. Inspired to pursue design after seeing beautiful Italian cars while living abroad as a young child, Saul regards his work in aeronautical design as one of his contributions to society. Similarly, he traced his strengths of fairness and perspective to experiencing different cultures while growing up and living internationally.

Knowing his top strengths and remembering when they first were manifest in his life helped Saul to let go of his imposter-syndrome and live in alignment with what matters most to him. In the third session, he shared that he wanted to bring more fun into his life and was planning a mini-vacation that evening with his wife. In the final session, Saul stated that he is feeling amazing, having made progress beyond his expectations, especially in self-confidence for leading his new team. The insights from values clarification and knowledge of character strengths helped to change his assumptions about what is possible for how he shows up at work.

Erica

Erica is a 54-year-old, Latinx, female-identifying regional sales manager for a national specialty retail store, who lives with her partner of eight years. She was only six months into her new role overseeing seven stores in the Pacific Northwest when COVID-19 restrictions commenced.

Erica started coaching with a stated desire to reduce stress, improve work-life balance, and "find out what makes me happy." During the pandemic, her company's stores remained open and their sales declined. Her organization's upper-management did not adjust the metrics used to define salesperson and manager success, despite the change in consumer demand. In response, Erica felt pressure to "press her team members harder for results." However, Erica's insistent efforts did not improve sales, and, instead, led to lower morale, reduced trust, and team alienation.

The second session focused on the exploration of her character strengths using the VIA survey. Her most prominent strengths were fairness, kindness, forgiveness, honesty, and social intelligence. Through exploration of her strength of fairness, Erica realized that she felt estranged from this character strength, particularly as it was manifest in her work role. Desiring to act in ways that aligned with her strength of fairness, Erica prioritized relating to team members as people first and numbers second. Despite the ongoing pressure for sales, Erica possessed genuine concern for her team, and began creating a culture that celebrated birthdays, acknowledged significant events, and encouraged team members to bring well-being into the workplace.

Erica's understanding of her strengths evolved further as she dealt with a work incident. Due to the stressors of the pandemic, a team member experienced a mental health crisis. Erica quickly and accurately assessed the situation and helped the person get to safety. She attributed her appropriate response to her sense of herself as a kind person.

Through awareness of another top strength, forgiveness, Erica reestablished her relationship with her brother who had judged her harshly after she came out about her sexual orientation many years ago. She shared that the positive change in the relationship with her brother led to feeling more integrated, and propelled her to bring her success with difficult conversations into the workplace. Leveraging her strength of honesty, Erica had direct and challenging conversations with team members that were also transparent and vulnerable. Through these interactions, she integrated team members into roles that were better fits for their strengths thereby improving the functionality of the stores that she oversaw.

Through exploration of her values, Erica prized "putting people first" and authenticity, feeling a deeper sense of connection to herself and others when acting in alignment with these values in the workplace. Ultimately, Erica decided to move out of the specialty retail sector entirely in order to bring her retooled sense of self into a different sphere of work. Today, Erica enjoys a new career in nonprofit sustainable organic farming.

Alison

Alison is a 27-year-old, white, first-generation American, female-identifying Human Resources Coordinator working at a multinational media firm in a large midwestern city. Married for two years, Allison lives in a small apartment in the city with her husband and an occasional dog they foster through a pet rescue.

The COVID-19 pandemic had a significant impact on Alison personally and professionally. She sought coaching with the support of her employer to address resilience. Like many people with white collar jobs, Alison shifted to remote work during the pandemic, as had her husband. A primary concern in the first coaching session was her notable feeling of disconnect from her leadership and the key stakeholders she was assigned to support with human resources services. In her work role, she focused on execution of tasks rather than building trust and healthy work relationships. During the pandemic, the quiet of working from home created space for Alison to become aware that she was more disengaged from her work partners than she realized. During in-person work, the distraction of the office and her focus on goal attainment, masked the reality of the state of her work connections. Alison shared that she also felt overwhelmed with little sense of purpose. These experiences exacerbated her stress and isolation, posing risks for burnout and diminished well-being.

Alison wanted work on emotional regulation to develop a sense of empowerment. As a starting point, and to gain a sense of who she was outside of her job, Alison completed the VIA survey to identify her personal strengths. Her top five character strengths were prudence, kindness, fairness, judgment, and love. She was asked to engage in a "strength spotting" exercise to remember the times in her life when she used her strengths or observed someone else displaying the strengths. The purpose was to better understand how her strengths connected to her deeper self, and how they could be called into action in her everyday life.

Upon reflection, Alison discovered a new insight that revealed the connection between her strengths of fairness, kindness, and love with her family lineage, and her original reason for choosing a career in human resources. Her deceased grandfather was a Holocaust survivor. He lived out these values and imparted them to her. Recollection of her earliest memory using the strength of kindness brought her back to befriending and helping a classmate with a learning disability when she was in preschool. Alison remained friends and acted as an advocate for her classmate from that early meeting through her secondary education. In addition, she explored how her strengths of prudence and judgment supported her people-focused work role. Identification of her character strengths was empowering, enabling her to draw a connection between acting in ways that aligned with her strengths and their impact on fostering positive emotions that support well-being.

Encouraged by her experience with the VIA strengths, Alison continued exploration of her inner landscape through concepts from the PERMA model. She experimented with positive emotion by starting work phone calls with a quick check-in about what was going well before diving into problem-solving. Reframing her work relationships to encompass human-centric interpersonal interactions (rather than simply executing work tasks) enhanced her experiences of relationships, engagement, meaning, and accomplishment and reduced her sense of isolation and overwhelm.

Uncovering and articulating her core values was the next step Alison chose on her coaching journey. Values identification, like strength spotting, proved empowering. She resonated with the values of clear communication, a harmonious work-life balance, and, overlapping with her VIA strengths, kindness and fairness. While maintaining these principles, she realized that she was doing little to intentionally act on them in her personal or professional life, and was motivated to create a plan. She started the intentional implementation of her values slowly, cooking a meal with her husband, and keeping her laptop closed after her workday ended. As with her experience of enacting her strengths, Alison noted an increase in positive emotions when her behaviors were in alignment with her values, and was motivated to explore additional ways to consciously enact her values.

Subsequent sessions built upon the strengths-based foundation that Alison identified, with consideration of how her strengths could support retooling her understanding of herself in relation to work. She began to function more effectively in her work role by using her strengths and values as guiding principles rather than always looking to supervisors for direction. She connected more personally with internal partners, made decisions without second-guessing herself, and established boundaries around her work and personal life. Alison's understanding of herself and her agency shifted. Instead of perceiving control outside of herself (e.g., with supervisors), she understood that she also possessed agency in both her work role and personal life. Using her strengths and values as touchstones enhanced Alison's self-efficacy.

Miguel

Miguel is a 31-year-old, Latinx, male-identifying singer and dancer working in the theater industry in New York City. He was waiting tables at a famous restaurant and working at a fitness gym part-time to pay the rent between acting jobs. Miguel lives alone, having amicably parted ways with his live-in partner shortly before the COVID-19 pandemic began.

All three of Miguel's work roles abruptly ended as theaters went dark and restaurants and gyms closed during the pandemic. Unemployment compensation helped him to pay the rent and Miguel decided to stay in New York anticipating that the COVID-19 lockdowns would last several weeks to six months at most. More than one-year later, with vaccines widely available and lockdowns slowly receding, the theater industry was still dark. Miguel reached out for coaching to find greater focus and increase his resilience as he charted a new path. His primary challenges presented in coaching included addressing the sense of languishing that he was experiencing, hoping to catch it before it turned to burnout, and identifying and securing meaningful work.

Miguel started the first session by taking the VIA survey. His top strengths were love, bravery, appreciation of beauty and excellence, kindness, and hope. Shortly after the first session, Miguel recalled that his top strength of love came from his grandmother who cared for him when he was a young child. His grandmother supported his interest in the arts and brought him to his first Broadway show traveling from the Midwest to New York to see *The Lion King* when he was seven-years-old. His grandmother's encouragement and support set the foundation for his lifelong pursuit of a career in the performing arts. He further connected his passion for the arts to his strength of appreciation of beauty and excellence.

Uncertainty about the viability of a career in the theatre following the COVID-19 pandemic was a major blow to Miguel's experiences of positive emotion, engagement, relationships, meaning, and accomplishments--all of the elements of the PERMA model of well-being. Miguel shared that he experienced positive emotion and a sense of connection and purpose when performing. He drew satisfaction from offering a theatre audience a short reprieve from their daily lives as they entered into the story unfolding onstage. His relationship to himself and others had been through his identity as an actor ever since he was a young child. His sense of meaning and accomplishment, similarly, came from performing and from being of service to the audience.

Aware that it may be a long time before he might be in front of an audience again, Miguel was open to exploring his values and aligning his next steps with what was most important to him. Miguel resonated with the values of nurturing close relationships and creating a sense of belonging. Further, he identified that he valued family, and caring for his health through nutrition and exercise. He began his reorientation to work by focusing on his physical self-care with renewed attention to his exercise and nutrition regime. This change brought about increased well-being. He chose to fill the gap between where he was after the third session and where he wanted to be by tapping into his character strength of bravery and exploring work outside the arts, waiting tables and starting a social media marketing business with the gym where he had formerly worked as his first client. He was quickly hired by two more businesses and is going strong growing his client base. While it is unclear when or how the arts will re-emerge post-pandemic, Miguel hopes to return to the arts as opportunities expand. For now, he is focused on living daily life in ways that are true to his values, nurturing his relationships, and savoring the joys he experiences in his new relationship with a partner he met shortly after beginning coaching.

DISCUSSION

These case studies represent individuals situated within particular personal and work-related circumstances impacted by the COVID-19 pandemic. While the macro-level social and economic forces shaping the pandemic were largely out of their control, they possessed individual agency to clarify and amplify knowledge about the self to move forward in new ways. Through pandemic challenges and responses to them, persons have changed. Stanford University sociologist Marianne Cooper observes, "The employees returning to the office are not the same people who left in March [2020]" (in Youn, 2021, np).

Self, Work, and Well-Being

With Prachi, we see a person struggling with team communication, coordination, and cohesion due to the constraints of pandemic work from home modalities. After identifying and leaning into her character strength of honesty and vulnerability, her teams were empowered to take an increased role in problem-solving. Prachi received a promotion and her teams flourished. Even more significantly, Prachi realized that being herself at work is okay, that she is more than her work, and that time with friends and family matters for her well-being.

Saul was resilient in the face of COVID-19 lockdowns and the demands of new leadership responsibilities. His discomfort with remote work led him to address his long-standing imposter-syndrome directly. While self-doubt still creeps in, he uses the knowledge of his strengths and values to keep a realistic perspective.

For Erica, the work-related effects of COVID-19 meant questioning all aspects of her work identity. With insights about her strengths of fairness, kindness, forgiveness, honesty, and social intelligence and her values of "putting people first" and authenticity, her understanding of self was transformed. She left her corporate retail sales job for work in nonprofit sustainable agriculture, a role that better aligns with her values of community and one that affords more free-time.

While Alison was executing and achieving at work during COVID-19, she was also languishing with little personal connection or vision about how work related to her as a person. A "work-in-progress," Alison's self-knowledge continues to unfold as she increasingly uses her self-awareness to engage in more person-centered relationships at work.

As a millennial in the performing arts, Miguel's relationship to work was completely turned upside down by COVID-19. He is adapting, and for now, is choosing not to return to service-industry jobs. Instead he is exploring working in arts administration and digital marketing. Whether this current adaptation is a stopgap measure until theatres reopen or a pivot to a new line of work will be revealed in time. What is known is that his self-identity in relation to work has shifted. He now thinks of himself more in terms of *who* he is rather than *what* he does, taking time to make sure his life is balanced and he is nurturing important relationships, recognizing that for his situation time, like money, holds value.

Shifting perspectives

Such shifting perspectives of self may be a hallmark of the post-pandemic reorientation to work.

Who one *is* rather than what one *does* may take precedence. With work consuming the majority of waking hours for most people, the work role, itself, may be understood differently. Prachi discovered that her preconceived notions of what a team leader should be were too narrow. Saul, grappling with impostor-syndrome, learned that vulnerability showed strength and was an asset to his leadership. Working as a corporate team manager in the retail sector, Erica was able to engage in difficult but open conversations that transferred power to her team members. While currently not in the career of his choice, Miguel found that he can still live out his values.

Orientations toward time may also be shifting. Prachi gained a newfound appreciation for time and self away from work as well as financial benefits. Erica's career pivot afforded time to nurture her burgeoning painting talent that nourishes her self-expression. Alison established new boundaries for work-life harmony. Even Miguel, while stymied by the lack of theatre work, welcomed the time to take care of himself physically and emotionally.

In the nexus of self, work, and well-being, time may offer the opportunity for exploration of the self including awareness of feelings and emotions associated with the self and work roles. However, time, itself, is not necessarily the primary goal. By itself, time does not guarantee awareness or transformation of the self. But, if coupled with knowledge, tools, and strategies, time can hold the potential for self-reflection affording space to connect with others beyond the workplace. Time may have restorative effects for the self and well-being. It may create capacity for the exploration of who one is beyond the often limited presentation and enactment of the work self where presenting a "good" image to achieve results is paramount, but not necessarily in alignment with one's strengths and values.

The importance of time and its relationship to employee inner-selves and well-being may be gaining attention. Internet company *Mozilla* instituted a "Wellness Week," shutting down so that employees could use the time as they wished. Similarly, *Bumble* and *LinkedIn* closed for a week, while e-commerce company *Shopify* commenced "Rest & Refuel Fridays" one day each month. *Marriott International*, the largest hotel firm in the world, added "TakeCare Days Off'' on the three days before Memorial Day, July Fourth, and Labor Day (Youn, 2021). Whether such temporary and relatively minor alterations can instill meaningful well-being for employees or recast the culture of workplaces that produced disaffection in the first place remains to be seen.

It is likely that more deeply transformative initiatives are needed. Other than intermittent time-off, what can workplaces do to foster opportunities for self-awareness and the professional and personal growth that comes with it? Organizations, at all levels, might consider building more avenues for the development of work cultures characterized by greater attention to ways of interacting that foster self-development and well-being including dynamics like positive emotion, engagement, relationships, meaning, and accomplishments--the elements of PERMA--along with opportunities for employees to acquire knowledge about their strengths, identify their values, and build resilience. Such knowledge of self must also have pathways available for persons to perform work roles in ways that are in alignment with their strengths and values.

FUTURE DIRECTIONS

Adopting these orientations to workplace dynamics and practices would involve connecting values with work processes, recognizing individuals' strengths, and fostering greater employee agency for empowerment where trust, authenticity, and open communication allow people to explore aspects of the self within the workplace rather than having to go outside of the workplace or leave it altogether in order to enact their strengths and values. Organizations might also invest time and attention to the development of approaches for workflows and practices that build conscious awareness of the ways in which communication, coordination, and collaboration are achieved. For example, *how* are work groups acting together? *How* are members communicating with each other--not simply what is the output of the work group.

More specifically, organizations might seek ways to establish greater clarity regarding individual work roles, with a shared vision that reinforces the value of each role and its place in supporting the larger organizational strategy. As appropriate, employees should have the freedom to use their own good judgment on a day-to-day basis to make necessary changes in stressful or overwhelming situations. The freedom to work with flexibility, sufficient resources, clear guidelines, and support is also essential. The actions of team members should be recognized and appreciated in ways that foster a sense of belonging and accomplishment, fueling further motivation. Team members and leaders might ask themselves whether they can name the strengths of the people around them. Orientations and practices such as these could bolster morale and productivity while decreasing turnover and attrition as they support the self and promote well-being.

Future research might continue to examine the impact of strengths-based and values-based strategies in the post-pandemic workplace for the development of self and its effects on organizational success. Additional research could explore how novel work arrangements initiated during the pandemic may contribute to greater agency and resilience.

CONCLUSION

The pandemic moments of reflection, time, and space away from usual activities offered opportunities to look inward in search of greater knowledge of the self for positive growth and change, for resetting priorities to ask, what works? What does not work? It may be that we are discovering anew what we value, what we can do without, what brings us purpose, meaning, connection to self and to others at work. This chapter identifies and elucidates four conceptual frameworks, along with their tools and strategies, that individuals can use for understanding self-identity in relation to work. The five case studies demonstrate use of the strategies to reset the self for the post-pandemic economy.

Looking to the post-pandemic future, it is instructive to look to the past. Seligman (2021) has observed that, after the Black Plague swept through Afro-Eurasia in the fourteenth-century taking with it nearly one-third of the human population, a mere fifty years later the Renaissance commenced. Where do we go from here? We may be at a unique historical juncture, on the brink of a new era. What will the post-pandemic time give rise to? Nascent changes in workplace and entrepreneurial opportunities may be emerging.

What else might be born? As we come out of this period of pandemic disturbance, we can regard it as an opportunity for learning about and working with the concepts and tools for identifying, understanding, and applying our character strengths, fostering positive emotions, engaging in meaningful work that aligns with personal values, and building resilience. Through use of these ideas and strategies, we can gain newfound agency for shaping the conditions of our lives in ways that enable the self to flourish in relation to work.

REFERENCES

Agenor, C., Conner, N., & Aroian, K. (2017). Flourishing: An evolutionary concept analysis. *Issues in Mental Health Nursing*, *38*(11), 915–923. doi:10.1080/01612840.2017.1355945 PMID:28876964

Arnink, C. L. (2020). A quantitative evaluation of shame resilience theory. *Inquiries Journal, 12*(11).

Bronfenbrenner, U. (2009). *The ecology of human development: Experiments by nature and design*. Harvard University Press.

Brown, B. (2006). Shame resilience theory: A grounded theory study on women and shame. *Families in Society*, *87*(1), 43–52. doi:10.1606/1044-3894.3483

Brown, B. (2012). *Daring Greatly*. Avery.

Campbell, C., Shollen, S. L., Egan, C., & Neilson, B. G. (2019). The capacious model and leader identity: An integrative framework. *The Journal of Leadership Studies*, *13*(1), 6–19. doi:10.1002/jls.21622

Cary, P. (2000). *Augustine's invention of the inner self: The legacy of a Christian Platonist*. Oxford University Press.

Chia, A., & Kern, M. L. (2020). Subjective wellbeing and the social responsibilities of business: An exploratory investigation of australian perspectives. *Applied Research in Quality of Life*, 1–28.

Chia, A., Kern, M. L., & Neville, B. A. (2020). Corporate social responsibility for happiness: Corporate determinants of societal happiness as social responsibility. *Business Ethics (Oxford, England)*, *29*(3), 422–437. doi:10.1111/beer.12274

Csikszentmihalyi, M., & LeFevre, J. (1989). Optimal experience in work and leisure. *Journal of Personality and Social Psychology*, *56*(5), 815–822. doi:10.1037/0022-3514.56.5.815 PMID:2724069

Davis, P. (2021). *Beating burnout at work*. Wharton School Press.

Fredrickson, B. L., Grewen, K. M., Coffey, K. A., Algoe, S. B., Firestine, A. M., Arevalo, J., Ma, J., & Cole, S. W. (2013). A functional genomic perspective on human wellbeing. *Proceedings of the National Academy of Sciences of the United States of America*, *110*(33), 13684–13689. doi:10.1073/pnas.1305419110 PMID:23898182

Gander, F., Gaitzsch, I., & Ruch, W. (2021). The relationships of team role and character strengths balance with individual and team-level satisfaction and performance. *Frontiers in Psychology*, *11*, 566222. doi:10.3389/fpsyg.2020.566222 PMID:33329199

Gander, F., Hofmann, J., & Ruch, W. (2021). Character strengths: Person–environment fit and relationships with job and life satisfaction. *Frontiers in Psychology*, *11*, 1582. doi:10.3389/fpsyg.2020.01582 PMID:32793038

Gonzales, M. (2020). The Bronfenbrenner micro-and meso-systems. In M. Gonzales (Ed.), *Systems thinking for supporting students with special needs and disabilities* (pp. 81–92). Springer. doi:10.1007/978-981-33-4558-4_6

Huber, A., Strecker, C., Kachel, T., Höge, T., & Höfer, S. (2020). Character strengths profiles in medical professionals and their impact on well-being. *Frontiers in Psychology*, *11*, 11. doi:10.3389/fpsyg.2020.566728 PMID:33424679

Integrative Life Center. (2021, February 22). *Shame Resilience*. https://integrativelifecenter.com/wellness-blog/shame-resilience/

Jimenez, J. (2021). *The burnout fix: Overcome overwhelm, beat busy, and sustain success in the new world of work*. McGraw Hill.

Kegan, R. (1982). *The evolving self: Problem and process in human development*. Harvard University Press.

Kern, M. L., Waters, L., Adler, A., & White, M. (2014). Assessing employee wellbeing in schools using a multifaceted approach: Associations with physical health, life satisfaction, and professional thriving. *Psychology (Irvine, Calif.)*, *5*(06), 500–513. doi:10.4236/psych.2014.56060

Kun, Á., Balogh, P., & Krasz, K. G. (2017). Development of the work-related wellbeing questionnaire based on Seligman's PERMA model. *Periodica Polytechnica Social and Management Sciences*, *25*(1), 56–63. doi:10.3311/PPso.9326

Lavy, S., & Benish-Weisman, M. (2021). Character strengths as "values in action": Linking character strengths with values theory–An exploratory study of the case of gratitude and self-transcendence. *Frontiers in Psychology*, *12*, 202. doi:10.3389/fpsyg.2021.576189 PMID:33613375

Lee, M. A., & Kawachi, I. (2019). The keys to happiness: Associations between personal values regarding core life domains and happiness in South Korea. *PLoS One*, *14*(1), e0209821. doi:10.1371/journal.pone.0209821 PMID:30625160

Lindgreen, A., Di Benedetto, C. A., & Beverland, M. B. (2021). How to write up case-study methodology sections. *Industrial Marketing Management*, *96*, A7–A10. doi:10.1016/j.indmarman.2020.04.012

Littman-Ovadia, H., Dubreuil, P., Meyers, M. C., & Freidlin, P. (2021). VIA character strengths: Theory, research and practice. *Frontiers in Psychology*, *12*, 2. doi:10.3389/fpsyg.2021.653941 PMID:33897563

Littman-Ovadia, H., Lazar-Butbul, V., & Benjamin, B. A. (2014). Strengths-based career counseling: Overview and initial evaluation. *Journal of Career Assessment*, *22*(3), 403–419. doi:10.1177/1069072713498483

Lund, S., Madgavkar, A., Manyika, J., Smit, S., Ellingrud, K., Meaney, M., & Robinson, O. (2021). *The future of work after COVID-19*. McKinsey Global Institute.

Martínez-Martí, M. L., Theirs, C. I., Pascual, D., & Corradi, G. (2020). Character strengths predict an increase in mental health and subjective well-being over a one-month period during the COVID-19 pandemic lockdown. *Frontiers in Psychology*, *11*, 2790. doi:10.3389/fpsyg.2020.584567 PMID:33192913

Niemiec, R. M., & McGrath, R. E. (2019). *The power of character strengths: Appreciate and ignite your positive personality*. VIA Institute on Character.

Patterson, O. (2006, December 26). Our overrated inner self. *The New York Times*.

Peterson, C., Ruch, W., Beermann, U., Park, N., & Seligman, M. E. (2007). Strengths of character, orientations to happiness, and life satisfaction. *The Journal of Positive Psychology*, *2*(3), 149–156. doi:10.1080/17439760701228938

Peterson, C., & Seligman, M. (2004). *Character strengths and virtues: A handbook and classification*. Oxford University Press.

Reivich, K. J., Seligman, M., & McBride, S. (2011). Master resilience training in the US Army. *The American Psychologist*, *66*(1), 25–34. doi:10.1037/a0021897 PMID:21219045

Robertson-Kraft, C., & Duckworth, A. L. (2014). True grit: Trait-level perseverance and passion for long-term goals predicts effectiveness and retention among novice teachers. *Teachers College Record, 116*(3).

Seligman, M. (2018). PERMA and the building blocks of wellbeing. *The Journal of Positive Psychology*, *13*(4), 333–335. doi:10.1080/17439760.2018.1437466

Seligman, M. E. (2012). *Flourish: A visionary new understanding of happiness and well-being*. Atria.

Seligman, M. E. (2021, June 1). *Positive Psychology, Agency, and Human Progress* [Video]. YouTube. https://youtu.be/TjWrL1MJbj0

Tellis, W. (1997). Application of a case study methodology. *Qualitative Report*, *3*(3), 1–19.

Tugade, M. M., & Fredrickson, B. L. (2004). Resilient individuals use positive emotions to bounce back from negative emotional experiences. *Journal of Personality and Social Psychology*, *86*(2), 320–333. doi:10.1037/0022-3514.86.2.320 PMID:14769087

Youn, S. (2021, June 29). America's workers are exhausted and burned out and some employers are taking notice. *The Washington Post.*

ADDITIONAL READING

Donaldson, S. I., Heshmati, S., Lee, J. Y., & Donaldson, S. I. (2020). Examining building blocks of well-being beyond PERMA and self-report bias. *The Journal of Positive Psychology*, 1–8. doi:10.1080/17439760.2020.1818813

Goodman, F. R., Disabato, D. J., Kashdan, T. B., & Kauffman, S. B. (2018). Measuring well-being: A comparison of subjective well-being and PERMA. *The Journal of Positive Psychology, 13*(4), 321–332. doi:10.1080/17439760.2017.1388434

Huber, A., Strecker, C., Hausler, M., Kachel, T., Höge, T., & Höfer, S. (2020). Possession and applicability of signature character strengths: What is essential for well-being, work engagement, and burnout? *Applied Research in Quality of Life, 15*(2), 415–436. doi:10.100711482-018-9699-8 PMID:32457814

Niemiec, R. M., & Pearce, R. (2021). The practice of character strengths: Unifying definitions, principles, and exploration of what's soaring, emerging, and ripe with potential in science and in practice. *Frontiers in Psychology, 11*, 11. doi:10.3389/fpsyg.2020.590220 PMID:33584426

Ruch, W., Niemiec, R. M., McGrath, R. E., Gander, F., & Proyer, R. T. (2020). Character strengths-based interventions: Open questions and ideas for future research. *The Journal of Positive Psychology, 15*(5), 680–684. doi:10.1080/17439760.2020.1789700

Seligman, M. E., & Csikszentmihalyi, M. (2014). Positive psychology: An introduction. In M. Csikszentmihalyi (Ed.), *Flow and the foundations of positive psychology* (pp. 279–298). Springer.

Wagner, L., Gander, F., Proyer, R. T., & Ruch, W. (2020). Character strengths and PERMA: Investigating the relationships of character strengths with a multidimensional framework of well-being. *Applied Research in Quality of Life, 15*(2), 307–328. doi:10.100711482-018-9695-z

Wagner, L., Pindeus, L., & Ruch, W. (2021). Character strengths in the life domains of work, education, leisure, and relationships and their associations with flourishing. *Frontiers in Psychology, 12*, 12. doi:10.3389/fpsyg.2021.597534 PMID:33967881

KEY TERMS AND DEFINITIONS

Bronfenbrenner's Ecological Systems Theory of Self-Identity: The theory that the self exists in relation to five dimensions of the social world including the microsystem, mesosystem, exosystem, macrosystem, and chronosystem.

Empathy: The ability to understand the feelings of others.

Flow: The state of being fully engrossed in an activity.

Inner-Self: The fixed-basis of a person's subjectivity and autonomy in the world.

Positive Emotion, Engagement, Relationships, Meaning, Accomplishments (PERMA): A process and tool for gaining self-awareness and agency.

Resilience: The ability to bounce back from adverse circumstances.

VIA Inventory of Strengths: A heuristic and tool for discovery of an individual's character strengths.

Well-Being: More than basic functioning, the flourishing of the self.

Chapter 2
Entrepreneurship Education as a Driver for Economic Recovery in the Post-Pandemic Era

Mufaro Dzingirai
https://orcid.org/0000-0002-1518-8275
Midlands State University, Zimbabwe

Rodgers Ndava
https://orcid.org/0000-0002-0070-1830
Midlands State University, Zimbabwe

ABSTRACT

Entrepreneurship appears to be a lucrative career in the post-COVID-19 era given the scaling down of big companies owing to the negative effects of the COVID-19 pandemic. Although much has been said and written on the role of entrepreneurship in economic development and growth, scant is known about its role in economic recovery from crises. Therefore, this chapter aims to investigate how entrepreneurship education can act as a catalyst for economic recovery in the post-COVID-19 pandemic era. It was observed that entrepreneurship plays a catalyst role in promoting economic recovery through producing enterprising graduates and promoting divergent thinking in solving wicked problems in the post-pandemic era. Nonetheless, it was also observed that the theoretical approach of teaching entrepreneurship was dominant at the expense of the practical approach due to limited resources. The outcomes of this study help practitioners and policymakers in making evidence-informed decisions.

DOI: 10.4018/978-1-7998-8626-6.ch002

INTRODUCTION

The twenty-first century has seen the widespread recognition of entrepreneurship education as a driver of entrepreneurial intention and economic development (Zhang & Huang, 2021). However, entrepreneurship is now regarded as the driver of economic recovery in the post-COVID-19 pandemic era. According to Langston (2020), for the past two decades or so higher education institutions have been embedded into entrepreneurship education practices to develop graduates' skills, knowledge and entrepreneurial competencies. Interestingly, higher education institutions across the globe are embarking on preparing enterprising graduates well-versed with innovative solutions and ideas that are aimed at improving the economic status in their respective countries and beyond. For the past 20 years, higher education institutions have been considered to be a part of the economic stakeholders. Notably, the 2008 global economic crisis only increased the awareness of entrepreneurship education given the agility of Small and Medium Enterprises (SMEs) as well as microenterprises. It is well-documented that institutions of higher education are becoming important actors in entrepreneurship discourse as they inculcate the most important entrepreneurial skills and competencies that are needed by society to improve the performance of the enterprises (Lackeus, 2019).

Despite the fact that entrepreneurship education dating back to more than twenty years ago, this concept is considered to be still at the early stage of development (Langston, 2020). The recent pandemic outbreak and its impact has been considered as a catalyst for accelerating the efforts to improve entrepreneurship through education and learning approaches. In this regard, entrepreneurship is now being considered a crucial career in the global economic recovery from the detrimental effects of the pandemic and economic crisis (Igbinakhase, 2021; World Health Organisation, 2020; World Bank, 2020; Langston, 2020). Despite the lucrative nature of entrepreneurship as a career in the post-pandemic era, Dzingirai, Tshuma, and Sikomwe (2021) observed that online marketplaces, cost-cutting measures, innovation and creativity, leveraging of technology, collaborations and partnerships, and sustainable culture act as the main post-pandemic sustainability strategies for SMEs. Unfortunately, little is known about how entrepreneurship can drive economic recovery in the post-COVID-19 pandemic era. Hence, this study aims to assess how entrepreneurship education can drive economic recovery after the pandemic.

BACKGROUND

The COVID-19 pandemic outbreak has undeniably detrimental effects on business and has caused a serious global economic downturn leading to massive job losses

(Dzingirai, Chagwesha, & Mudzurandende, 2021). In this respect, International Labour Organisation (ILO) estimated that there is going to be a fall in employment income between $860 billion and $3.4 trillion and between 5 million and 25 million job losses and more than 70 million people are probably going to fall into extreme poverty as a result of the daunting COVID-19 outbreak (ILO, 2020; United Nations (UN), 2020). This sorry state of affairs emerging from the outbreak of the COVID-19 pandemic has marked the increase in the pursuit of entrepreneurship as a lucrative career. For decades, entrepreneurship education has been taught in higher education institutions. Notably, the current economic crisis accelerated by the emergence of the pandemic has witnessed the importance of entrepreneurship education since most people are being retrenched and fresh graduates are failing to secure jobs.

It is in the public domain that the lockdown measures have negatively affected the operations of many businesses in different sectors of the economy. With this in mind, entrepreneurship education appears to be of paramount importance when it comes to the creation of employment, innovation, identification and exploitation of opportunities in the post-COVID era. Given this information, entrepreneurship can play a catalyst role in the economic recovery process in the post-COVID-19 pandemic era. Interestingly, many governments around the world have tried to encourage entrepreneurship activities as part of the initiatives to address the economic disruptions (Hardie et al., 2020). Therefore, there is now an urgent need to interrogate how entrepreneurship education can promote the speed of economic recovery in the post-COVID-19 pandemic era. In this regard, we can extend the mainstream entrepreneurship and economic recovery literature.

Although the COVID-19 pandemic started as a health crisis, it ended up having some noticeable spillover negative effects to the economy of many countries especially developing countries. It is worrisome to note that Baker, Bloom, Davis, and Terry (2020) lamented that the pandemic has caused an economic recession that is equivalent to the Great Depression if not worse than that with stringent lockdowns confining people to their homes. Worryingly, many workers are losing their jobs since a plethora of companies is shutting down without the possibility to be operational again. In response to the lockdown measure, many institutions of higher education have resorted to online teaching and learning but organizations in other sectors such as manufacturing, agriculture and mining cannot rely on online platforms (Akkermans et al., 2020; Fernandes, 2020).

The formation of SMEs and microenterprises in the entrepreneurial spirit has been on the rise and individuals are engaging in street entrepreneurship just to survive the economic negative effects of the pandemic. Public awareness on entrepreneurship education thus becomes of paramount importance as these entities create employment and fill in the void created by large companies when they laid-off employees. To improve the performance of entrepreneurs and their entities, entrepreneurship education is the most appropriate approach that is adopted worldwide (Dzingirai, 2020a). Ho et al. (2018) applauded the relevance of entrepreneurship in Singapore among other Asian and European countries. In Sweden, the curriculum for all levels includes entrepreneurship education (Fejes et al., 2019). The widespread credit of entrepreneurship education has also gained popularity in Africa where the focus on SMEs is increasing rapidly. Hence, the global community has seen that institutions of higher education can intensify entrepreneurship education.

The impact of the COVID-19 pandemic on the global economy and society has been unprecedented to the extent that both the public and private enterprises, governments and non-governmental organizations come together to support people and the business community to eliminate the daunting effects of the pandemic (Maritzl, Parenyi, Dewaal, & Buck, 2020; UN, 2020). The pandemic crippled many if not all economies around the world and extensive efforts are being exerted towards eradicating the virus that poses serious challenges not only in terms of business but health-wise. Massive rollouts of vaccines underway paves the way for economies to open and thrive to work towards economic recovery. Governments around the world are determined to come up with effective ways of creating enabling environment that is conducive for economic recovery. According to the Government of Ireland (2021), the Economic Recovery Plan 2021 also aims to invest in business and workers where training and education will be provided targeting specific sectors that are lagging behind. These include the SMEs as entrepreneurs that can drive the economy to greater heights. As part of the SME and Entrepreneurship Growth Plan the government of Ireland aims to improve the export sector by supporting start-ups and micro-enterprises. Economic recovery will include scaling down the unemployment levels that escalated due to the pandemic outbreak hence relentless efforts are needed to help people get back to work.

As economies work towards recovery, it is not certain that all jobs lost are going to be created again. It is worth mentioning that creation of other job opportunities through entrepreneurship is the ultimate goal of many economies worldwide (Naume, 2020). New lucrative job opportunities could be created if entrepreneurial opportunities are fully and efficiently utilized (Maritz et al., 2020; World Bank, 2020). Given this information, there is an urgent need to extend our understanding of the role of entrepreneurship not in economic development and growth only but also in the economic recovery process in the post-COVID-19 pandemic era. Therefore, this study aims to bridge this gap by gathering evidence from a Zimbabwean perspective.

CONCEPT OF ENTREPRENEURSHIP EDUCATION

It is necessary to conceptualize entrepreneurship in order to fully understand how it can be linked to economic recovery in the post-Covid-19 pandemic era. With this in mind, Lackeus (2019) emphasize that encouraging students to become more entrepreneurial is perhaps the most difficult yet important task. One of the first responsibilities of lecturers and teachers is to describe what entrepreneurship education is all about. In the United Kingdom, the term enterprise education is often used in place of entrepreneurship education hence the terms are used interchangeably. In other countries like the United States of America, the term entrepreneurship education is preferred as more practical. Some opinions put forward to suggest that the term entrepreneurship education is a unification of both enterprise and entrepreneurship education hence the term entrepreneurship education is used extensively. According to Lackeus (2015), in Eastern and Northern Europe, other terms referring to entrepreneurship education are used, for instance, in Sweden entrepreneurial learning is often used in place of enterprise education while in Finland the term internal entrepreneurship is widely used. The idea of entrepreneurship basically entails entrepreneurial entities creating innovative organizations that create value even if they are set for profit or not. Both new and existing organizations need entrepreneurship education to succeed as entrepreneurship is not a one-time activity but a continuous process. Changes that take place in the business environment require new ideas and ways of doing things to be learned. Hence, higher education institutions are used as innovation hubs in coming up with entrepreneurial strategies, innovative ways and cost-effective ways of production and service provision (Lackeus, 2019; Nabi et al., 2018; Sieger et al., 2019).

Broad and Narrow View of Entrepreneurship Education

The broad and narrow views of entrepreneurship education are linked to two different perspectives. According to Hardie et al., (2020), the narrow perspective on entrepreneurship education is confined to business aspects that help to gain opportunities on human resources, acquiring capital, finance and marketing. The broader perspective, on the other side, requires the development of entrepreneurial competencies through designs and schemes that resort to chances or opportunities in the surrounding community. Entrepreneurship education is designed to educate students or business practitioners and the community at large about entrepreneurship (Hardie et al., 2020; Nabi et al., 2018). Notably, entrepreneurship education mainly focuses on preparing learners to develop skills and competencies to become entrepreneurs and start their own businesses.

One of the most important goals of entrepreneurship education is to develop entrepreneurial competencies, particularly the competencies that are considered to be necessary for enterprises to be successful (UN, 2020; Maritz et al., 2020). These competencies include the skills, knowledge and understanding of the attitudes that induce the ability and willingness to partake in activities that create value. These competencies are not just restricted to the business idea but also include other aspects of the business that are important such as marketing, human resources, dynamic capabilities as well as production and finance among other necessary competencies for sustainable development (UN, 2020). In this regard, according to Blanda, and Urbancikova (2020), sustainable development aims to cater for the needs of the present-day generation without compromising the needs of future generations. Hence, this concept of sustainable development aims to produce growth benefits at the same time protecting and preserving the environment so that future generations are not deprived of the same opportunities.

Going forward, it is of paramount importance to capture the need for entrepreneurship during and after economic crises. To build new foundations for economic recovery, entrepreneurship education has become a fertile ground upon which entrepreneurship education will flourish in the post-COVID-19 pandemic era (Naume, 2020). Therefore, entrepreneurship as a career appears to be attractive in the global economic recovery process provided that institutions of higher education are delivering high-quality entrepreneurship education (Dzingirai, 2020b; Lackeus, 2015; Sieger et al., 2019). The idea is to develop motivated students who are eager to create value based on the knowledge acquired and the collective efforts to create value towards economic activities that improve the standards of living. This can go a long way in increasing per capita income. The aggregate engagement and participation of entrepreneurs contribute towards employment, Gross Domestic Product (GDP) and standards of living through value creation hence turning around the economy.

To increase the participation of individuals in economic activities through the provision of entrepreneurship education in the post-COVID pandemic era, people can be taught and motivated to engage in activities that create economic value hence improving the economic wellbeing of the society which is the ultimate goal of every government (Zhang & Huang, 2021). Large organizations including well-known transnational corporations started as small companies with few individuals with entrepreneurial activities but they grow to become large firms. This description acknowledges the aspects of self-reliance, personal development, creativity and generally becoming an entrepreneur (Rieckmann, 2020; Nabi et al., 2018).

Entrepreneurship education also prepares students to be adaptive, resilient, and entrepreneurial in line with the changes in the business environments. Maritz et al., (2020) also confirm that entrepreneurship education is relevant as far as developing and preparing students to deal with the constantly changing environment. Evidence from the literature confirms that entrepreneurship education is indeed effective when it comes to the development of students for entrepreneurial purposes and the success of many economies now relies on the entrepreneurial expertise of the future generation (Dzingirai, 2020b). However, there is also a growing concern over the quality of entrepreneurship education and its influence on the development of students to become entrepreneurs. Some graduates from universities prefer to become employed somewhere else instead of becoming entrepreneurs themselves. Sierger et al., (2019) also confirmed this employment perspective of many graduates.

Entrepreneurial Education and Economic Recovery

Entrepreneurship education has been a widely accepted phenomenon in a bid to improve the livelihoods of many through the avenues to better living provided by entrepreneurship such as employment and value creation. One of the best approaches to enhance entrepreneurship understanding is through higher education institutions' involvement in teaching entrepreneurship so as to give entrepreneurs, potential entrepreneurs and students the requisite knowledge and skills. The role of entrepreneurial education on economic sustenance and the growth of the global economy is undoubtedly imperative hence the subject has become a worldwide phenomenon taught in business schools. In the United States alone, Lackeus (2015) reported that around 1200 business schools were teaching entrepreneurial education as a way of promoting economic growth through entrepreneurship. Currently, many economies are adopting entrepreneurial education as part of their education and industrial policies with most high education institutions offering entrepreneurship modules as compulsory subjects for all varsity students.

UN (2020) reported that entrepreneurship is relevant as far as addressing social, economic and environmental challenges is concerned hence making entrepreneurial education relevant in creating an enabling environment for economic growth. One of the United Nations 2030 Agenda for Sustainable Development resolutions acknowledges the importance of entrepreneurship by SMEs and micro-enterprises in addressing the economic challenges caused by the COVID-19 pandemic (UNb, 2020). UN (2020a) advocates for the establishment of SMEs and entrepreneurial entities that advance economic development initiatives for the economic resurgence in the post-pandemic era.

There is a growing consensus among scholars concerning the issue of value creation as the main goal of any entrepreneurial activity be it the economic activity undertaken for-profit motive or not (Zhang & Huang, 2021; Lackeus, 2015). Value creation through entrepreneurship requires some kind of novelty or innovativeness of the entrepreneurs and this often involves consumption of resources. Value creation occurs not only for making a living but as well through meaningful participation, involvement, or engagement for wellbeing and satisfaction. In this regard, value creation and entrepreneurship are grounded on operational competencies including incremental improvements and management processes in light of routine value creation while explorative value creation is grounded on entrepreneurial competencies (IMF, 2020; UN, 2020a)

The collapse of many corporates globally witnessed massive rolling out of policies, strategies and efforts by administrations around the world to strengthen enterprises. These efforts include entrepreneurship education, grants and financial assistance. SMEs and microbusinesses are considered to be the backbone for most economies globally hence the entrepreneurial education and financial assistance are mainly focused on resuscitating these enterprises to turn around the deteriorating economies (Naume, 2020). According to ILO (2020a), SMEs and microbusinesses, both in the formal and informal sector contribute about two-thirds of the global employment proportion and between 80% and 90% of employment in developing countries. In order for administrations to respond to the disruptions caused by the pandemic outbreak, it is necessary to educate the owner-managers of the SMEs, the young generation and the general public about the entrepreneurial processes (IMF, 2020; UN, 2020b).

The pandemic outbreak shifted the focus of everyone as the health threats continue to cause havoc in every country and the business environment for both SMEs and microbusinesses. The pandemic reduced the demand for some products and services with some markets completely shutting down especially those products that are non-essential like tourism, entertainment and recreational businesses (Naume, 2020; UN, 2020c). In underdeveloped countries where around 90% of employment was provided by SMEs, shutting down these entities simply means shutting down the economy as these entities are the major contributors of tax money to the central government (IMF, 2020). This is the main reason why the governments in developing nations as much as developed countries make countless efforts to try and improve the entrepreneurial activities by their citizens (IMF, 2020; OECD, 2020; ILO, 2020).

In Africa, UN (2020a) reported that 80% or more were affected as compared to a lesser proportion of large enterprises that were affected within the range of 50 to 60 percent (Economic Commission for Africa and International Economics Consulting, 2020). This empirical evidence clearly shows the relevance of entrepreneurship in any given economy hence entrepreneurship education is becoming the central point of focus for administrations around the globe in an effort to excel in economic recovery efforts, especially after the COVID-19 pandemic era. Coronavirus significantly contributed towards high unemployment or job losses and drastic declines in revenues. Subsequently, UN (2020b) reported that Foreign Direct Investment (FDI) dropped by 40% in the year 2020 and if the pandemic is not controlled the situation may continue to deteriorate. Both developed and developing countries continue to suffer.

Hence, entrepreneurial education is at the heart of the economic recovery agenda whereby the institutions of higher education can play a leading role in the economic recovery process through the delivery of relevant entrepreneurship education.

Despite the challenges brought about by the COVID-19 pandemic outbreak, progressive changes were also brought economic transformation that is associated with opportunities especially in terms of innovation and electronic or digitalization of operations (World Bank, 2020; UN, 2020c). The use of online shopping has escalated significantly encouraging consumers and suppliers to reduce contact time. Rapid response to restrictive lockdowns and health threats drive the widespread digitalization across all nations. The entrepreneurial organizations embrace these technological advancements to bypass the coronavirus lockdown restrictions which are aimed at minimizing the spread of the daring coronavirus (Naume, 2020). Despite the efforts by governments to save enterprises from collapsing by offering financial assistance, central governments also aim to revive the struggling economies through offering advice and education also known as enterprise education or entrepreneurial education.

The central governments as the responsible authorities through state universities and colleges can scale up the provision of entrepreneurship education to both students and the general public in an effort to accelerate economic recovery in the post-COVID-19 pandemic era. Universities are spearheading the programs in some public universities in Zimbabwe when it comes to the provision of entrepreneurship education. Some institutions of higher education are offering entrepreneurship education as a compulsory course for all university students from all faculties and departments so as to educate and motivate students and even university staff about the importance of entrepreneurship (Dzingirai, 2020a; UN, 2020; World Bank, 2020). This can go a long way in promoting economic recovery after the COVID-19 pandemic which causes a cocktail of economic challenges that are affecting the economic performance of both developed and developing countries.

The pandemic outbreak came at a point where most countries in Africa among other developing countries in the world were still struggling with the finance-related issues and the outbreak of the pandemic worsened the already sorry state of most countries falling under the bracket of the less developed countries. The economic crisis induced by the emergence of the COVID-19 pandemic has witnessed nations' debt escalating to unmaintainable levels but the UN (2020b) projected that some countries are slowly beginning to recover and 2021 might see some progressive changes. However, inadequate resources may slow the recovery efforts and this calls upon the need for entrepreneurs to be more innovative and creative so as to come up with other ways of staying in business. Not only financial aid is needed but entrepreneurship education to improve the acumen of people in business.

Besides the burden on national governments to help entrepreneurs to revive the businesses, development assistance in form of other non-monetary forms such as opportunities and education is needed by the citizens (Naume, 2020). The pandemic exerts too much pressure on the central government as far as health and economic crisis is concerned with the business community looking up to the government during these difficult times while the government looks up to the business community to help to fight the pandemic (UN, 2020b; World Bank, 2020). The troubled governments expect the business community to participate as part of the Corporate Social Responsibility (CSR) while the financially troubled businesses consider that it's time for the government to support the businesses using the tax monies previously contributed by businesses. Unfortunately, most of the administrations in the developing counties does not have enough finances due to maladministration, corruption and misappropriation of public funds to the extent that these administrations always clamor for more revenue collections but the progress does not match the revenue collected (World Bank, 2020; UN, 2020c).

UN (2020c) emphasize the relevance and importance of technology and innovation infrastructure in light of entrepreneurship education in this COVID-19 crisis arguing that innovation and technology help to build a better future for everyone. Excellent innovation systems come with packages that make it easy for entrepreneurs to conduct business and provide services over digital platforms that are risk-free when it comes to the spread of the deadly coronavirus (Naume, 2020). Efforts to accelerate entrepreneurship education are also part of the innovative systems where mentors and lecturers can interact with their students and associates virtually without violating lockdown gathering restrictions. Digitization also breaks the distance barrier and makes it possible for decisions to be made as soon as possible. Innovative systems also enable entrepreneurship to break the international boundaries with the digital platforms making it easy for consumers to reach global markets online and this is not a new phenomenon but entrepreneurship education courses such as e-commerce improve economic activities even under lockdown restrictions. (UNCTAD, 2020; UN, 2020a).

Given the unprecedented challenges of the COVID-19 pandemic, it appears to be the right time to interrogate how the provision of entrepreneurship can drive economic recovery in the post-COVID-19 pandemic era. It is worth mentioning that economic transformation after the pandemic requires committed and dedicated entrepreneurs (Naume, 2020). Entrepreneurship education has emerged as the leading spectacle of late due to the high unemployment rate created by the global pandemic that has forced employers to scale down their operations with many companies shutting down. Therefore, the provision of entrepreneurship education by higher education institutions can allow the respective governments to speed up economic recovery. Before the pandemic outbreak, the awareness of permeating entrepreneurship into education has prompted much job creation, societal resilience and economic growth for many economies. Therefore, this study aims to investigate the relevance and practicality of entrepreneurship education in enhancing economic recovery in the post-pandemic era.

RESEARCH METHODOLOGY

A qualitative investigation into the subject was done in observation of the COVID-19 lockdown restrictions. The applicability and relevance of entrepreneurship education as a driver for economic recovery in the post-pandemic era were investigated qualitatively. The use of digital platforms and ICT alternatives was relevant in this study although the use of such technologically advanced platforms is not so easy due to technological gaps associated with connectivity and logistical challenges in developing countries like Zimbabwe (Teti et al., 2020; Adedoyin, 2020).

Research philosophy

This qualitative study on entrepreneurial education as a driver for economic recovery in the post-pandemic era is supported with interpretivism philosophy. Interpretivism is widely accepted as a philosophy that supports qualitative research similarly to social constructivism (Bogna, Raineri, & Dell, 2020). As such, this philosophy allows qualitative investigation and analysis of the topic under study so as to come up with credible and accurate results that are also easy to understand. This philosophy is widely accepted and used by many scholars and researchers on entrepreneurship and it is considered relevant as far as providing in-depth analysis and understanding of qualitative aspects (Doern, 2017).

Research design

In conformity with the interpretivism paradigm employed is the exploratory research design that was adopted in an attempt to explore and investigate the relevance of entrepreneurship education as a driver for economic recovery in the post-COVID-19 era. Research design is generally considered to be the plan that is to be followed when carrying out research and, in this study, the exploratory research design was the most appropriate hence it was used (Creswell, 2014).

Sampling procedure

The sample for the research was made up of 10 respondents from the Business Management department and the Entrepreneurship department who have experience in teaching entrepreneurship courses in higher education. The respondents were selected from these departments since they are the experts in entrepreneurship as a subject hence their contribution and responses are considered to be more reliable and informed by their high level of expertise as far as entrepreneurship education is concerned. Three respondents were selected from the department of business management and seven from the entrepreneurship department. Purposive sampling also known as judgmental sampling was used to select respondents since this non-probability sampling method improves credibility and precision data given that the selected participants perfectly were in a better position to give candid and reliable responses (Ames et al., 2019).

Data collection techniques

Focus group discussions and in-depth interviews were used as methods of collecting data. Focus groups were used as the main research instruments in this study. According to Gundumogula (2020), the use of focus groups is increasingly dominating in qualitative research, academic and management research as well as in applied research. In this research, focus groups with respondents were used to gather information concerning the relevance, significance and practicability of entrepreneurship education as a driver for economic recovery in the recent post-pandemic era. Gundumogula (2021) reiterates that focus groups are not really different from interviews except that focus groups give rooms for many participants to interact with the researcher and use the group discussion to learn and share business-related aspects from one another. According to Gundumpgula (2020), focus groups are more relevant when collecting qualitative data as they allow the researcher to get more information and learn other new aspects pertinent to the research as respondents interact during the discussion. As the participants interact, the researchers get deeper information about the subject matter hence rich data was collected. Moreover, in-depth interviews were used for the purpose of seeking clarification on some aspects that needed distinct insights. According to Adedoyin (2020), interviews should be conducted in a systematic way where ambiguous questions should be avoided and precise questions that add value to the study be asked in a friendly and convenient way.

Data analysis

Thematic analysis was used as a basic approach for data analysis and qualitative interpretation. Thematic analysis is the widely accepted method of analyzing qualitative data in research. Braun, Clarke, Hayfield, & Terry (2019) similarly applaud the use of thematic analysis as a systematic way of analyzing qualitative data that is flexible and accessible.

Results and discussions

This section presents the key findings and discussions on entrepreneurship education as a driver for economic recovery in the post-pandemic era citing evidence from higher education. The following aspects were examined and responses recorded.

Significance of Entrepreneurship Education

Respondents vividly agreed with the practicability and relevance of entrepreneurship education as a panacea that can be used to drive economic recovery in the post-pandemic era. Empirical evidence suggests that most businesses fail within the first five years of their establishment and the main reason behind the failure of the business is non-other lack of entrepreneurial expertise hence the respondents agreed that the use of entrepreneurship education in higher learning institutions can be a preparatory activity for students who often become the captains of the industry after graduation as supported by the following quotes from the participants:

"Entrepreneurship education is one of the best ways that can be used to prepare for the future success of enterprises after this COVID-19 thing" (R5).

"Of all the strategies available to the government, entrepreneurship should be the best of them all since it prepares entrepreneurs to be experts in business dealings. Financial aspects are relevant but without entrepreneurship education, most enterprises continue to fail." (R9)

"It is better to prepare the potential entrepreneurs first before giving them financial assistance. Education should be the starting point of any entrepreneurial activities and we have enrolled many prominent business people who appreciate the importance of entrepreneurship education when it comes to making informed decisions. As you may know, entrepreneurs will earn a lot after the pandemic as compared to employees." (Focus Group Participant, FG3).

Enterprising Students

The study sought to investigate the use of entrepreneurship education as a driver of economic recovery in the post-pandemic era. The respondents confirmed that convincing students to become entrepreneurial is one of the most difficult things to do as far as teaching entrepreneurship is concerned. One way to measure if one has convinced students to become entrepreneurial is ensuring that learners apply what has been leaned into practical. Notably, some responses of the interviewees were as follows:

"Delivering a lecture on entrepreneurship and convincing one to become an entrepreneur are two different things." (R3)

"Some students are really excellent when it comes to understanding the entrepreneurial concepts but are hesitant to implement the ideas even if they have a potential to become successful entrepreneurs." (Focus Group Participant, FG1)

"Almost all students agree that entrepreneurship is the way to sustainable livelihoods but the idea of starting one's entity is not an option for a recent graduate who has the desire to work for large and already established organizations" (R1)

Teaching and Learning Approaches

The teaching and learning approaches used to develop the entrepreneurial capabilities for students include networking, case studies, consultancy and generally digital simulation. Besides the satisfactory qualifications of many lecturers, the study found that it takes more than just a qualification to motivate students to pursue entrepreneurial initiatives and opportunities. The theoretical aspects are considered to be simple by many students but the implementation part of the learning process is lacking as some interviewees said:

"The pandemic outbreak changes a number of things and among these is the teaching and learning approach. Everyone has gone digital and so is the education system." (R10)

"The traditional approach of face-to-face interaction has been replaced by technology and worse the restrictive lockdown makes it impossible for tutors and learners to meet regularly. The only way to meet is through virtual meetings which are frequently interrupted by connectivity and power challenges." (Focus Group Participant, FG2)

"Qualifications alone do not influence the students but the characters of the tutors are really important when it comes to lesson delivery." (R6)

"Theoretical aspects of entrepreneurship are not enough There is also a need for practical assessment based on the achievements of the students." (R5)

Entrepreneurship Promoting Divergent Thinking

All participants confirmed that entrepreneurship education should be aimed at promoting divergent thinking as an important skill in dealing with challenges and changes such as economic crises. 80% of the respondents, however, reported that the educators only try to promote divergent thinking but the practical aspect is only evident when the learners become entrepreneurs and intrapreneurs in the organizations. Participants also confirmed that divergent thinking helps entrepreneurs to act on time when faced with challenging situations that need urgent decision-making. The following responses were notable from the respondents:

"Promoting divergent thinking is one important aspect that needs to be mastered by entrepreneurs especially when the old ways of doing business are no longer viable." (R8)

"Divergent thinking is an entrepreneurial requirement that we aim to impart to our students so that they are able to maximize opportunities as they arise especially when there are changes in the business environment. Some opportunities may arise when the old tricks are no longer viable hence divergent thinking is needed to act fast." (R4)

Many scholars agree with the respondents concerning the importance of promoting divergent thinking in entrepreneurship education as a way of ensuring that entrepreneurs are able to respond swiftly to the dynamic changes in entrepreneurial ventures (Lackeus, 2019; Langston, 2020.)

Availability of Resources for Entrepreneurial Education

It has been noted that 80% of respondents reported that there are no enough resources to ensure the success of entrepreneurship education initiatives. The following responses were notable from the participants:

"The curriculum for entrepreneurship education is well-drafted but learning institutions lack resources for implementation hence most practical lessons are just theorized by the tutors". (R9)

"Resources are not as much important as the willingness to start a business and the ability to identify opportunities." (R2)

Many studies confirm the importance of identifying splendid opportunities but also confirm the importance of resource availability. Most SMEs especially in developing countries are run by individuals or families without enough funding and credit facilitates in developing countries are very limited hence family resources or personal belongings are used to finance entrepreneurial operations (OECD, 2020; World Bank, 2020; Langston, 2020).

Entrepreneurship experience

Work experience is now a prerequisite in teaching entrepreneurship education as practice experience helps in describing practical aspects of entrepreneurship that need clarification. There is ongoing debate as to whether entrepreneurship teachers should have practical experience in the subject or not. Each educator from the participants shared different stories and routes to their entrepreneurship education path and while the stories are different so are the approaches by the tutors on educating and influencing the lives and opinions of learners. Interestingly, most respondents were entrepreneurs although with less experience in mega-enterprises but SMEs and microbusinesses as capture in the following responses:

"Entrepreneurship is best learned through practice and that's how you get experience. When I joined the university, I did not have enough entrepreneurial or teaching experience but I manage to put the knowledge that acquired into practice to start my retail shop. Surprisingly the business is doing well beyond my expectations." (Focus Group Participant, FG4).

"I had a little experience from my work-related learning but I manage to gain a lot of experience through voluntary employment whilst I was looking for employment." (R7).

"I had more than 7 years experience of teaching and business-related experience when I joined the university but I continue to learn even from my colleagues in the business community. As a lecturer and an evaluator of students practicals I always

take every opportunity to evaluate and learn from organizations that recruit our students for work-related learning" (R1).

DISCUSSION

Different themes emerged from the data analysis as presented above. In terms of approach, it emerged that different approaches for teaching entrepreneurship education were being adopted. In this context, Langston (2020) also reported that entrepreneurship teachers come from different backgrounds and have different stories to tell about their professional life hence the approaches used by these tutors are slightly different. Entrepreneurship education can be used to model learners by improving their skills and knowledge to identify opportunities and solving problems that may arise in their business community. Through entrepreneurship education, students can improve their competencies and capabilities to manage and navigate through difficult environments such as the COVID-19 period. The ability of entrepreneurship education to improve the business acumen of students creates a viable business community that is able to turn around the situation by thinking outside the box and come up with economically sound and viable decisions. Hardie et al., (2020) also confirm that entrepreneurship education has the potential to improve the knowledge, skills and competencies of learners so that they are able to identify and take advantage of the opportunities that may arise in any situation. Riekmann (2020) also reported that universities and other learning institutions need urgent attention on entrepreneurship education so that the young generation is fully prepared to deal with the constantly changing environment.

RECOMMENDATIONS

Experimental Approach to Entrepreneurship Education: It is high time for universities and other higher education institutions to adopt the experimental approach to entrepreneurship education so as to improve the entrepreneurial activities of students and the public in general during the post-COVID-19 pandemic era. Results confirmed that the current teaching approach is more concentrated on the theoretical aspects hence most graduates end up being unemployed instead of becoming entrepreneurs. The experimental approach is more practical and motivates learners to become more practical as well as fostering value creation. Profound understanding of the entrepreneurial concepts is achieved through a practical or experimental approach where learners can enjoy the benefits of the projects as well as gaining experience.

Promoting Entrepreneurship as a Lucrative Career in the post-COVID-19 Era: To motivate the learners, lecturers could collaborate with entrepreneurial icons to model the students so that they are more connected to the practical aspects of entrepreneurship. Sharing practical stories and experiences from entrepreneurial role models can give the students the zeal and eagerness to follow suit in the post-pandemic era. These role models can also help students with practical experiences with respect to different industries and sectors. For instance, if the lecturer can organize workshops or seminars with entrepreneurial role models from mining, agriculture, engineering and retail to mention only a few sectors, learners get exposure to different industries which can open golden entrepreneurial avenues for students. This could offer the students a wide array of choices or options depending on their passion and interests. It is well-known that individual behavior can be easily influenced by role models. Hence, the use of entrepreneurial role models could improve the entrepreneurial passion of students in the post-pandemic era.

Establishment of Cooperative Entrepreneurship Hubs: To improve entrepreneurial activities, the governments should establish cooperative entrepreneurship hubs in the communities and urban areas that will promote intensification of entrepreneurship activities in the post-COVID-19 pandemic era. These community entrepreneurship hubs can be used as part of the entrepreneurship education departments for experimental and practical mentoring of students and the public in the post-COVID-19 pandemic era in pursuit of economic recovery. Moreover, entrepreneurship educators can utilize cooperative entrepreneurship hubs as part of their community engagement activities.

Recommendations for Further Research

The use of entrepreneurship education alone as a driver of economic recovery is not adequate to stimulate economic recovery in the post-COVID-19 pandemic era. Given this limitation, future studies could focus on the other strategies that can be adopted to address economic challenges in the post-pandemic era. Moreover, some quantitative studies on the impact of entrepreneurship education on economic recovery are welcomed.

CONCLUSION

This study aims to examine the role of entrepreneurship education as a driver for economic recovery in the post-COVID-19 pandemic era. Results recorded confirms that entrepreneurship education can play a catalyst role for economic recovery in the post-COVID-19 pandemic era. However, not much has been done to ensure that education becomes more practical than just theory as most students in higher learning institutions are ending up graduating without the zeal to start their own entrepreneurial activities. The main challenges presented show that entrepreneurship education is not being efficiently delivered due to the teaching approaches and the strategies used in learning institutions. The idea of emphasizing entrepreneurship education is to motivate, promote and encourage learners to peruse entrepreneurial activities that generate more employment and economic activities hence turning around the struggling economies. Despite the potential of entrepreneurship education to stimulate economic activities little has been done so far to ensure that entrepreneurship education is fully and efficiently executed. If more resources could be employed in entrepreneurship education and contingency approaches are implemented the practicality of entrepreneurship education could become more relevant as compared to present-day efforts by governments and higher learning institutions to stimulate economic recovery through entrepreneurship. With this in mind, it is recommended that management of institutions of higher education should promote an experimental approach to entrepreneurship education, the governments should establish cooperative entrepreneurship hubs, and promote entrepreneurship as a lucrative career in the post-COVID-19 pandemic era.

REFERENCES

Adedoyin, O. B. (2020). *Qualitative Research Methods*. Near East University.

Akkermans, J., Richardson, J., & Kraimer, M. (2020). The Covid-19 crisis as a career shock: Implications for careers and vocational behavior. *Journal of Vocational Behavior*, *119*(1), 1–5. doi:10.1016/j.jvb.2020.103434 PMID:32390655

Ames, H., Glenton, C., & Lewin, S. (2020). Purposive sampling in a qualitative evidence synthesis: A worked example from a synthesis on parental perceptions of vaccination communication. *BMC Medical Research Methodology*, *19*(1), 26. Advance online publication. doi:10.118612874-019-0665-4 PMID:30704402

Baker, S. R., Bloom, N., Davis, S. J., & Terry, S. J. (2020). *Covid-induced economic uncertainty* (Working Paper No. 26983). https://www.nber.org/papers/w26983

Blanda, J. & Urbancikova, N. (2020). Social Entrepreneurship as a Tool of Sustainable Development. *Quality Innovation Prosperity, 24*(3). . doi:10.12776/qip.v24i3.1463

Bogna, F., Raineri, A., & Dell, G. (2020). Critical realism and constructivism: Merging research paradigms for a deeper qualitative study. *Qualitative Research in Organizations and Management*, *15*(4), 461–484. doi:10.1108/QROM-06-2019-1778

Braun, V., Clarke, V., Hayfield, N., & Terry, G. (2019). Thematic Analysis. In L. Liamputtong (Ed.), *Handbook of Research Methods in Health Social Sciences* (pp. 843–860). Springer. doi:10.1007/978-981-10-5251-4_103

Creswell, J. W. (2014). *Research design: Qualitative, quantitative, and mixed-method approaches* (4th ed.). Sage.

Doern, R. (2017). Strategies for resilience in entrepreneurship: Building resources for small business survival after a crisis. Institute of Management Studies, Goldsmiths, University of London.

Dzingirai, M. (2020a). Design Thinking Perspective in Entrepreneurship Education. In N. Baporikar (Ed.), *Handbook of Research on Entrepreneurship Development and Opportunities in Circular Economy* (pp. 397–416). IGI Global. doi:10.4018/978-1-7998-5116-5.ch021

Dzingirai, M. (2020b). Barriers for quality management implementation in higher education. In M. Sony, K. Karingada, & N. Baporikar (Eds.), *Quality management implementation in higher education: practices, models, and case studies* (pp. 132–151). IGI Global. doi:10.4018/978-1-5225-9829-9.ch007

Dzingirai, M., Chagwesha, M., & Mudzurandende, F. (2021). Challenges and opportunities from COVID-19 vis-à-vis informal cross-border women entrepreneurs scenario in Zimbabwe. In N. Baporikar (Ed.), *Handbook of research on sustaining SMEs and entrepreneurial innovation in the post-COVID-19 Era* (pp. 40–59). IGI Global. doi:10.4018/978-1-7998-6632-9.ch003

Dzingirai, M., Tshuma, N., & Sikomwe, S. (2021). Post-pandemic sustainability strategies for Zimbabwean SMEs. In N. Baporikar (Ed.), *Handbook of research on strategies and interventions to mitigate COVID-19 impact on SMEs* (pp. 457–476). IGI Global. doi:10.4018/978-1-7998-7436-2.ch022

Economic Commission for Africa and International Economics Consulting. (2020). *Insights on African businesses' reactions and outlook to COVID-19.* Retrieved July 18, 2021, from https://www.uneca.org/publications/insightsafrican-businesses%E2%80%99-reactions-and-outlook-covid-19

Fejes, A., Nylund, M., & Wallin, J. (2019). How do teachers interpret and transform entrepreneurship education? *Journal of Curriculum Studies, 51*(4), 554–566. doi: 10.1080/00220272.2018.1488998

Fernandes, N. (2020). *Economic effects of coronavirus outbreak (COVID-19) on the world economy. 2020.* Retrieved July 15, 2021, from https://papers.ssrn.com/sol3/papers.cfm?abstract_id=3557504

Ferreira, C. C. (2020). Experiential learning theory and hybrid entrepreneurship: Factors influencing the transition to full-time entrepreneurship. *International Journal of Entrepreneurial Behaviour & Research, 26*(8), 1845–1863. doi:10.1108/IJEBR-12-2019-0668

Government of Ireland (GoI). (2021). *Economic Recovery Plan 2021.* Department of the Taoiseach gov.ie.

Hardie, B., Highfield, C., & Lee, K. (2020). Review Article Entrepreneurship education today for students' unknown futures. *Journal of Pedagogical Research, 4*(3), 401–417. doi:10.33902/JPR.2020063022

Ho, M. H., Uy, M. A., Kang, B. N. Y., & Chan, K. Y. (2018). Impact of entrepreneurship training on entrepreneurial efficacy and alertness among adolescent youth. *Frontiers in Education, 3*(13), 1–10. doi:10.3389/feduc.2018.00013

Igbinakhase, I. (2021). Determinants for SMEs and entrepreneurship success post-pandemic. In N. Baporikar (Ed.), *Handbook of research on strategies and interventions to mitigate COVID-19 impact on SMEs* (pp. 168–185). IGI Global. doi:10.4018/978-1-7998-7436-2.ch008

ILO. (2020). *ILO Monitor: COVID-19 and the world of work* (7th ed.). Retrieved July 15, 2021, from https://www.ilo.org/global/topics/coronavirus/impacts-and-responses/WCMS_767028/lang--en/index.htm

ILO. (2020a). *ILO Monitor: COVID-19 and the world of work* (4th ed). Retrieved July 15, 2020, from https://www.ilo.org/global/topics/coronavirus/impacts-and-responses/WCMS_745963/lang--en/index.htm

International Monetary Fund. (2020). *Policy responses to COVID-19.* Retrieve July 16, 2021, from https://www.imf.org/en/Topics/ imf-and-covid19/Policy-Responses-to-COVID-19

Lackeus, M. (2015). *Entrepreneurship in education.* OECD Paris France.

Lackeus, M. (2019) Making enterprise education more relevant through mission creep. In Enterprising education in UK higher education: Challenges for theory and practice. Routledge Studies in Entrepreneurship.

Langston, C. (2020). Entrepreneurial educators: Vital enablers to support the education sector to reimagine and respond to the challenges of COVID-19. *Entrepreneurship Education, 3*(3), 311–338. doi:10.100741959-020-00034-4

Maritz, A., Perenyi, A., De-Waal, G., & Buck, C. (2020). Entrepreneurship as the unsung hero during the current COVID-19 economic crisis: Australian Perspectives. *Sustainability*, *12*, 4612.

Nabi, G., Walmsley, A., Liñán, F., Akhtar, I., & Neame, C. (2018). Does entrepreneurship education in the first year of higher education develop entrepreneurial intentions? The role of learning and inspiration. *Studies in Higher Education*, *43*(3), 452–467. doi:10.1080/03075079.2016.1177716

Naude, W. (2020). *Entrepreneurial recovery from COVID-19: Decentralization, democratization, demand, distribution, and demography*. Discussion Paper Series, DP No. 13436.

OECD. (2020). *COVID-19: SME policy responses.* Retrieved 12 July, 2021, from https://read.oecd-ilibrary.org/view/?ref=119_119680di6h3qgi4x&title=Covid-19_SME_Policy_Responses

Rieckmann, M. (2020). *Innovative Learning Approaches to foster sustainable entrepreneurship competencies with regard to the SDGs in Higher Education* [Webinar]. Intrinsic project. Retrieved July 15, 2021, from https://www.intrinsic.eu/_media/rieckmann-innovative-learning-approaches-to-foster-sustainable-entrepreneurship-competencies.pdf

Teti, M., Schatz, E., & Liebenberg, L. (2020). Methods in the time of COVID-19: The vital role of qualitative inquiries. *International Journal of Qualitative Methods*, *19*, 1609406920920962. doi:10.1177/1609406920920962

UNCTAD. (2020b). *The need to protect science, technology and innovation funding during and after the COVID-19 crisis*. Policy Brief No. 80. Retrieved July 10, 2021, from https://unctad.org/webflyer/need-protect-science-technology-and-innovation-funding-during-and-after-covid-19-crisis

United Nations. (2020a). *Impact of the Pandemic on Trade and Development. Transitioning to a New Normal.* United Nations Conference on Trade and Development. Retrieved July 2, 2021, from https://unctad.org/webflyer/impact-covid-19-pandemic-trade-and-development-transitioning-new-normal

United Nations. (2020b). *Entrepreneurship for sustainable development.* United Nations General Assembly, Seventy-fifth session, A/75/257. Retrieved July 3, 2021, from https://digitallibrary.un.org/record/1639377

United Nations. (2020c). *External debt sustainability and development.* A/75/281. Retrieved July 16, 2021, from https://unctad.org/system/files/official-document/tc2015d1rev2_S04_P02.pdf

WEF. (2020a). *Challenges and opportunities in the post-COVID-19 world*. Retrieved July 15, 2021, from https://www.weforum.org/reports/post-covid-19-challenges-and-opportunities

WEF. (2020b). *Great Reset: What university entrepreneurship can bring to the post-COVID world?* Retrieved July 10, 202, from https://www.weforum.org/agenda/2020/07/university-entrepreneurship-post-covid-19-world/

World Bank. (2020). *Map of SME support measures in response to COVID-19*. Retrieved July 4, 2021, from https://www.worldbank.org/en/data/interactive/2020/04/14/map-of-sme-support-measures-in-response-to-covid-19

WTO. (2020). *E-commerce, trade and the COVID-19 pandemic*. Retrieved July 18, 2021, from https://www.wto.org/english/tratop_e/covid19_e/ecommerce_report_e.pdf

Zahra, S. A. (2021). International entrepreneurship in the post-Covid world. *Journal of World Business*, *56*(1), 101143. doi:10.1016/j.jwb.2020.101143

Zhang, J., & Huang, J. (2021). Entrepreneurial self-efficacy mediates the impact of the post-pandemic entrepreneurship environment on college students' entrepreneurial intention. *Frontiers in Psychology*, *12*, 643184. doi:10.3389/fpsyg.2021.643184 PMID:33995198

ADDITIONAL READING

Cazeri, G. T., Anholon, R., Rampasso, I. S., Quelhas, O. L. G., & Leal Filho, W. (2021). Preparing future entrepreneurs: Reflections about the COVID-19 impacts on the entrepreneurial potential of Brazilian students. *Journal of Work-Applied Management*, *13*(2), 277–283. doi:10.1108/JWAM-10-2020-0046

Gordana, D. P., & Biljana, I. S. (2021). Sustaining SME management and innovations in the post-COVID era. In N. Baporikar (Ed.), *Handbook of research on strategies and interventions to mitigate COVID-19 impact on SMEs* (pp. 588–608). IGI Global. doi:10.4018/978-1-7998-7436-2.ch029

Korber, S., & McNaughton, R. B. (2018). Resilience and entrepreneurship: A systematic literature review. *International Journal of Entrepreneurial Behaviour & Research*, *24*(7), 1129–1154. doi:10.1108/IJEBR-10-2016-0356

Naidoo, V. (2021). SME sustainability in South Africa post-COVID-19. In N. Baporikar (Ed.), *Handbook of research on sustaining SMEs and entrepreneurial innovation in the post-COVID-19 era* (pp. 419–437). IGI Global. doi:10.4018/978-1-7998-6632-9.ch020

Sheth, J. (2020). Impact of Covid-19 on consumer behavior: Will the old habits return or die? *Journal of Business Research, Elsevier, 117*, 280–283. doi:10.1016/j.jbusres.2020.05.059 PMID:32536735

KEY TERMS AND DEFINITIONS

COVID-19 Pandemic: It is a newly emerged infectious disease caused by a coronavirus.

Economic Crisis: It is a drastic fall in the economic performance of the country which is manifested in a decline in production and demand, rising unemployment and bankruptcy of businesses. This will automatically lead to high poverty levels in the country.

Economic Recovery: It is a business cycle stage characterized by improved demand following a recession in business activity.

Entrepreneurship: It is the process of starting and running a new profitable business by taking risks.

Entrepreneurship Education: It is the provision of skills, knowledge, and motivation to engage in successful business start-ups.

Microenterprises: These are very small businesses that are very common in developing countries that employ five or fewer people as they are supported by microcredit.

Unemployment: It is a term normally used to describe people in a specific country who are actively looking for a decent job but are not securing a job.

Chapter 3
Career Retooling in a Pandemic-Recovery Phase

Shalin Hai-Jew
https://orcid.org/0000-0002-8863-0175
Kansas State University, USA

ABSTRACT

The SARS-CoV-2/COVID-19 pandemic has been disruptive of various industries globally, due to the need for social distancing in the absence of effective vaccines and treatments in the first year and counting. As humanity has racked up losses, many people have been sidelined from the workforce, which was already under pressure with the incursions of high technology in the Fourth Industrial Revolution (4IR). To survive, people have had to raid savings, liquify whatever they have of value, and rely on family and friends and public charity to survive. Many have left bills unpaid, for rent, for auto loans, for credit card debt, and others. As the world slowly comes out of the pandemic, thanks to multiple effective vaccines (by BioNTech and Pfizer, Moderna, Johnson & Johnson, stateside), many are starting to reenter the job market, with varying outcomes. This work explores various career retooling paths in this moment based on content analysis of available formal and informal data. There is primary research from the Social Web.

INTRODUCTION

Workplaces have always been in a state of churn, with inflows and outflows of employees with varying tasks and positions, achieving various defined objectives, and advancing the work of the respective organizations. People have always had to work on building their respective skillsets and creating personal brands to communicate

DOI: 10.4018/978-1-7998-8626-6.ch003

their value to work places. People have always had to adapt to new workplace realities, with globalization (which brings on more competitors from around the world), technological innovations (with people's jobs being replaced by artificial intelligence and automation), and other challenges. The advent of the SARS-CoV-2 / COVID-19 pandemic (Oct. 2019 to present) is said to have accelerated many of the trends of the Fourth Industrial Revolution (4IR), with human jobs replaced by machines and machine processing of information. Those in manufacturing are at especial risk of having their jobs lost to automation and so need to "continue, shift, or re-orient their career paths" (Chin, Li, Jiao, Addo, & Jawahar, 2019, p. 523). In the early summer of 2021, in the U.S., as more and more of the population are being vaccinated, employers are engaging the "arduous process of recalling their employees" (Klotz, May 30, 2021). Some market sectors have changed fundamentally while others less so. Even if it is not yet apparent, much of the world has shifted on its axis.

What makes coming out of a global pandemic, in fits and starts, so different? And how should these differences be understood for those in the present moment? What does it mean to be adaptive in this time and in the fluid job markets?

This work explores what career retooling may look like in a pandemic recovery phase and in an environment of technological incursions in the job market. Initial reports suggest that women have borne an undue burden in this pandemic, with many who have left the workplace permanently to care for children. People are coming out of the pandemic less fit, in many cases, having avoided healthcare visits and not following doctor's guidance for various health issues and getting insufficient exercise. Some who have had the infection may be experiencing COVID-19 "long hauler" syndrome, with various continuing effects on various parts of the body: the brain, the heart, and so on.

After a year and a half of web conferencing, there are concerns about how colleagues may interact in person. After a year and a half of public health warning against interacting with others within six feet and in doors, and seeing so many become ill and many die, there is a sense that many have post-traumatic stress disorder (PTSD) and social anxieties. At the same time that the larger economy and work environments have changed, people are facing up to the brevity of life and their own mortality. They are struggling with a sense of lack of trust of others, whether fellow citizens or health professionals or government, or even all the prior. Perhaps some want meaningful work, or their goals have changed, and they want different things from life. Work may have been displaced from life's center, and perhaps personal or other goals have come to the fore.

Some sectors that were undergoing pressure, some in the coal mining industry, for example, have dwindled further. Supply chain interruptions have meant workplace interruptions, such as in car manufacturing. Restaurants and bars, casinos, and other locales long closed due to the health risks of close proximity to other people without sufficient masking have reopened to great fanfare. Tourism is starting up again. Institutions of higher education are still reeling from drops in enrollments.

Some are predicting a powerful rebound and burgeoning economy that is rising from enforced torpor. Others suggest that rampant inflation is on the horizon due to the government stimulus payment and pent-up demands and excess liquidity. In this crucial moment, there are efforts by government leaders to fund infrastructure buildouts, which may mediate the near- and mid-future present. In some locales, universal basic income is being provided by the government to citizens, for a time, to lower the pressure to go out to work and potentially become exposed to SARS-CoV-2 (the pathogenic virus) and COVID-19 (the disease caused by the virus).

Regardless, there are expectations that workplaces have changed, perhaps to enable more remote work and sparser people co-located in physical spaces. There are touchless ways to enter and exit rooms and elevators. There are plastic screens between peoples. There are signs advocating hand hygiene, social distancing, and masking. Work processes themselves have changed, with a focus on contactless-ness, Work relationships themselves may have changed, with employees trusted to do particular work without direct physical oversight. Trainings have gone virtual in many cases.

REVIEW OF THE LITERATURE

"We want a career that helps to avoid obsolescence, continually develops towards professional mastery, and retains our value to customers and clients."

Peter J. Denning, in "Career Redux: How can one design a career when career as an institution is dead? Entrepreneurs have an answer" in Communications of the ACM [Sept. 2002 45(9), 21 - 26]

"Education can lower the barriers to opportunity in a way that nothing else can. It offers everyone the chance not only to develop knowledge and learn skills but also to continue to transform themselves and their communities and both adapt and rise to new demands and challenges."

Fiona Hill, There is Nothing for You Here (2021, p. 352)

The general narrative about preparedness for the work world goes like this. Each person has particular interests and capabilities, and as they move through formal education (K-12 into higher education), they acquire knowledge, skills, and abilities (KSAs) that can be applied to the workplace. Each person may be thought of as having core competencies and then peripheral ones. Their core strengths may refer to KSAs that they use often, and the peripheral ones may be less used and less practiced. They develop soft skills to enable them to work with other people collaboratively. People need to maintain a running inventory of their skills and enable an objective analysis of what they can offer value-wise to employers. If they identify needs, they need to fill those capability gaps.

People apply for jobs for which they have the requisite skills, and they acquire skills on-the-job and on-their-own along the way. People are expected to constantly upskill and reskill, to have a set of capabilities that can be transferred to other organizations, as needed. There can be formal (accredited), nonformal (non-accredited), and informal (non-course-based learning) learning opportunities. Teachers themselves need to retool through professional development to acquire cutting-edge knowledge, skills, and abilities (KSAs) to support their students (Wetherill, Burton, Calhoun, & Thomas, Dec. 2001 – Jan. 2002, p. 54). The idea is that skills date out quickly. Those in Career and Technical Education (CTE) face the challenge of preparing future workers when "the types of work those people will perform does not yet exist" (Rojewski & Hill, 2014, p. 137), which requires constant reframing the curriculum. There is the sense that work is more "short-term, project-based efforts encompassing multiple tasks, part-time or transient, sporadic and subject to global factors, international in scope, structured around a 24 hours per day/7 days per week schedule, rapid change, being harder to predict the future, a network developed via social media, staffed with aging workers, and union-unfriendly. The emerging world of work requires higher intellectual skills and postsecondary education or training for initial entry into the workplace because of an increasing dependence on technology. Constant retooling throughout life is becoming the norm rather than the exception" (Rojewski & Hill, 2014, p. 143). To wit: "career navigation, work ethic, and innovation" are to be infused in the curriculum and in CTE research (Rojewski & Hill, 2014, p. 146), from K-12 onwards. There can be learning from internships and volunteer work. Based on different life needs, they may have to move or reposition. They may climb various career ladders and both actualize themselves and achieve their own goals… and support the objectives of the organizations for which they work. Many also engage in "gig work" or side jobs; they are freelancers. These gigs not only enable another source of funds but also job experiences.

For those for whom work fulfills part of their identities, people often have to seek the professional positions that enable the fulfilment of those ambitions. For some, this may mean starting their own businesses. An enduring idea is that of E.H. Schein, who originated the concept of a "career anchor" or a "pattern of self-perceived talents, motives, and values…guide, constrain, stabilize, and integrate the person's career" (Schein, 1978, p. 127). He explained further:

The concept of 'career anchor' grew out of several decades of longitudinal research to capture some of the essential components of how career occupants define themselves in relation to their work. A person's career anchor is the evolving self-concept of what one is good at, what one's needs and motives are, and what values govern one's work related choices. One does not have a career anchor until one has worked for number of years and has had relevant feedback from those experiences. But once a career anchor evolves, roughly five to ten years after one has gone to work, it becomes a stabilizing force in the total personality that guides and constrains future career choices. (Schein, 1990, p. 2)

A more recent questionnaire-based study found that "the practice of work values have a significant positive impact" on career success (Zhu, Tan, & Li, 2020, p. 266), affecting both subjective and objective senses of career success. The individual self is considered important for strategic career management, given the power of intrinsic motivations. A "self-centered approach to strategic career management" (McCray & Rawlins, 2015, p. 55) begins with the individual and optimally results in a fit between the person and the organization (p. 56), where the needs of both are met. People need to plan for contingencies for various possibilities in the career experience (McCray & Rawlins, 2015, p. 57). People need to have a sense of "self-efficacy" for "career progress" (Alexander & Twinomurinzi, 2012, p. 295). One study considered various variables students use to select a job; these include the following: "interest, security, self-efficacy, computing self-efficacy, status, flexibility, quality of life, and career progress" (Alexander & Twinomurinzi, 2012, pp. 300). A topline finding is that students consider "genuine interest in their career subjects and job security" as very important (Alexander & Twinomurinzi, 2012, p. 303).

Another consideration is what macro phase of work people are in: early, mid, or late career. Some typical organizational career development activities for those in their "early-, mid-, and late-career" phases follow: For early-career employees, there are supports like "informal guidance, counseling, and mentoring" and "increased focus on variety of assignments" (Feldman, Summer 1996, p. 146) For those in mid-career, there are "periodic skill assessment, retraining and cross-training, (and) protection against age discrimination" (p. 146). For those in the late stage, human resources may provide "pre-retirement counseling, 'open window' programs, (and) bridge employment and 'outward' career tracks" (p. 146). Organizations maintain the twin concerns of "organizational growth and increased opportunities for individual advancement" (Feldman, Summer 1996, p. 146) simultaneously. Those working in a time of downsizing need to maintain technical competence (p. 153) and work as an "outstanding performer" (p. 154).

In terms of practicalities, people are at various employment states. Some have kept their jobs that they had prior to the pandemic and may be in various stages of satisfaction / dissatisfaction in their work. Some have had hours cut or been temporarily furloughed. Some have part-time work. Some have no work at all. In terms of compensation, these may vary, and these may fulfill all or only part of people's living needs. From whatever starting point, people are advised to make efforts to understand the state-of-the-job market and to apply for the jobs that are available. They are asked to make profiles in online job sites. They are asked to use their social connections to create job-seeking opportunities.

One recent pre-pandemic study examined the use of Q&A forums for career advice. Such forums are designed "for sharing expertise, where individuals can pose questions and receive multiple responses from a broad set of individuals" (Tomprou, Dabbish, Kraut, & Liu, 2019, p. 653:2). The questions and answers are generally public, and participants' identities are not usually validated. These researchers found three types of support: "socio-emotional, instrumental, and informational" (Tomprou, Dabbish, Kraut, & Liu, 2019, p. 653:3). They write:

Socio-emotional support focuses on personal growth, such as boosting a protégé's self-confidence. Instrumental support involves helping protégés improve career visibility and offering sponsorship. Informational support involves providing relevant information on specific issues. Some research has reported role modeling as a fourth function of mentoring, which refers to individuals' identification with a senior or an expert acting as the role model. (Tomprou, Dabbish, Kraut, & Liu, 2019, p. 653:3)

The support does not indicate any insider knowledge of a protégé or any continuing relationship. The interactions are often light and fleeting. The researchers found that people going to such online forums for various reasons: to validate offline mentoring feedback, for the time-based immediacy of feedback, for the diversity of feedback, and for having access to expertise or experiences that the questioner would not have otherwise (Tomprou, Dabbish, Kraut, & Liu, 2019, p. 653:5). As for those who mentor others, they experience reciprocity in the community, so there is give-and-take. Many also mentor others to improve their own skills through that advice offering (Tomprou, Dabbish, Kraut, & Liu, 2019, p. 653:5), so there are benefits in multiple directions.

A taxonomy of career advice requests involving three main areas of best practices, threats to career progress, and "time-sensitive decision making" (Tomprou, Dabbish, Kraut, & Liu, 2019, p. 653:6). The researchers identify the need for follow-on forum design to "better support online career mentorship around critical events, ongoing relationships, response structuring, and response reuse" to further improve the value of such Q&A forums for career advice (Tomprou, Dabbish, Kraut, & Liu, 2019, p. 653:10).

Another earlier work offers a dedicated recommender system to advise on horizontal career change. They write: "Employees suffering from high mental or physical stress may use the online portal in order to find new occupations with less or different kinds of stress involved while preserving the employee's social status" (Buschner, Schirru, Zieschang, & Junker, 2014, p. 1). This tool is a matrix-based approach for employment recommendation.

Even prior to the pandemic the awareness of economic instability and the need to acquire the skills to "pivot" has been a focus of study (Freer, 2019, p. 20). There is the sense that all people in the workforce need to be entrepreneurial and develop their careers on multiple tracks (Gray, 2001), to actually compete in a globalized world. Long-running "careers" belong to a time when "professional knowledge changes relatively slowly" (Gray, 2001, p. 65), but with accelerated change, people will need to adapt and be capable of engaging the "wired life" in a time of ubiquitous computing (Gray, 2001, p. 69). Through workshops, people have studied how to remain "true to yourself in the face of change" but also practice "strategic vulnerability" and engage various opportunities (Freer, 2019, p. 21). Those who hold ideas of a "career" in the traditional sense may experience "promise and…potential disillusionment" (Baruch & Vardi, 2016, p. 355). Present-day work involves both "thrill and agony" (p. 359); specifically, downsizing has personal costs for people: ambitions, health, lifestyles, and even "family safety" (p. 360). For others who expect careers to only have rising trajectories, career plateaus may be difficult. An earlier work observes the personal toll of employment in an "age of transition" with "job dislocation and decline" and experienced "lay-offs, threats of downsizing, or being trapped in an unrewarding career" (Cutshaw, 2011, p. 45). Employees may experience various emotions like "pain, fear, and anger" (p. 45) during downturns like recessions. Retooling a career is about bringing "form and focus" to a career (Carliner, 1999, p. 283).

People cannot let the past year and a half of a pandemic be a lost one. If people become less marketable, they will end up with lesser jobs and end up lesser skilled and less competitive. People need to develop career management competencies, especially if they are to transition effectively from academia into the work world. One learning assignment in this space involves university students making videos about work for 9 to 12 year-old schoolchildren and acquiring KSAs in "personal management, learning and work exploration, as well as career building areas" along the way (Ikeda, Assilmia, Angelina, & Okawa, 2019, p. 127). Various studies have been conducted to understand the determinants of job satisfaction in various domains.

- Is the compensation (wages and benefits and perks) fair? Better than the going market rate? Worse?
- Is the work load manageable? Higher or lower than perceived average?
- Is there room to develop and grow as a professional? As a person?
    - Is there space for pursuing some personal interests in work?
- Is there a path for professional advancement?
- Are there opportunities for professional development? Is there organizational interest in having the individual grow?
- Is the employee sufficiently challenged with the work? Is there a sense of satisfaction with the work?
- Are there sufficient equipment and supplies to achieve the necessary work?
- Is the management effective?
- Is the management personable? Relatable?
- Do the workplace values align with those of the individual?
- Is there conflict between work and life? Are these resolved in positive ways?

Other studies are more case-based. Another study explores career satisfaction of professionals in the information systems (IS) field, with a finding that those in "consulting firms are more satisfied with their choice of careers than those who work for non-consulting firms" (Ballou & Huguenard, 2008, p. 50).

Even if workers themselves are prepared, there may be age, race, religious, or other forms of discrimination. One research work posits the "aging advantage." Multiple studies show "older workers to be more engaged, more loyal, less likely to quit, less likely to be absent voluntarily, more willing to work hard, and just as adaptable *when given the opportunity,* compared with their younger colleagues" (Newman, 2011, p. 137). Older workers tend to be "better qualified, more interested in accomplishment, more interested in doing meaningful work, more motivated by autonomy and flexibility and less interested in promotions than their younger coworkers" (p. 137). Certain characteristics of work make for "sustainable careers": being renewable (with "renewing assignments, refocusing, re-education"), flexible ("continuous learning, changeable, adaptable, more options, variable engagement"), and integrative ["bring(ing) disparate information together, perspective, knowledge management"] (Newman, 2011, p. 140). Managers need to engage intergenerational management and better manage talent, such as the Baby Boomers and Gen Y employees (Newman, 2011, p. 142).

Some are turning to their peripheral knowledge, skills, and abilities (KSAs), perhaps from leisure activities and hobbies (including serious ones), to develop new paths for their work lives. Some hobbies are "lifetime" ones (Hegde, Aug. 2016), which enable people to develop serious skillsets. Skills can also develop based on a do-it-yourself (DIY) culture. Still yet, skills may develop out of need, such as contexts of privation.

If avocations involved creative pursuits (Root-Bernstein, 2020), perhaps these may translate into creative objects that may be sold on online markets. Or the skills may be shared on social media (as tutorials). Adults engage in activities including formal (accredited), nonformal (non-accredited), and informal (non-learning-based activities) learning. Any one of those threads may lead to something for which others may pay: knowledge, skills, training, and created products. There is always space for consulting, trainings, applied skills, and some handmade products. Certainly, it is not unheard of for amateurs to contribute to serious research and innovation. What people want and value (what they are willing to pay for) may differ given the times and the state of the world on the other side of the pandemic. Stebbins (1982) observed that people who did not find satisfactory work have turned to "serious leisure" to "express their abilities, fulfill their potential, and identify themselves as unique human beings" (Stebbins, 1982, p. 251). In times of less work, job satisfaction may also be less given the lack of wider choices. Transferring KSAs from one context to another may not be that much of a stretch. (There is a switch from the generally non-commercial to the commercial.) Interestingly, however, so-called "hobby-jobs" have been found to be associated with burnout of the individual, who may be self-employed but working in a passion field (Volpone, Perry, & Rubino, 2013).

The work will capture some of the learning based on the only global pandemic in recent memory for living generations. This work is based on content analysis of available published journalism and social media data.

CAREER RETOOLING IN A PANDEMIC-RECOVERY PHASE

The SARS-CoV-2 / COVID-19 pandemic disrupted humanity globally. It roiled markets. It contributed to social strife. In late May 2021, many people coming out of the pandemic did a surprising thing: they started quitting jobs en masse.

First, due to the uncertainty caused by the pandemic, many employees who would have otherwise quit their jobs stayed put. Indeed, using the Bureau of Labor Statistics Job Openings and Labor Turnover Survey to examine total (nonfarm) quits over the past two years there were close to 6 million fewer resignations in 2020 than there were in 2019. (Klotz, May 30, 2021)

Starting in March 2021, there was a 2.4 percent resignation rate, what one professor termed "the highest quit rate recorded for that month in 20 years" (Klotz, May 30, 2021). These were backlogs of resignations that were temporarily stopped by the pandemic because people did not want to be in transition or jobless during this mass-scale emergency. With the economy improving, the utility of staying at an undesirable job fell, and people recalculated. Some Americans reduced their spending and paid off debt during the pandemic, in part due to government stimulus funds and unemployment funds for inflow and limited places to spend in terms of outflow.

Others have built up a fear of being around others during the year-and-a-half of cyclic lockdowns and reopenings, and they have lessened interest in returning to work. Some want all their coworkers to be fully vaccinated, too, before they would feel safe enough to return to a physical workplace (Klotz, May 30, 2021). Humanity is predicted to have to continue shadow-boxing the deadly virus for years yet globally. Indeed, there are many "hiring" signs out. Many of the highest performers in a workplace are moving on (Klotz, May 30, 2021). And yet, on job sites, many of the jobs on offer are temporary ones. In these setups, "talent agencies" serve as middle organizations to find talent for companies, which can save on the cost of benefits and on the risk of hiring full-timers. It is possible that the available jobs are lower-wage ones, which have kept many unemployed on the sidelines.

DISCUSSIONS

The research focus of this work includes the following questions:

What makes coming out of a global pandemic, in fits and starts, so different? And how should these differences be understood for those in the present moment? What does it mean to be adaptive in this time and in the fluid job markets?

Coming out of a global pandemic, it is clear that an environmental scan is necessary to understand what the available work is and how to acquire and align knowledge, skills, and abilities to that work. The predictions about which fields would come back strong vs. those that will not have been fairly prescient. However, it is important to check the research and plan accordingly.

In general, people have to "sense make" and then decide how they want to proceed work-wise. This decision making is depicted in Figure 1. They have to position themselves to be competitive.

This is an early work which probes the need to retool and adapt in the early recover phase of the COVID-19 pandemic, for which there is no recent human analog. There will certainly be much more thorough learning as time passes and more research is conducted. How this manifests will differ widely based on whether the persons are in developed vs. developing countries, the work domains, and other factors.

Figure 1. Work-Related Decision-making Coming out of a Pandemic

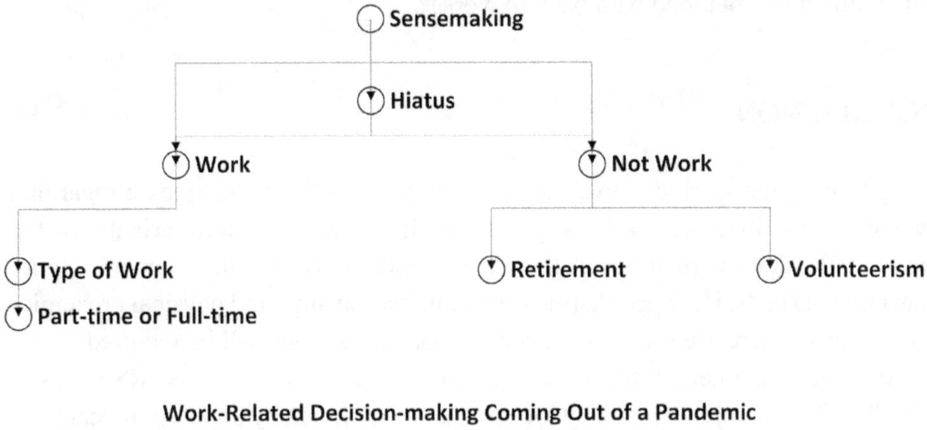

FUTURE RESEARCH DIRECTIONS

Some important work will have to be done to help mass swaths of the human population come out of mass-scale trauma, since people have been living under threat of serious illness and death for the past year and a half. There has been research on how to make workplaces more biosafe, but that is currently still a contested space. In time, there will be more work on management and leadership in such times.

As noted above, there are differences expected between developed and developing countries and their management strategies.

While many are retooling to return, a subset of people will never return to the workplace. According to some news accounts, some parents have chosen to make rearing children full-time (unpaid) labor. Others feel that they are "of age" to retire, whether or not their finances are sufficient for such a crucial life decision. Others have been planning to retire for a long time, and the pandemic has just accelerated their personal timelines. Still others have lost their livelihoods; their careers may have been replaced by technologies or are no longer required. Perhaps their positions were filled by others. Future research may probe some questions including the following: What factors went into the personal decision-making to leave the workforce for good? How did they arrive at the penultimate decision? What issues did they consider? What prior work fields were these individuals in? What are the demographics of these individuals? How did the pandemic affect the decision making directly? How ready were these individuals for post-work lives? What resources did they have set aside: financial, housing, social, and others? Are there any factors that could change their minds? In these cases, how will these individuals retool for a life without work (and without any planned path back to work)?

CONCLUSION

Regardless of the work context, the work retooling will require finesse regarding hygiene, sanitation, and masking, given the rise of various viral variants. At the moment, the delta variant out of India is of concern given higher transmissibility than other variants. How people finesse social relationships and physical proxemics also matters. There are relevant "pandemic soft skills" that will be required.

As humanity emerges from the other side of the devastating SARS-CoV-2 / COVID-19 pandemic, location by location, and population by population, many are finding their prior livelihoods gone. For others, their livelihoods have fundamentally changed. They are finding that their skills are no longer in high demand. They are finding that the predicted Fourth Industrial Revolution (4IR) has made inroads in the economy and resulted in the disappearance of various jobs that were filled by people. They are also finding that there are many service industry jobs that people are no longer willing to work due to low wages. They are finding many positions of management responsibility being filled by younger people who are able to withstand some of the risks and who have some of the requisite skills. The current employment picture is confusing, and the predictions by economists and other professionals are all over the board. Humanity is returning to some sort of "new normal" but with less recognizable than they might have hoped.

REFERENCES

Alexander, P. M., & Twinomurinzi, H. (2012). Changing career choice factors as the economic environment changes. *Proceedings of SAICSIT '12*, 295 – 305. 10.1145/2389836.2389872

Ballou, D. J., & Huguenard, B. R. (2008). Personal and situational predictors of IS professionals' career choice satisfaction. *Proceedings of SIGMIS-CPR '08*, 50 – 57.

Baruch, Y., & Vardi, Y. (2016). A fresh look at the dark side of contemporary careers: Toward a realistic discourse. *British Journal of Management*, *27*(2), 355–372. doi:10.1111/1467-8551.12107

Buschner, S., Schirru, R., Zieschang, H., & Junker, P. (2014). Providing recommendations for horizontal career change. *Proceedings of I-KNOW '14*, 1 – 4. 10.1145/2637748.2638440

Carliner, S. (1999). Industry meets academia: My year of retooling from practicing professional to tenure-track professor. In *Communication Jazz* (pp. 281–288). Improvising the New International Communication Culture. doi:10.1109/IPCC.1999.799135

Chin, T., Li, G., Jiao, H., Addo, F., & Jawahar, I. M. (2019). Career sustainability during manufacturing innovation. *Career Development International*, *24*(6), 509–528. doi:10.1108/CDI-02-2019-0034

Cutshaw, O. (2011). First you grieve: job loss, job stagnation, and job burnout in an age of transition. In *O. Cutshaw's Surviving an information career crisis in a time of change* (pp. 45–55). Chandos Publishing. doi:10.1016/B978-1-84334-632-6.50004-2

Feldman, D. C. (1996, Summer). Managing careers in downsizing firms. *Human Resource Management*, *35*(2), 145–161. doi:10.1002/(SICI)1099-050X(199622)35:2<145::AID-HRM1>3.0.CO;2-Y

Freer, L. M. (2019). Strategies for career resilience in the face of economic uncertainty. *Proceedings of SIGUCCS '19*, 20 – 22. 10.1145/3347709.3347811

Gray, J. (2001). The end of career. *Communications of the ACM*, *44*(11), 65–69. doi:10.1145/384150.384163

Hegbe, S. (2016). Developing hobbies for a lifetime. *Journal of Social Welfare and Management*, *8*(2), 111–121.

Ikeda, R., Assilmia, F., Angelina, E., & Okawa, K. (2019). Job digital storytelling program for university students to develop career management competencies. *Proceedings of ICDTE 2019*, 127 – 131. 10.1145/3369199.3369220

Klotz. (2021, May 30). *The Covid vaccine means a return to work. And a wave of resignations*. NBC News.

McCray, R. R., & Rawlins, J. L. (2015). Be the leader of your career: A self-centered approach to strategic career management. *Proceedings of SIGUCCs '15*, 55 – 57. 10.1145/2815546.2815575

Newman, K. L. (2011). Sustainable careers: Lifecycle engagement in work. *Organizational Dynamics*, *40*(2), 136–143. doi:10.1016/j.orgdyn.2011.01.008

Rojewski, J. W., & Hill, R. B. (2014). Positioning research and practice in career and technical education: A framework for college and career preparation in the 21st century. *Career and Technical Education Research*, *39*(2), 137–150. doi:10.5328/cter39.2.137

Root-Bernstein, M. (2020). *Avocations. In Encyclopedia of Creativity* (3rd ed., Vol. 1). Elsevier.

Schein, E. H. (1978). *Career dynamics*. Addison-Wesley.

Schein, E.H. (1990). *Career anchors and job/role planning: The links between career pathing and career development*. Academic Press.

Stebbins, R. A. (1982). Serious leisure: A conceptual statement. *Pacific Sociological Review*, *25*(2), 251–272. doi:10.2307/1388726

Tomprou, M., Dabbish, L., Kraut, R. E., & Liu, F. (2019). Career mentoring in online communities: Seeking and receiving advice from an online community. Proceedings of CHI 2019, 1 – 12.

Volpone, S. D., Perry, S. J., & Rubino, C. (2013). An exploratory study of factors that relate to burnout in hobby-jobs. *Applied Psychology*, *62*(4), 655–677. doi:10.1111/j.1464-0597.2012.00502.x

Wetherill, K., Burton, G., Calhoun, D., & Thomas, C. C. (2002, January). Redefining professional career development in the twenty-first century: A systemic approach. *High School Journal*, *85*(2), 54–66. doi:10.1353/hsj.2001.0026

Zhu, Q., Tan, R., & Li, L. (2020). Relationship between practice of work values and career success: based on the regulating of career adaptability. *Proceedings of ICCMB 2020*, 266 – 270. 10.1145/3383845.3383854

Chapter 4
Equipping Higher Education Students with Digital Skills for the Post-Pandemic World

Aslı Günay
Social Sciences University of Ankara, Turkey

ABSTRACT

The Covid-19 pandemic has led to a digital transformation in global higher education because universities were forced to close, and higher education students faced interrupted education processes. Currently, online learning in higher education is a new phenomenon, and the pandemic has highlighted the importance of digital skills for higher education students for both new distance teaching and learning methods and the new labor market. The longer universities remain closed, the more higher education students will lose their future, resulting in a permanent loss of digital skills for the post-pandemic world. Accordingly, this study presents the current situation of higher education students relative to the pre-pandemic period and offers recommendations about the importance of equipping them with digital skills. In this context, this study overviews the level of digital skills of higher education students by synthesizing and comparing current data from reliable international institutions and provides an overall assessment.

INTRODUCTION

The fast and wide dissemination of information and communication technologies (ICTs) has created completely new economic competition conditions for countries since the beginning of the knowledge-based economy. While ICTs have altered or

DOI: 10.4018/978-1-7998-8626-6.ch004

eliminated numerous work settings, jobs, industries, and socio-economic activities, they have also created new labour market conditions (Nyiri, 2002). Today, new technologies have continued to be the main drivers of disruption in labor markets around the world. For example, new technological innovations such as 3D printing, artificial intelligence and the Internet of Things have already had a widespread impact on the existing workplace (World Economic Forum [WEF], 2016). Furthermore, digitalization in working life is growing and changing rapidly, and it is apparent that the new types of employment that are being created and those that are being lost are not the same (Organisation for Economic Co-operation and Development [OECD], 2018).

The Covid-19 pandemic was discovered in China in November 2019. Globally, as of 22 October 2021, there have been 242.348.657 confirmed cases of Covid-19, including 4.927.723 deaths (World Health Organization [WHO], 2021). However, the Covid-19 pandemic is not only a health crisis, it has also changed the world economy forever and impacted the lives of most people. Global output is projected to rise by 5.7% in 2021 after a 3.4% contraction in 2020, but the recovery still remains uneven (OECD, 2021a). Moreover, digitalization and access to ICT infrastructure for remote work have become more important than ever before. Before the pandemic, overall, global competitiveness improved by 1.3 points in 2019, driven mainly by the increase in ICT adoption (WEF, 2019). Globally, internet users have doubled since 2010, surpassing 50% of the world population, and every sector of the economy has seen a fast uptake of digital technologies (WEF, 2020a). Despite this progress, the digital divide, the gap between individuals with regard both to their opportunities to access ICT and to their use of the internet for a wide variety of activities, is still on the rise around the world since only 53.6% of the global population can use the internet (OECD, 2001; WEF, 2020a). As people adapt to living and working online, internet usage has nearly doubled since the pandemic began, with OECD countries having roughly twice the number of high-speed mobile Internet subscriptions per inhabitant as non-OECD countries (OECD, 2020). This digital divide between countries is one of the main challenges for countries to rebound their economies during the Covid-19 pandemic, and some people and firms will most probably be worse off than in the pre-pandemic world due to the huge digital divide around the world.

The Covid-19 pandemic has also had a severe impact on higher education as universities closed their premises and countries shut their borders in response to lockdown measures (Schleicher, 2021). After a massive expansion in higher education in the last few decades, more than 227 million students were suddenly disrupted in 2020 by university closures due to the Covid-19 pandemic (United Nations Educational, Scientific, and Cultural Organization [UNESCO], 2021). The pandemic has forced universities to explore new ways of teaching and learning, including distance and online learning (United Nations [UN], 2021). Globally, the number of online courses has risen steeply during the pandemic. However, the long-term closure of universities poses a great risk for students' future since they will probably fall below the minimum proficiency levels in both theory and practice (UN, 2020). In particular, students who don't have access to digital devices and/or web access at home due to the digital divide are at risk of falling behind. Currently, most universities around the world are preparing for a safe and effective digital learning environment by altering their normal schedules and organization at the institutional and national levels (Aristovnik et al., 2020). Therefore, the pandemic has also dramatically changed higher education with the distinctive rise of online learning or the global dependency on digital technology, whereby teaching is undertaken remotely and on digital platforms.

On the other hand, the Covid-19 pandemic has made it more difficult to transition from universities to the labor market due to the significant reduction in job opportunities in the labor market. Global unemployment increased by 33 million in 2020, with the unemployment rate rising by 1.1% points to 6.5% (International Labor Organization [ILO], 2021a). Moreover, the pandemic-induced shortfall in jobs is projected to amount to 75 million in 2021 and 23 million in 2022 (ILO, 2020b). The World Economic Forum's Future of Jobs Report 2020 estimated 85 million jobs could be lost, while 97 million new roles may emerge due to the wave of automation in 2025 (WEF, 2020b). Regardless of the economic climate, higher education systems should aim to ensure that individuals have the skills the labour market needs (OECD, 2021b). Particularly, accelerating automation in the labor matket has forced people to have digital skills to succeed in their work or find a job. Recent developments are projected that digitalization is driving greater demand for digital skills in the post-pandemic labor market (WEF, 2020b). Hence, equipping higher education students with a digital skills is currently more important than before to survive in the new labor market considering the lack of available jobs for both re-entrants and new labor market entrants.

Briefly, the Covid-19 pandemic has highlighted the importance of digital skills for higher education students in the new world order. Since university closures have caused disruption to students, there is no time to waste in putting comprehensive rules in place to prevent a lost generation and further disadvantages for them. Thus, the objective of this study is to characterize the current state of higher education students in relation to the pandemic circumstances, to synthesize the findings on the level of digital skills, particularly in OECD countries, and to make recommendations for their digital skills acquisition and improvement. The OECD, founded in 1961, is a group of 38 countries ranging from North and South America to Europe and Asia-Pacific (OECD, 2021c). It is important to note that OECD member countries account for 63% of world GDP, and OECD countries and key partners represent about

80% of world trade and investment (Office of the United States Trade Representative [USTR], 2021; OECD, 2021c), and also OECD statistics and analysis can help guide policy decisions and play a crucial role in country reviews aimed at improving performance. Therefore, it is thought that OECD data, analysis, and surveys can be used as a good proxy for evaluating digital skills among university students around the world. In addition, European Commision (EC) data, analysis, and surveys are also used for evaluation of the digital skills of young adults, along with some other resources such as the ILO and WEF. In short, this study comprehensively analyzes existing databases and other sources to identify the current state of the digital skills level of university students.

In this context, the organization of the paper is as follows. The next section discusses the necessity of digital skills for higher education students during the pandemic. While the third section is related to information about the level of digital skills of students, the fourth one addresses the digital skills that are in demand in the labor market today and in the post-pandemic era. The next one is about future research directions, and finally, the study is concluded.

BACKGROUND

The Covid-19 pandemic has led to a digital transformation of global higher education because universities were forced to shut their facilities, and students have suffered with interrupted training processes (Aristovnik et al., 2020). The significance of adequate digital skills has increased as learning activities have shifted from face-to-face to online learning. During the pandemic, many universities used digital technologies for the first time in their teaching and learning (European Institute of Innovation & Technology [EIT], 2020). Although online learning is not entirely new in universities (Cheng et al., 2017; Zarzour, Bendjaballah, and Harirche, 2020; França and Marques, 2021), globally, neither the universities nor the students were ready for such an unexpected move to digital activities to deliver classes off-campus like mobile apps, webinars, video conferencing, YouTube etc (Diab and Elgahsh, 2020; França and Marques, 2021). However, the digital divide between and within countries, as well as the level of ICT infrastructure, have a significant impact on the achievement of rapid digital transformation in universities. Not all students have the same abilities, resources or opportunities to participate in online learning.

Advances in connectivity, widespread use of devices and digital applications, the desire for individual flexibility, and the ever-increasing demand for digital skills are driving the digital transformation in higher education (EC, 2020). In this context, some recent studies, such as Lazányi, Vincze, and Szikora (2021), Ravelj and Murko (2021), and Uleanya and Alex (2021), discuss the state of digital skills in higher education during the Covid-19 pandemic and make recommendations for improving them.

Digital skills are defined as a range of abilities to use digital devices, communication applications, and networks to access and manage information. They allow people to create and share digital information, communicate and collaborate, and solve problems in order to achieve effective and creative self-fulfillment in life, learning, work, and social activities (UNESCO, 2018). Digital skills are critical for dealing with the challenges of online learning that characterize higher education systems during the pandemic (European Parliamentary Research Service [EPRS], 2015). The European Commission recognized the importance of equipping digital skills to survive in today's knowledge-based society before the Covid-19 pandemic. In this regard, in 2006, the European Parliament and the European Council named digital competence as one of eight essential skills for active citizenship and social life (EC, 2006). The 2018 European Council recommendation on key competences for lifelong learning defines digital competence as the 'confident, critical and responsible use of, and engagement with digital technologies for learning at work, and for participation in society. It includes information and data literacy, communication and collaboration, digital content creation (including programming), safety (including digital well-being and competences related to cybersecurity), and problem solving' (EC, 2018). Within this framework, digital skills relevant for the development of digital competence comprise 'the ability to use, access, filter, evaluate, create, program and share digital content' (Council of the European Union, 2018).

The higher education market has expanded globally as a result of globalization and a knowledge-based economy, and it has become an economically relevant notion, mostly in national politics. The digital economy is now primarily driven by digital skills. As a result, if anyone wants to thrive in the post-pandemic society, they must be digitally skilled, especially students who will be looking for a job in the near future. Nearly 90% of jobs in all sectors will require some sort of digital skills in the future, but only 35% of EU workers have such skills. The demand for digital skills will increase in areas such as artificial intelligence, data literacy, supercomputing, and cybersecurity (EC, 2020; Ravjeli and Murko, 2021). Because the Covid-19 pandemic calls into question the value of a university degree, universities will have to reinvent their learning environments by speeding up their digital transformation (Schleicher, 2020).

DIGITAL SKILLS OF STUDENTS IN HIGHER EDUCATION

The Covid-19 pandemic has already had an unprecedented impact on higher education worldwide in virtually all aspects of its functioning. The pandemic transformed the way teaching took place, accelerating a transformation that was already taking place in the form of online learning and teaching (Farnell, Matijević, and Schmidt, 2021). As a result, education has changed dramatically, with the distinctive rise of e-learning, whereby teaching is undertaken remotely and on digital platforms (Li and Lanani, 2020). Most universities provide some sort of support to the teaching and learning process in the form of training and technical support. However, some universities have faced problems with their capacity for delivering online classes in terms of technology and tools for the suddenly increased demand (European University Association [EUA], 2020, Farnell, Matijević, and Schmidt, 2021). Access to online communication tools and the internet remains a challenge for some students, as does their level of digital skills.

In the European Students' Union (ESU) poll, 80.7% said they were confident in using online learning platforms when asked about their digital skills. Despite this, 7.9% of students expressed a lack of confidence in using online learning platforms, with the remaining 11.4% staying neutral. Students also stated that they preferred to study on "one online platform in a consistent manner for all courses" (Doolan, et al., 2021). Furthermore, Aristovnik et al. (2020)'s global survey confirms that students are mostly confident in their use of online communication platforms, though when asked about their least developed digital skills, respondents singled out "those connected with adjusting the advanced settings of some software and programs and using online teaching platforms." As a result, in terms of digital skills, students' capacity for online learning is diverse (Farnell, Matijević, and Schmidt, 2021).

Since the Covid-19 pandemic has forced many young people (aged 16–24) to study online, having digital skills is a major phenomenon during the pandemic and in should be seen as an investment for the skills of higher education students that need while entering the labour market (Ruseva, 2015; Lauder and Mayhew, 2020). This means that one of the most important factors to consider when developing university curricula is their possibility to help produce graduates who are employable in light of current societal demands, particularly with the advent of the digital economy, which emphasizes the use of digital skills for everyday use and problem-solving. Digital skills, in particular, are predicted to become required for students in order for them to remain relevant both in university and beyond graduation. (Uleanya and Alex, 2021). However, according to Ruseva (2015), having basic level digital skills is insufficient for young people to find decent jobs. Figure 1 shows that 80% in the European Union (EU) have basic or higher levels of digital skills. This was 24% higher than the percentage of people aged 16 to 74 (56%). It comes as no surprise that young people's digital skills vary based on their country's economic situation.

Students were not prepared for the world of digital learning opportunities in the OECD's Programme for International Student Assessment (PISA), which measures 15-year-olds' ability to use their reading, mathematics, and science knowledge

Figure 1. Share of young people with basic or above basic digital skills, 2019 (% of individuals aged 16 to 24)
Source: (Eurostat, 2019)

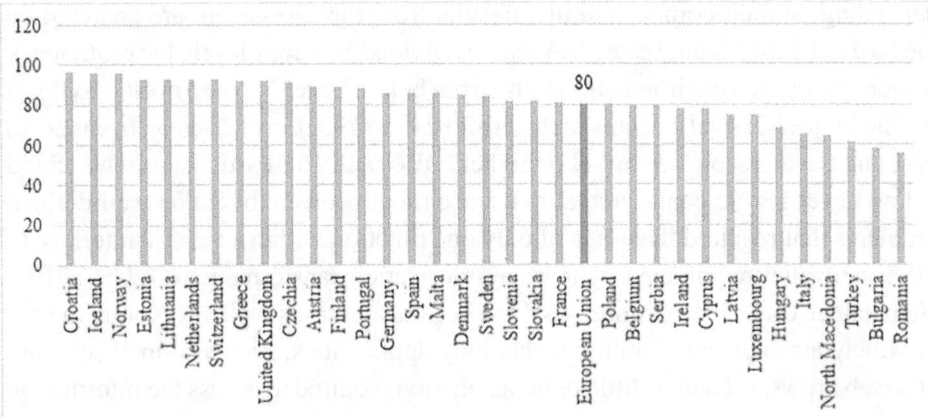

and skils to face real-life issues. The OECD's 2018 round of the PISA indicates a quarter of school principals across the OECD claimed that shortages or inadequacy of digital technology had hampered learning quite a bit or a lot, ranged from 2% in Singapore to 30% in France and Italy (OECD, 2019a).

Moreover, the OECD's Programme for the International Assessment of Adult Competencies (PIAAC) measures the proficiency of working-age adults (aged 16-65) in three key information-processing skills: literacy, numeracy, and problem solving in technology-rich environments (OECD, 2016). PIAAC defines problem solving in technology-rich environments as "using digital technology, communication tools and networks to acquire and evaluate information, communicate with others and perform practical tasks" (PIAAC Expert Group in Problem Solving in Technology-Rich Environments, 2009). It focuses on "the abilities to solve problems for personal, work and civic purposes by setting up appropriate goals and plans, and accessing and making use of information through computers and computer networks" (OECD, 2012). It assesses problem-solving skills as well as basic computer literacy; in other words, the capacity to use ICT tools and applications. Individuals' fundamental workplace skills for engagement in society and economic growth are assessed in this global survey, which was conducted in over 40 nations (OECD, 2016). As a result, it could be a useful proxy for demonstrating the level of digital skills of higher education graduates in OECD countries prior to the Covid-19 pandemic. This could advise governments on the level of digital skills that university graduates should have today.

The survey was administered to the respondents under the supervision of expert interviewers. Following the completion of the background questionnaire, respondents took the assessment test on a laptop computer or on paper using printed test booklets, depending on their computer skills. Results from the assessment are analysed on the basis of a 500-point scale. The scale is divided into four levels for proficiency in technology-rich environments skills (from below Level 1 – the lowest – to Level 3 – the highest). Level 1 scores ranged from 241 to 290, Level 2 scores from 291 to 340, and Level 3 scores were 341 or higher (OECD, 2016). Participants who scored below Level 1 were considered at risk since the tasks were based on well-defined problems that required the usage of only one function within a generic interface to meet one explicit requirement without any information transformation (OECD, 2019b; Hämäläinen et al., 2019). Moreover, Level 1 indicates tasks typically require the use of widely available and familiar technology applications, such as e-mail software or a web browser. There is little or no navigation required to access the information or commands required to solve the problem. At Level 2, tasks typically require the use of both generic and more specific technology applications, and some navigation across pages and applications is required to solve the problem. Adults at Level 3 can complete tasks involving multiple computer applications, a large number of steps, and the discovery and use of ad hoc commands in a novel environment (OECD, 2019b). In this regard, Hämäläinen et al. (2019) defined adults in Levels 1, 2, and 3 as weak, moderate, and strong performers, respectively.

Educational attainment positively affects the proficiency levels of adults' problem solving in technology-rich environments (OECD, 2016; Xiao et al., 2019). In other words, adults with higher education diplomas are probably more proficient at problem solving in a technology-rich environment skill than people with only a high school diploma. Figure 2 shows the proficiency levels of adults' problem solving in technology-rich environments for higher-educated adults. Considering this, the shares of higher educated adults are 37.83% scored at Level 2 and 9.88% scored at Level 3 on average across OECD countries. While on average, 48% of higher educated adults across OECD countries scored at Level 2 or 3 in the problem-solving assessment, this share was much lower in some countries, including Peru (14%), and Mexico and Turkey (26%). In contrast, 52% of higher-educated adults scored at Level 2 or 3 in problem solving in Hungary and 49% in the United States. On the other hand, basic digital skills are nearly universal among higher-educated adults, and across OECD countries, only 4% of adults in this group were not able to participate in the problem-solving assessment. Figure 2 also reveals that this percentage was slightly higher in Mexico and Turkey (7%), and Peru (12%). Therefore, when compared to adults in other OECD countries, higher-educated adults' digital skills were lower in developing and middle-income countries. As a result, the government in these countries should focus more on equipping university students with digital skills for the post-pandemic world.

Figure 2. Level of problem solving in technology-rich environments proficiency, by higher education attainment (aged 16-65)
Source: (OECD, 2016)

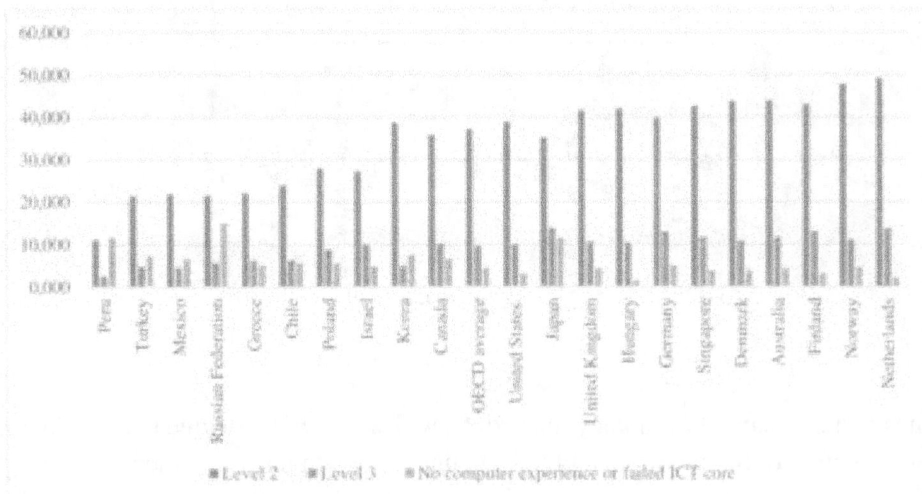

THE IMPACT OF DIGITAL SKILLS ON STUDENT EMPLOYABILITY IN HIGHER EDUCATION

Today, expanded and diversified educational options have enlarged the pool of skilled people across countries, and those with higher qualifications, as opposed to those with lower qualifications, are more likely to find work (OECD, 2021b). Since unemployment has almost certainly been rising as the Covid-19 pandemic spreads, individuals with lower educational attainment may be the most disadvantaged, in contrast to others. From this perspective, younger adults (aged 25-34) with a university degree are less likely to be unemployed (7%) compared to those with upper secondary or post-secondary non-higher education (9%) as their highest attainment in several OECD and partner countries (OECD, 2021b). Figure 3 displays the unemployment rates among younger adults with a university degree in 2019 and 2020. Regarding this, the positive effect of university attainment on unemployment rates is particularly high in the United Kingdom, the United States, Hungary, and the Netherlands, with the lowest unemployment rate (3%) during the pandemic. Greece, Colombia, Spain, South Africa, and Italy have the highest unemployment

Figure 3. Trends in unemployment rates by higher educational attainment (aged 25-34 olds)
Source: (OECD, 2021b)

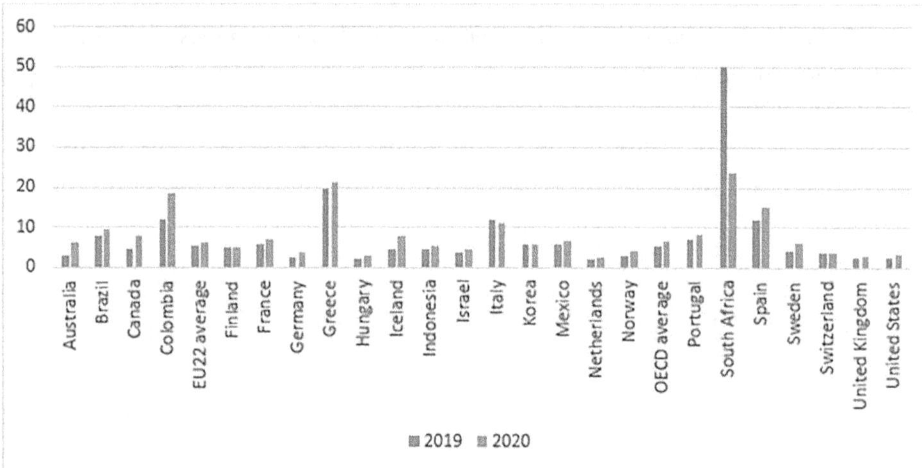

rates of more than 10% among young adults with a university degree in 2020. With the exception of South Africa and Italy, countries' youth unemployment rates with a university degree increased or remained unchanged after the pandemic in 2020.

Higher education attainment is associated with higher employment rates for younger adults (aged 25-34) on average across OECD countries (Figure 4). Before the Covid-19 pandemic in 2019, young adults with a university degree had an average employment rate of 85%, which was greater than the 76% for those with upper secondary or post-secondary non-higher education attainment (OECD, 2021b). However, Figure 4 shows that the employment rate by university attainment fell by 2% to 83% in 2020 during the pandemic on average across OECD countries. In general, many countries experienced a drop in employment rates, with Colombia experiencing the greatest drop (8%). However, South Africa was the only country to show a 30% increase in the employment rate among young adults with a university degree (Figure 4).

Figure 5 displays that higher-skilled workers accounted for the lowest share of employment worldwide among all the occupational categories in 2019, namely 20.6%, but as a group they also exhibited the lowest decline in employment relative to the pre-pandemic period, at 3%. In other words, higher-skilled workers were far more likely to be able to work from home during the pandemic than workers in middle-skilled and low-skilled occupations (ILO, 2021). Hence, if high-skilled workers are associated with university graduates, it might be said that adults with university degree may be less harmed than other education level degree graduates.

Figure 4. Trends in employment rates, by higher educational attainment (aged 25-34)
Source: (OECD, 2021b)

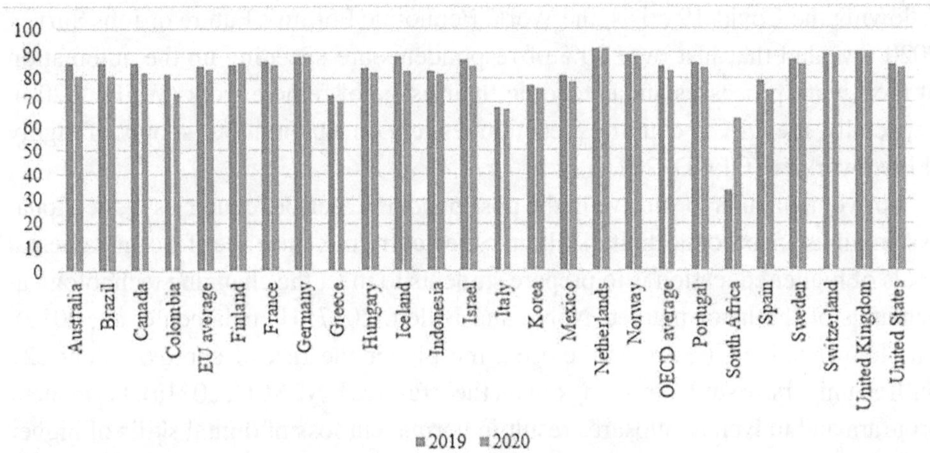

Figure 5. Distribution of employment by occupational skill level (%)
Source: (ILO, 2021b)

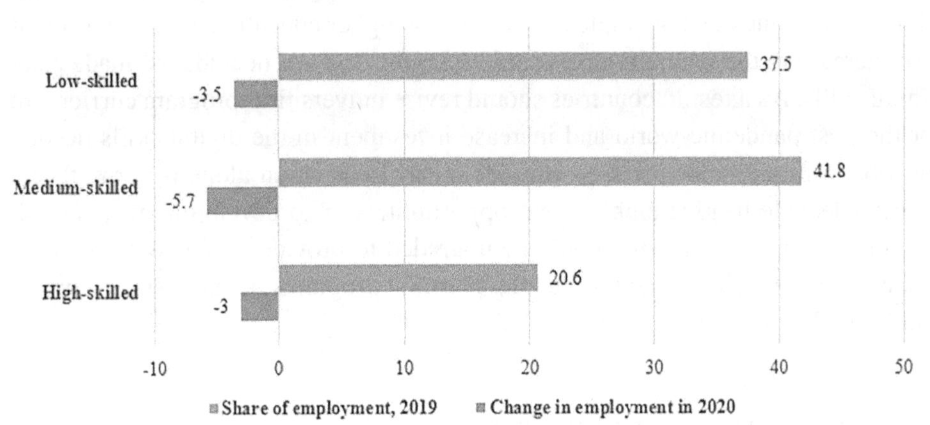

Employers' perceptions of digital skills have fallen by 3.4% in advanced economies and increased by 1.8% in emerging and developing economies since 2017 (WEF, 2020a). The lack of basic digital skills not only hinders ICT adoption, but it also increases the likelihood of job losses as a result of automation. At least 14% of all jobs in OECD countries are at "high risk" of automation, and 32% of all jobs are at "significant risk," making it more difficult for employees to shift to new roles in the labor market (WEF, 2020a). Therefore, as technology disrupts labor markets, there is a particular shortage of digital skills in the new economic structure. Furthermore, following the Covid-19 crisis, the World Economic Forum's Future of Jobs Survey 2020 revealed that just over 80% of respondents are speeding up the automation of their work processes and extending their usage of remote work (WEF, 2020b). Especially, the OECD countries' economies rely on a continuous supply of highly skilled workers (OECD, 2021b).

For young adults to survive in the post-pandemic period, countries' educational systems must incorporate digital skills into their curricula, since one of the fundamental goals of higher education is to prepare students to meet the changing technological demands of the labor market (Noble and Billett, 2017; Hämäläinen et al., 2019). The longer universities remain closed, the higher the risk of approximately 227 million university students losing out on their future (UNESCO, 2021a). Permanent program and university closures result in permanent loss of digital skills of higher education students.

Moreover, the adequacy of universities to meet the needs of employment is rated at 68 points (out of 100) in advanced economies and 55 points (out of 100) in emerging and developing economies over the last decade (WEF, 2020a). Hence, it is obvious that human capital development across countries has slowed, although a number of countries have made investments in basic upgrading of training systems. This result implies that unemployment rates by higher education attainment might also increase in the medium-term (until 2025) due to current students' inadequate digital skills. As a result, countries should revise universities' program curriculum for the post-pandemic world and increase investment in the digital skills needed for jobs in future labor markets. Besides, formal education alone is currently no longer adequate to give employment opportunities or to develop human capital. Rather, university programs should be upgraded to provide digital skills through universities, as well as ongoing lifelong learning programs, to address the current and future labor shortfall of digital skills.

FUTURE RESEARCH DIRECTIONS

It is difficult to assess the pandemic's impact on higher education around the world because the impact is unprecedented and the pandemic is ongoing. There is presently no more data or analysis available that would allow for more accurate projections about Covid-19's future impact on higher education. Hence, alternative measurements might be developed for measuring the digital skills proficiency level of university students to make evaluations and recommendations. However, the rapid transition to online learning in universities has prompted concerns about the quality of teaching. Therefore, it would be interesting for future research to assess of the quality of teaching during the Covid-19 pandemic. In addition, creating a lifelong learning culture in higher education to improve the digital skills of students and staff might be the subject of another study with the finance of the digital transformation of universities.

CONCLUSION

The Covid-19 pandemic has created unprecedented disruptions on all levels of society, including higher education. In this context, the Covid-19 pandemic has affected approximately 227 million higher education students globally. Along with higher education students, academicians and learning and teaching methods in higher education systems around the world have been affected, with many having turned to online learning to complete the academic year due to the closure of universities. Although some universities had open education or distance education programs prior to the pandemic, online learning is the major development trend in universities due to the Covid-19 pandemic. But emergency remote teaching as a global response to the Covid-19 pandemic is unprecedented, and difficult to predict the medium-term (until 2025) implications because there is no previous experience to resort to in terms of lessons learnt (Farnell, Matijević, and Schmidt, 2021). Lack of data or analyses that would allow for more accurate predictions about the possible future impact of Covid-19 on higher education is the main limitation of current studies.

The potential medium-term (until 2025) risks are explored in the World Bank [WB] (2020) report, which identifies possible permanent closures of universities as a result of the impact of the pandemic. In terms of teaching and learning, the impact of the pandemic may result in a permanent movement of more study programs to online or remote platforms. In the medium term (until 2025), graduate unemployment may increase due to, among other things, decreased confidence in the quality of remote education as a result of lower exam requirements and potential learning losses. This in turn raises a number of questions about the skills of graduates demanded in the labor market.

Today, digital transformation in higher education is more important than in the pre-pandemic period, since the longer universities remain closed, the higher the risk of higher education students losing out on their future, resulting in permanent loss of their skills. Since technology is an integral part of the workplace experience today, and as these technologies grow, this will impact the digital skills students need to succeed in the workplace of the future. Current reports show that on average, only 48% of higher-educated adults across OECD countries have sufficient problem solving skills in technology-rich environments, which is a proxy for digital skills.

Since it is unclear what the future holds, it is more important than ever to make sure that university students should have the digital skills to benefit from the new employment opportunities to survive in a post-pandemic world.

Neverthless, the digital transformation in higher education has also had some socio-economic impact on students' life due to the digital divide among them. University closures during the Covid-19 pandemic have plunged some students further into hardship, living in poverty with no digital resources at home, or located in remote areas with a lack of learning materials or school supplies. As a result, the digital gap is a further risk in the medium term (until 2025) to equity in teaching and learning in universities. Additionally, the situation has been harder for vocational education and training (VET) in higher education since the work-based component of education and training has been interrupted.

Academicians are tasked with the critical role of equipping students with the digital skills required for the post-pandemic workplace. Academicians should be equipped with the digital skills to help students develop or improve their basic digital skills. Besides, universities and academia should upgrade their curricula to provide digital skills through digital education during the Covid-19 pandemic. Moreover, both university students and academicians will also need to be committed to continuous digital training as a part of lifelong learning to ensure reskill and upskill of their digital skills. Lifelong learning is important tool for digital skill development to help today's university students prepare for a future of work. In addition, universities might provide additional university-level financial support for at-risk students to access equipment, internet services, and to improve their digital skills (Doolan et al., 2020; Montacute and Holt-White, 2020).

Although the digital transformation around the world was accelerating prior to the pandemic as an increasing number of governments prepared and placed their national digital strategies. In addition to the national strategies, the pandemic has drawn attention to the need for coordinated strategic development around the world to increase the performance of universities during the Covid-19 pandemic. Considerable regulatory steps are needed until 2025 to support the growth in distance learning, including addressing privacy concerns and increasing funding for university infrastructure to increase broadband access (Picker, 2021). This requires effective digital infrastructure, high-quality curriculum, and digitally competent and confident academic staff in universities (EC, 2020).

REFERENCES

Aristovnik, A., Keržič, D., Ravšelj, D., Tomaževič, N., & Umek, L. (2020). Impacts of the Covid-19 pandemic on life of higher education students: A global perspective. *Sustainability, 12*(20), 8438. doi:10.3390u12208438

Cheng, H. N., Liu, Z., Sun, J., Liu, S., & Yang, Z. (2017). Unfolding online learning behavioral patterns and their temporal changes of college students in SPOCs. *Interactive Learning Environments, 25*(2), 176–188. doi:10.1080/10494820.2016.1276082

Council of the European Union. (2018). *Council recommendation of 22 May 2018 on key competences for lifelong learning*. https://eur-lex.europa.eu/legal-content/EN/TXT/PDF/?uri=CELEX:32018H0604(01)&rid=7#:~:text=The%20Reference%20Framework%20sets%20out,social%20and%20learning%20to%20learn

Diab, G. M. A. E.-H., & Elgahsh, N. F. (2020). E-learning during Covid-19 pandemic: Obstacles faced nursing students and its effect on their attitudes while applying it. *American Journal of Nursing Science, 9*(4), 295. doi:10.11648/j.ajns.20200904.33

Doolan, K., Barada, V., Burić, I., Krolo, K., & Tonković, Ž. (2021). *Student life during the COVID-19 pandemic lockdown: Europe-wide insights*. European Students' Union (ESU).

European Commission. (2006). *Recommendation of the European Parliament and of the Council*. https://eur-lex.europa.eu/LexUriServ/LexUriServ.do?uri=OJ:L:2006:394:0010:0018:en:PDF

European Commission. (2018). Competences for lifelong learning. *Official Journal of the European Union, 189*, 1–10.

European Commission. (2020). *Digital education action plan 2021-2027*. European Commission.

European Institute of Innovation & Technology. (2020). *Public consultation: Digital education during the Covid-19 recovery period and beyond*. https://eit.europa.eu/news-events/news/consultation-digitaleducation-action-plan

European University Association. (2020). *European higher education in the Covid-19 crisis*. https://eua.eu/downloads/publications/briefing_european%20higher%20education%20in%20the%20covid-19%20crisis.pdf

European Parliamentary Research Service. (2015). *Bridging the digital divide in the EU*. https://www.europarl.europa.eu/RegData/etudes/BRIE/2015/573884/EPRS_BRI(2015)573884_EN.pdf

EUROSTAT. (2019). *Share of young people with basic or above basic digital skills*. https://ec.europa.eu/eurostat/web/products-eurostat-news/-/edn-20200715-1

Farnell, T., Skledar Matijević, A., & Šćukanec Schmidt, N. (2021). *The impact of COVID-19 on higher education: a review of emerging evidence*. NESET report. Luxembourg: Publications Office of the European Union. . doi:10.2766/069216

França, T., & Marques, B. P. (2021). Gender and digital skills in Portuguese higher education during the Covid-19 Pandemic. In N. Tomaževič, D. Ravšelj, & A. Aristovnik (Eds.), *Higher education policies for developing digital skills to respond to the Covid-19 crisis: European and global perspectives* (pp. 59-71). European Liberal Forum.

Hämäläinena, R., De Weverb, B., Nissinen, K., & Cincinnatod, S. (2019). What makes the difference – PIAAC as a resource for understanding the problem solving skills of Europe's higher-education adults. *Computers & Education*, *129*, 27–36. doi:10.1016/j.compedu.2018.10.013

ILO. (2021a). *COVID-19 and the world of work*: Seventh Edition. https://www.ilo.org/global/topics/coronavirus/impacts-and-responses/WCMS_767028/lang--en/index.htm

ILO. (2021b). *World employment and social outlook – Trends 2021*. https://www.ilo.org/global/research/global-reports/weso/trends2021/WCMS_795453/lang--en/index.htm

Lazányi, K., Vincze, A., & Szikora, P. (2021). The digital skills in the Hungarian higher education during the first wave of Covid-19. In N. Tomaževič, D. Ravšelj, & A. Aristovnik (Eds.), *Higher education policies for developing digital skills to respond to the Covid-19 crisis: European and global perspectives* (pp. 4-18). European Liberal Forum.

Lauder, H., & Mayhew, K. (2020). Higher education and the labour market: An introduction. *Oxford Review of Education*, *46*(1), 1–9. doi:10.1080/03054985.2019.1699714

Li, C., & Lalani, F. (2020). *The COVID-19 pandemic has changed education forever. This is how.* https://www.weforum.org/agenda/2020/04/coronavirus-education-global-covid19-online-digital-learning/

Montacute, R., & Holt-White, E. (2020). *COVID-19 and social mobility impact brief# 2: University access & Student finance*. https://www.suttontrust.com/wp-content/uploads/2020/05/COVID-19-and-Social-Mobility-Impact-Brief-2.pdf

Noble, C., & Billett, S. (2017). Learning to prescribe through co-working: Junior doctors, pharmacists and consultants. *Medical Education*, *51*(4), 442–451. doi:10.1111/medu.13227 PMID:28164385

Nyíri, L. (2002). Knowledge-based society and its impact on labour-market values. *Society and Economy*, *24*(2), 201–218. doi:10.1556/SocEc.24.2002.2.3

OECD. (2001). *Information and communication technologies and rural Development*. www.sourceoecd.org

OECD. (2012). *Literacy, numeracy and problem solving in technology-rich environments: Framework for the OECD survey of adult skills*. OECD Publishing. doi:10.1787/9789264128859-

OECD. (2016). *Skills matter: Further results from the survey of adult skills, OECD skills studies*. OECD Publishing.

OECD. (2018). *Transformative technologies and jobs of the future*. https://www.oecd.org/innovation/transformative-technologies-and-jobs-of-the-future.pdf

OECD. (2019a). PISA 2018 results: Vol. I. *What students know and can do?* OECD Publishing. doi:10.1787/5f07c754-

OECD. (2019b). *Skills matter: Additional results from the survey of adult skills, OECD skills studies*. OECD Publishing. doi:10.1787/1f029d8f-

OECD. (2020). *OECD digital economy outlook 2020*. OECD Publishing. doi:10.1787/bb167041-

OECD. (2021a). *OECD economic outlook 2021*. OECD Publishing. doi:10.1787/edfbca02-

OECD. (2021b). *Education at a glance 2021: OECD indicators*. OECD Publishing. doi:10.1787/b35a14e5-

OECD. (2021c). *Where: Global reach*. https://www.oecd.org/about/members-and-partners/

Office of the United States Trade Representative. (2021). *Trade Organizations: OECD*. https://ustr.gov/trade-agreements/wto-multilateral-affairs/oecd

PIAAC Expert Group in Problem Solving in Technology-Rich Environments. (2009). *PIAAC problem solving in technology rich environments: A conceptual framework*. OECD Education Working Papers, 36. Paris: OECD Publishing. doi:10.1787/19939019

Picker, R. C. (2021). *COVID 2025: How the pandemic is changing our world.* https://news.uchicago.edu/story/covid-2025-how-pandemic-changing-our-world#education

Ravšelj, D., & Murko, E. (2021). Higher education policies for developing digital skills in response to the Covid-19 crisis: Evidence from Slovenia. In N. Tomaževič, D. Ravšelj, & A. Aristovnik (Eds.), *Higher education policies for developing digital skills to respond to the Covid-19 crisis: European and global perspectives* (pp. 72-82). European Liberal Forum.

Ruseva, G. (2015). *Digital skills and youth employability.* https://all-digital.org/wp-content/uploads/2017/10/Telecentre-Europe-Youth-employability-policy-paper-Dec2015.pdf

Schleicher, A. (2020). *The impact of COVID-19 on education: Insights from education at a glance 2020.* OECD Publishing. https://www.oecd.org/education/the-impact-of-covid-19-on-education-insights-education-at-a-glance-2020.pdf

Uleanya, C., & Alex, J. (2021). Higher education policies for developing digital skills: Lessons learnt from the Covid-19 crisis in South Africa. In N. Tomaževič, D. Ravšelj, & A. Aristovnik (Eds.), *Higher education policies for developing digital skills to respond to the Covid-19 crisis: European and global perspectives* (pp. 110-119). European Liberal Forum.

UN. (2020). *Policy brief: Education during COVID-19 and beyond.* https://www.un.org/development/desa/dspd/wp-content/uploads/sites/22/2020/08/sg_policy_brief_covid-19_and_education_august_2020.pdf

UN. (2021). *COVID-19 and higher education: Education and science as a vaccine for the pandemic.* https://www.un.org/en/academic-impact/covid-19-and-higher-education-education-and-science-vaccine-pandemic

UNESCO. (2018). *Digital skills critical for jobs and social inclusion.* https://en.unesco.org/news/digital-skills-critical-jobs-and-social-inclusion#:~:text=Digital%20skills%20are%20defined%20as,to%20access%20and%20manage%20information

UNESCO. (2021). *Institute of statistics: Education statistics.* http://data.uis.unesco.org/

WEF. (2016). *The future of jobs employment, skills and workforce strategy for the fourth industrial revolution.* Geneva: World Economic Forum. https://www3.weforum.org/docs/WEF_Future_of_Jobs.pdf

WEF. (2019). *The global competitiveness report 2019.* Geneva: World Economic Forum. https://www3.weforum.org/docs/WEF_TheGlobalCompetitivenessReport2019.pdf

WEF. (2020a). The global competitiveness report 2020. Geneva: World Economic Forum. https://www.weforum.org/reports/the-global-competitiveness-report-2020

WEF. (2020b). *The future of jobs report 2020*. Geneva: World Economic Forum. https://www.weforum.org/reports/the-future-of-jobs-report-2020

WHO. (2021). *WHO coronavirus (COVID-19) dashboard*. https://covid19.who.int/

World Bank. (2020). *The COVID-19 crisis response: Supporting tertiary education for continuity, adaptation, and innovation*. World Bank. https://documents1.worldbank.org/curated/en/621991586463915490/The-COVID-19-

Xiao, F., Barnard-Brak, L., Lan, W., & Burley, H. (2019). Examining problem solving skills in technology-rich environments as related to numeracy and literacy. *International Journal of Lifelong Education, 38*(3), 327–338.

Zarzour, H., Bendjaballah, S., & Harirche, H. (2020). Exploring the behavioral patterns of students learning with a Facebook-based e-book approach. *Computers & Education, 156*, 103957. https://doi.org/10.1016/j.compedu.2020.103957

ADDITIONAL READING

Abad-Segura, E., González-Zamar, M. D., Infante-Moro, J. C., & García, G. R. (2020). Sustainable management of digital transformation in higher education: Global research trends. *Sustainability, 12*(5), 2107. doi:10.3390u12052107

Bond, M., Marín, V. I., Dolch, C., Bedenlier, S., & Zawacki-Richter, O. (2018). Digital transformation in German higher education: Student and teacher perceptions and usage of digital media. *International Journal of Educational Technology in Higher Education, 15*(48), 48. Advance online publication. doi:10.118641239-018-0130-1

Pham, H., Tran, Q.-N., La, G.-L., Doan, H.-M., & Vu, T.-C. (2021). Readiness for digital transformation of higher education in the Covid-19 context: The dataset of Vietnam's students. *Data in Brief, 39*, 107482. doi:10.1016/j.dib.2021.107482 PMID:34712758

Nurhas, I., Aditya, B. R., Jacob, D. W., & Pawlowski, J. M. (2021). Understanding the challenges of rapid digital transformation: The case of COVID-19 pandemic in higher education. *Behaviour & Information Technology*, 1–17. Advance online publication. doi:10.1080/0144929X.2021.1962977

KEY TERMS AND DEFINITIONS

Covid-19 Pandemic: A disease caused by a new coronavirus, which has not been previously identified in humans, discovered in China in 2019.

Digital Divide: Disparity between individuals with regard both to their opportunities to access ICT and to their use of the internet for a wide variety of activities.

Digital Skills: Ability to use, access, filter, evaluate, create, program, and share digital content.

Higher Education: Educational qualification awarded upon successful completion of specific educational programs in universities and equivalent institutions.

Labor Market: Place where workers and employees interact with each other.

Lifelong Learning: Any learning activity that an individual engages in throughout his or her life to develop his or her knowledge, skills, interests, and qualifications with an emphasis on personal, social, and occupational aspects.

Problem Solving in Technology-Rich Environments: Using digital technology, communication tools and networks to acquire and evaluate information, communicate with others and perform practical tasks.

Unemployment: Individuals who are employable and actively seeking a job but are unable to find a job.

Section 2

A New Post-Pandemic Workplace

Chapter 5
Returning to the In-Person Workplace in a (Post?) Pandemic Context

Shalin Hai-Jew
https://orcid.org/0000-0002-8863-0175
Kansas State University, USA

ABSTRACT

The SARS-CoV-2/COVID-19 pandemic has been with humanity since late 2019 (based on new information) and has cost close to four million lives globally (and counting) and resulted in chronic health conditions for many tens of millions of others with "long COVID." As humanity acquires some level of biosafety with several highly effective vaccines, many are returning to work in physical buildings and in the proxemic company of others (in shared interpersonal airspace). This return to normalcy aims to ramp up social creativity and work productivity. Some are returning to changed physical spaces with "social distancing" which is empirically, perhaps, not so effective. This work explores what it is like to return to the in-person workplace based on contemporary research, journalistic coverage, social media narratives, and a light auto-ethnography, with global research included but a particular focus on the U.S.

INTRODUCTION

Connectivity in the world—such as "globalization, travel, and trade"—are accelerants of pandemics (Joseph, Angeline, & Arasu, 2020, p. 133), even as these practices have slowed based on travel bans against non-essential travel and biosafety measures

DOI: 10.4018/978-1-7998-8626-6.ch005

have been emplaced. The pandemic disrupted various supply chains, but human needs for PPE and other goods mean business continuance in some fields (Chinniah, Taylor, & Proches, June 25, 2020, p. 2). Globally, the SARS-CoV-2 / COVID-19 pandemic has infected some 200 million people. This pandemic has cost close to four million deaths (and counting) from its start in late 2019. Many millions more are experiencing "long COVID" health effects, which may be permanent, with major effects on brains, hearts, and other organs. The current numbers are thought to be undercounts by potentially several orders of magnitude. Some estimate that actual counts would show well over 10% of the world's population or 800 million as having been infected. Even as many questions remain about the origins of the pathogenic "severe acute respiratory syndrome – coronavirus 2" and "coronavirus disease 2019," a traumatized world is slowly coming out of various lockdowns.

Social distancing at social scale has been found to be effective in lowering the spread of an airborne transmissible pathogen between people. Social distancing at societal scale refers to endeavors like "school closure, workplace non-attendance, increased case isolation, and community contact reduction" (Milne & Xie, Mar. 21, 2020, p. 1). Another proposal to lower the number of people in close proximity to each other is "hybrid telecommuting," which seems to change up scheduling for people's work. This method to limit contacts between people affect "real-life contact networks stemming from a workplace, a primary school and a high school" (Mauras, et al., 2020, p. 1) and so may disrupt potential viral transmission chains. Such endeavors, when modeled out, show some flattening of the epidemic curve and a lowering of the daily infection case numbers and lengthening the outbreak duration (to "buy time" for mitigations). These can be effective even under some conditions of uncertainty, such as in the early phases of an outbreak with a novel as-yet unknown pathogen.

One important observation is that "the original COVID-19 always keeps in a constant transform in different places and periods, respectively" based on constant mutations (Estrada, Feb. 2021, p. 1) and different instantiations among different populations. To acknowledge the changes, one researcher suggests renaming the COVID respiratory disease annually, such as "COVID-20," "COVID-21," to capture annual differences in "transmission, treatments, eradication, and vaccination" (Estrada, Feb. 2021, p. 1).

Such government lockdowns—set up to lower the number of proxemic human contacts—have not been socially costless. They have slowed economies, decimated various industries, prevented more effective schooling, led to various lack of attention to health, and other challenges. With the mass vaccination of populations in the U.S., however, reopenings are occurring at a rapid pace in the spring and summer of 2021. Governments are communicating a need to make up for lost time. The Work-from-Home (WFH or WfH) phenomenon in early days seemed to harness various practices that work (George & George, Apr. 2020, p. 269), based on some guidance from public health professionals. Now, it is about Return-to-Work (RtW). The changing workplace geographies may mean different things to different people based on their local contexts, which are unevenly distributed. Homeworking in the Global North differs from other locales (Reuschke & Felstead, 2020, pp. 208-209):

The privileged socio-economic profile of homeworkers before the COVID-19 crisis is associated with living in well-off neighbourhoods, in particular inner-city neighbouurhoods with high proportions of professional workers as well as suburban areas with large properties and high proportions of homeowners" (Moos & Skarbursis, 2007, as cited in Reuschke & Felstead, 2020, p. 211), but the new homeworkers had to improvise in the face of the pandemic and were likely much less able to have suitable spaces for homeworking. (p. 211)

Analogically, return to work will likely vary depending on geographical locales. Many of the employed are returning to shared physical work spaces with shared personal and interpersonal airspace. At this time, there is the sense that this transition is part of a mass-scale experiment, without clarity about what exactly will happen with the loosening of facemask rules and in-person gatherings. For many, the social-physical distancing is still respected in indoor spaces. Where there were emotional stresses, extreme mindfulness, and high cognitive load for biosafety in all spaces prior to the broader rollout of the respective vaccines (Pfizer/BioNTech, Moderna, Johnson & Johnson, currently, in the U.S.), the new current stresses relate to the cognitive load of navigating the new social spaces and readjusting to each other's physical (vs. virtual) presence. Social dynamics have been upended. Where employees have chafed at company policies forcing the turning on of cameras for online meetings (Kelly, Sept. 24, 2021), the additional challenges now have to do with face-to-face social distancing and senses of personal respect. Those who have started working in buildings are providing early test case data for *in vivo* research.

With human lives still under threat and humanity on alert (and in fight or flight mode), the stress can be debilitating. This work explores what it means to be returning to a workplace as a society is slowly coming out of a pandemic, based on a review of the research literature, journalistic articles, social media narratives, and a light auto-ethnography.

REVIEW OF THE LITERATURE

During the first year and a half (and counting) of the SARS-CoV-2 / COVID-19 pandemic, the academic research has been comprised of lab studies of the virus, epidemiological studies in the world (*in vivo*), various models and simulations, studies of media and social media, and other works. Given the broad reach of the pandemic, there have been studies in particular domains that overlap with topics of interest. One common intervention related to work involved the reduction of "nonemergency access to workplaces" (Ng, 2020, 1).

To be clear, essential workers (in healthcare, in meat production, in grocery stores, in law enforcement, in postal services, in package delivery, and others) have never truly stopped working during the pandemic. Their services were considered so critical to the functioning of society that people in these roles worked on the frontline and took on the brunt of the health risks in the face of a pathogenic and deadly virus against which humanity had no actual pharmacological defense. In the U.S., workplaces were relatively slow in addressing actual defenses against the pathogen. Over time, they did set up various mitigations: plastic barriers against aerosols, PPE, remote thermal tests, limited entrances to workplaces, workplace hygiene, safer waste management, and others. Employees were asked to wear facemasks, practice hand hygiene, and respect social distancing. Throughout this time, many engaged in denialism (which is not a defense), and some people were super spreaders of the deadly virus. The very thin trust of others turned out to be the right response, given how irresponsibly many behaved. With the digitalization of work places, there were numerous changes to various aspects of businesses: "labor and social relations, marketing and sales, and technology" (Almeida, Santos, & Monteiro, 2020, p. 97) and expected new digital products to enable such work flexibility and the need for new talent that can work the telecommuting angle. Employee retention is expected to be challenging in the post-COVID-19 era (Jayathilake, Daud, Eaw, & Annuar, 2021). Many are choosing to be stay-at-home parents. Many are still too traumatized to look for work. Many have resigned. Many who held off on quitting their unsatisfying jobs prior to the pandemic but held on as the pandemic loomed are also resigning in order to look for more satisfying work. A surgeon who became infected with COVID-19 and nearly died shares his sense of limited time and the need to pass on his innovative surgical procedures and learning to others (Grady, June 3, 2021). The various contexts of a working population are varied.

The digital transformation in the work place requires companies to have "smart capital allocation for digital initiatives, engagement of appropriate digital tools, talent recruitment, and brand permission" (Olokundun, Ibidunni, Ogbari, Falola, & Salau, 2021, p. 41). The idea is that the long-term effects of a long-present pandemic may mean that work itself has changed, worker expectations have changed, and future pandemics have to be considered. One study involved a multi-state American company and how it fared from March – August 2020, with non-pharmaceutical interventions (NPI) against COVID-19 only. The company was able to keep SARS-CoV-2 infection rates on par with community prevalence through testing campaigns, policies for face masking, hand hygiene, and social distancing, and progressive policies such as increasing paid sick leave (Haigh & Gandhi, April 2021, n.p.). The coauthors write: "Among 586 employees at three sites, only 1.5% employees developed severe illness over the study duration" (Haigh & Gandhi, April 2021, n.p.).

Without information and communication technologies (ICT), the pandemic itself would have been a lot more costly in lives. ICT enabled people to hunker down, continue livelihoods from home, order groceries, and survive, until functioning vaccines became available. The return to work is really about the rest of the population, which telecommuted or engaged in remote work…or who sat out the year and a half (so far) of the pandemic.

The shock of the COVID-19 pandemic has meant paradigm shifts for both "work from home" and "return to work," and the future may result in a "new work order" (Kaushik, May – June 2020, p. 27677). Where work places initially helped employees adjust to working from home, now they are helping their employees re-acclimate to a new work-based reality. The workplace logistics are complex and multi-dimensional, with health security as a central concern, including the "mental well-being" of staff (Kaushik, May – June 2020, p. 27679). These endeavors occurred in the midst of the pandemic, in a time of uncertainty when little was known about the novel pathogen.

At the societal level, social distancing endeavors like lockdowns are seen as the most effective interventions, based on simulations. This requires a nimble government, with a critical observation: "The highest reduction in the infection attack rate is achieved by the rapid activation of all available social distancing interventions, and with the highest rates of compliance" (Milne & Xie, Mar. 21, 2020, p. 6). This also assumes cooperation by the general public. In the modeling for various scenarios, the researchers assumed that the policies and practices could "be held for as long as a year" (Milne & Xie, Mar. 21, 2020, p. 12), which does not seem to be an accurate assumption based on human behaviors in various locales. Of the four endeavors, in terms of stand-alone efforts, school closure was found to be "the least effective single social distancing measure considered…(and) highly disruptive as adults are needed to care for younger children" (Milne & Xie, Mar. 21, 2020, p. 14).

Another more holistic approach involves the "Community-Workplace" model. This simulation-based work finds that "continuous testing can help a workplace avoid an outbreak by reducing undetected infectiousness even in high-contact environments" (Poole, et al., 2020, p. 1). Compared to other workplaces, university campuses require "more testing to remain safe" because of more time spent on the campus and with higher interactivity among people on campus (Poole, et al., 2020, p. 1). It is important to consider "the level of interaction of employees with non-employees in the community" (Poole, et al., 2020, p. 2) to understand workplace risks since community spread can affect employees. This research team theorizes a level of testing regime at which infection rates may be kept at 3% (vs. a no-testing scenario). Various testing scenarios are posited and simulated, such as only an initial test, only when symptoms appear, every work day regardless of symptom (in terms of percentages of the target population) (Poole, et al., 2020, p. 5). One identified weakness of the simulation is that a homogeneous population is assumed in the scenario (Poole, et al., 2020, p. 11). Another research work advocates for "high quality daily testing" for SARS-CoV-2 virus. The co-researchers write about their model-based study: "We show that reduction in overall infected-person-days, IPD, by significant percentages can be achieved, for fixed numbers of tests per day of 5% and 10% of the population, of 30% and 50% in the IPD numbers, respectively" (Hernandez & Valentinotti, 2020, p. 1). Ironically, only some minority of organizations instantiated workplace-based testing, according to journalistic articles (some "bubbled" sports teams and a few others).

The International Organization for Standardization (ISO) released the ISO/PAS 45005 "Safe Working" technical standard to codify ways to keep employees safer during a pandemic. This is a new ISO standard for "maintaining business operations in the context of the coronavirus pandemic" and is informed by two main concepts:

1. Reasonable measures must be undertaken by employers to manage the risks arising from COVID-19 are, or will be, implemented to protect the health and safety of workers and visitors; 2. Workers should not be required to work unless appropriate measures have been implemented. (Sandle, Jan. 29, 2021, p. 1)

Indeed, there are risks to employees getting to and from work (in transportation systems of all sorts), being a work, interacting with others at work, engaging in work activities, and others. Different occupational settings and types of work pose different risks. It is important to identify risk factors "for susceptibility to adverse and mortality outcomes" to enable public health interventions (Leso, Fontana, & Iavicoli, 2021, p. 1). Many people in a population have pre-existing health conditions, which have to be considered to calculate actual risks to employees of contracting COVID-19 at work (p. 6). Other research focused on case-based viral exposure controls in work places, specific to healthcare settings, border protection, airline operations, laboratories, grocery stores, restaurants, meat packing plants, ophthalmology, solid waste work, wastewater workers, and others. A case-based study showed the need for forensic pathologists and other staff to wear PPE when conducting autopsies (Puzović, Baković, Bubalo, & Mayer, 2020). Workplaces are being "re-imagined, re-improved and re-invented" both during and after the pandemic (de Lucas Ancillo, del Val Núñez, & Gavrila, 2020, p. 6) to ensure "occupational health and safety" even against an airborne pathogen (p. 8).

Partway into the pandemic, researchers found that aerosols were one type of transmission route, with the attendant risks of "coughing, sneezing, talking, singing and breathing" (Lindsley, et al., 2020, p. 1118) and toilet flushing (p. 1120) and medical procedures (p. 1120). Engineering efforts were deployed to prevent human transmission through "droplet, fomite and short-range aerosol routes" like "ventilated headboards" and intubation boxes" and "germicidal irradiation" (Lindsley, et al., 2020, p. 1121). Transparent barriers were also set up. And there were various changes to ventilation systems (Lindsley, et al., 2020, p. 1122). Many used facial respirators to filter out some particulates. Some wore eye covers to prevent ocular exposures. Personal protective equipment (PPE) may also include a "splash guard visor" and single-use isolation gowns (Cirrincione, et al., 2020, pp. 11 - 12).

Policies are only as good as they are applied. One study engaged trial testing of various COVID-19 compliance measures in work places, in a 12-week intervention study. Not surprisingly, they found a disparity between reports of one's own compliance vs. others' observations of that (non)compliance (Arroyos-Calvera, Drouvelis, Lohse, & McDonald, 2021, p. 14). They observe that it may be more effective to "nudge" those "low in compliance, instead of targeting the entire population" (p. 14). They also observe the risks that the interventions against infection are "short-term" ones, which entail other risks (p. 1). This would suggest that even if people adhered closely to the proper biosafety procedures, they would need to adhere perfectly into perpetuity.

Stressors in the COVID-19 Era

COVID-19 in the workplace has been anticipated to have various effects on employees and work organizations. One research team explored the literature in work and organizational psychology to anticipate how the major psychological stressors related to the pandemic will affect employees, even as they work from home and as virtual teams (Kniffin, et al., Aug. 10, 2020, pp. 3 - 4). Such work-based practices in the pandemic may lead to the "loss of social connection" and loneliness (Kniffin, et al., Aug. 10, 2020, p. 5). There are socio-psychological effects of unemployment and social inequality (Kniffin, et al., Aug. 10, 2020, p. 7).

Employee mental health has come to the fore in workplaces. Common stressors include the "perception of safety, threat and risk of contagion, infobesity (information overload) versus the unknown, quarantine and confinement, stigma and social exclusion as well as financial loss and job insecurity" (Hamouche, 2020, pp. 1 and 4). Other works have borne out the sense of psychological stress. The heightened pressures on nursing staff and workplace conditions have resulted in mental health impacts (Havaei, Ma, Staempfli, & MacPhee, Jan. 2021, p. 1). COVID-19 mental stressors can lead to potential failure of "the individual's mental and physical systems" (Makhbul & Rawshdeh, Mar. 2021, p. 194), with reactions like "sorrow, anxiety, misperception, fear and anger" in response to the pandemic (p. 195).

Some negative reactions include the following: "the overuse of gadgets and the Internet among children and teenagers" (Makhbul & Rawshdeh, Mar. 2021, p. 197); xenophobia and fear of the foreign "related to a group, race or nation" (p. 197), and other challenges. Another study found reports of depression, insomnia, anxiety, and other signs of stress for those with "direct contact with patients with COVID-19" (Liu, et al., 2021, p. 1).

Ways forward

At workplaces, most interventions for COVID-19 exposure controls involve administration, policy, communications, engineering controls, personal protective equipment, and other elements, in various combinations for occupational health and safety (Viramgami, Pagdhune, Sarkar, & Balanchandar, 2020).

The remote work is thought to have created a sense of disconnection between employees and their employers. Some predict a post-COVID "a new world, a new lexicon, a new social norm with far reaching economic and social destruction" (Kaushik & Guleria, 2020, p. 9) along with people feeling disconnected from their work places when engaging in work from home (p. 13). As large numbers of people are anticipated to start heading back to work in shared physical spaces, some are calling leaders to start documenting workplace culture more explicitly in order to share insights with employees to help in the adjustment (Mukhopadhyay & Mukhopadhyay, Jan. 2021). Another work suggests the importance of problem-based learning in the post-COVID-19 workplace, to enable collaborative working through challenges. The co-authors suggest problem-based learning around issues of "social and personal communications" and "security policies" and dealing with stress during a pandemic and stopping future COVID-19 like pandemics (Buheji & Buheji, 2020, p. 37).

Various organizations are designing a "back to work protocol" to repopulate buildings safely (Rastogi, Sobek, Jephson, & Allison, 2020, p. ii), with engineering and administrative controls and methods to measure and verify the effects. The efforts involve work in general ventilation, air treatment and filtration, local air treatment, source control / elimination (such as regarding toilets), and indoor environmental quality (including temperature, humidity) (Rastogi, Sobek, Jephson, & Allison, 2020, p. 5). Employees are trained to practice "cough hygiene" and various forms of "access control" to limit overcrowding (Rastogi, Sobek, Jephson, & Allison, 2020, p. 11). As schools reopen, there are social restrictions and space reconfigurations to achieve some level of biosafety (D'Angelo, et al., 2021, p. 1).

More permanent changes?

Some critical research throughout the pandemic has been the epidemiological monitoring of critical statistics, such as those verified as infected, recovered, susceptible, and dead. Hospital numbers also were collected and were used to inform on the state of the pandemic. One study mapped out the time dynamics of COVID-19 and enabled forecasting of case counts, which could suddenly explode given exponential spread (Carroll, et al., 2020, p. 1). Different countries' performances could be more objectively observed. This study involved data from 64 countries. Four time patterns were identified: "They are either (1) consistently higher than average (e.g., Switzerland), (2) consistently lower than average (e.g., India), (3) initially lower but then experience a dramatic increase over time (e.g., the US), or (4) initially higher before entering a period of control (e.g. Slovenia)" (Carroll, et al., 2020, p. 2). The numbers could be analyzed in relation to various national policies and practices.

Analysis of Successes and Failures

The numbers of infections, illnesses, and deaths in the United States points to systemic failures:

The United States (US) has been among those nations most severely affected by the first—and subsequent—phases of the pandemic of COVID-19, the disease caused by SARS-CoV-2. With only 4% of the worldwide population, the US has seen about 22% of COVID-19 deaths. Despite formidable advantages in resources and expertise, presently the per capita mortality rate is over 585/million, respectively 2.4 and 5 times higher compared to Canada and Germany. As we enter Fall 2020, the U.S is enduring ongoing outbreaks across large regions of the country. Moreover, within the US, an early and persistent feature of the pandemic has been the disproportionate impact on populations already made vulnerable by racism and dangerous jobs, inadequate wages, and unaffordable housing, and this is true for both the headline public health threat and the additional disastrous economic impacts. In this article we assess the impact of missteps by the Federal Government in three specific areas: the introduction of the virus to the US and the establishment of community transmission; the lack of national COVID-19 workplace standards and enforcement, and lack of personal protective equipment (PPE) for workplaces as represented by complaints to the Occupational Safety and Health Administration (OSHA) which we find are correlated with deaths 16 days later …and the total excess deaths in 2020 to date already total more than 230,000, while COVID-19 mortality rates exhibit severe—and rising—inequalities in race/ethnicity, including among working age adults. (Hanage, et al., 2020, p. 995)

The missteps involve border controls, lack of occupational health protections, uncontrolled community spread, leading to premature mortality and various inequitable social outcomes (Hanage, et al., 2020). In journalistic coverage, the U.S. government failed to set up testing effectively when the outbreak could still be controlled. They did not put into place face masking, which could have saved many lives. They did not follow the pandemic playbook created by the National Security Council in 2016 (Hanage, et al., 2020, p. 1003).

Many of the illnesses occurred in workplaces in the U.S. By contrast, another study focused on workplace infections in Ontario, Canada, from Jan. 21 – June 30, 2020. The researchers write:

There were 199 outbreaks with 1245 cases, and 68% of outbreaks and 80% of cases belonged to i) Manufacturing, ii) Agriculture, Forestry, Fishing, Hunting, iii) Transportation and Warehousing" with a median size of outbreaks at 3 cases (and a min-max range of 1 – 140) (Murti, Achonu, Smith, Brown, Kim, Johnson, Ravindran, & Buchan, 2020, p. 2)

The length of time of outbreaks were a median of 7 days (a min-max range of 0 – 119) (Murti, Achonu, Smith, Brown, Kim, Johnson, Ravindran, & Buchan, 2020, p. 2). In the time frame, there were 608 household cases. This level of surveillance suggests some effectiveness in terms of public health entities in government.

In the Republic of Korea (South Korea), researchers advocate having a health examination system for employees include transmissible diseases in light of the COVID-19 pandemic (Seo, Mu, Kim, & Lee, July 2020, p. 1).

Another study proposes a phased return of people to Beijing, the capital of the People's Republic of China, in a way that would keep down the reproductive number (R_0 or r-nought). SARS-CoV-2 was first identified in Wuhan, China. Beijing is a high risk region given that it is the center of so much of the life of the country, with people from all provinces (Zhang, et al., 2021, p. 481) of a highly populous country. The city was shut down to prevent a massive outbreak, and the question is how to restart the city safely. The solution—which worked—was to bring back people "batch-by-batch in terms of their profession" (Zhang, et al., 2021, p. 485). Stage 1 involved resumption of work at 50% by February 20, 2020, "including Accommodation Services, Governmental Organization, Financial and Insurance Services, Commercial Business, and Enterprises" and so on, with Shopping added in Stage 2 and others until 100% by Stage 6 in April 10, 2020 (Zhang, et al., 2021, pp. 485-486). This work involves modeling out different dates and percentages of sub-population returns to the city and offers spatio-temporal predictions of infection spread and prevalence (Zhang, et al., 2021, p. 488). The available numbers give credence to the benefits of having had prior experiences with pandemics and bureaucratic measures in place to enforce quarantine and other policies.

A study out of Hong Kong found a high level of dissatisfaction with workplace policies related to COVID-19, with unhappiness on policy "comprehensiveness, timeliness, and transparency" (Wong, et al., Mar. 2020). This dissatisfaction does not seem to have been limited to any one locale, given employee concerns about their health and a sense of lack of care of many employers and the management class.

Changes to the built environment. There are changes proposed to the built environment. One study listed ten expected changes post-COVID in the construction sciences (including architecture, civil engineering, urbanism, and others), based on learning from previous pandemics and the current one. There are an anticipated decline in car-based transportation infrastructure, "a push for information-based construction management methods," off-site construction and engineering, an increase in lightweight structural systems, new materials for insulation, "revisions in density and compact design," More adaptive spatial planning (including hygiene consideration), "smaller and individual internal layouts" such as for "public buildings, commercial buildings, retail, and offices," meso-scale strategies at the community level, and "new opportunities for non-centralized building systems" (Cheshmehzangi, 2021, n.p.).

COVID-19 may transform how people use public built spaces less because of awareness of biosafety risks of shared air, especially in large groups. COVID-19 is projected to have effects on "future design, use and perceptions of public space" and city design (Honey-Rosés, et al., Apr. 21, 2020, p. 1). As part of this study, the researchers ask: "How will the needs of vulnerable groups such as women, racial minorities, immigrants, low-income residents, the elderly, children and the homeless be accounted for in future public space designs, practices, and rules? Will cities in the Global South attempt to constrain or regulate the informal street economy? Will the pandemic permanently disrupt the interconnected global settlement system?" (Honey-Rosés, et al., Apr. 21, 2020, p. 4) The potential "aversion to large crowds" is projected to affect "concerts, cultural events, sporting events, ceremonies, markets and political protests" (Honey-Rosés, et al., Apr. 21, 2020, p. 7). There are concerns that people may reject public transit due to fears of contagion. There are concerns about the potential infringement on civil liberties of people in public spaces as part of policies to control pandemic spread (including remote temperature checks, health checkpoints, release of personal health data, and others), based on COVID-19 interventions in some countries (p. 12).

In this time, there have been various technological innovations, including various types of face masks and mobile apps to track possible exposures, air cleaners, and others. One proposal involves a spatial-aware sensor net to enable safer workplace reopenings dubbed the "Internet of COVID-19 Things" platform (IoCT). This technology is designed to provide situational awareness that enables "interoperability through the open geospatial standards for indoor COVID-19 person-to-person place risk assessment" (Liang, et al., 2021, p. 77).

Social justice issues

Social pressures have mounted with the disruptions of the pandemic. Some public health officials have worked hard to avoid stigmatizing those with COVID-19. They have worked to maintain people's privacy in terms of health status. The more prescient leaders have worked to maintain the social fabric, even as it was under strain. Researchers suggest the importance of preparing people for a post-COVID world by creating "positive person-to-person relationships that will craft a more harmonious social situation" (Makhbul & Rawshdeh, Mar. 2021, p. 199).

One glaring issue involved the lack of protections for essential workers. To achieve "true health justice for all," structural disparities in the treatment of various dispossessed workers need to be addressed. For example, the home healthcare worker population is 90% women, and two-thirds of these are women of color (Yearby & Mohapatra, May 29, 2020, p. 1). Yet, such workers are low-wage ones with high risks. Workers at meat processing plants worked during the pandemic without workplace protections for long periods before some changes were made (Yearby & Mohapatra, May 29, 2020, p. 2). There should be common-sense workplace protections, paid sick leave, the disallowing of "any bonuses based on lack of absenteeism," free health care for employees and their families, childcare support, and other practical considerations (Yearby & Mohapatra, May 29, 2020, pp. 4-5) for essential workers.

The shock of the pandemic is seen as a potential opportunity to reconfigure urban mobility to address gender gap issues and enable environmental sustainability (González-Sánchez, Olmo-Sánchez, & Maeso-González, 2021). Women work more in sectors that require physical presence (p. 5). A Strengths, Weaknesses, Opportunities, and Threats (SWOT) analysis of urban mobility "from the perspective of sustainability and gender equity in the context of the coronavirus pandemic" (p. 6) found that gender sensitivity was not present in many mobility policies (p. 8). A lack of work flexibility in working hours often require driving during traffic congestion periods (González-Sánchez, Olmo-Sánchez, & Maeso-González, 2021, p. 9). This study proposes various creative opportunities such as building a "15-minute city" and autonomous vehicles for commuting and drones for parcel delivery (p. 10). Responsible transportation may be reconfigured to "benefit of the global environment and individual citizens alike" (Budd & Ison, 2020, p. 1). Part of the sustainability piece may involve more telecommuting. Certainly, many are suggesting that settling into a "new normal" should not be done unthinkingly and should include the redefining of "transformative smart work and space" (Hu, 2020, p. 277).

COVID-19 has had outsized effects on marginalized populations. There have been "inequities in access to decent work and experiences of discrimination resulting in many of the vulnerable populations in the United States (Kantamneni, 2020, p. 1). Many of those most effective are in highly impacted sectors: "restaurants/bars, travel and transportation, entertainment, personal services, and certain types of retail and manufacturing" (Vavra, 2020, as cited in Kantamneni, 2020, p. 2). The pandemic has had outsized effects on women who often also have more "household and caretaking responsibilities" than men (Kantamneni, 2020, p. 3). Those in minority communities have experienced harsher economic impacts like job loss, lack of healthcare, homelessness, and other challenges. Certain target groups like Asian Americans have experienced increased discrimination and violent attacks.

Some have studied how people communicate about the pandemic on social media. In a nationally representative sample of US adults, one team found that "members of racial and ethnic minority groups were most likely to report posting COVID-19 content on social media" (Campos-Castillo & Laestadius, 2020). These included those "traditionally less likely to use social media" such as "men and older adults" (Campos-Castillo & Laestadius, 2020). This may perhaps suggest the need for public health personnel and other strategic communicators to use social media more effectively to engage the broader population. There are some challenges, too, however, with digital divides.

Others are calling for "just transitions" regarding energy in the post-COVID world. As the world moves away from coal power, for example, the transitions should include "income support for workers" and "local economic development tools for affected communities" and "realistic training / retraining programs that lead to decent work" and sharing of best practices (Henry, Bazilian, & Markuson, 2020, p. 2). Policies should mitigate potential harms to impacted workers and the larger communities.

RETURNING TO THE IN-PERSON WORKPLACE IN A (POST?) PANDEMIC CONTEXT

Returning to a physical workspace is a sign of normalcy that is welcome to many. Social media show some of the messaging shared among the users of the respective platforms.

Figure 1. Sociogram of #backtowork Discussants on Twitter Microblogging Platform

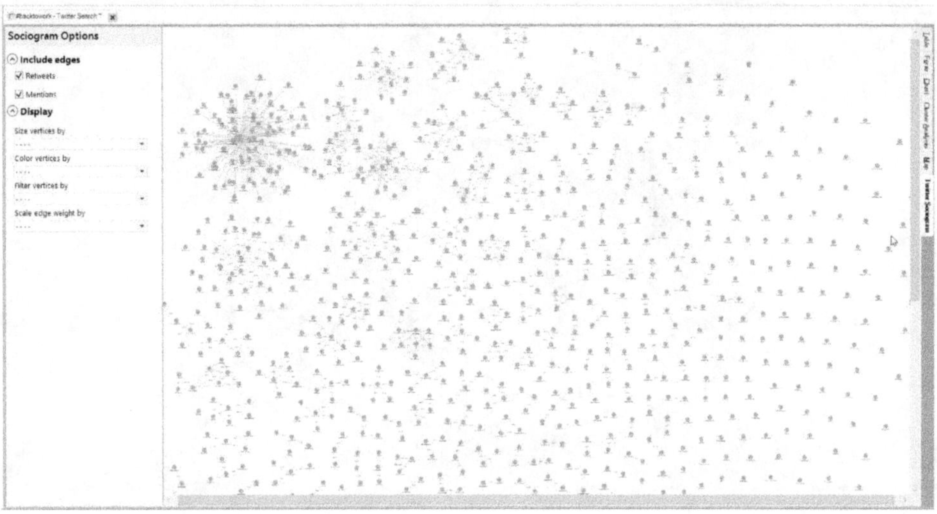

SAMPLING SOCIAL MEDIA

Social media come in various types. This sampling involved a microblogging site, a social image sharing site, and a news sharing site.

A #backtowork Hashtag Network on a Microblogging Site

A search on Google for "return to work hashtags" found the following top 10, in descending order: #backtowork (67%), #covid (9%), #backtoschool (5%), #staysafe (2%), #coronavirus (2%), #work (2%), #newnormal (2%), and #love (2%). The top one was used to seed the extraction of a hashtag network, which resulted in 1,100 Tweets for #backtowork, on the Twitter microblogging site. The social network graph of the communicators around this hashtag show one larger graph, a number of smaller ones, a few motifs, and numerous isolate nodes.

A global map of this #backtowork network shows a global distribution (Figure 2).

In terms of word similarity analysis between the communicators, a few conversations are being had among the social media accounts (Figure 3).

As to some general focuses, a word cloud was created from the 1,000 most commonly used terms in the shared messages among the communicators.

Themes and subthemes were autocoded from the hashtag network. These may be seen in the treemap diagram (Figure 5) and the codebook (Table 1). The themes and subthemes were coded at cell level (vs. sentence or paragraph levels) given the structure of the extracted data from Twitter in a data table.

Figure 2. Global Map of #backtowork Discussants on Twitter Microblogging Platform

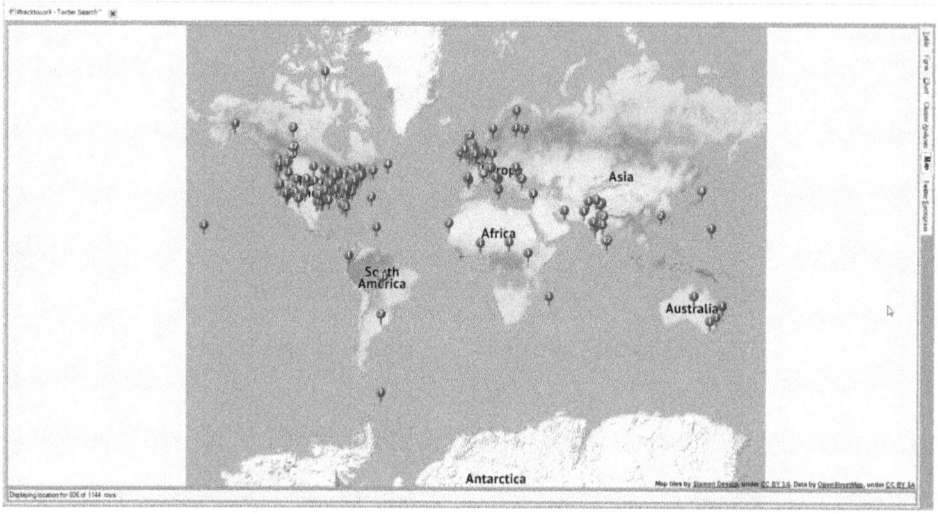

An automated sentiment analysis was run over the #backtowork hashtag network's communications. A majority of the text was neutral. The text that included sentiment found mostly positive sentiment.

The sentiment-bearing text trends mostly "very positive" and moderately positive," not "negative". This may be seen in the 3D bar chart in Figure 7.

Figure 3. Ring Lattice Graph of #backtowork Discussants on Twitter Microblogging Platform

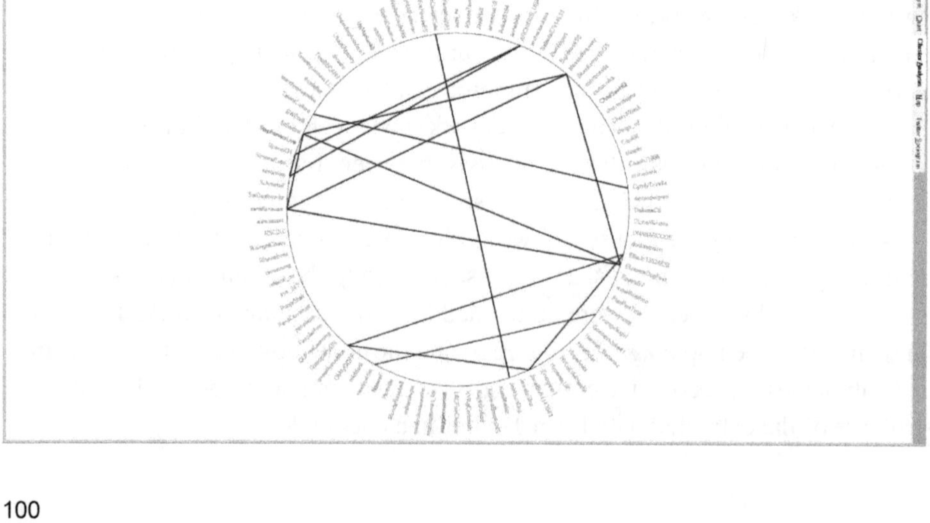

Figure 4. Word Cloud of #backtowork Discussants on Twitter Microblogging Platform

A word tree shows some of the concerns around COVID-19. These include various ways that work places are dealing with the current concerns.

A Related Tags Network

Another approach to looking at this present moment is to look at a “work” related tags network on Flickr. Here, the folk tags applied to shared social imagery on Flickr shows neutral labeling text and more practical concerns.

Figure 5. Treemap Diagram of Autoextracted Themes and Subthemes from #backtowork Hashtag Network

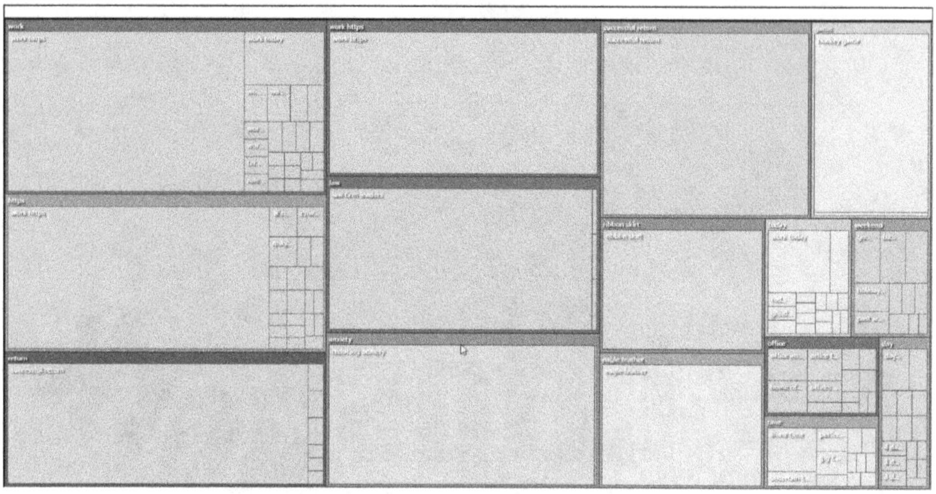

News sharing site

Finally, there were some light read-throughs of Reddit threads around returning to offices…and many of these involve requests for information. A consensus seems to be that the "hybrid" model is in play, with some returning to the office and others telecommuting. Some seem to have light concerns, one noting that this person just has to "wear a mask around the office." Working from home is seen as a "trial" for some. The trigger point for companies is described as "vaccine widely available" as a phase. Several threads were copied, but the one found most valuable was one based on human resource professionals.

TURN RIGHT AT MATISSE

I have been visiting my cubicle about twice a month during the pandemic in order to access particular technologies. My office had shifted to one on the periphery of campus due to an accidental fire caused by roofing activities back in 2018. Then, the pandemic hit, and leaders restricted access to campus. By mid-Spring 2021, my cubicle was ready, and I received keys. I moved to the cubicle in early April and started showing up at work at the end of April and have been working in my cubicle in the university library since. (I learned to find my way to my new office by turning right at the book shelf with a number of volumes about French artist Henri

Table 1. Codebook of Autoextracted Themes and Subthemes from #backtowork Hashtag Network on Twitter Microblogging Platform

Topics	Subtopics
anxiety	
	anxiety dreams
	reducing anxiety
day	
	1st day
	3 day holiday weekend
	3 day weekend
	4 day week
	4 day weekend
	consecutive days
	couple days
	day weekend
	exciting day today
	half days
	hot day
	idle days
	normal day
	productive day
	rehearsal day
	sunny day
eagle feather	
	eagle feather
game	
	game win streak
	hockey game
https	
	➡ https
	✸ https
	19 orders https
	acvhrbzbff https
	bioscience perspective https
	conference room https
	equipment https
	heat https
	huddersfield https
	limousine fleet https
	mainstream https
	oqsef2kkal https
	pères https
	playlist dès maintenant https
	qnkyv1blg8 https
	reopening https
	support https
	today https
	top bag https
	visit https
	work https
	z9iw7d8tcc https
law	
	big issues leaders
	issues firms
	law firm leaders
	medical law expert
office	

continued on following page

Table 1. Continued

Topics	Subtopics
	amazing office space
	at-work office
	flexible offices
	home office
	office desk
	office face time
	office impact
	office life
	office spaces
	office today
	office work
	offices things
	physical office
return	
	big return
	broad return
	eventual return
	peoplehum return
	safe return
	staff return
	successful return
ribbon skirt	
	ribbon skirt
successful return	
	successful return
time	
	1st time
	alone time
	face time
	full time
	gig times
	looooong time
	office face time
	perfect time
	response times
	spare time
	time detours
	uncertain times
today	
	2021 edits today
	exciting day today
	free today
	friend today
	grind today
	job today
	later today
	office today
	online today
	pledge today
	purpose today
	thing today
	tired today
	today https
	work today
	world today
weekend	
	3 day holiday weekend

continued on following page

Table 1. Continued

Topics	Subtopics
	3 day weekend
	4 day weekend
	bank hol weekend
	bank holiday weekend
	cracking weekend
	day weekend
	exciting weekend
	good weekend
	holiday weekend
	past weekend
work	
	at-home workers
	frontline workers
	hybrid work
	hybrid work schedules
	office work
	part-time workers
	remote working hours
	role work
	term work
	work attire
	work environment
	work https
	work place
	work productivity
	work today
	work trip
	work week
	work
	working chair
	working face
	working mill
	working necessities
	working space
	working tomorrow
work https	
	work https

Matisse.) I have been masked for most of that time until our campus released all those who had been vaccinated from wearing masks. Organizations are following U.S. Centers for Disease Control and Prevention (CDC) guidance in setting policies and practices. There are interests in protecting the workforce and also for defending against potential legal exposures. (I'd received my doses in March and April and was fully protected by early May. I was not in the first or second tranches of recipients. I would have been willing to have even taken experimental versions of the vaccines given my general confidence in the scientists in this case. I did sign up to take part but was not called.) There are still only a few people on campus. There is a palpable sense of relief and joy at returning to work. However, at this moment, only some 42% of citizens in the state have received their vaccinations against SARS-CoV-2.

Every day, there are more and more of the "You have arrived" moments after the two weeks of the second inoculation. There's buying food out of a vending machine

Figure 6. Treemap Diagram of Autocoded Sentiment from #backtowork Hashtag Network on Twitter Microblogging Platform

using actual money (dollars and coinage). There's purchasing a cup of coffee in a recyclable cup. There's watching a movie with others unmasked in a movie theatre (and with children present) at the end of May. There is a lot more regular exercise.

Being in the presence of colleagues is at once both joyful and a little stressful, particularly when distances are closed (closer and closer), and then people are in one's airspace. By early June, most people wear masks only haphazardly or just sort of hold it in front of their faces as a sign of politeness. We are benefitting from the quiet period at a university with fewer students on campus. This is our time to adapt.

There is a sense that we are in the post-acute phase of the SARS-CoV-2 / COVID-19 pandemic. There are wildcard factors, such as viral variants and other challenges, but if things hold, the country may be emerging from a devastating phase.

Update in October 2021. As the saying goes, the bloom is off this (work) rose. With the various financial pressures, administrators are asking faculty and staff to do more with less. They are pressuring employees to work nights and weekends, in order to meet deadlines. While the amount of work that can be done is magnified on campus (I'm more productive and efficient while working on campus), and a majority of colleagues is warm and polite, some administrators have gone feral in their time away from the office. One in particular has become verbally abusive and threatening, and he has expressed racist microaggressions (including pulling "chink eyes" to me directly during a one-on-one web conferencing meeting). At minimum, this is a racist microaggression; at worst, this is a sign of anti-Asian hatred, disrespect, and callousness—which also shows up in biased and discriminatory supervisory

Figure 7. 3D Bar Chart of Autocoded Sentiment from #backtowork Hashtag Network on Twitter Microblogging Platform

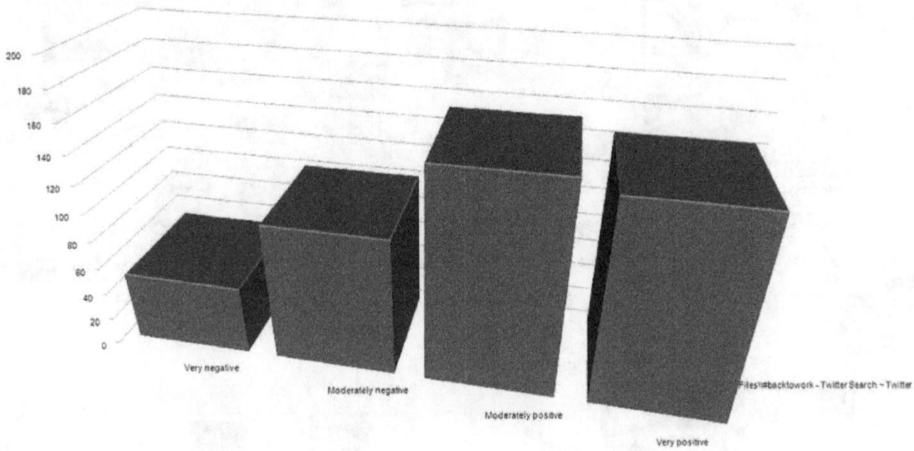

Figure 8. Word Tree around "COVID" from #backtowork Hashtag Network on Twitter Microblogging Platform

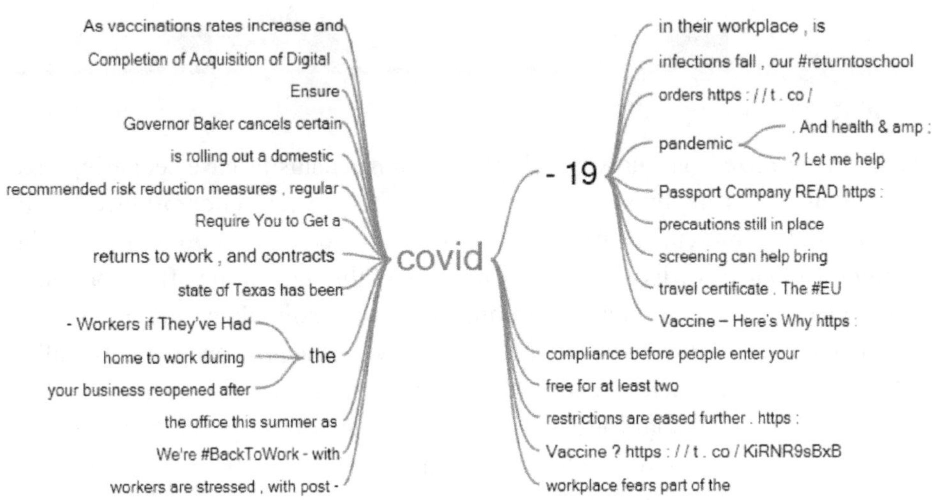

decision-making. He is insistent that the multiple full-time equivalencies (FTEs) of responsibilities have to be maintained. While he had been working the issue of standing up a team to take on some of the workload for the past two years, none of

Figure 9. "Work" Related Tags Network on Flickr (1.5 deg)

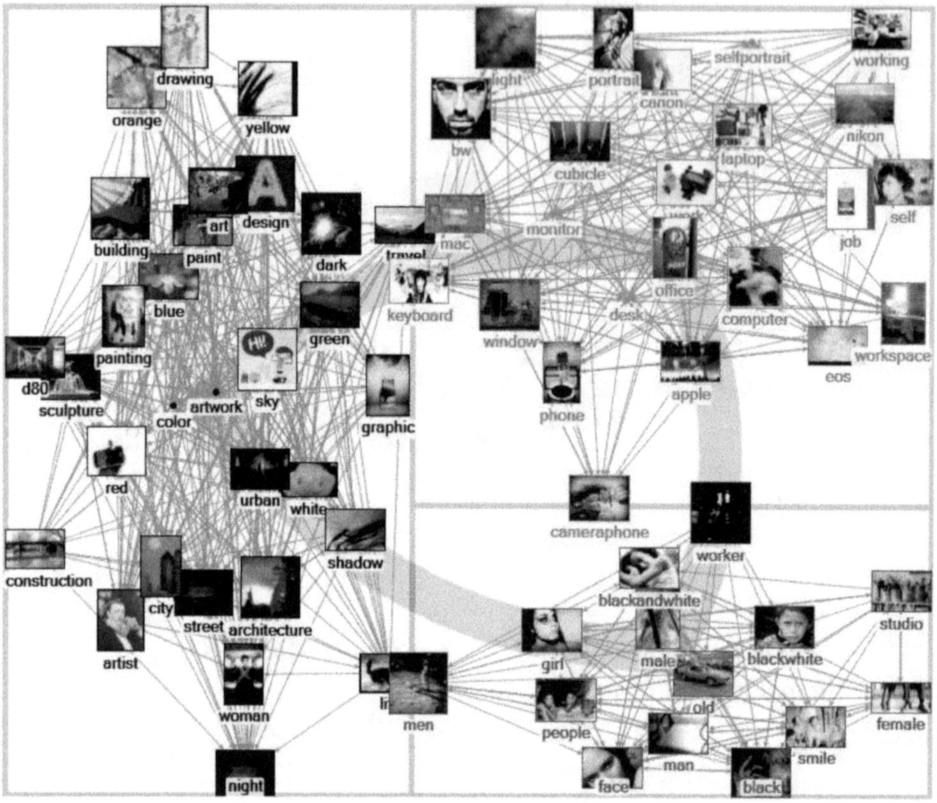

that has materialized. The university's complaint mechanisms have been triggered, but little change is likely going to occur, given the current circumstances (with everyone web conferencing meetings) and the university's inordinate financial pressures. Colleagues wince when they hear about the state of the office, but there are also challenges in a litigious environment. At what point do wrongs escalate to settlement in a court of law, which will be expensive monetarily and reputationally?

November 2021. Then, in early November, in the library's lounge, an incident occurs which seems to capture just how much has changed in two years of a rampaging pandemic. It is just prior to lunchtime, and the lounge, with its socially distanced tables, are empty except for one person. The author starts the water heating pot and goes to a nearby room for a quick errand. When she returns, the one diner is gone, and another masked person is heating something in the microwave. People are purposefully avoiding each other's presence, and it is still the wise thing to do, in terms of biosafety. It is no longer rude when another person leaves as one enters

Table 2. "Work" Related Tags Network on Flickr (1.5 deg)

Graph Metrics	Values
Graph Type	Directed
Vertices	68
Unique Edges	1680
Edges With Duplicates	0
Total Edges	1680
Self-Loops	0
Reciprocated Vertex Pair Ratio	0.304347826
Reciprocated Edge Ratio	0.466666667
Connected Components	1
Single-Vertex Connected Components	0
Maximum Vertices in a Connected Component	68
Maximum Edges in a Connected Component	1680
Maximum Geodesic Distance (Diameter)	2
Average Geodesic Distance	1.413495
Graph Density	0.368744513
Modularity	Not Applicable
NodeXL Version	1.0.1.336

because it is not post-pandemic yet. It is hard to say when that day will actually come. Perhaps mid-2022.

DISCUSSION

The past year and a half has been a time of unprecedented stress, with the threat of a deadly virus hanging over humanity. It has only been in the past few months that people have had access to the vaccinations stateside, and other countries have it even slower. Some hiring personnel suggest that there is a preference for those who have been vaccinated. How long COVID-19 will be with humanity is as-yet unknown, but the projections are that it may be a permanent part of the biological landscape given its capabilities and the mass endemicity of its spread in humanity. There are questions about whether this is a zoonotic spillover event from animals into humans or whether this was from a lab leak.

FUTURE RESEARCH DIRECTIONS

There will certainly be research on how to reopen with consideration for social justice, employee health, healthy productivity for work places, and other topics. In this early moment of the return to work, there is optimism and perhaps some learning from a year-and-a-half of challenges.

CONCLUSION

To capture a sense of return-to-work from a devastating pandemic, this work drew on the research literature, journalistic articles, social media narratives, and a light auto-ethnography. This found some level of thinking and planning for the re-opening in the research literature and journalistic articles and also optimism on social media. There are hopes that this difficult period will be in the rearview mirror for humanity, if it can only work together for everyone's collective betterment. Certainly, societies need healthy economies and employed persons, and these next months will determine how well the U.S. as a major country and economic engine fares.

REFERENCES

Almeida, F., Santos, J. D., & Monteiro, J. A. (2020). The Challenges and Opportunities in the Digitalization of Companies in a Post-COVID-19 World. *IEEE Engineering Management Review*, *48*(3), 97–103. doi:10.1109/EMR.2020.3013206

Arroyos-CalveraD.DrouvelisM.LohseJ.McDonaldR. (2021). *Improving compliance with COVID-19 guidance: a workplace field experiment*. doi:10.2139/ssrn.3760562

Budd, L., & Ison, S. (2020). Responsible Transport: A post-COVID agenda for transport policy and practice. *Transportation Research Interdisciplinary Perspectives, 6*, 1 - 5.

Buheji, M., & Buheji, A. (2020). Characteristics of 'problem-based learning' in post-COVID-19 workplace. *Human Resource Management Review*, *10*(2), 33–39.

Campos-Castillo, C., & Laestadius, L. I. (2020). Racial and ethnic digital divides in posting COVID-19 content on social media among US adults: Secondary survey analysis. *Journal of Medical Internet Research*, *22*(7), e20472. doi:10.2196/20472 PMID:32568726

Carroll, C., Bhattacharjee, S., Chen, Y., Dubey, P., Fan, J., Gajardo, A., Zhou, X., Muller, H.-G., & Wang, J. L. (2020). Time dynamics of COVID-19. *Scientific Reports*, *10*(1), 1–14. doi:10.103841598-020-77709-4 PMID:33273598

Cheshmehzangi, A. (2021). Revisiting the built environment: 10 potential development changes and paradigm shifts due to COVID-19. *Journal of Urban Management.*

Chinniah, B. M. N., Taylor, S., & Proches, C. G. (2020, June 25). COVID-19: The New Normal for the Workplace. *UKZNDABAonline*, *8*(21), 1–3.

Cirrincione, L., Plescia, F., Ledda, C., Rapisarda, V., Martorana, D., Moldovan, R. E., Theodoridou, K., & Cannizzaro, E. (2020). COVID-19 pandemic: Prevention and protection measures to be adopted at the workplace. *Sustainability, 12*(9), 1 – 18.

D'Angelo, D., Sinopoli, A., Napoletano, A., Gianola, S., Castellini, G., del Monaco, A., Fauci, A. J., Latina, R., Iacorossi, L., Salomone, K., Coclite, D., & Iannone, P. (2021). Strategies to exiting the COVID-19 lockdown for workplace and school: A scoping review. *Safety Science*, *134*, 1–8. doi:10.1016/j.ssci.2020.105067 PMID:33162676

de Lucas Ancillo, A., del Val Núñez, M. T., & Gavrila, S. G. (2020). Workplace change within the COVID-19 context: a grounded theory approach. *Economic Research-Ekonomska Istraživanja*, 1-20.

Estrada, M. A. R. (2021, Feb.). *From COVID-19 to COVID-21*. Preprint.

George, R., & George, A. (2020, April). Prevention of COVID-19 in the workplace. SAMJ. *South African Medical Journal*, *110*(4), 269–270. doi:10.7196/SAMJ.2020.v110i4.14723 PMID:32657736

González-Sánchez, G., Olmo-Sánchez, M. I., & Maeso-González, E. (2021). Challenges and Strategies for Post-COVID-19 Gender Equity and Sustainable Mobility. *Sustainability, 13*(5), 1 - 19.

Grady, D. (2021, June 3). 'I had never faced the reality of death': A surgeon becomes a patient. *The New York Times.*

Haigh, K. Z., & Gandhi, M. (2021, April). COVID-19 Mitigation With Appropriate Safety Measures in an Essential Workplace: Lessons for Opening Work Settings in the United States During COVID-19. In Open Forum Infectious Diseases (Vol. 8, No. 4). Oxford University Press.

Hamouche, S. (2020). *COVID-19 and employees' mental health: Stressors, moderators and agenda for organizational actions.* Emerald Open Research.

Hanage, W. P., Testa, C., Chen, J. T., Davis, L., Pechter, E., Seminario, P., Santillana, M., & Krieger, N. (2020). COVID-19: US federal accountability for entry, spread, and inequities—lessons for the future. *European Journal of Epidemiology, 35*(11), 995–1006. doi:10.100710654-020-00689-2 PMID:33136249

Havaei, F., Ma, A., Staempfli, S., & MacPhee, M. (2021, January). Nurses' Workplace Conditions Impacting Their Mental Health during COVID-19: A Cross-Sectional Survey Study. *Health Care, 9*(1), 1–14. PMID:33467080

Henry, M. S., Bazilian, M. D., & Markuson, C. (2020). Just transitions: Histories and futures in a post-COVID world. *Energy Research & Social Science, 68*(101668), 1–4. doi:10.1016/j.erss.2020.101668 PMID:32839696

Hernandez, X., & Valentinotti, S. (2020). On an optimal testing strategy for workplace settings operating during the COVID-19 pandemic. medRxiv. 1 - 18. doi:10.1101/2020.12.22.20248752

Honey-Rosés, J., Anguelovski, I., Bohigas, J., Chireh, V., Daher, C., Konijnendijk, C., Litt, J., Mawani, V., McCall, M., Orellana, A., Oscilowicz, E., Sánchez, U., Senbel, M., Tan, X., Villagomez, E., Zapat, O., & Nieuwenhuijsen, M. (2020, Apr. 21). *The impact of COVID-19 on public space: A review of the emerging questions.* Academic Press.

Hu, R. (2020). COVID-19, smart work, and collaborative space: A crisis-opportunity perspective. *Journal of Urban Management, 9*(3), 276–280. doi:10.1016/j.jum.2020.08.001

Jayathilake, H. D., Daud, D., Eaw, H. C., & Annuar, N. (2021). Employee development and retention of Generation-Z employees in the post-COVID-19 workplace: A conceptual framework. *Benchmarking, 28*(7), 2343–2364. doi:10.1108/BIJ-06-2020-0311

Joseph, B., Angeline, N. G., & Arasu, S. (2020). COVID-19—Practicing prevention in the workplace. *Indian Journal of Occupational and Environmental Medicine, 24*(3), 133–136. doi:10.4103/ijoem.ijoem_460_20 PMID:33746423

Kantamneni, N. (2020). The impact of the COVID-19 pandemic on marginalized populations in the United States: A research agenda. *Journal of Vocational Behavior, 119*(103439), 1–4. doi:10.1016/j.jvb.2020.103439 PMID:32390658

Kaushik, M. (2020, May-June). Post COVID-19 world: A paradigm shift at workplace. *TEST Engineering & Management*, 27675 – 27687.

Kaushik, M., & Guleria, N. (2020). The impact of pandemic COVID-19 in workplace. *European Journal of Business and Management, 12*(15), 9–19.

Kelly, S.M. (2021, Sept. 24). *Stop making employees turn on webcams during meetings*. CNN.

Kniffin, K. M., Narayanan, J., Anseel, F., Antonakis, J., Ashford, S. P., Bakker, A. B., Bamberger, P., Bapuji, H., Bhave, D. P., Choi, V. K., Creary, S. J., Demerouti, E., Flynn, F. J., Gelfand, M. J., Greer, L. L., Johns, G., Kesebir, S., Klein, P. G., Lee, S. Y., ... Vugt, M. (2020, August 10). COVID-19 and the Workplace: Implications, Issues, and Insights for Future Research and Action. *The American Psychologist*. Advance online publication. doi:10.1037/amp0000716 PMID:32772537

Leso, V., Fontana, L., & Iavicoli, I. (2021). Susceptibility to coronavirus (COVID-19) in occupational settings: The complex interplay between individual and workplace factors. *International Journal of Environmental Research and Public Health, 18*(3), 1 - 16.

Liang, S. H., Saeedi, S., Ojagh, S., Honarparvar, S., Kiaei, S., Jahromi, M. M., & Squires, J. (2021). An Interoperable Architecture for the Internet of COVID-19 Things (IoCT) Using Open Geospatial Standards—Case Study: Workplace Reopening. *Sensors (Basel), 21*(1), 50–82. doi:10.339021010050 PMID:33374208

Lindsley, W. G., Blachère, F. M., Burton, N. C., Christensen, B., Estill, C. F., Fisher, E. M., Martin, S. B., Mead, K. R., Noti, J. D., & Seaton, M. (2020). COVID-19 and the workplace: Research questions for the aerosol science community. *Aerosol Science and Technology, 54*(10), 1117–1123. doi:10.1080/02786826.2020.1796921

Liu, T., Zheng, Z., Sha, X., Liu, H., Zheng, W., Su, H., Xu, G., Su, K.-P., So, K.-F., & Lin, K. (2021). Psychological impact in non-infectious disease specialists who had direct contact with patients with COVID-19. *BJPsych Open, 7*(1), 1–4. doi:10.1192/bjo.2020.147 PMID:33283699

Makhbul, Z. K. M., & Rawshdeh, Z. A. (2021, March). Mental stress post-COVID-19. *International Journal of Public Health Science, 10*(1), 194–201.

Mauras, S., Cohen-Addad, V., Duboc, G., la Tour, M. D., Frasca, P., Mathieu, C., Opatowski, L., & Viennot, L. (2020). Mitigating COVID-19 outbreaks in workplaces and schools by hybrid telecommuting. medRxiv. 1 - 40. doi:10.1101/2020.11.09.20228007

Milne, G. J., & Xie, S. (2020). The effectiveness of social distancing in mitigating COVID-19 spread: a modelling analysis. MedRxiv. 1 - 16. doi:10.1101/2020.03.20.20040055

Mukhopadhyay, B.R., & Mukhopadhyay, B.K. (2021, Jan.). *The leader's guide to new workplace culture during Covid-19*. Academic Press.

Murti, M., Achonu, C., Smith, B. T., Brown, K. A., Kim, J. H., Johnson, J., Ravindran, S., & Buchan, S. A. (2020). COVID-19 Workplace Outbreaks by Industry Sector and their Associated Household Transmission, Ontario, Canada, January to June, 2020. medRxiv. doi:10.1101/2020.11.25.20239038

Ng, W. T. (2020). COVID-19: Protection of workers at the workplace in Singapore. *Safety and Health at Work*, 1–3. PMID:33052261

Olokundun, M., Ibidunni, S., Ogbari, M., Falola, H., & Salau, O. (2021). COVID-19 Pandemic and Antecedents for Digital Transformation in the Workplace: A Conceptual Framework. *Open Access Macedonian Journal of Medical Sciences, 9*(F), 41-46.

Poole, S. F., Gronsbell, J., Winter, D., Nickels, S., Levy, R., Fu, B., . . . Fromer, M. (2020). A holistic approach for suppression of COVID-19 spread in workplaces and universities. medRxiv. doi:10.1101/2020.12.03.20243626

Puzović, V., Baković, M., Bubalo, P., & Mayer, D. (2020). Accidental death from a fall from height at workplace turned out to be a COVID-19 death. *Forensic Science International: Reports*, *2*(100139), 1–4.

Rastogi, P., M., Sobek, O. N., Jephson, G.. & Allison, J. (2020). *A Data-driven Indoor Air Quality Framework for Post-COVID-19 Workplace Re-entry*. Academic Press.

Reuschke, D., & Felstead, A. (2020). Changing workplace geographies in the COVID-19 crisis. *Dialogues in Human Geography*, *10*(2), 208–212. doi:10.1177/2043820620934249

Sandle, T. (2021, Jan. 29). *International recommendations for COVID-19 workplace safety*. ISO/PAS 45005.

Seo, E., Mun, E., Kim, W., & Lee, C. (2020). Fighting the COVID-19 pandemic: Onsite mass workplace testing for COVID-19 in the Republic of Korea. *Annals of Occupational and Environmental Medicine*, *32*(1), 1–4. doi:10.35371/aoem.2020.32.e22 PMID:32802338

Viramgami, A., Pagdhune, A., Sarkar, K., & Balachandar, R. (2020). Occupational Health and Safety Practices at workplace during COVID-19 Pandemic. *Journal of Comprehensive Health*, *8*(2), 77–82.

Wong, E., Ho, K. F., Wong, S. Y., Cheung, A. W., & Yeoh, E. (2020). Workplace safety and coronavirus disease (COVID-19) pandemic: survey of employees. Bulletin of the World Health Organization. doi:10.2471/BLT.20.255893

Yearby, R., & Mohapatra, S. (2020). *Structural discrimination in COVID-19 workplace protections.* Health Affairs Blog.

Zhang, W. B., Ge, Y., Liu, M., Atkinson, P. M., Wang, J., Zhang, X., & Tian, Z. (2021). Risk assessment of the step-by-step return-to-work policy in Beijing following the COVID-19 epidemic peak. *Stochastic Environmental Research and Risk Assessment*, *35*(2), 481–498. doi:10.100700477-020-01929-3 PMID:33223954

Chapter 6
Skills, Practices, and Emotions for Teaching in Times of Pandemic:
An Analysis of Pre-School, Primary, and Secondary School Teachers (Argentina, 2020)

Gabriela Vergara
National University of Rafaela, Argentina

Constanza Faracce Macia
University of Palermo, Argentina

ABSTRACT

This chapter describes how Argentine teachers at the pre-school, primary, and secondary levels adapted to emergency distance education during the Preventive and Compulsory Social Isolation (ASPO) that was established in Argentina due to the COVID-19 pandemic in 2020. From an exploitative-descriptive strategy, a non-probabilistic survey was carried out through an online questionnaire during June 2020, whose sample consisted of 411 cases. Among the results, it is highlighted that the teachers applied their knowledge and skills prior to the pandemic, but they also had to learn to use new resources to adapt to the educational conditions of the pandemic, which led to greater effort and difficulties for older teachers. In accordance with this, the predominance of joy and pride in the younger teachers indicates that they were more satisfied than the older ones. It is concluded that despite the fact that all teachers expressed having adapted, the older ones encountered greater difficulties and, consequently, had to resort to a greater diversity of adaptation strategies.

DOI: 10.4018/978-1-7998-8626-6.ch006

INTRODUCTION

This chapter describes how Argentine teachers at the pre-school, primary and secondary levels adapted to emergency distance education (Baptista Lucio et al., 2020) during the Preventive and Compulsory Social Isolation (ASPO, for its acronym in Spanish) that was established in Argentina due to the Covid-19 pandemic in 2020.

In Argentina, ASPO came into effect on March 20, 2020, in order to prevent the circulation of the Covid-19 virus. All inhabitants of the country were ordered to remain in their usual residences without going to their workplaces, in addition to the prohibition of travel on roads, highways and public spaces, with the exception of activities and services considered essential (Decree 296/2020).

Within this framework, the Ministry of Education ordered "the suspension of face-to-face classes at the initial, primary and secondary levels in all its modalities, and higher education institutes" (Resolution 108/2020). This measure was extended throughout 2020 and forced teachers to adapt to a virtual education, in order to maintain the continuity of the school calendar in the heterogeneity of contexts present throughout the country.

In the context of the knowledge society (Stehr, 1994), the network society (Castells, 2006) or the 4.0 society (Scribano and Lisdero, 2019), social relations are changing rapidly, so it is interesting to understand to what extent the process of "lifelong learning" (Fenwick, 2001) can be understood in the short and abrupt period in which teachers in Argentina (as in much of Latin America) had to readapt their teaching practices, moving from the classroom as a physical workspace face to face with the students to a virtual modality and their different ways to teach.

BACKGROUND

Formal system education in the context of 4.0 society is an important vehicle to develop skills, abilities and attitudes about technology and digital tools and guarantee the integration of children for the future decades. It is considered part of an individual's well-being, avoiding that technology controls people or that people could be isolated from their local or global communities. Moreover, digital skills have a snowball dynamic as it allows to increase pathways to another's learning and skills. That is to say, in 4.0 societies it's not sufficient to know how to read and write if not moreover it must be how to use the power of technology and the internet (West, Kraut and Wi Chew, 2019).

Before the Covid-19 pandemic, studies analyzed distance education and "blended learning" (Gossenheimer et al., 2017; Hsu & Hsieh, 2014), focusing both on aspects related to students' experiences and intellectuals skills required for distance learning

(Ateya et al., 2015; Arroyo et al., 2015; Terras & Ramsay, 2015), as in the difficulties or barriers identified by educators in the teaching processes (Kowalczyk, 2014). Some of them showed that students of the net generation or digital natives used technology to stay connected and entertained, but their Internet literacy skills were scarce. This implied a challenge for educational institutions to adequately teach the use of electronic sources that would allow satisfactory future development (Combes, 2008). Possibilities of implementing digital resources for learning in preschool children were also analyzed (Ciolan, et al., 2014), or using social networks such as Facebook for teaching foreign languages, finding that it can become an area of genuine communication for the completion of homework (Buga, et al., 2014). In cultural terms, an integration of values from the Asian tradition was considered to take advantage of the potential of the digital society (Kim, 2002).

In a report on Latin America and the Caribbean situation about technology and education, has detected a "second gap". It wasn 't by the technological devices instead grasps on topics, use of technology and skills, so there was a need to move forward in processes of learning and technology. In 2010, 9 countries out of 17, had TIC policies in education. In Argentina, in 2009, 87% students of 15 years have access to a computer in educational centres, but there were only 27 students per computer while in OECD (Organisation for Economic Co-operation and Development) countries the relation were 7 students by computer (Sunkel et al., 2013).

These debates and discussions acquired a new nuance after the isolation measures implemented by the Covid-19 pandemic, which directly affected the face-to-face classroom modality, specifically in countries of Global South, where various situations of social, economic and labor precariousness subsist since before the pandemic. The Philippines has measured levels of stress in teachers, finding that women had higher levels of stress than men and a relationship between self-perception of health and perceived risk of contracting Covid-19 (Oducado et al., 2020). In Paraguay, virtual classes for teachers implied adapting part of the study plan and the attempt to replicate the face-to-face classroom experience. The absence of synchronous tools for direct communication in real time and the need for training in access to stable digital media was evidenced (Picón et al., 2020).

In Mexico, the National Survey of Teachers before Covid-19 (END-Covid-19) applied during 2020 to 2253 basic education teachers (preschool, primary, secondary and high school) of the National Education System, showed the coexistence of digital tools (Whatsapp, Facebook) and traditional resources (photocopies and textbooks). It was found that teachers were willing to receive support in digital environments, although at the primary level, greater hesitation in training in digital tools and platforms was identified (Baptista Lucio et al., 2020). In continuity with the investigations of the adaptation of teachers to the new conditions of isolation and the difficulties that this implied, this chapter focuses on the particularities that this acquired in the Argentine case.

MAIN FOCUS OF THE CHAPTER

This chapter describes the characteristics acquired by teachers' learning and adaptation to technological resources, based on the results obtained in 411 cases the "Survey about teaching in times of quarantine for teachers of Initial, Primary and Secondary Education (Argentina, 2020)" applied online during June 2020.

The central questions are these: How did the teachers adapt to the new way of teaching in times of pandemic?; What resources did they have to cope with daily classes? and How is the relationship between digital competencies and their age and place of residence from a sociological perspective of bodies/emotions?

To answer this, the following argumentative strategie is proposed: First, the principal concepts of Sociology of bodies/emotions are exposed, which are the theoretical framework from which to analized empirical data. Second, the survey and general characteristics of sample and surveyed cases are described. Third, the data is analyzed with contingency tables, relating two main variables: age and place where the teachers lived (according to the number of inhabitants). Fourth, in the conclusions it is stated that despite the fact that all teachers expressed having adapted, the older ones encountered greater difficulties because they had less resources and skills and, consequently, had to overcome a lot of obstacles to achieve the adaptation. Emotions coupled this practices and experiences with higher levels of insatisfaction (fear, shame, anger, etc.) or mixed emotions (pride and fear i.e.). A continuous monitoring to describe how teachers follow teaching in the post-pandemic time is considered relevant, at once caracterize in what level of digital literacy are children in Argentina ranked to advance policies in this aspect.

Bodies in a New Space/Time

The present analysis is developed from a Sociology of Bodies and Emotions (Scribano, 2012) that assumes the intrinsic relationship between the bodily condition of human agency, with the social/natural construction of emotions that become social practices.

Social agency is crossed by the vectors of space and time allowing society to go through processes of social structuring (Giddens, 2003). The world is knowed from the bodies by impressions that shock during the interchanges with the socio-environmental context. In this sense, are differentiated between individual-body, social-body and subjective-body (Scribano, 2008). If an individual-body is the interchange between physiological systems and biological processes that guarantee an acceptable level of bodily energy in the relationship between organism and environment (Scribano, 2007), social-body is the resulting of socialization process that becomes body with a social energy that is the potency to plan, execute and resolve agency actions (Scribano, 2007b).

The body seen on a temporal axis implies the configuration of a biography as a condensation and synthesis of the experiences that articulate, in turn, the particular and individual of each agent with the socio-historical processes in which he or she has lived. The body seen on a spatial axis, supposes places as positions, conditions and dispositions of action, from where the way of knowing and feeling the world is also constituted.

According to the analysis proposed in this chapter the age is a variable that use to an indicator of the time of biological-body but in the dialectic with social and subjective dimensions of body. In the same sense, the other main variable to analyze the data, context or place where people live in terms of number of residents is an indicator of ways of sociabilities where the social-body has become and where the impact of technologies is different.

For the purpose of this chapter these categories are fundamentals to understand practices of teachers in Argentina of "lifelong learning" that made possible the adaptation to an emergency distance education considering age and residence place.

For this reason, age (in a social-generational sense strongly impacted by the digital society, but without neglect the complex combinations with social class) is relevant for the understanding of teaching practices, as well as spatial location (or place where they live), in terms of teachers' residence, assuming that technologies are able to connect and transmit technological resources across physical distances.

Emotions in practices

Emotions result from the dialectic relationships between impressions, perceptions and sensations, combining neurophysiological aspects and others derived from social constructions (Elías, 1998; Scribano, 2007a), so the sensations do the unnoticed work of incorporating the social as emotion.

Analyzing emotions, insofar as they are social practices (Sartre, 2005), makes it possible to account for the actors' sense of agency and, therefore, explain social production (Giddens, 2003). Contrary to the conception of emotions as individual states or internal feelings of subjects, they are understood in their social character: as incorporated and constructed from the interaction of subjects with the world and with others (Luna Zamora, 2005; Scribano, 2012) In this process, they affect the regulation of social order.

Society 4.0 and Digital Skills

"Society 4.0" refers to the economic and social processes that were structured from the so-called "Fourth Industrial Revolution". Although the advent of 4.0 companies emerged at the end of the last century, it has been strongly radicalized in recent years, driving the rapid development of social networks and the consequent increase in their commercial value. Thus, in recent years, information and communication technologies have begun to be present in multiple dimensions of social life, from production processes and new forms of work to daily interaction with others. These changes on a planetary scale have been reconfiguring social experiences, practices, bodies and emotions, by and through the massive use of digital platforms and social networks, causing a constant hybridization between online and offline worlds that characterizes the social life of the 21st century (Leurent & Boer, 2018; Scribano & Lisdero, 2019).

In the framework of the expansion of digital technology and Industry 4.0, which represents the Fourth Industrial Revolution, the structure, dynamics, nature, character of communication, consumption, production, employment and learning are changing. This impacts on new jobs and new ways of learning but also for any citizen. This leads to the need for basic digital literacy skills to live, share, work, learn and actively participate. In this context it becomes necessary to have a digital learning programme otherwise a part of the population will be digitally illiterate, unable to cover minimum work requirements (Tsekeris, 2019).

In other sense, ICTs (Information and Communication Technologies) are a central part of the fifth techno-economic paradigm of informatics and telecommunications, tools and processes for managing information by electronic means, including hardware, software and telecommunications. Their emergence in developed countries has highlighted technological and social gaps between countries, but also within countries and between social groups (Sunkel, 2006; Pérez, 2004).

A first approximation to understand the meaning of digital skills is to start from "digital literacy". UNESCO defines it as the process that involves many practices from the access and to manage through understanding, evaluate and create information using digital devices to resolve situations at work or social life. There are seven competence areas with their own specific competencies: device and software operations, information and data literacy, communication and collaboration, digital content creation, safety, problem-solving and career-related competencies. Furthermore, has been identified three skills levels: in the first basic functional skills to access in digital technologies; in the second, generic skills to relevant use, and the last, higher-level skills in transformative ways (West, Kraut and Ei Chew, 2019).

Some authors also consider that along with digital literacy, knowledge and skills, but above all attitudes of commitment and interest should be considered in order to perform well (Law, Woo, de la Torre and Wong, 2018). Within the digital divide, access, use and appropriation of ICTs have been identified as progressive phases (Selwyn, 2004). Appropriation includes skills in daily productive, leisure and relational activities (Winocur, 2006; Crovi & López, 2011).

If we connect the last topics, bodies and emotions in the real time/space where their practices have taken place, it is clear to understand that they were living in a digital society before the pandemic in different levels, forms and intensities. In the context of Argentina in general, and on the education of the formal system (at pre-school, primary and secondary levels that are part of compulsory education) they had small, fragmentary and discontinuous experiences in digital literacy. Thus, this new context made it necessary to make immediate use of available and nearby resources to enable the continuity of the school system. It implied translating or adjusting some everyday skills for the specific field of education.

It is important to consider this in the post-pandemic context and into the future, where digital will not disappear from everyday life, the world of work and education, but will be increasingly necessary - along with devices and concrete access to internet connection - in order not to add a further disadvantage to those who are most disadvantaged.

Particularly in education again, there is a need to consider a serious programme of teacher training and apprenticeship in digital literacy, otherwise this endeavour will only be an anecdotal experience while they go back to pens, pencils and blackboards.

The survey did not include variables to measure the socioeconomic level of teachers, but the place of residence variable is intended to show a certain structural heterogeneity within a group of people engaged in the same work activity, despite the differences that may exist between income and working conditions.

Hypothesis

In the context of the above, the following hypothesis is formulated: Social agency is affected by a social history that it did embody, in form of dispositions, perception schemes, implicit knowledge and emotions that are intrinsic part of practices. In this case, age is an important vector not only to the adaptive capabilities, instead like the objective component of the body that indicates different ways of socializations, more or less nearby to the technology, and their consequent sensibilities in relation to this.

The place where teachers live is another important vector to map the experiences in times of the pandemic Covid-19. The processes of urbanization in the countries of the Global South -as an expression of the situation of dependency in which they find themselves- imply a socio-spatial division based on a system of specific, asymmetric and hierarchical social relations (Castells, 1974). In Latin American urban centers (administrative centers, more populated and wealthy), access to economic opportunities, as well as the availability of certain goods and services, tend to be concentrated, and "as one moves from the central nucleus towards the periphery of the Metropolitan area of large cities, the equipment and service infrastructure are more precarious or do not exist" (Oszlak, 2017: 35, 36). In this sense, Argentina is a heterogeneous country in relation to the economic activities, socioeconomic levels of development an with a spatialized difference in conditions of life -for example the region called "Big North'' (Norte Grande) (Bolsi et al., 2009)- and the existence of inequalities in internet access and quality has been studied according to geographical location, being more favorable in urban areas than in rural areas (Rojas & Poveda, 2017; Lloyd, 2020). Regarding the speed of the Internet connection, the National Communications Agency reports openly on its website that the average download speed of fixed internet in a quarter for Ciudad Autónoma de Buenos Aires was 68 mbps in 2021, while in the province of San Juan it was only 7. The processing speed of the technological devices implies a lot of situations in which teachers should be adapted to teach in emergency distance education.[1]

Methodological strategy

An exploratory study of descriptive scope was carried out within the guidelines of the mixed strategy. The non-probabilistic sample of 411 cases was made up of 87% women. The mean age was 40.94 (SD= 8.67). Forty-four percent had been working for up to 9 years; 30% had been working for 10-19 years and 19% for 20-29 years. Sixty-eight percent were living with another person (in a couple or marriage), while 22% were single. In the 19-29 age group, half declared themselves single, while in the 30-39 age group, 70% were married; in the 40-49 age group, 75% were married, and in the 50 and over age group, 62% were married, with the presence of separated/divorced persons increasing to 23%. Forty-one percent had no children, while 51% had 1-2 children. The 19-29 age range showed the highest value of no children (74%), while the 40-49 age range had the highest value of 2 children (38%). In 68% of the cases there were 2 providers in the household. Between 30-50 years of age the percentage of 2 providers was 73%. Twenty-five percent of the sample stated that there was only one provider in the household, with the highest percentage of 36% in the 50 years and older age group (coinciding with the age group with the highest percentage of separated/divorced persons). Almost half of those who responded to the survey perceived themselves as the head of household in terms of income, but 42% said they were the spouse or partner. Within the 30-50 age group, almost half stated that the head of household by income was the spouse or partner (i.e., two-parent nuclear households, with 2 providers and with 2 children primarily). Sixty-eight percent of the cases worked in a publicly managed establishment and 25% in a privately managed establishment with state contribution. Fifty-seven percent worked at the secondary level, 33% at the primary level and 10% at the pre-school level.

Survey

Based on the concepts of practices, perceptions and emotions, a closed questionnaire was designed, which consisted of six modules. The first covered sociodemographic information (gender, age, marital status, teaching position, seniority, level of teaching, type of school management, among others). From the conceptual distinctions, we inquired about practices such as content development, activities to solve, corrections, evaluations and communication with students' parents, with the management team and with teaching peers. Regarding perceptions, questions were asked about the amount and criteria for content selection, the format or type of activities proposed to students, the feelings experienced in relation to the classes, the criteria for correction and feedback to students, the selection of content to be evaluated and the emotions experienced during corrections and evaluation instances. In addition, a set of statements were elaborated to evaluate levels of agreement regarding the use of technology in teaching, the possibilities of correction, and the relationship with peers, among others. The last module of the survey addressed aspects related to the use of certain tools, programs and applications before quarantine, such as video calls, social networks, home banking, cloud data storage and online shopping. Information was also collected in relation to those technological devices acquired and implemented in the teaching work during the quarantine. On the other hand, this section inquired about the type of virtual resources and the purpose for which they were used during the quarantine for teaching work, about the emotions experienced when implementing these technological resources and about the perceptions regarding the use of various technological/virtual resources that they began to use during the quarantine.

Analysis of data

The information collected was analyzed according to age and place of residence. Numeric variable called age registered continuous values that be recoded into a new interval variable of 10 years for the present analyse. About place of residence, nominal variable -name of town or city- was recoded into a new numeric variable that contained the quantity of inhabitants that were in 2010, according to the last National Population and Housing Census. In a third moment, this new numeric variable was recoded one again according to the classification of cities by number of inhabitants, in connection with the idea that well-being and living conditions vary in relation to the urban hierarchy in proportion to the size of the population

Table 1. Urban Scale Created

Urban category	Size (inhabitants)
Big Cities	>1,000,000
Big MSA[3]	500,000 - 1,000,000
Small MSA	50,000 - 500,000
Small Cities	1-50,000

Source: own elaboration.

(Velázquez y Celemin, 2020). Although there are various urban scales, such as the one proposed by The Organization for Economic Co-operation and Development (OECD)[2] (Chai-Lee Goy, 2017) or the classic work by Vapñarsky and Gorojovsky (1990), in this case a classification of cities was created that made it possible to differentiate and group the different urban realities of the surveyed teachers, given that there was not so many cases in large cities or metropolises. Then, the variable was defined like as follows in Table 1:

Considering the level of measurement used for the variables of interest (nominal or ordinal and interval), contingency tables and association tests were computed using Pearson's chi-square statistic. SPSS software version 23 was used to perform the analyses.

Results and interpretations

For the purpose of this chapter, the following are characterized: a) digital skills and the use of technological tools (before and during the pandemic) for teaching; b) practices associated with the learning of these resources and ways to access and, c) emotions in relation to these virtual resources, that teachers have used last week. The aforementioned analysis is carried out considering two relevant variables, such as age and place of residence.

The relationship between that social agents brought in the sense of skills and dispositions in their bodies before the pandemic, with the practices that they did and the strategies to learn and add options to resolve the distance teaching are connected with ways to feel or emotions that are in their own practices.

Digital Skills Before and During the Pandemic

The survey asked about a range of digital tools as a way of finding out whether teachers used them before the pandemic and the skills involved in using these

Table 2. Digital skills according to age before quarantine 2020

Frequent Use	Home banking computer	Home Banking Mobile Phone	WhatsApp	Social Networks	YouTube (upload videos)	Online Storage (Google Drive, etc.)	Online Shopping (Amazon, etc)	Video-calls
19-29	60.90%	65.20%	87.00%	93.50%	43.50%	52.20%	47.80%	15.20%
30-39	67.20%	65.60%	76.80%	82.40%	28.80%	60.00%	56,80%	12.00%
40-49	62.30%	54.30%	75.90%	77.80%	30.20%	53.10%	44.40%	9.30%
50 and over 50	50.60%	37.70%	75.30%	70.10%	31.20%	50.60%	29.90%	14.30%

Source: Own elaboration based on survey.

tools. The options included communication applications, data storage and banking transactions, among others.

Regarding digital skills prior to the pandemic according to age, the use of social networks and WhatsApp in teachers of all ages stands out and in third place is home banking in its two variants. In the case of social networks, it can be observed that the gap between young and old respondents is higher than other skills in 23 points.

In the second category -Whatsapp-, it is more pronounced in the youngest (19-29), since for these exceeds 85% of the responses, while in the older age group (over 50), WhatsApp is located with 75% and social networks 70.10%. It is also interesting to note that, compared to WhatsApp and social networks, among the two youngest groups (19-29 and 30-39), there is less use of YouTube to upload videos (43.50% and 56.80%, respectively) and even less use of video calls (15.20% and 12%) before the pandemic as can be seen in Table 2:

Although this does not directly relate to teaching practices, the use of home banking from computer or mobile phones indicates a nearby higher percentage in young than old teachers with the last device. The access to home banking by mobile phone almost doubled to 19-29 group (65.2%) compared with 50 and more (37.7%). But there is a smaller difference in home banking by computer with just 10 points between these groups.

Considering the place of residence, in cities with more than 1 million people the main digital skills are in social networks and data storage with 71%. In medium-sized cities and small cities social networks and WhatsApp stand out: both in the big MSA and small MSA the use of social networks and WhatsApp is higher than 74%, and in the small towns (less than 50,000 inhabitants) the use of social networks was 79% and of Whatsapp 82%. Thus, no significant differences were observed in pre-quarantine skills according to the size of the cities, as presented in Table 3:

Table 3. Digital skills according place of residence before quarantine 2020

Frequent Use	Home Banking Computer	Home Banking Mobile Phone	WhastApp	Social Networks	YouTube (upload videos)	Online Storage (Google Drive, etc.)	Online Shopping (Amazon, etc)	Video-calls
Big cities	52.40%	57.10%	66.70%	71.40%	33.30%	71.40%	33.30%	9.50%
Big MSA	66.70%	41.70%	75.00%	75.00%	16.70%	41.70%	25.00%	0.00%
Small MSA	66.20%	58.90%	74.90%	81.70%	33.30%	57.10%	45,70%	11.00%
Small Cities	56.10%	51.00%	81.90%	78.70%	29.00%	49.00%	47.70%	14.20%

Source: Own elaboration based on survey.

In the above, it stands out that social networks and WhatsApp in the use they had. Then it is necessary to describe what skills and digital applications have been used by teachers during the mandatory and preventive isolation by Covid-19.

Because of its status as a social body, skills, dispositions and practices can be (re)produced in differing circumstances daily so it makes it possible to connect with the practices that teachers performed during the pandemic.

In the tension between continuity or interruption in their practices before/during the pandemic the question arises how teachers resolved the day-to-day business of education in the compulsory isolation that emptied classrooms and forced teachers to maintain the learning remotely.

The survey asked for technological resources that teachers applied to teach in the last week. Teachers relied on this pre-pandemic knowledge and skills to "teach classes", communicate with their students for consultations and to send materials, receive assignments and send corrections, with some differences depending on the age, as observed in the Table 4:

When observing the resources used to teach, communicate with students for inquiries, send materials and corrections and receive activities, differences are also observed according to the age of the teachers. A high percentage of teachers use WhatsApp, however their use is even more pronounced in the youngest, between 19 and 29 years old (84.90%) and 75% in older ones. In turn, these indicate greater use of YouTube (upload videos) with 61%, video calls with 54%, social networks (26%) in the last but less use of E-mail and Data Storage, compared to teachers over 30 years of age.

Table 4. Use to teach, communicate with students for inquiries, send materials and corrections and receive activities in quarantine, according to age

Use to teach...	19 a 29	30 a 39	40 a 49	50 and over
Video calls	54.40%	63.20%	52.40%	48.10%
E-mail	49.90%	64.80%	61.70%	54.60%
Classroom	43,50%	47.20%	41.50%	35.10%
Youtube (upload video)	60.90%	42.40%	38.30%	49.40%
WhatsApp	84.90%	72.00%	75.40%	75.40%
Google docs, drive	32.60%	40.80%	40.10%	40.30%
Social Networks	26.10%	16.00%	13.50%	22.10%

Source: Own elaboration based on survey.

Among the youngest (19-29 years), 60.90% used YouTube, which decreased to 42.40% among those aged 30-39, to 38.30% in those aged 40-49 and 49.40% in those of 50 or more. In the same sense, 26.10% of the youngest teachers use social networks, 16% of those aged 30-39, 13.50% of those aged 40-49 and 22.10% of those 50 or more.

If it compared younger and older teachers the latter outnumber the former in only two categories: e-mail (5 points of difference) and on-line storage (8 points approximately). It is relevant to note that young teachers had 3 principal ways to maintain distance education: Whatsapp, upload videos and video calls, but in 50 and over it stands out Whatsapp, email and upload videos. However in adult teachers (30-49) the use of e-mail was higher than in the older group.

In the older group, some differences are observed. E-mail was used by 55%, youtube 49% and video calls 48%. Again Whatsapp shows a continuity prior and during the pandemic but it appears other resources to complement it. The use of these new strategies are different according to age.

According to the place of residence stands out in small cities the use of Whatsapp (82%) while video calls are more used in cities with more than 1 million (76.2%) as described in the Table 5:

In sum, if Whatsapp was used before and during the pandemic in big cities with a higher percentage it is surprising the growing use of video-calls (9.5% before to 76% during the pandemic). It was part of lifelong-learning because bodies substantially modified some of their teaching practices to ensure the realization of synchronous classes, emulating the classroom context. But it was possible because the connection speed to the internet is higher in the big cities surveys that affect both students and teachers.

Table 5. Use to teach, communicate with students for inquiries, send materials and corrections and receive activities in quarantine, according to place of residence

Use to teach...	Big Cities	Big MSA	Small MSA	Small Cities
Video calls	76.20%	66.70%	53.90%	53.50%
E-mail	57.20%	66.70%	67.10%	50.20%
Classroom	47.70%	41.70%	54.90%	24.50%
Youtube (upload video)	52.40%	58.30%	42.20%	44.50%
WhatsApp	66.80%	58.30%	73.10%	81.90%
On line storage	42.80%	33.30%	47.20%	29.60%
Social Networks	19.10%	33.30%	18.30%	14.10%

Source: Own elaboration based on survey.

Another relevant aspect is many options to teach in these big cities: video calls (76.2%), Whatsapp (66.80%), E-mail (57.2%), Up load videos (52.4%), Classroom (47.7%), etc. Four digital resources were up to 50% with a small gap between them.

Instead, 8 of 10 teachers that lived in small cities used Whatsapp, and just 5 video calls. Main percentages in these cities are concentrated in 3 resources (up to 50%) but with an important gap between the first (whatsapp) and the second (video calls). In MSA cities teachers have applied more Whatsapp in small than in big, where the main resources were video calls and e-mail (both 66.70%).

Practices Associated with the Learning of These Resources and Ways to Access

Regarding strategies related to lifelong learning, it was found that they had to learn to use new technological resources for teaching, adapting their practices and knowledge to the conditions associated with isolation. About the behaviors that account for this learning, significant differences were observed according to the age of the teachers as presented in Table 6:

Among the youngest (19 and 29 years of age), only 4.4% indicated that it was difficult for them to learn to use new resources and the same percentage received help from their families to do so, while 26.6% were learning about these resources every day. All these percentages rise with increasing age. In the same sense, 45.5% of those aged 50 and over indicated that they are learning to use the new resources, with a percentage difference of more than 20 points with respect to the other age categories.

Table 6. Learning and use of technological resources according to age

	At the least one resource it is new to me, and I learned to use it in quarantine	At the least one resource it is new to me and I am learning to use it	At least one resource is new to me and it is hard for me to learn how to use it	At least one resource is new to me, someone from my family helps me	All I use now already knew prior to quarantine	I am learning every day about these resources
19-29	67.6%	19.7%	4.4%	4.4%	19.6%	26.2%
30-39	69.6%	20.8%	5.4%	10.2%	14.4%	43.2%
40-49	65.4%	23,5%	6.6%	16.7%	12,3%	52.4%
50 and over 50	53.3%	45.5%	13%	25.3%	7.8%	59.8%

Source: Own elaboration based on survey.

Skills and dispositions according to age show that after three months from start the ASPO 5-7 out of 10 teachers learned at least one resource. The lifelong learning in this case is more evident in those 50 and over who stand out in keep learning (45.5%), need help from someone in their family (25.3%), have difficulty (13%) and use new resources from knowledge prior to the pandemic (just 7.8% in "All I use now already knew prior to quarantine").

But in young teacher it is evident that they had more resources previous the pandemic and a fast skill to incorporate new digital applications but it is striking that they registered the smaller percentage in the category "I am learning every day about these resources" (26.2%) as if it were a situation overcome or resolved.

In general, this indicates that isolation meant a greater effort to adapt to technological skills and tools for older teachers.

When observing the place of residence, the incorporation of at least one new resource that has already been learned to use stands out, with a percentage greater than 60% in cities of all sizes as introduced in Table 7:

Both the teachers in the big cities and the Big MSA were helped by someone from the family to use the new resources to a greater extent than those living in the Small MSA and Small Cities.

Also, in comparison to the rest, teachers in Big cities highlight all resources currently used prior to quarantine (23.8%). However, given that the categories are not mutually exclusive, it is relevant to mention that only 10.5% of teachers surveyed said only that everything currently used already knew before the quarantine, while 2.2% combined that answer with "I am learning every day about these resources." The rest of the teachers who responded that they already knew everything they used during

Table 7. Learning and use of technological resources according to residence

	At the least one resource it is new to me, and I learned to use it in quarantine	At the least one resource it is new to me and I am learning to use it	At least one resource is new to me and it is hard for me to learn how to use it	At least one resource is new to me, someone from my family helps me	All I use now already knew prior to quarantine	I am learning every day about these resources
Big cities	71.5%	19.2%	9.6%	28.7%	23.8%	38.2%
Big MSA	74.9%	33.2%	24.9%	24.9%	0%	66.6%
Small MSA	65.8%	24.4%	10.7%	15.3%	14.2%	51.7%
Small Cities	62.9%	26.9%	6.3%	11.5%	16.6%	47.5%

Source: Own elaboration based on survey.

quarantine combined this response with one or more of the remaining categories, showing that it involved new learning and an adaptation effort in almost all cases.

Emotions in Relation to These Virtual Resources

The survey asked for emotions feeled last week in relation to virtual resources. The pre-determinate options were seven and people could choose up to three between joy, pride, shame, sadness, helplessness, anger and fear.

According to the answers obtained they were grouped as follows: joy and pride (satisfaction); shame, sadness, helplessness, anger and fear (dissatisfaction) and combinations to both (emotions mix, for example pride and fear).

The emotions in the different groups of age presented a complex scenario to the people with more than 50. In effect, young teachers (19-29) asserted that joy and pride were emotions that described their experiences in 61% of respondents further than emotion mix (22%) and dissatisfaction (11%). But in the aged 50 and over

Table 8. Emotions to use virtual resources by age

	Satisfaction	Emotions mix	Dissatisfaction	No apply / no answer
19 - 29	63.00%	21.70%	10.90%	4.30%
30 - 39	51.20%	15.20%	20.80%	12.80%
40 - 49	57.40%	10.50%	18.50%	13.60%
50 and more	37.70%	20.80%	31.20%	10.40%

Source: Own elaboration based on survey.

Table 9. Emotions to use virtual resources by place of residence

	Satisfaction	Emotions mix	Dissatisfaction	No apply / no answer
Big cities	38.10%	19.00%	42.90%	0%
Big MSA	25.00%	25.00%	25.00%	25.00%
Small MSA	49.80%	13.20%	22.80%	14.20%
Small Cities	61.30%	15.50%	14.20%	9.00%

Source: Own elaboration based on survey.

answers claimed a non clear emotional context: 38% were satisfied, 31% dissatisfied and 21% emotion mix.

In this case, these results are congruent with the practices and skills to affront the process of teaching in pandemic and with a process to learning technological resources. Young teachers were more satisfied with the technological devices and resources because they had more skills and dispositions to add new ways for their work. It was the opposite situation in the 50 and over.

Emergent category in the analyses of data, "emotion mix" had a similar percentage in young and old teachers and less in 30-39 and 40-49 groups of ages. Maybe it is possible that the imprevisible and uncertain situation of a pandemic put teachers in front of new practices, with previous knowledge and satisfaction for managing to sustain education in a non-standard way.

Considering the place of residence, in cities with more than 1 million people the main emotions were dissatisfaction with 43%, but satisfaction were 38%. In contrast, in small cities (less than 50,000 inhabitants) last emotions registered the higher percentage with 61% while 15% were emotion mix and 14% dissatisfaction.

Emotion mix is a category interesting to further because although it is not a relevant or high value, shows a persistent percentage in a range to 13-25 points by cities but in Table 8, there is a similar percentage. It could be due to the new situation, uncertainty, confusion and fear in the meantime teachers comply with obligation and responsibility to maintain the education in any event. More satisfaction in small cities may be connected to achieving respect to technological resources and digital skills. In that context achieves may appear highlighted or oversized.

CONCLUSION

During the first year of the pandemic, isolation and social distancing as the main (and, at that time, the only) preventive measures, highlighted the situations of social, labor and economic insecurity that accumulate in the societies of the Global South, as well as the centrality of the virtual/digital/mobile to continue with daily actions in the different dimensions of life (Scribano, 2020). In this context, to ensure the continuity of obligatory education, there was an abrupt transition from an almost totally face-to-face modality towards an emergency distance education, which implied not only a deepening of the inequalities related to the digital gap, but also an adaptation of both students and teachers to a new way of teaching and learning.

By focusing on teachers, this chapter suggests, in conclusion, that in Argentina the appropriation of new digital resources and skills by teachers at the pre-school, primary and secondary levels, and their consequent integration into the teaching process, is affected by multiple factors such as the digital skills of teachers prior to the pandemic, but also by institutional aspects, among others, not addressed in this analysis. As for age, there is a notorious incidence, not so much in the absence of adaptation but in the fact that the older the age, the less diversification of resources or the greater difficulties. In response to this, other strategies from the social environment (a family member, a teacher, someone from the institution, etc.) are resorted to. The differences by place of residence are not more significant than age, which would indicate that the processes of social structuring of 4.0 societies unfold beyond the distances and the number of inhabitants of a city or town. The planetarization of the 21st century shortens distances at the same time that social inequalities become more complex (Scribano, 2020).

It is undeniable that the mobile/virtual/digital is going through more and more aspects of our lives and that its deepening will not end after the pandemic. The use of digital resources in education, as well as the teaching and learning of digital skills, become central elements in the training of citizens and workers in the 21st century. With this we wonder about the future of education in 4.0 societies, but also in the Global South, as is the case of Argentina, in terms of possible digital divides that may be generated or deepend around digital education. Some fundamentals points to keep investigated are inequalities in access to devices and connectivity as the first stage of digital literacy which is still unresolved in Argentina, let alone the systematic and planned development of digital skills from the formal education system.

Respect to teachers it will be relevant monitoring how increase the lifelong learning in teachers before the pandemic and in a more global dimension to investigate how, in addition to the age and generational variable, socioeconomic variables, state policies on education and the concrete action of the educational institutions in which these teachers work, operate. And its counterpart it must ask about the impact on student learning, according to the multiple difficulties experienced by their teachers to adapt to these new forms of teaching.

The pandemic in the South Global has evidenced structural inequalities, generational factors and ways of resolution that work but do not ensure that the pathways to further digital literacy have been started.

REFERENCES

Arroyo, A. T., Kidd, A. R., Burns, S. M., Cruz, I. J., & Lawrence-Lamb, J. E. (2015). Increments of transformation from midnight to daylight: How a professor and four undergraduate students experienced an original philosophy of teaching and learning in two online courses. *Journal of Transformative Education*, *13*(4), 341–365. doi:10.1177/1541344615587112

Ateya, M., Khalil, E., Rasheed, S., & Asokan, G. V. (2015). A protocol for literature triage in online learning for the net-generation nursing and allied health care students. *Nursing Reports*, *5*(1), 22–23. doi:10.4081/nursrep.2015.5134

Baptista Lucio, P., Almazán Zimerman, A., Loeza Altamirano, C. A., López Alcaraz, V. A. & Cárdenas Domínguez, J. L. (2020). Encuesta Nacional a Docentes ante el COVID-19. Retos para la educación a distancia [National Survey of Teachers to COVID-19. Challenges for distance education]. *Revista Latinoamericana De Estudios Educativos*, *50*(ESPECIAL), 41-88. doi:10.48102/rlee.2020.50.ESPECIAL.96

Bolsi, A., Longhi, F., & Paolasso, P. (2009). Pobreza y mortalidad infantil en el Norte Grande Argentino. Un aporte para la formulación de políticas públicas [Poverty and infant mortality in the Great North of Argentina. A contribution to the formulation of public policies]. Cuadernos geográficos, 45(2), 231-261.

Buga, R., Capeneata, I., Chirasnel, C., & Popa, A. (2014). Facebook in foreign language teaching – a tool to improve communication competences. *Procedia*, *128*, 93–98. doi:10.1016/j.sbspro.2014.03.124

Castells, M. (2006). *La sociedad red: una visión global* [The network society: a global vision]. Alianza.

Castells, M. (1974). *La cuestión urbana* [The Urban Question]. Siglo XXI.

Goy. (2017). *The impact of technological innovation on building a sustainable city.* https://jqualityinnovation.springeropen.com/articles/10.1186/s40887-017-0014-9

Ciolan, L., Petrescu, A., Radulescu, C., & Bucur, C. (2014). Training Teachers to Use Digital Resources for the Knowledge Society. *Procedia - Social and Behavioral Sciences*, *128*(22), 415-419. doi:10.1016/j.sbspro.2014.03.180

Combes, B. (2008). *The Net Generation: Tech-savvy or lost in virtual space?* ASL, Berkeley, USA. research papers. doi:10.29173/iasl7966

Crovi, D., & López, R. (2011). Tejiendo voces: Jóvenes universitarios opinan sobre la apropiación de internet en la vida académica [Weaving voices: young university students give their opinion on the appropriation of the internet in academic life]. *Revista Mexicana de Ciencias Politicas y Sociales*, *56*(212), 69–80.

Decree 296/2020. *Aislamiento Social Preventivo y Obligatorio* [Preventive and Compulsory Social Isolation]. https://www.boletinoficial.gob.ar/detalleAviso/primera/227042/20200320

Elías, N. (1998). *La civilización de los padres y otros ensayos* [The civilisation of parents and other essays]. Editorial Universidad Nacional y Grupo Editorial Norma.

Fenwick, T. (2001). *Experiential Learning: A Theoretical Critique from Five Perspectives*. Information Series No. 385.

Giddens, A. (2003). *La constitución de la sociedad* [The constitution of society]. Amorrortu.

Gossenheimer, A. N., Bem, T., Carneiro, M. L. F., & De Castro, M. S. (2017). Impact of distance education on academic performance in a pharmaceutical care course. *PLoS One*, *12*(4), e0175117. doi:10.1371/journal.pone.0175117 PMID:28384362

Hsu, L., & Hsieh, S. (2014). Factors affecting metacognition of undergraduate nursing students in a blended learning environment. *International Journal of Nursing Practice*, *20*(3), 233–241. doi:10.1111/ijn.12131 PMID:24888995

Kim, C. Y. (2002). Teachers in Digital Knowledge-Based Society: New Roles and Vision. *Asia Pacific Education Review*, *3*(2), 144–148. doi:10.1007/BF03024907

Kowalczyk, N.K. (2014). *Perceived barriers to online education by radiologic sciences*. Academic Press.

Oducado, R. M., Parreño-Lachica, G. & Rabacal, J. (2021). Estrés percibido debido a la pandemia de COVID-19 entre los profesores profesionales empleados [Perceived stress due to the COVID-19 pandemic among employed professional teachers]. *Revista Internacional de Investigación e Innovación Educativas*, (15), 305–316. doi:10.46661/ijeri.5284

Oszlak, O. (2017). *Merecer la Ciudad* [Deserve the City]. EDUNTREF.

Pérez, C. (2004). *Revoluciones tecnológicas y capital financiero* [Technological revolutions and financial capital.]. Siglo XXI.

Picón, G. A., González de Caballero, G. K., & Paredes Sánchez, J. N. (2020). Desempeño y educators. *Radiologic Technology*, *85*(5), 486–493.

Law, N., Woo, D., de la Torre, J., & Wong, G. (2018). *A Global Framework ofReference on Digital Literacy Skills for Indicator 4.4.2*. UNESCO.

Leurent, H., & Boer, E. (2018). *The Next Economic Growth Engine Scaling Fourth Industrial Revolution Technologies in Production*. World Economic Forum.

Lloyd, M. (2020). *Desigualdades educativas y la brecha digital en tiempos de COVID-19* [Educational Inequalities and Digital Gap in times of Covid 19]. Universidad Nacional Autónoma de México. Instituto de Investigaciones sobre La Universidad y la Educación

Luna Zamora, R. (2005). *Sociología del miedo. Un estudio sobre las ánimas, diablos y elementos naturales* [Sociology of fear. A study on the souls, devils and natural elements]. Universidad de Guadalajara. formación docente en competencias digitales en clases no presenciales durante la pandemia COVID-19. doi:10.1590/SciELOPreprints.778

Resolution 108/2020. *Ministerio de Educación* [Ministry of Education]. https://www.boletinoficial.gob.ar/detalleAviso/primera/226752/20200316

Rojas, E.F. & Poveda, L. (2018). *Estado de la Banda Ancha en América Latina y el Caribe* [Status of Broadband in Latin America and the Caribbean]. Publicación de las Naciones Unidas (CEPAL).

Sartre, J.-P. (2005). *Bosquejo de una teoría de las emociones* [Sketch for a theory of emotions]. Alianza Editorial.

Secretaría de Evaluación e Información Educativa. (2020). *Evaluación Nacional del Proceso de Continuidad Pedagógica. Informe preliminar de la Encuesta a Docentes* [National Evaluation of the Pedagogical Continuity Process. Preliminary report of the Teacher Survey]. https://www.argentina.gob.ar/educacion/evaluacion-e-informacion-educativa/evaluacion-nacional-del-proceso-de-continuidad-pedagogica

Selwyn, N. (2004). Reconsidering political and popular understandings of the digital divide. *New Media & Society*, *6*(3), 341–362. doi:10.1177/1461444804042519

Scribano, A. (2007). *Mapeando interiores: Cuerpo, conflicto y sensaciones* [Mapping Interiors: Body, Conflict, and Sensations]. Córdoba: José Sarmiento Editor

Scribano, A. (2007a). *Policromía Corporal, cuerpos, grafías y sociedad.* [Bodily Polychrome: Bodies, spellings and Society] Córdoba: José Sarmiento Editor

Scribano, A. (2008). Sensaciones, conflicto y cuerpo en Argentina después del 2001 [Sensations, Conflict and Body in Argentina After 2001]. *Espacio Abierto, 17*(2), 205-230.

Scribano, A. (2012). Sociología de los cuerpos/emociones [Sociology of body/emotions]. *Revista Latinoamericana de Estudios sobre Cuerpos, Emociones y Sociedad, 10*(4), 93-113.

Scribano, A., & Lisdero, P. (2019). *Digital labor, Society and Politics of Sensibilities*. Palgrave Macmillan. doi:10.1007/978-3-030-12306-2

Scribano, A. (2020). La guerra de las curvas: pandemia, sensibilidades y estructuración social [The war of the curves: pandemic, sensibilities, and social structuration]. Simbiótica, 7(1).

Stehr, N. (1994). *Knowledge societies*. Sage.

Sunkel, G. (2006). *Las tecnologías de la información y la comunicación (tic) en la educación en América Latina: una exploración de indicadores* [Information and communication technologies (ict) in education in Latin America: an exploration of indicators]. Naciones Unidas. https://www.cepal.org/socinfo/noticias/documentosdetrabajo/9/27849/Serie126final.pdf

Sunkel, G., Trucco, D., & Espejo, A. (2013). *La integración de las tecnologías digitales en las escuelas de América Latina y el Caribe. Una mirada multidimensional* [The integration of digital technologies in schools in Latin America and the Caribbean. A multidimensional look]. Santiago de Chile: Naciones Unidas. https://repositorio.cepal.org/bitstream/handle/11362/21681/S2013023_es.pdf

Terras, M. M., & Ramsay, J. (2015). Massive open online courses (MOOCs): Insights and challenges from a psychological perspective. *British Journal of Educational Technology, 46*(3), 472–487. doi:10.1111/bjet.12274

Tsekeris, C. (2019). Surviving and thriving in the Fourth Industrial Revolution: Digital skills for education and society. *Homo Virtualis, 2*(1), 34–42. doi:10.12681/homvir.20192

Vapñarsky, C., & Gorojovsky, N. (1990). El crecimiento urbano en la Argentina [Urban Growth in Argentine]. IIED.

West, M., Kraut, R., & Wi Chew, H. (2019). *I'd blush if I could. Closing gender divides in digital skills through education*. UNESCO.

Winocur, R. (2006). Internet en la vida cotidiana de los jóvenes [Internet in the daily life of young people]. *Revista Mexicana de Sociología, 68*(3), 551-580. http://www.scielo.org.mx/scielo.php?script=sci_arttext&pid=S0188-25032006000300005&lng=es&nrm=iso

ADDITIONAL READING

Castells, M. (1997). *La era de la información* [The informational age]. Alianza.

Cena, R. & Dettano, A. (2020). Políticas sociales y emociones en el marco del COVID-19: sobre viejos "nuevos" debates e intersticios. [Social policies and emotions in the framework of COVID-19: about old "new" debates and interstices]. *Cuadernos del pensamiento crítico latinoamericano,* (80). Consejo Latinoamericano de Ciencias Sociales, CLACSO.

De Sena, A., & Scribano, A. (2020). *Social Policies and Emotions. A look from the Global South.* Palgrave Macmillan. doi:10.1007/978-3-030-34739-0

Feenberg, A. (1991). *Critical Theory of Technology.* Oxford University Press.

McCutcheon, K., Lohan, M., Traynor, M., & Martin, D. (2015). A systematic review evaluating the impact of online or blended learning vs face-to-face learning of clinical skills in undergraduate nurse education. *Journal of Advanced Nursing, 71*(2), 255–270. doi:10.1111/jan.12509 PMID:25134985

KEY TERMS AND DEFINITIONS

Bodies: Dialectic between a phylogenetic logic, which articulates the organic and the environment, a subjective dimension from the self-reflection of the self as the centre of gravity and a dimension of socialisation of the body, from habits, gestures and hexis.

Digital Skills: Skills to use digital devices, communication applications and networks to access, manage and exploit information. They enable individuals to produce and share digital content, communicate and collaborate, and solve problems for effective and creative self-fulfillment in life, learning, work, and wider social activities.

Digital Teaching Practices: Concrete actions that aim to concretise the formal teaching process, such as content development, problem-solving activities, corrections, evaluations and communication with parents, management, and peers.

Distance Education: Formal education situation where there is a separation of teachers and learners in space and time and where pedagogical strategies are determined by the technologies available at any given time.

Emotions: In its social character, emotions are understood as built and constructed from the interaction of the subject with the world and with others, affecting the production and regulation of the social order.

Isolation: Implies physical separation to prevent the spread of the virus. For example It implied that people were forced to stay at home and go out only to basic needs without going to their workplaces, in addition to the prohibition of travel on roads, highways and public spaces, with the exception of activities and services considered essential.

Perceptions: Naturalised ways of organising the set of impressions that impact on the social agent, in his or her exchanges with the socio-environmental context, and which are accumulated and reproduced.

Sociedad 4.0: Economic and social processes that were structured by the so-called "Fourth Industrial Revolution" from the rapid development of social networks and the consequent increase in their commercial value. The information and communication technologies present in multiple dimensions of social life, from productive processes and new forms of work to everyday interaction with others, reconfigure social experiences, practices, bodies and emotions between online and offline worlds.

ENDNOTES

1 https://datosabiertos.enacom.gob.ar/dataviews/245546/velocidad-promedio-de-bajada-de-internet-fijo-por-provincia (08/26/2021).

2 The Organisation for Economic Co-operation and Development (OECD) also classified the size of cities based on four categories. First, a large metropolitan area has a population of 1.5 million or more. Second, the metropolitan area has a population between 500,000 and 1.5 million people. Third, a medium-sized urban area has a population of about 200,000 to 500,000 people. Fourth, a small-sized urban area has a population of about 500,000 to 200,000 people (Chai-Lee Goy, 2017).

3 Medium Sized Agglomerations.

Chapter 7
Collaborative Trade Exchange and the COVID-19 Event:
Barter in the Andean Subregion of Ecuador

Jessica Silvana Matute-Petroche
https://orcid.org/0000-0002-4598-3026
Universidad Católica de Santiago de Guayaquil, Ecuador

Uriel Hitamar Castillo-Nazareno
Universidad Católica de Santiago de Guayaquil, Ecuador

Luis Fernando Pazmiño-Crespo
Universidad Católica de Santiago de Guayaquil, Ecuador

ABSTRACT

While the most serious part of the pandemic was taking place, key economic variables were aggravated such as unemployment, cost of the basic food basket, precariousness of the basic salary, and distribution of wealth (Gini). The objective of this chapter is to analyze the emergence of bartering during the pandemic as an anti-crisis measure and an initiative of mutual support, which originates from the population in the central highlands of Ecuador (the Andes), an area with social, cultural, and economic importance for the country. To achieve this objective, a methodology with a quantitative approach was applied with descriptive scope and non-probabilistic sampling, consisting of direct observation, interviews, and surveys. The results obtained reveal that bartering is a collaborative commercial exchange practiced to minimize the economic effects caused by COVID-19 and to compensate for the inefficiency of an absent state.

DOI: 10.4018/978-1-7998-8626-6.ch007

INTRODUCTION

Bartering, or collaborative exchange, has had a transcendent insurgence in the economic depression generated by the COVID-19 pandemic. This phenomenon, bartering, has been present in Ecuador in some areas more than others, leading to the question: why is it present now with particular intensity, and how deep is it? To answer this question, a study of four provinces located in what is known as the central highlands of this South American country is presented.

There are four provinces (Cotopaxi, Chimborazo, Tungurahua and Bolivar) that, despite having a great endowment of natural resources, an enviable geography and an ancestral culture of farmers, cannot overcome social precariousness. This is very evident that, in pandemic conditions, and in the absence of public support policies, they have had to resort bartering as a solution to the need for surviva006C. The immediate thing, therefore, is to know the socio-economic structural nature of these provinces: their weaknesses and level of vulnerability.

The area where these provinces are located is the Andean[1] subregion, also known as "The Avenue of Volcanoes" (Santillán and Lozada, 2013). Its altitude ranges from 1 800 m to 6 268 m, in this specific geography there are parallel rows of massive volcanic peaks. This is why the chains of large conical volcanoes are named as the provinces: Chimborazo, Tungurahua and Cotopaxi. Active volcanoes covered with glaciers, makes the cartography of this part of the South American mountain range unique (Chávez, 2012). But on the economic level, it is only possible to generate yields, with this peculiar landscape, often touristy, which was demolished with the COVID-19.

In addition, in these provinces there are three of the five most important national parks in the country, due to their pre-Hispanic and Inca content: Cotopaxi Park, Llanganates Park, and the Chimborazo Wildlife Reserve. These parks are open to the public in an attempt to generate incomes through tourism. The tourism region stands out for preserving unique ecosystems of the high Andean paramo, peaks and valleys of great scenic value, which is complemented by handicrafts, gastronomy and cultural expressions. However, none of these aspects were useful to solve the central issue of socioeconomics: family or community income.

A province of cultural and commercial importance in this area is Cotopaxi. It has a surface area of 6 071 km^2, a population of 303 489 inhabitants and an average annual temperature of 12 °C. However, it contains a climatic peculiarity: it has a temperate, cold and warm-humid environment. For this reason, its ecosystem is home to several arboreal species, especially pines, which makes the place unique in South America, since it is more reminiscent of an alpine forest than a forest of the Andes, which makes it very visited according to the Development Plan and Land Management (*Plan de Desarrollo y Ordenamiento Territorial PDOT by its acronym in Spanish*) of Cotopaxi (2015). Extraordinary natural resource, but that makes it dependent on the possibility of the displacement of people to the place.

Its productive area is mainly agricultural, among its crops are barley, wheat, corn, legumes, vegetables and a great variety of fruits. In the western sector of the province, the cultivation of tropical products is favorable. Finally, the forest wealth is considerable, since there are wooded areas composed of walnut, alder, laurel, oak, among others. This variety of agricultural products shows the wide range of possibilities for a collaborative exchange when the neoclassical markets that work with coins are closed. The barter gene is hidden there.

Tungurahua is a province with an area of 1 200 km^2 and a population of 297 011 inhabitants. It has interesting geographical features (peaks, gorges, hot springs, fast rivers, trails) and agricultural production based on tubers, roots, vegetables, fruits and flowers. Another important source of income are its tourist attractions, among which are: The Ambato Fair, which celebrates both the Carnival and the Flowers and Fruits Festival, which includes cultural and artistic activities, the international folklore festival, the book fair. In addition, in this province is located the city of Baños de Agua Santa, famous for being one of the cities more attractive for tourists in Ecuador.

Festivals, natural wonders and ancestral mystique, this constitutes a structure of undertakings that requires, to have results, the concurrence of strangers (national and foreigners) who leave coins. Additionally, this province stands out for its Micro Small and Medium Enterprises (MSMEs, for its acronym), according to the Decentralized Autonomous Government of Tungurahua (PDOT, 2018). Among the main industries are: footwear, leather, garments, textiles, furniture, chemicals, food and beverages. This helps, but their coverage is very local. MSMEs have no national and less international scope, additionally, more than 60% depend on tourism.

The other locality studied is Chimborazo, located at the foot of the active volcano that bears its name. According to Chimborazo's PDOT (2020), this province has an area of 6,569 km^2 and a population of 403,632 inhabitants. The climate varies with temperatures ranging from 6 to 20 degrees Celsius. Hence, its main income comes from agriculture whose products (fruits, vegetables, grains) are sold in raw material and food markets throughout the country. It has MSMEs engaged in the production of ceramics, carpets, food products, dairy products, and various manufactured goods, although they do not constitute a major source of income for this province. It is trapped in its small and precarious productive world, which makes it vulnerable and, consequently, it is always ready for collaborative exchange as a mechanism that contributes to expand the market.

Finally, there is the province of Bolívar. According to information from its PDOT (2015), this has an area of 3 939.9 km2 and a population of 183 665 inhabitants. The climate ranges between 8 and 20 degrees Celsius. The western zone reaches the tropical sub-Andean with permanent humidity, which allows for successful agriculture. Although it has MSMEs (in armory, mining and dairy) is less endowed than the other provinces in this aspect, in this province agriculture is decisive. The main resources on which its income depends are the following: diversified agriculture, livestock, mining, industry, manufacturing and handicrafts. Without productive variants, but with abundant primary production, it presents the same situation as its neighboring provinces: very weak capacity to generate income.

It is important to note that, as a transversal aspect, these provinces share a culture of cooperativism[2] and mingas[3], which permanently promotes collaborative processes. Cooperativism has boosted MSMEs, marking a slight difference, especially in Tungurahua and Cotopaxi. However, the organizational base of the economy is agricultural, so they are very dependent on primary markets and short-term credit. This was dramatically affected by COVID-19. The vulnerability of these economies is evident.

Commercial agricultural and tourism activities are the most affected by the restriction of human mobility as a consequence of the COVID-19 pandemic. These activities dropped to levels never seen before, causing a breakdown in the economy of the central highlands. These are the socio-economic structural conditions in these four provinces that make this type of collaborative exchange possible. It seems that their culture makes it possible for this commercial practice to be easily adopted. As the capitalist economy falls, collaborative exchange is born and grows, in an inversely proportional relationship and in the opposite direction, but one confirming the existence of the other.

In this perspective, the predisposition to carry out barter activities has always been present. Therefore, this chapter is structured as follows: section I, which presents an economic and productive diagnosis of the provinces studied; section II refers to the reality of collaborative exchange by analyzing some key cases; section III, by explaining the community and economic meaning of barter, a theoretical approach to the phenomenon under study is constructed; finally, in section IV, the interpretation of results is made. This set of elements is considered sufficient to demonstrate the transcendence, validity and complexity of this topic in the current socioeconomic context.

I. DESCRIPTION OF THE ECONOMIC-PRODUCTIVE BREAKDOWN THAT DRIVES BARTERING

Specifically, what level of poverty exists in this sub-region and how have they been affected by COVID-19, and what role does barter play in these circumstances? Is it a situation of survival? Or is it an ideological situation against capitalist markets?

Table 1. Evolution of Income Poverty in Ecuador

Year	2016	2017	2018	2019	2021
Poverty	23,70%	23,10%	24,50%	25,50%	32,20%
Extreme poverty	8,60%	8,40%	9,00%	9,50%	14,70%
Total	32,30%	31,50%	33,50%	35,00%	46,90%
Gini	0,465	0,462	0,472	0,478	0,493

Source: Prepared by the authors with data from INEC (2021).

Looking at the position of poverty that Ecuador occupies in Latin America, it is possible to dimension the precariousness, economic vulnerability and the relations of poverty in which the barter insurges.

In the eyes of the Economic Commission for Latin America and the Caribbean (ECLAC) (2020), in its report Social Panorama of Latin America, the situation is not at all encouraging. According to this report, Latin America has the following balance sheet one year after the start of COVID-19: a 7.7% drop in GDP and the closure of 2.7 million companies. This results in a critical economic situation that has caused a 12-year setback in poverty and a 20-year setback in extreme poverty. With this, vulnerability increases with respect to 2019: from 467 to 491 million people living with incomes up to 3 times the poverty line. The data show that Latin America is the most affected in the world, because, with only 8.4% of the world population, it registered 27.8% of deaths due to COVID-19.

Within this worrisome framework, the following data for Latin America is presented: poverty represents 30.5% of the population and extreme poverty 11.3%, which together total 41.8%, measured as of 2019. An increase of no less than 5% is projected for 2021, which leads to the possibility of having a poverty rate of approximately 46% by December. In the same line, we can observe the evolution of the Gini index, which is located at 0.46, and this indicator is expected to worsen to a value of 0.48 for the region.

Faced with this situation, Ecuador presents a worrying evolution of poverty, exceeding the Latin American average. From 2016 to 2021, poverty data are as shown in the table below.

Table 1 shows how Ecuador, from 2019 to 2021, with an increase from 35% to 4x6.9%, respectively, exceeds the poverty data of the Latin American region. To this, it is important to add the situation of the Gini indicator gotten worse from 0.478 to 0.493 in the same time span, confirming a worsening trend since 2016, which registered 0.465. This is a data visibly worse than the one raised by ECLAC for the subcontinent, which stood at 0.46 in 2020.

Table 2. Poverty Level in the Central Highlands

Province	Income poverty (December 2020)	Extreme poverty by income (December 2020)		Total
Cotopaxi	44,00%	23,20%		67,20%
Chimborazo	55,10%	34,50%		89,60%
Bolivar	52,30%	25,70%		78,00%
Tungurahua	27,90%	14,50%		42,40%
National	32,70%	14,20%		46,90%
Latin America	30,50%	11,30%		41,80%

Source: Prepared by the authors with data from INEC (2021) and ECLAC (2020).

The reality that drives the need to modify the way of exchanging is intimately linked to monetary circulation and, of course, to family income. Bartering is an aspect that denounces the extreme contraction of the money supply of a population and also makes explicit a failed state. In the provinces of the central highlands of Ecuador this is evident. The situation of high scarcity becomes life or death in the pandemic and after it as well. The following is a statistical perspective of the tragic dimension of poverty and extreme poverty in the area referred to. Table 2 describes a poignant reality typical of the poorest people in the world.

The critical situation of these provinces is shown by the data. These show that the total poverty of Chimborazo is 89.60% (including poverty and extreme poverty), that of Bolivar is 78% and that of Cotopaxi 67.20%, well above the Ecuadorian and Latin American average. With these data, it is possible to assure that these provinces have been deeply affected by the pandemic, although before it, they were already in a situation of worrisome poverty. Therefore, the question is born in the heart of the misery and a failed state presence: What to do to live?

But answering the question also implies knowing in detail some critical components, such as the illiteracy rate and the level of internet use in households; this, specifies the practical difficulty faced in that area of the country. Information from the Institute of Statistics and Census (INEC, 2021) can be observed in Table 3.

The number of families with internet access in Bolivar is 5.26%, Chimborazo 9.15% and Cotopaxi only 6.28%. On the other hand, the level of illiteracy reaches approximately 14% in the province of Bolivar and 13.51% in Chimborazo. When reviewing the number of MSMEs by province, Chimborazo has 27,123 enterprises, or approximately 2.5%, and Bolivar has 12,144, which corresponds to 1.25% of the national total of MSMEs. Combining these three aspects, the answer sought can be

Table 3. Critical Components Aggravated During the Pandemic

Province	Population	Economically active population	Households with internet	Number of MSMEs	Illiteracy rate
Tungurahua	504.583,00	284.741,00	13,93%	41.490,00	7,47%
Bolivar	183.641,00	95.751,00	5,26%	12.144,00	13,92%
Cotopaxi	409.205,00	204.137,00	6,28%	25.364,00	13,62%
Chimborazo	458.581,00	233.768,00	9,15%	27.123,00	13,51%

Source: Multidimensional Statistics - Institute of Statistics and Census (INEC, 2021).

clarified. This reality indicates that one is tied to the proximity (neighborhood or community) and to the apparently "elementary", which implies bartering for survival.

The situation is aggravated if we measure the number of active MSMEs, those that have a Single Taxpayer Registry (RUC) and file taxes. The following table shows the inclement impact of the pandemic, according to data from the Internal Revenue System (SRI, 2021). This shows that the affectation has broken family economies.

Table 4. Active Companies with Registration and Tax Returns

Province	2015	2016	2017	2018	2019	2020	2021
Bolivar	1.309	1.248	1.662	1.835	2.635	1.870	1.513
Chimborazo	3.062	3.033	3.639	4.548	6.283	5.058	3.933
Cotopaxi	2.768	2.633	3.279	3.817	5.307	4.132	3.340
Tungurahua	4.337	4.221	4.931	5.911	7.219	6.425	4.917

Source: Prepared by the authors with data from the Internal Revenue Service (SRI, 2021).

The data in Table 4 indicates that the province of Bolivar, in 2019, showed an increase with respect to previous years. This reached 2 635 MSMEs active in 2019, then decrease to 1 513 active companies in 2021, data that represents a drop of 43%. Chimborazo, has a drop from 6 283, in 2019, to 3 933 in 2021, which means 37.4%. Tungurahua is another province in critical situation, which falls from 7 219 to 4 917 that means 31.88%. The four provinces total 13 703 active MSMEs in 2021, which represents approximately 6.71% of the national total (SRI, 2020).

Undoubtedly, there are plenty of reasons for the population to run out of income and look for ways to generate collaborative exchanges.

In that same perspective, it is possible to review with data from the SRI (2021) how much has been the impact on tax collection in which the following can be observed:

Table 5. Revenues from Taxes

Province	2017	2018	2019	2020	2021
Bolivar	11.178.140	11.856.569	11.049.503	9.808.128	5.138.366
Chimborazo	76.528.054	77.924.108	66.063.128	56.364.628	32.629.908
Cotopaxi	115.075.906	121.558.028	113.570.249	102.218.795	59.702.509
Tungurahua	226.908.221	240.873.569	243.387.726	182.411.417	102.530.724
Total	**8.420.350.835**	**8.746.037.087**	**8.679.766.860**	**6.939.749.589**	**3.642.852.052**

Source: Prepared by the authors with data from the Internal Revenue Service (SRI, 2021).

The drop in tax returns by province, from 2019 to 2021, averages 50%. But, when calculating the total collected from the four provinces, the contraction is approximately 60% by 2021, which can be attributed to the Covid effect19. It seems that there is no other way than bartering.

Given the serious situation of poverty in this region of Ecuador, the doors are open to a dynamic of survival that forces the organization of ways to obtain basic foodstuffs. Bartering is the activity of choice, when communities and citizens reach a consensus to exchange, in the absence of the State. At this point, it is important to confirm and highlight the capacity of families and communities to deny the state and emancipate themselves from it, forcing us to answer the question: What happens in the territory when barter takes place? It is discovered that they are more than citizens, that the transcendent for living is realized by the subject in its territory.

II. THE REALITY OF COLLABORATIVE EXCHANGE IN THE CENTRAL HIGHLANDS

Collaborative exchange takes on greater relevance when the crisis caused by the COVID-19 pandemic deepens, especially in these four provinces. One of the forms that this activity takes, in the Ecuadorian Highlands, are the *barter fairs*[4]. This activity is executed, despite being a complex event to carry out, due to the coordination for the commercialization of the diversity of products, culture, values and times.

One of the most striking for its popularity is “El trueque del Sol”, in Pimanpiro (city of Ibarra); this is promoted by announcing that the exchange here is without currency and that surely no one will be sad, the compensation is total. Another is the “Fair of Hope”, in Imbabura, with the same content of social and commercial promotion. To carry out an event of this type implies a high level of organization and social-productive consensus, which brings with it a leadership that could be called interesting. It is evident that a new criterion for conducting the exchange is born in the midst of extreme poverty. It is a leadership that, in this area, replaces the failed State.

In these fairs you can find products from cold climates, which are exchanged with others that come from temperate climate zones. You can also find cattle, pork, poultry and others. In this way, more than 500 products from all parts of the country and mainly from the central highlands are offered. This requires a place, a regulation accepted by all, a mechanism of free access, an authority to resolve conflicts and ensure continuity. In other words, community leadership is required.

In the barter fairs, which also take place in the central highlands, the products require different production times and culture. However, everything here manages to be solved not by setting a price, but by assigning a value. This finds synchronization and commercial simultaneity, with other products, in conditions of totally different time and culture. To specify, it is worth giving an example: making a collaborative exchange between cassava or oranges is highly complex. This complexity is intrinsic[5], since it is necessary to build equivalence of value permanently. From this, progress is made towards social and community brotherhood (Dimas & Herrera, 2020).

As already mentioned, what is crucial in bartering is not the price, but the work and the need for consumption implicit in the products being exchanged (Abeledo, 2014). The producer participates with the conviction that the value of his work is useful for him, his family and the community, this ensures the continuity of the exchange. This is evidenced in the interviews conducted with the inhabitants of the central highlands.

I have always used barter when I came to sell my products, I have been selling in the plaza for ten years, I used to exchange with other producers for what was needed in my house, but now with the COVID-19 pandemic I do it much more because people have no money, so they prefer to exchange, although sometimes I lose out...before it was fairer, nobody lost, now I lose, but it is better than having to return with my products. Sometimes guys from the fields also come to help me load and in exchange I give them products because it is not convenient for me to pay them...now that there is no money or work, it is better to pay them like this. The exchanges are carried out in an itinerant way, house to house, in a personal way and when there is a need to do it; and not in a previously established place and day. Participation in bartering is reciprocal, sometimes people go out to other houses in search of exchanges and, at other times, they wait at home for them to arrive to exchange. Most of those who go out do so because they also aspire to sell their products (María, Alausí, August 2021).

The lady's testimony is very relevant, as it shows in particular the social vicissitudes to be able to consume. There is a clear economic phenomenon that arises when one reaches the situation of not having money to buy in a capitalist country. This is an instance beyond extreme poverty. Here is another story from an inhabitant in this area of Ecuador.

I don't like bartering because they don't give what they should really give, there is a lot of injustice, it should be regulated by someone because bartering well done is good because we could all exchange without the need to have money. Here in the plaza it is difficult to do it, with the people in my community we do it, they also have their crops and we exchange products, they give me what they harvest and in exchange I give them what I have as well, so we all win. The products that are most exchanged are those destined for food, including: tomatoes, cucumbers, corn, eggs, beans, lima beans, peas. In second place are poultry, such as chickens and guinea pigs. Finally, there is the exchange of services such as manure in exchange for products (Amira, Achupallas, August 2021).

The barter community, since it is created to solve the food crisis, is better than the food market as it is defined today. Although there must be regulation, collaborative activity is better than the model that forces currency at times when it is impossible to use price as a unit of exchange. The testimony marks the great need in the face of a life and death situation (to eat or not to eat). Individual exchange, through barter, takes place around basic consumer goods by the producer and the direct consumer. In this, there are no secondary markets, there is no accumulation and there is no speculation since the simultaneity of value[6] regulates everything. It is then necessary to analyze a third testimony.

I am retired and for more than thirty years I have been doing welding work here in my house, many people come from the countryside to weld their appliances or do a "little job" but they do not always have money and as they are known, they bring me products in exchange for the work. For example, for a welding job that costs two dollars, they leave me potatoes, carrots, beans, which together cost more than two dollars. So we help each other, sometimes I tell them not to give me too much, but they say that they don't want to carry weight and then they get damaged because people don't want to buy the products...there is no money. Bartering is mostly done through the exchange of low value goods. The exchange of products with high economic values is not viable, local production is generally for basic and immediate consumption (Eleuterio, Huigra, August 2021).

Here the collaborative exchange is done to cover the needs of the basic basket when income disappears. It is different from the spirit of barter fairs in times of "normality". In this case, which analyzes the provinces of the central highlands, the situation is focused on times when there is no family income. In this particular circumstance, families are not in poverty or extreme poverty, they are outside the system, this is another category. The family, as a subject of exchange, is excluded in this neoliberal economic organization. Community leadership and barter also deconstruct this system because it is the redoubt of the marginalized.

The physical distancing and increased stay at home, forced by the pandemic, with the consequent loss of family purchasing power, has led these populations to rely on each other to save themselves from hunger. Collaborative association of local producers, increase of productive initiatives and family enterprises, is the last hope. It does not occur to anyone to think of the State or its government.

III. THE COMMUNITY AND ECONOMIC MEANING OF BARTERING

Barter is a practice that has been considered typical of populations with backward, inefficient and culturally precarious economies (Pimentel, 2017). In this sense, the economic surprise is given when the solution to the dramatic crisis, at a time of pandemic, is generated from the people and in a non-classical economic framework (Sundararajan, 2016). The solution is found in the "pure" social consensus of collaborative exchange. Therefore, the elements of accumulation or capitalist preferences are left out of the picture in this perspective (Gregory, 2012). Especially in indigenous[7] community sectors in the provinces, the aforementioned reality is much more frequent.

This part of the country carries out, within the framework of barter, transactions without currency as a form of payment or compensation using mingas. This practice has been taken up and generalized since the recent COVID-19 pandemic to minimize the effects caused by the *lack of liquidity*[8]. Thus, it is once again becoming a contemporary phenomenon that facilitates transactions, on a small or large scale, between actors in the liquidity trap (Rodríguez, Gallón & Gómez, 2019). Consequently, one aspect to highlight is the fact that this type of transactions forces to look for a fair exchange of even goods. But what does this phenomenon represent from a social-economic perspective? (Sundararajan, 2016).

a) A community economic authority is constituted that facilitates the continuity of barter; sometimes this authority is implicit as a moral reference when barter is carried out between families outside of a fair;
b) Goods are demanded and compensated with goods, which belong to different classes (different origins), in other cases, they may be items exchanged for merchandise or other services;

c) Information is "perfect", all participants have access to the same information about the products;
d) The protagonists are essentially free to enter or exit the negotiation and are at the same level of trading power, at the end of the deal they remain in the same patrimonial conditions as before negotiating;
e) Value is exclusive to those who barter; there is no way of interpreting it outside this dynamic of exchange. Moreover, there may be bargaining, but not with respect to some abstract numerical measure of price, since each simply desires the good that the other possesses;
f) The two parties to the transaction act simultaneously, although the two may be separated by time (they might commit future production or services), or by place, if the bargaining is in networks; and,
g) Finally, the act is transformative, moving objects between "value regimes" (Appadurai, 1986), held by the two actors (Gregory & Halff, 2017).

This demonstrates high economic efficiency at times when markets do not function. When currency is scarce, the socio-economy presses for the generation of circuits with circulation of value, price is annulled and barter replaces it (Frenken, 2017). In a catastrophe due to loss of income, such as the one experienced by these four provinces, it is interesting that this population denies the system and takes refuge in a community leadership that promotes consensus in order to consume (Comisión Europea, 2016). However, these elements are not registered in an accounting system, they are not registered in the SRI, nor do they appear in the Gross Domestic Product (Rodríguez, Gallón, & Gómez, 2019).

This dynamic, bartering uncovers an immense breach in the heart of accumulative and consumerist capitalism; but, at the same time, it becomes an extraordinary lever to maintain its validity (Brändle, 2017). It opens a door in parallel line that builds economy based on exchanges that sustain family and community life (González, 2018). This practical strength implies two conceptually transcendent aspects: a) the redefinition of poverty, since it is executed in the absence of income; and, b) it expresses a social subject that surpasses the citizen by constructing the economic reality denying the State. It can be said, then, that barter is best understood when viewed in the light of its social context of consensus (Hamari, Sjöklint & Ukkonen, 2016). To the extent that this context of consensus varies, so will its exchange characteristics (Patiño, Gómez-Álvarez & Plaza-Angulo, 2017).

Table 6. Current Activity

Activity	Percentage	Cumulative percentage
Farmer	15,3	15,3
Student	9,3	24,7
Self-employed (self-employed).	16,3	40,9
Employee	33,5	74,4
Unemployed	16,7	91,2
Retired.	8,8	100,0
Total	**100,0**	

IV. ANALYSIS OF THE SURVEYS CONDUCTED IN THE CENTRAL HIGHLANDS

In order to reach the target population in a relevant way, the questionnaire was prepared digitally, using the Google Forms application, to avoid contact and respect sanitary measures. It consists of 17 questions divided into six sections: the first section allows the collection of demographic information of the surveyed population; the second explores knowledge about collaborative exchange and possible use during the pandemic; the third asks if any exchange has taken place; the fourth aims to find out about the exchange carried out (analyzes variables such as products exchanged, frequency, place and medium used for the exchange) and about the fairness of the exchange; The fifth, collects the perception of the possibility of continuing to use barter as a means of exchange; and finally, it inquires about the affiliation of the villagers to any exchange network and the frequency of possible transactions.

The response rate to the questionnaire was 71.67%. The data was generated on the Google Forms site and processed in the SPSS version 2.6 program to generate the frequency tables for each variable that made up the questionnaire. The reality that manifests itself in this territory of the central highlands of Ecuador can be simplified from the analysis of a survey consisting of 13 questions asked to 215 inhabitants of this Andean sub-region. The methodological questions that this paper seeks to answer are: How deep is this barter activity? And to what extent was it used now? The survey provides important complementary answers.

Taking into account the aforementioned conceptual context, the first step is to inquire about the employment situation, to find out if they are in a circumstance of socioeconomic urgency. Within this framework, the respondents are distributed as shown in the following table:

According to Table 6, 33.5% are employed, 16.7% unemployed, and 16.3% self-employed, which implies economic[9] informality. Another important percentage to highlight are those who are engaged in agriculture, with 15.3%. Finally, 9.3% of respondents are students and 8.8% are retired. In the context of the pandemic, all those who were not employed were left without formal income, in this case, approximately 67%. In accordance with the previous question, the level of study of the respondents is also relevant in this research in order to establish a relationship, if possible, between bartering and academic training. In other words, barter is usually considered as a precarious exchange criterion of less educated societies.

In terms of educational level, 29.3% are in high school, 26.0% are professionals and 21.4% have a bachelor's degree. Finally, 15.3% have elementary school and only 7.9% have fourth level studies. It can be affirmed, with these statistics, that this is a population that is very well informed about what barter is and what markets mean. Along these lines, when asked about the effect that COVID-19 has had on the family income, the position of the respondents was 99.5% (including employees), confirming the critical situation that has been generated by the pandemic. This, for obvious reasons, leads to the need to search for ways to maintain the food supply through mechanisms that compensate for the drop in income (Delgado and Delgado, 2014).

In terms of educational level, 29.3% are in high school, 26.0% are professionals and 21.4% have a bachelor's degree. Finally, 15.3% have elementary school and only 7.9% have fourth level studies. It can be affirmed, with these statistics, that this is a population that is very well informed about what barter is and what markets mean. Along these lines, when asked about the effect that COVID-19 has had on the family income, the position of the respondents was 99.5% (including employees), confirming the critical situation that has been generated by the pandemic. This, for obvious reasons, leads to the need to search for ways to maintain the food supply through mechanisms that compensate for the drop in income (Delgado and Delgado, 2014).

This search leads to the proximity to barter, which has been corroborated as a widely known exchange criterion. Of the total number of people surveyed, 78.6% say they are completely familiar with this particular exchange, and an additional 19.1% say they know what it is, although before the pandemic they had not been familiar with it. When these two percentages are added together, 97.7% know about barter and have practiced it in some way. That is why, when asked directly if they have used it during the pandemic, the answer is a resounding 81%, who answer in the affirmative. Leaving 8.8% who have not used it, but could do so at any time.

This turns out to be one of the key revelations because it shows how the population has clung to barter in the absence of the state, which has not provided any way to solve the crisis. Bartering is real and is the basis of efficient social organization that shows that other territorial initiatives can be carried out without the participation of the State. But there is still more, it was specifically asked if they had obtained food using this community collaborative approach. The following table describes the positions in response to the question.

Table 7. Use of Barter with Groceries

Criteria	Percentage	Cumulative percentage
Totally agree	40,0	40,0
All right.	18,6	58,6
Indifferent	7,9	66,5
Disagree	7,0	73,5
Strongly disagree	26,5	100,0
Total	**100,0**	

According to Table 7, 40.0% used bartering as a collaborative means to obtain food on a recurrent basis and 18.6% used it in times of critical shortages and, finally, 7.5% indicated that they are prepared to do so at any time. To understand the response, it is important to know that here it was aimed at specifying the provisions for daily food consumption only. In the corroboration of the food demanded, which leaves the previous question unanswered, it was asked which were the most exchanged products.

Of the 66.5% of respondents who indicated that they had used barter as a means of obtaining food during the pandemic, 28.8% indicated that they bartered only for vegetables and fruits, and 20.5% also bartered for non-perishable foodstuffs. But this bartering goes much further than just food. In addition, 7.9% bartered clothes and 3.3% bartered medicines and 1.4% bartered school supplies.

Regarding other barter items, 4.2% of the respondents stated that they exchanged large animals for small animals, household goods, furniture, used furniture, technology and telephones. This demonstrates that we are facing a phenomenon that seeks to capture the integral part of the community's economic activity. This is impressive since everything is self-regulated and without currency. There is a complex exchange of specific value.

A transcendent evaluation, to verify the depth that bartering has taken in these provinces, is to know how many times it has been done during this pandemic period. The result is reflected as follows: as in the previous question, of the 66.5% of respondents who indicated that they used barter as a means of obtaining food during the pandemic, 38.6% mentioned that they did it between 0 and 3 times, followed by 15.3% who did it between 4 to 6 times, 7.0% did it between 7 to 10 times and finally, more than 10 times with 5.6%. It is clear that use increases as the need becomes more acute.

In other words, 38.6% were at least 3 times without monetary resources, at all, to buy (with zero income). Attention must be paid to this phenomenon. We are invited to recall what has already been said: extreme poverty is determined when one has less than $2 for daily consumption. Well, in this case, these families have found themselves on 3 occasions, with absolutely no income to buy, the answer: bartering. This has worsened so much that 5.6% have been in this situation more than 10 times during the pandemic. The frequency with which this phenomenon appears indicates that it is important to theoretically redefine poverty and extreme poverty in this context.

Knowing whether or not the exchange was "fair" is relevant, since in this extreme crisis it is essential that once the barter has been carried out, the immediate need is resolved:

Table 8. Do you think the barter was fair?

Criteria	Percentag e	Cumulative percentage
No response	33,5	33,5
Totally agree	27,4	60,9
All right.	23,3	84,2
Indifferent	3,3	87,4
Disagree	8,8	96,3
Strongly disagree	3,7	100,0
Total	**100,0**	

Following Table 8[10], of the 66.5% who carried out a collaborative exchange during the pandemic, 27.4% totally agree in considering that the barter was fair, 23.3% agree that the result was good, although it could be better. There were 3.3% who considered that it was neither bad nor good. There were 8.8% who disagreed and 3.7% who would have preferred not to do this barter.

It could be that the means by which the barter was made may have influenced some people not to achieve satisfaction or others to achieve what they were looking for. Therefore, the following question is asked: What means did you use to contact your counterpart to make the exchange? As with the previous question, of the 66.5%, 36.7% made the exchange in person, 11.2% through neighbors, 10.2% by telephone and 7.4% through social networks. Other means were used by 0.9%. In addition to the above, we can ask: What was the place chosen for the barter? Of the 66.5% who carried out a collaborative exchange during the pandemic, 43.7% mentioned having done it at home, while 10.7% did it on public roads, 7.9% in open squares, 2.3% in markets and the remaining percentages did it in other spaces.

There is no doubt that it is a family phenomenon. It is not a call that has as its center the traditional squares, although that expression also exists, it is the need of each family that determines the environment and the place. The need is the guide in the face of the absolute absence of the Ecuadorian state. So much so, that when asked about the possibility of maintaining barter as a form of formal exchange, the response was overwhelming, given that 98% agreed.

Given this reality, it is necessary to reflect on the spontaneity and informality of these exchanges. Respondents were asked if they were affiliated to any exchange network or something equivalent. In response, 94% said they were not affiliated with any network. It is a bit of a reflection of these societies, they only rush in the face of urgency. This leads to the objective of this article: to formally propose the possibility of promoting collaborative exchange networks, holding fairs or family activities where it is possible to barter as a diversification of what we know as a market today.

CONCLUSION

Three important aspects emerge from this form of bartering and that it is possible to ensure it: (a) understanding that barter arises when capitalist exchange breaks down, this is always present to the extent that there is always the crisis, it has been proven that it is not an isolated aspect; (b) the state is absolutely replaced by a community and family leadership that is much more efficient and committed, and in that line, the social subject is redefined beyond a citizen; and (c) the negation, also absolute, of the classic capitalist system, by managing to transfer value without transferring currency, which cancels accumulation and imposing collective welfare. These are three criteria that together can trigger one or more rigorous investigations on the relevance of this state model and new criteria for organizing production, the market and consumption in provinces such as those of the central highlands of Ecuador.

Two instances were identified in the practice of bartering: one is historical, linked to the ancestral nature of the concept in the indigenous peoples of the Ecuadorian highlands, which can be witnessed in the fairs. The other, related to the urgency of the daily coexistence of families in a situation of economic vulnerability (Bergesio & González, 2020). A third practice could be added, related to the use of platforms and social networks to carry out the exchange agreement. According to Finau and Scobie (2021), indigenous peoples have resumed bartering supported by technology and social networks to carry out the exchange process, which could be promoted in the new normality.

In extreme precariousness, what this research shows are that, in the economic model of these provinces, the need for personal contact prevails, hence the vulnerability of their reality. To improve this circumstance, it is possible to promote more efficient ways of bartering in the perspective of saving time, as proposed by Quiña-Mera,

Saransig-Perugachi, Trejo-España, Naranjo-Toro, Guevara-Vega (2019), focused on promoting the exchange of goods and services through the use of platforms without the use of currency.

In this line, the conformation of each exchange network depends on: a) the geographic location between provinces, within each parish or community; b) the distance between houses, c) family and community ties, d) quantity and value; and, e) the type of products offered and demanded. Thus, the implicit question is answered: barter is established as an anti-crisis mechanism post COVID-19 that ensures the survival of these provinces.

REFERENCES

Abeledo, S. (2014). Territorio, caminos y prácticas culturales de los viajes de intercambio del último siglo (departamento de Los Andes, provincia de Salta). In Espacialidades en las tierras altoandinas. Avances de investigación desde el noroeste argentino (pp. 29-62). Buenos Aires: CONICET - Instituto Interdisciplinario Tilcara, FFyL, UBA.

Appadurai, A. (1986). *The Social Life of Things*. Cambridge University Press. doi:10.1017/CBO9780511819582

Bergesio, L., & González, N. (2020). Los viajes de intercambio y las ferias. Relatos y vigencia del trueque en la Puna jujeña (Argentina). *Estudios Atacameños*, (65), 407–427. doi:10.22199/issn.0718-1043-2020-0034

Bieniek, M. (2021). Bartering: Price-Setting Newsvendor Problem with Barter Exchange. *Sustainability*, *13*(12), 6684. doi:10.3390u13126684

Brändle, G. (2017). Controversias en torno al impacto social del consumo colaborativo: Algunos elementos para la discusión. Redes.com. *Revista de Estudios para el Desarrollo Social de la Comunicación*, *15*, 122–143. doi:10.15213/redes.n15.p123

Chávez, L. (2012). Implementación de tres rutas turísticas en la Zona Sierra Centro del Ecuador. Tesis de grado. Universidad Politécnica de Chimborazo. Chimborazo, Ecuador.

Comisión Europea. (2016). *Una Agenda Europea para la economía*. Retrieved from https://tinyurl.com/y3y8xugv

Delgado, F., & Delgado, M. (2014). *El vivir y comer bien en los andes bolivianos. Aportes de los sistemas agroalimentarios y estrategias de vida de las naciones indígena originario campesinas a las políticas de seguridad y soberanía alimentaria*. AGRUCO -Plural Editores.

Dimas, D., & Herrera, J. (2020). La práctica del trueque en una comunidad mazahua del Estado de México. *Otra Economía, 13*(24), 77–94.

Finau, G., & Scobie, M. (2021). Old ways and new means: Indigenous accountings during and beyond the pandemic. *Accounting, Auditing & Accountability Journal*. https://www21.ucsg.edu.ec:2117/10.1108/AAAJ-08-2020-4753

Frenken, K. (2017). Political economies and environmental futures for the sharing economy en Philosophical Transactions of the Royal Societ. *Philosophical Transactions of the Royal Society A, 375*(2095), 20160367. Advance online publication. doi:10.1098/rsta.2016.0367 PMID:28461431

Gobierno Autónomo Descentralizado de la Provincia de Bolívar. (2015). *Plan de Desarrollo y Ordenamiento Territorial de Bolivar 2015- 2020*. Tomado de https://multimedia.planificacion.gob.ec/PDOT/descargas.html

Gobierno Autónomo Descentralizado de la Provincia de Chimborazo. (2020). *Plan de Desarrollo y Ordenamiento Territorial de Chimborazo 2020- 2030*. Tomado de https://multimedia.planificacion.gob.ec/PDOT/descargas.html

Gobierno Autónomo Descentralizado de la Provincia de Cotopaxi. (2015). *Actualización del Plan de Desarrollo y Ordenamiento Territorial de Cotopaxi 2025*. Tomado de http://app.sni.gob.ec/sni-link/sni/PORTAL_SNI/data_sigad_plus/sigadplusdocumentofinal/0560000110001_FINAL-PDYOT-COTOPAXI-2015_17-08-2015_18-17-17.pdf

Gobierno Autónomo Descentralizado de la Provincia de Tungurahua. (2015). *Informe Técnico para la Alineación Plan de Desarrollo y Ordenamiento Territorial PDOT Provincial - al Plan Nacional de Desarrollo 2017 - 2021*. Tomado de https://multimedia.planificacion.gob.ec/PDOT/descargas.html

González Cabrera, I. (2018). La economía colaborativa del intercambio entre pares a una nueva economía de mercado. Revista de derecho mercantil (Madrid).

Gregory, A., & Halff, G. (2017). Understanding public relations in the 'sharing economy'. *Public Relations Review, 43*(1), 4–13. doi:10.1016/j.pubrev.2016.10.008

Gregory, Ch. (2012). On money debt and morality: Some reflections on the contribution of economic anthropology. *Social Anthropology, 20*(4), 380–396. doi:10.1111/j.1469-8676.2012.00225.x

Hamari, J., Sjöklint, M., & Ukkonen, A. (2016). The sharing economy: Why people participate in collaborative consumption. *Journal of the Association for Information Science and Technology, 67*(9), 2047–2059. doi:10.1002/asi.23552

Instituto de Estadísticas y Censos (INEC). (2021). *Boletín Técnico N°03-2021-IPC*. Tomado de https://www.ecuadorencifras.gob.ec/documentos/web-inec/Inflacion/2021/Marzo-2021/Boletin_tecnico_03-2021-IPC.pdf

La Comisión Económica para América Latina y el Caribe (CEPAL). (2020). *Panorama Social de América Latina 2020*. CEPAL. Tomado de https://www.cepal.org/es/publicaciones/46687-panorama-social-america-latina-2020

Patiño, D., Gómez-Álvarez, R., & Plaza-Angulo, J. (2017). Caracterización económica y cuantificación de la economía colaborativa. In Economía colaborativa y trabajo en plataforma: realidades y desafíos [Sharing economy and platform work: realities and challenges] (pp. 51-101). Bomarzo.

Pimentel, G. L. (2017). La personalización de las relaciones económicas a través de la economía colaborativa: los límites al supuesto de no-turismo: the limits to the assumption of non-turism. *Revista Académica ECO, 17*, 107-115. Retrieved from https://tinyurl.com/y4hqvxgr

Quiña-Mera, J., Saransig-Perugachi, E., Trejo-España, D., Naranjo-Toro, M., & Guevara-Vega, C. (2019). Automation of the Barter (Exchange Management in Ecuador Applying Google V3 API for Geolocation. In Á. Rocha, C. Ferrás, & M. Paredes (Eds.), *Information Technology and Systems. ICITS 2019. Advances in Intelligent Systems and Computing* (Vol. 918). Springer. doi:10.1007/978-3-030-11890-7_21

Rodríguez Triana, M. A., Gallón Vargas, N., & Gómez Zapata, Y. (2019). *La contabilidad en propuestas de economía solidaria y alternativa*. Academic Press.

Santillán, K., & Lozada, V. (2013). Diseño y diagramación de una guía turística para difusión de los destinos turísticos de la Zona Sierra Centro Ecuatoriana. Tesis de grado. Universidad Politécnica Nacional. Quito, Ecuador.

Servicio de Rentas Internas (SRI). (2021). Recuperado de https://srienlinea.sri.gob.ec/saiku-ui/#cancel

Sundararajan, A. (2016). *The sharing economy: The end of employment and the rise of crowd-based capitalism*. MIT Press.

ADDITIONAL READING

Anderson, R., Ashlagi, I., Gamarnik, D., & Kanoria, Y. (2017). Efficient dynamic barter exchange. *Operations Research*, *65*(6), 1446–1459. doi:10.1287/opre.2017.1644

Gómez Terán, M., Echeverría Almeida, J., Naranjo Toro, M. E., & Oviedo Pantoja, W. G. (2018). *El trueque en San Pedro de Pimampiro, alternativa actual de una práctica ancestral*. Editorial Universidad Técnica del Norte.

Hua, G., Zhang, Y., Cheng, T., Wang, S., & Zhang, J. (2020). The newsvendor problem with barter exchange. *Omega*, *92*, 102149. doi:10.1016/j.omega.2019.102149

Ikeda, K., & Hamid, M. N. (2018). Applications of blockchain in the financial sector and a peer-to-peer global barter web. *Advances in Computers*, *111*, 99–120. doi:10.1016/bs.adcom.2018.03.008

Jairo, T. F. (2008). El trueque: Tradición, resistencia y fortalecimiento de la economía indígena en el Cauca. *Revista de Estudios Sociales*, (31), 146–161. doi:10.7440/res31.2008.10

Jorge, W. C. (2021). Corrales y el intercambio comercial en el anexo de Ranracancha, distrito de Vinchos, provincia de Huamanga: Trueque, ganadería y productos. *Alteritas*, *10*(11), 83–92.

Rojas, J. R. A., Andrade, R. I. M., Espinoza, M. S. M., & Tirado, P. S. O. (2017). El trueque como sistema de comercialización-Desde lo ancestral a lo actual. *Revista Uniandes Episteme*, *4*(3), 288–300.

Vercoe, R. A. (2018). Trueque Chilote: Traditional Barter Networks Connect Nature and Society in Northern Patagonia. In A. Daughters & A. Pitchon (Eds.), *Chiloé. Ethnobiology*. Springer. doi:10.1007/978-3-319-91983-6_5

KEY TERMS AND DEFINITIONS

Collaborative Exchange: Active and cooperative participation of two people who exchange one good or product for another of the same or equivalent value.

Community: Group of human beings who have certain elements in common or who have the same interests.

Cooperativism: Is the action that determines the cooperation of a group of members as a means to obtain a greater benefit for the satisfaction of their needs.

Fair: A space for open and inclusive participation where sellers and buyers of products, generally brought from the countryside, meet.

Income Crisis: A situation of changes caused by the instability of the economic income from an activity, which is subject to evolution.

Indigenous: Collectivities that assume an ethnic identity that defines them as the autochthonous peoples of the country, descendants of pre-Hispanic societies.

Minga: Voluntary and free community or collective work for the purpose of achieving a common work or objective.

Pawkar Raymi: In Quechua language means many colors. It is the exact point at which they can offer their fruits to be consumed.

Plaza: Uncovered public urban space in which a wide variety of activities take place, generally used for fairs.

Taita: Quechua word meaning father, father, God.

ENDNOTES

1 Andean because it belongs to the Andes Mountains in Ecuador.

2 They are closely linked to the financing provided by the Savings and Credit Cooperative to achieve the enterprise, to which they always turn to in associations. They have advantages in terms of credit costs, credit times and guarantees.

3 Typical of the Andean indigenous culture. Voluntary and free community or collective work for the purpose of achieving a common goal.

4 Commercial space where *collaborative exchange* is carried out without the use of currency; this is an open and inclusive space where sellers and buyers of products, which are generally brought from the countryside, interact.

5 It is natural to collaborative exchange (barter).

6 The simultaneity of value requires the existence of an equivalent product in order to be able to barter. Having more or less does not offer any advantage.

7 These are the collectivities that assume an ethnic identity that defines them as the autochthonous peoples of the country, descendants of pre-Hispanic societies.

8 Refers to the circumstance in which monetary circulation is weak or null and paralyzes exchange.

9 An urban micro commerce activity that has no formal links with the State and is used as a survival channel.

10 The 33.5% that did not answer this question corresponds to the percentage of the population that did not make any exchange during the pandemic, this variable was asked in question 9 of the questionnaire.

Section 3

Sector-Level Changes to Work Post-Pandemic

Chapter 8
Permanent Changes in the Tourism Industry:
The case of Galicia, Spain

Andrea Areán Magnou
Universidade de Vigo, Spain

Noelia Araújo-Vila
https://orcid.org/0000-0002-3395-8536
Universidade de Vigo, Spain

ABSTRACT

The world as we knew it has changed forever as a result of the COVID-19 pandemic. Tourist service providers had to adjust their services to the mandatory changes imposed by authorities' regulations and consistently with the demand of service users. This chapter focuses on detecting those potentially lasting changes and mark the new parameters in the tourism sector. The qualitative research chosen consisted of in-depth interviews with hotel and restaurant managers in the tourism industry of the four provinces of Galicia (Northwest Spain). Based on the theoretical review, the first conclusion is that, although tourism has been affected many times, whether by pandemics, economic crises, or even terrorist attacks, it is an industry that bounces back quickly and so far, regardless of the magnitude of the events that have affected it, always goes back to its previous level. In that regard, the answers obtained in the empirical part of the study show a great passivity in the industry. The supply has not made, nor do they foresee any structural changes to address the changes in the demand.

DOI: 10.4018/978-1-7998-8626-6.ch008

INTRODUCTION

In late 2019, a new type of coronavirus that causes COVID-19 was discovered in Wuhan, China. Although the way first humans got infected has not been fully confirmed, what we do know is that the virus is transmitted in humans through the respiratory tract with an incubation period that ranges from 1 to 14 days. In most cases it presents as a respiratory infection that can vary depending on the risk groups, progressing to severe pneumonia or multiorgan failure, being generally fatal in the elderly (Pérez et al., 2020).

The rapid spread of the disease led the World Health Organization (hereinafter WHO) to declare a health emergency of international concern on January 30, 2020, based on the impact the virus could potentially have on developing countries. On March 11, 2020, WHO recognized it as a pandemic (Pérez et al., 2020). In an unprecedented situation, due to the rapid spread and form of contagion (via the respiratory tract), most countries urged their citizens to return home and not to travel unless it was strictly essential, starting in March 2020 (the travel ban started in January in China). International travel bans and widespread restrictions on public gatherings and mobility have affected more than 90% of the world's population. Cruise ships were the extreme case, with people struggling to return home with no ports allowed them to dock (Gössling et al., 2020).

The general objective of this chapter is to learn which of the changes seen in the tourism sector as a result of the COVID-19 pandemic in Galicia could become permanent. The sub-objectives are to determine the main changes in consumer behavior, to determine whether the pandemic will lead to changes in the types of tourism chosen, to determine whether there will be changes in the services offered by providers and whether the fear caused by the pandemic will lead to the demand for new products or services. This research included an initial theoretical review of the existing scientific literature on the changes derived from the COVID-19 situation in tourism to date, as well as the expected changes.

The study presents the primary results of in-depth interviews (qualitative analysis) and some final conclusions. The research is justified to know the effects that trigger this unprecedented situation. One of the implications is that by anticipating long-term changes, the industry stakeholders can prepare and improve the range of services offered in the tourism sector from now and better plan the adaptation to the new environment. While various papers are being published regarding the consequences of COVID-19 in the tourism sector, it is relevant to know if the changes in consumer behaviors are strictly due to the current circumstance or whether it will motivate a deeper analysis and behavioral change. The main motivation for conducting this research was that we still do not know whether there will be irreversible changes in the industry, both from the point of view of supply and demand. Other crises have affected the industry in the past as shown below; yet none reached the scale of the current global situation.

BACKGROUND

Before the outbreak of the COVID-19 pandemic, tourism accounted for 10% of the global Gross Domestic Product (GDP) and employed 20% of the economically active population; in Spain in particular, tourism accounted for 12% of GDP and employed 12.7% of the economically active population (Bauzá & Melgosa, 2020), with revenues reaching 71,200 million euros in 2019 (Ortega, 2021). In Galicia, tourism represented 10.4% of GDP and provided 11% of the jobs in 2019 (Expansión, 2020). Almost one third (1.4 million) of the total number of tourists received by Galicia that year were foreign (Faro de Vigo, 2020a).

With the reduction of international travel and mobility, both domestic and international tourism sank abruptly. The immediate effects on the air travel, cruise and hospitality sector were devastating. Governments understood that tourism is a perishable good, since what was not billed in a season cannot be recovered (Gössling et al., 2020). Although tourism has already suffered several crises, whether due to other pandemics (including SARS or bird flu), terrorist attacks (such as 11-S) or economic crises (including the one caused by the fall of Lehman Brothers), there has never been a crisis with the characteristics of the current one, since mobility had never been globally limited to the extent that it has been on this occasion. This forced the industry to implement changes, not only related to health, but also in terms of flexibility of supply (La Vanguardia, 2020).

In Spain, tourism GDP fell by 69% during 2020 (Díaz, 2021). The World Travel and Tourism Council's prediction warns that 50 million jobs could be lost worldwide due to the pandemic (Mesa, 2020). The main consequences will be suffered by the most tourist-dependent countries, since in addition to the problems in the sector, during economic crises people restrict superfluous spending, a category that includes the tourism industry (Mooney & Zegarra, 2020).

Previous health crises

In recent decades other pandemics have occurred, all of them had an impact on both the economy and tourism, so it is presumed that what happened could serve as a predictive model. However, the impact of those does not compare with the current situation. Restrictive measures on human mobility have never been implemented in so many places simultaneously. In this sense, the changes in the behavior of tourists in previous health crises were so specific to the destination that the studies focus on later economic crises, but not on the tourism sector (Huertas et al., 2020). On the other hand, although these crises help us to understand the panorama, it is necessary to clarify that none of them has had an impact on tourism in Galicia.

Five health alerts have already been declared in this century; in addition to the current one:

1. SARS in 2002. WHO defined it as epidemic in 2003. Most of the cases occurred in China. While short-term tourism was affected, the consequences were not as severe as the Chinese Government had expected.
2. Bird flu in 2009; although it was defined as pandemic, it had a relatively mild effect on tourism.
3. MERS pandemic started in 2012 and is still active. It was first detected in Saudi Arabia, and according to WHO, its mortality rate was 30% and it spread mainly through direct interpersonal contact. In 2015, 9 people died in South Korea and 2,800 were quarantined. As a result, travels to that country fell by an average of 55% from May 20 to June 5, that year. The most affected countries of origin were Hong Kong, Taiwan and China, with a 102%, 83% and 72% reduction, respectively. These countries had been the worst hit by SARS in 2002, which would justify the overreaction compared to other countries in 2012 pandemic (Canalis, 2015).
4. Ebola was declared pandemic in 2000 and peaked between 2013 and 2014. It is still active, and its mortality rate is 50%. The first outbreaks occurred in Democratic Republic of Congo and Sudan in 1976; subsequent outbreaks were seen in West Africa between 2014 and 2016 and in Democratic Republic of Congo between 2018 and 2019. As for tourism, there is evidence proving that Ebola negatively influences the choice of destinations by tourists, even to countries in Africa that have never had any cases, since the disease is associated with the entire continent (Gössling et al., 2020).

These four health alerts plus the terrorist attacks of September 11, 2001, and the 2008-2009 global financial crisis suggest that tourism is a resilient industry, and those historical examples can be used as a reference in predictive models. On one hand, tourism may recover faster than expected, as happened in China in 2002 with SARS. On the other hand, people may associate the virus with the countries based on their level of control, as happens with Ebola. In this sense, Seychelles, Sweden or New Zealand are considered to be the countries that are coping with the COVID-19 pandemic best, and this will surely have an impact on the speed of the recovery of tourism in those countries. However, it is estimated that the magnitude of the global impact of COVID-19 will be far greater than that caused by the aforementioned events (Gössling et al., 2020).

It is also noteworthy that, although there have been other pandemics in history of mankind, this one in the twenty-first century is more serious for three reasons (Gössling et al., 2020):

- Growing and highly mobile world population
- Trend towards urbanization and concentration of people
- Highly global transport network that acts as a propagation vector

Impact of COVID-19 and New Regulations

Due to the magnitude of the current pandemic, one of the key aspects of society is the change in behavior linked to the perception of the risk that covid-19 represents. According to the theory of protection motivation, assessing the severity of a threat is one of the cognitive processes behind the decision to adopt a protective behavior (Parady et al., 2020; Rogers, 1975). Given the importance of behavioral factors in pandemic management, it is crucial to assess behavioral responses to the situation and determine how perceived risk is related to engaging in protective behaviors (Wise et al., 2020).

Following WHO's declaration of the pandemic, a series of measures have been implemented globally in order to minimize the spread of the covid-19 virus. Among the main measures are social distancing, self-isolation and quarantine of positive and potentially positive persons. Due to the relative rarity of pandemics, research on the psychological effects of these measures and the current pandemic itself is scarce, but growing rapidly (Bo et al., 2020; Zhou et al., 2020). In fact, recent research has used an approach that addresses the mental health needs of frontline health workers, one of the groups that has experienced this situation firsthand. Others have also emphasized how the implementation of psychological support systems during the pandemic is essential to guarantee emotional stability (Zaka et al., 2020). Studies are even being carried out in order to understand the psychological consequences derived from these measures, mainly mental health consequences that people may experience as a result of isolation and quarantine. (Holmes et al., 2022).

Currently, we have been in a pandemic for more than a year, with periods of partial and even practically total closures (except for essential needs and medical assistance). This situation has affected practically all individuals in some way, changing their daily routines and habits radically. Several important theories emphasize the importance of social relationships as key drivers of human behavior and optimal psychological functioning, such as the theory of self-determination (Deci et al., 2000), Seligman's PERMA model (2011) and Diener's tripartite model of subjectivity (1999). Taken together, these theories identify the important constituent elements of subjective well-being (BS), something that during the last year has been largely limited due to bans on social gatherings, affecting many individuals in a negative way.

In a very short time, society was forced to change its habits, as well as to implement a series of sanitary measures that would prevent the further spread of the virus. Teleworking was established in all possible cases, thus avoiding physical interaction with other individuals. Trips and flights were canceled, as a result of the reduced mobility imposed. The big question that experts are asking themselves is whether any of these changes will be established from now on, or whether society will return to the pre-pandemic situation.

In a matter of months, the framing of the global tourism system shifted from over-tourism (Dodds et al., 2019) to not tourism, with the transformation that this has meant for certain destinations and, especially, the image we have in mind of certain places, now empty. Even so, the general belief is that tourism will recover as it has from previous crises (CNN, 2020). A year after the start of the pandemic, there is still uncertainty regarding the recovery of the economy and social life. Tourism and hospitality are key sectors in the recovery of the economy of many countries, especially where these sectors represent a significant percentage of their economy. Williams and Kayaoglu (2020) point out that almost a tenth of European non-financial economic activities were linked to tourism and accounted for 9.5% of employment among the EU workforce in 2016. Williams and Kayaoglu (2020) also indicate that the accommodation and food and beverage sectors in the EU contributed 19.7% and 58.7%, respectively, of overall employment in the tourism industry. On this basis, it is clear that the large tourism-related companies and companies supporting this sector after the covid-19 pandemic have had an unprecedented socio-economic impact (Qiu et al., 2020).

As reported by administración.gob.es, there are several regulations in force in Spain due to the pandemic as of April 2021. These include but are not limited to the state of alarm declared to curtail the spread of the virus, the requirements imposed on both accommodation and restaurant businesses, the mobility restrictions, the mandatory use of masks, and the mandatory quarantine for people entering from certain countries (Bauzá & Melgosa, 2020).

What is currently expected is that these regulations will be gradually tapered until a "new normal" is reached. This would include the opening of borders and the lifting of travel restrictions. On the other hand, there could also be actions derived from the resumption of the activities, for example, the training of workers in the sector, specific hygiene measures, distancing in certain types of venues or spatial location strategies (Gómez et al., 2020). If these measures were adopted, they could be classified into two types. On one hand, consumer behavior changes resulting from the pandemic, and on the other new government regulations aimed to prevent the spread of the virus, to ensure health safety and avoidance of crowds (Bauzá & Melgosa, 2020).

Impact of COVID-19 on the Tourism Sector

According to the Chinese Government, sectors with the worst economic losses during this pandemic were restaurants and movie theaters that were closed by decree, public transport that underwent significant restrictions and tourism (Ma et al., 2020). From the economic point of view, experts expect it to be the biggest crisis since the Second World War; in addition, this will mark a before and after in the tourism sector. While the industry has already been exposed to other crises, none of these affected tourism in long term (Gössling et al., 2020).

Globally, in March 2020, 65% of the companies in the tourism sector had difficulty to pay their bills, being restaurants, cafes and accommodation facilities the most affected. It was especially bad for restaurants and cafes, since this industry usually lacks solid liquidity, and the situation favors big food chains (Gössling et al., 2020). UN expects that, by mid-2021, instead of growing by 2.5% as planned, economy will retract by 0.9% and the 2030 sustainable development goals will not be achieved. WTO had originally forecast a 3-4% growth in international arrivals, and on March 6 it revised that forecast down to 1-3%. On March 26 they corrected the forecast again, estimating a 20-30% reduction. This new adjustment confirms how difficult it is to forecast a situation in an unprecedented context. According to UN, the reduction in international arrivals considering only 2020 produced a reduction from $300 million to $450 million in monetary terms (Gössling et al., 2020).

In the accommodation sector, it is estimated that bookings fell by at least 50% in all countries, with the worst situations in Italy, Greece and Germany. As of May 2021, some countries remain closed to tourism, others have opened with origin-based restrictions, and some require mandatory quarantine upon arrival (Gössling et al., 2020). All tourism-associated services are likely to be bound to special regulations (such as requiring vaccination certificate and PCR testing); such requirements will probably become an unavoidable requirement for employees in the tourism sector (Sharfuddin, 2020).

After the prolonged quarantines, consumers of tourist services will be willing to resume their activities but will choose areas considered safe. The recommendations issued by developed countries on destinations will then play a key role. This can lead to negative consequences if this power is used with political intentions, if they turn it into an instrument of international politics as a way to obtain favors (Sharfuddin, 2020). This will favor destinations already associated with a natural flavor, not crowded and endowed with good health care systems, such as Australia (Wen et al., 2020). The cruise sub-industry will probably be the slowest to recover, since to resume operations, people will be required to be vaccinated or to present negative PCRs. The problem with PCRs is that people may be already incubating and transmitting the virus while their results remain negative (Gössling et al., 2020).

Not all types of tourism were equally affected. For example, Norway reported that the camping subsector was better spared than traditional accommodations, as they offer more space between people. This suggests that in the future people might change the way they choose destinations, and the degree to which those changes will be permanent is still to be determined (Gössling et al., 2020). The situation could favor typologies of tourism that were already experiencing growth, such as sustainable tourism (Hall et al., 2020), independent travel and health and wellness tourism (Baum et al., 2020), since many of these types tend to be practiced outdoors (Gössling et al., 2020). Transport also plays a role; people are likely to move away from crowded means of transportation so common in cities and opt for places with an alternative circulation plan, such as bicycles or even horseback riding (Wen et al., 2020).

From the point of view of industry, changes in the structure of companies are also expected. As SMEs were the companies facing the worst liquidity issues, large groups have engaged in buying small companies, so the sector could be restructuring (Khan et al., 2020). While there are many studies trying to predict what will happen to tourism, for example, in the wake of climate change, there has never been a study predicting how the tourism industry would react to an event of the magnitude of the current pandemic, so literature available is relatively scarce, albeit recent. The fact that the world has also previously gone through various pandemics and crises that affected the industry and that tourism never collapsed means that perhaps the current situation is not being given the importance that it warrants (Gössling et al., 2020). This crisis is also a good opportunity to restructure and make a shift towards more sustainable tourism (Gössling et al., 2020) as it is likely that two of the consequences will be moving away from seasonality to avoid crowds and putting an end to group travel (Wen et al., 2020).

New Post-COVID Regulations

From a political point of view, although each country passes its own legislation, tourism is expected to recover as it has always done after each crisis. As a result, all associated service sectors, such as airlines, hotels, and restaurants, are also expected to recover. However, there is enough evidence suggesting that certain changes are here to stay (Gössling et al., 2020). One of the measures most likely to be adopted by most countries will be the establishment of a new health and hygiene protocol in tourim facilities, to include, among others, vaccination certificates, reducing capacity and implementing social distancing measures in hotels, restaurants and airlines.

On the other hand, it is expected that visa schemes will be tightened, that migration services will begin to request vaccination certificates, medical certificates or even that will not allow entrance of people at risk, so that the most affected tourism would be that of the elderly (Sharfuddin, 2020). In fact, six countries -Bangladesh, Bhutan, Iran, Laos, Malay and Myanmar- that did not require a visa before the pandemic, require one now. Currently, many countries require confinements of around 14 days upon arrival and fine tourists who fail to abide the requirements (Sánchez, 2020).

Nationalisms could also be fostered, especially in developed countries that vaccinate faster (Gössling et al., 2020). Travel insurance covering COVID-19 assistance is likely to be required in near future, and this would benefit the travel-related health coverage sector (Wen et al., 2020). The pandemic could also deepen the gap between rich and poor countries, considering the disparity of resources each country can devote to handle it. The countries that will be safer are precisely those that assign more resources on vaccination and subsidies. Many developing countries where tourism was flourishing will be among those that suffer the most (Gössling et al., 2020).

Changes in Tourism Consumption During and After the Crisis

One of the main consequences of the COVID-19 pandemic is that consumers may continue to fear contagion (García, 2020). Hence, one of the most important changes expected in the sector is that they may opt for safe destinations. In terms of accommodation, this implies choosing certified places, or those that offer safety measures adapted to new normal. Large chains will be in better position, as they tend to have more spacious facilities and can afford the implementation of new protocols (Bauzá & Melgosa, 2020). Trends expected inside accommodation facilities include the reduction of contact with staff, both during check-in and check-out, and in room service. Companies that already have the necessary technology will find it easier to implement changes required. On the other hand, both restaurants and accommodation will need to adapt to trends to avoid buffet service (Cruz et al., 2021).

Many studies show that in times of uncertainty and crisis tourist flows do not disappear, but mutate and head towards rural areas, far from cities; therefore, rural tourism, adventure tourism and alternative tourism are typologies that are benefited in the COVID-19 context (Korstanje, 2020). By way of contrast, activities that are typical of cultural tourism, such as visits to museums, theaters or other closed or crowded places will be the most affected (Zumbana, 2021). In that regard, in China (the first country to address the aftermath of this pandemic), they found that as consumers began to regain confidence, they preferred ecological tourism products (Gössling et al., 2020).

According to a study conducted by Expedia Group, distances people are ride to travel may also vary, since only 22% of the tourists consulted expressed interest in traveling beyond 1,500 miles. When asked about means of transport they would use, most mentioned their own car (50%), followed by plane and then by rental car. In this same study, 87% of the tourists consulted stated that they would consider the health safety of the destination and 73% mentioned the tourist activities and attractions (Sánchez, 2021).

Another expected change refers to the flexibility of reservations, since, in the midst of a changing situation, people will not be willing to buy options that do not accept changes, even if that implies to pay more (Bauzá & Melgosa, 2020). These changes will obviously increase the costs for service providers, so one of the biggest questions is whether these increases will be passed on to consumers (and how much more the latter will be willing to pay) or whether the industry will bear the brunt losing profitability, whenever possible (Paisant, 2020).

Situation in Galicia, Spain

The first two cases of COVID-19 recorded in Galicia came from Madrid, and were detected in A Coruña and Vigo, on March 9, 2020. On March 10, while the Central Government prohibited the arrival of flights from Italy and events attended by over 1,000 people, suspended the IMSERSO program (tourism program for senior citizens and retirees) and decided that sports events should be held without any public, Galicia decided to limit visits to hospitals and long-term care facilities (La Voz de Galicia, 2021).

Two days after WHO declared pandemic on March 11, president of the government Pedro Sánchez, decreed the state of alarm in Spain, suspending all non-essential activities. One day earlier, the president of the Xunta de Galicia, Núñez Feijóo, had suspended education activities and closed bars and shops (La Voz de Galicia, 2021). Tourism is the main activity in Spain, and in Galicia in particular, mobility restrictions caused 44% of the companies in the sector to close, 8% permanently and 36% temporarily (Gómez et al., 2020).

On March 11, Galician Tourism Cluster prepared a report with actions to be implemented by the sector *vis à vis* the imminent crisis, also including responses to queries some companies had already begun to raise. The following day, a meeting was held with representatives of the tourism sector to decide future steps to overcome the looming crisis (Galician Tourism Cluster, 2021). On March 14, 2020, five days after the detection of the first two cases, Galicia recorded its first two COVID-19-related deaths. Both the 92-year-old woman in Vigo and the 81-year-old man in Pontevedra had comorbidities (La Voz de Galicia, 2021). The lady's family also tested positive for the virus. By the time there were 153 people infected in Galicia; 27 patients had been admitted to hospital and 7 to ICUs (La Voz de Galicia, 2020).

On June 21, 2020 with the end of the state of alarm, some actions were taken to prevent contagion on beaches. One case was the plots in Sanxenxo, where Silgar Beach was divided into 780 little plots with a total maximum capacity of 2,340 people (Faro de Vigo, 2020b). In A Coruña they implemented the traffic light system, whereby you may visit the website to check vacancies before you go to the beach (Cadena SER, 2020). Also, this day the Xunta decided to close A Mariña area due to an outbreak that affected more than 100 people (La Voz de Galicia, 2021).

One of the measures adopted included postponing the elections of the Galician Parliament, originally to be held on April 5 to elect President and 75 representatives of the XI legislature. Elections were finally held on July 12, with a new victory of the incumbent President Núñez Feijóo and an absolute majority of the Popular Party for the fourth time in a row (La Voz de Galicia, 2021). On August 7, 2020, as a result of an outbreak in a gym in Arteixo, where 17 new cases ensued the first detection, new restrictions were applied in A Coruña, as they decreed the closure of nightlife activities, including the prohibition of parties and festivals. On August 12 Galicia became the first autonomous community to ban smoking in the streets if the safety distance could not be ensured (La Voz de Galicia, 2021).

On September 12, schools were reopened owing to the Xunta's reluctance to delay the start of classes. The measures enforced were the mandatory use of masks and classroom ventilation. In addition, the Servizo Galego de Saúde (Sergas) carried out serology testing to all the staff of nursery schools and preemptive screenings to the rest of the staff (La Voz de Galicia, 2021). On October 8, the Xunta decided to confine Ourense, due to an increase in cases because of an outbreak in the city. The outbreak had begun in August and could not be curbed, leading to the prohibition of gatherings of non-cohabitants and trans-municipality mobility, keeping work-related activities as the sole exception. This confinement would last until November 24 (La Voz de Galicia, 2021).

On October 25, government declared a new state of alarm that would continue until May 2021 across the national territory, allowing each Autonomous Community to adopt the restrictive actions they deemed appropriate, such as curfews. The Xunta de Galicia decreed the closure of hostelry services and the perimeter confinement on November 7, and also establishing that gathering could only include people living in the same household in the high-incidence areas (La Voz de Galicia, 2021).

However, for Christmas, New Year and Epiphany, Galicia reduced some mobility restrictions, leading to the so-called "third wave", which peaked on January 23, with 1,889 positive cases recorded in 24 hours. Given this increase in cases and the fact that Galicia accumulated almost 20,000 positive cases at the time, the Xunta decided to tighten restrictions by closing the entire hostelry industry again, limiting business hours and decreeing municipal closures (La Voz de Galicia, 2021).

On March 26, 2021, the Galician Government started de-escalating the measures adopted for the third wave, allowing the reopening of the accommodation industry and recovering mobility (La Voz de Galicia, 2021). Vaccination in Galicia began on December 27, 2020 in long-term care facilities (La Voz de Galicia, 2021). As of May 2021, 100% of people over 80 and 94% of people between 70 and 79 years had already been vaccinated.

According to Galicia tourism website, the Xunta de Galicia has adopted several measures for the reactivation of tourism, both to encourage demand and to ensure health. On one hand, they launched the program "Galicia Destino Seguro" (secure destination) to raise confidence in the demand side. For the supply side, this program is based on four pillars:

- Information and manuals that include the hygiene and health protocols to be applied
- Training through free and certifiable courses
- Counselling
- Funding for companies to afford the implementation of the new health measures

Everything was geared to ensure a safe feeling among the tourists arriving in Galicia. On the other hand, Sergas opened a dedicated hotline to enable non-residents with assigned family doctor to receive care in the Community free of charges if they presented any COVID-19 symptoms. In addition, to ensure health safety, anyone coming from a high-incidence territory had to provide their data to the Galician health authorities within 24 hours of arrival, regardless of whether or not they presented any symptoms (Turismo de Galicia, 2021).

To reactivate tourism and the cultural sector, on April 30 the Xunta approved the voucher Quedamos En Galicia, a shared effort between the Public Administration and the Tourism Cluster to promote recovery. This aims to inject liquidity into companies in the sector, as well as to encourage consumption. Vouchers are prepaid cards that can be used to pay in any of the companies participating in the programme (Turismo de Galicia, 2021).

On May 18, addressing the audience at the Hotusa Explora Forum on tourism innovation held in Madrid, the president of the Xunta, Núñez Feijóo proposed to reduce the VAT applicable to the tourism sector to encourage consumption., In his view, this industry should now be a political and economic priority; he went on to add that safety is the most important thing that can be offered to tourists (Caínzos, 2021). Finally, from May 19 to May 23, at the International Tourism Fair (FITUR) held in Madrid, Galicia was presented as a safe destination from the point of view of health, a destination that targets a public that prioritizes safety and calm in their holidays. The Community's booth was the most active at the trade show (Xunta de Galicia, 2021).

Tourism Reactivation Plan in Galicia

Galicia exceeded 5.1 million visitors in 2019, being the autonomous community with the highest growth in Spain, with 6.2% more than the previous year. Total overnight stays last year were 11 million (INE, 2019), thus reaching one of the most positive data in its history. In addition, it represents around 10.4% of Galician GDP and 11% of employment in this community. 2019 was the year with the highest increase in hotel income, reaching almost 315 million euros. Likewise, Spain is the seventh community in arrival of international tourists, with more than 1.5 million.

For this reason, a strategy is necessary to reactivate the economy in this sector, once goverment allow mobility of individuals and reopening of establishments and businesses. Public administration itself, aware of the situation and needs of the sector, publishes on May 5, 2020 through the *Consellería de Cultura e Turismo da Xunta de Galicia* (2020) its post-COVID-19 reactivation plan for two key sectors: culture and tourism. This plan includes an investment of 27 million euros and about 50 measures for both sectors, with three main objectives:

- promote employment
- generate liquidity
- reactivate consumption

The document proposes 9 lines of action with an investment of 11 million for tourism and 10.6 million for the cultural sector, in addition to 5.1 million for cross-cutting measures included in the *Xacobeo 2021*. 4 of these areas are focused on the tourism sector, including a total of 24 measures.

- Actions to promote Galicia in order to reactivate demand
- Creation of new tourism products
- Support for the business and maintenance of tourism employment
- Training, competitiveness and innovation

A priori it is observed that these axes are of help to reactivate the tourism activity after this circumstantial stop, but they should serve as a starting point to continue working on a tourism strategy in this community for medium and long term. An example of this are measures linked to training in the sector or creation of new products.

METHODOLOGY

The main objective of this work is to determine whether any changes brought about by the pandemic in the tourism sector of Galicia will remain over time. The secondary objectives are listed below:

- Determine the changes perceived from the side of the supply (means that on this occasion only the supply was taken into account to carry out the investigation, the research on demand has not been carried out), and whether they will become permanent
- Determine the changes expected in the behavior of tourism consumers
- Determine if the pandemic has caused any changes in the typologies of tourism picked.
- Determine whether fear of the pandemic has led to the demand for new products or services.

To respond to this objective, it has been chosen a qualitative research via in-depth interviews. These interviews have been semi-structured, that is, they are based on a script of questions on the objectives set, but the interviewees are allowed some leeway to add any comments they consider relevant. The rationale for choosing the method was that it allows to collect information of interest for the research and to direct the interview so as to meet the objectives of the study. As it is interactive, the method allows for explanations or probes that may be relevant for the purposes of the research (Ortega, 2020).

The research included five stages:

1. Search in secondary sources to gather information potentially relevant to this research already published by other people or government agencies. The objective at this stage was to consider facts or phenomena that could affect the hypothesis and that had already been examined in previous research. This stage was also important for the correct design of the guidelines for the interviews.
2. Setting the objectives.
3. Development of the guidelines to ensure that the in-depth interviews would meet the preset objectives.
4. Implementation of the interviews. Collection and transcription of data for the final assessment.

5. Presentation of the results and conclusions.

A total of 11 interviews were conducted from May 2 to May 13, 2021, involving managers of accommodation facilities and restaurants in the tourism sector of the four provinces of Galicia, Spain, seeking results representative of the entire Galician territory. Since the number of interviewees is small, this chapter results on being a first approach to the subject.

The interview consisted of 14 questions structured in 4 blocks:

- The first block is aimed at determining the changes perceived by the supply side and whether these will become permanent (questions 1 to 5).
- The second block probes on the expected changes in consumer behavior (questions 6 to 10).
- The third block responds specifically to the changes in the chosen types of tourism (questions 11 and 12).
- The fourth block addresses the fears that may persist in the wake of the pandemic (questions 13 and 14).

RESULTS

Changes in the Supply Side

Regarding the determination of the changes in the supply side and which of these would become permanent, the survey first inquired about the changes that had already taken place. All the interviewees stated that the only changes implemented in their facilities were those related to the incorporation of legally binding sanitary measures. They had to develop cleaning and disinfection protocols, install hydroalcoholic gel dispensers, control the maintenance of interpersonal distances and buy and install CO2 meters (Xunta de Galicia requirement for restaurants).

As to the management of the facilities, they reported that they had been forced to lower their rates, and that this had resulted in the lay off of staff. According to the interviews, the most affected places are the largest ones, as their cost structure is difficult to sustain when revenues decline; also receiving a greater number of customers hinders compliance with social distancing protocols. In this regard, the interviewee I1 stated that: "This has affected the big hotels more: although our turnover has dropped and we have fewer bookings, 50% less, having few rooms helps you resist better; as our business is a rural country house, it is small".

Table 1. Tourism experts interviewed in Galicia (Spain)

Code	Position	Company	Type of business	Province
I1	Owner	Casa das Capelas	Country house	Ourense
I2	Manager	Irixo	Hotel	Ourense
I3	Manager	Latino	Bar	Ourense
I4	Owner	Casa Currás	Restaurant	Pontevedra
I5	Owner	Caracas	Hostel	Pontevedra
I6	Manager	Naval do Espiño	Hotel	Pontevedra
I7	Manager	Mobydick2	Hostel	Ourense
I8	Owner	Verve	Hostel	Lugo
I9	Owner	ALÓ	Snack bar	Lugo
I10	Manager	A casa da Viña	Restaurant	A Coruña
I11	Owner	Oxford Suites	Hostel	A Coruña

Among the potentially permanent changes, hotel managers mention cleaning, since much progress was made in the implementation of protocols and products, and it would not make sense for the health authority to reverse that. Although from the point of view of supply they think that everything will return to normal, they notice that people have become accustomed to the use of hydroalcoholic gel and mask, so they intend to keep at least the hydroalcoholic gel dispensers, even if they cease to be a legal requirement.

In relation to whether the establishments will offer other assurances or guarantees, the answers indicate that they will only offer what is strictly required by law. Facilities had to adopt different rules to facilitate the coexistence between guests or diners, transmitted through various communiqués that specify the regulations followed by the venue and how the customers should act. For example, in the case of hotels, when the guests are not in the room, they must leave the windows open; in the case of restaurants, diners must keep their masks on when not eating or drinking.

With regard to changes in announcements to promote services, the only reference is to the communication of compliance with the regulations imposed and the existence of cleaning and disinfection protocols. Finally, and consistently with the belief that there will be no long-term changes in the supply side, none of the interviewees consider offering new services, not even the facilities that declare losing reservations due to their lack of certain services, such as food service.

Changes in demand

The second objective of this work is to respond to changes in demand, and to define which of these are expected to remain permanently. As for this point, the interviewees have replied that not being able to go on vacation, people go out more to restaurants and bars. In that regard, I11 said: "more people come to the bar downstairs, because as they can't travel, they just go out." They also order food and/or beverages to be served outdoors and opt for large venues with good ventilation.

Hotel and hostel managers believe that many tourists seek accommodation with food service so as not to have to leave the facilities; they also notice a greater influx of customers from nearby areas but consider that this is only due to restrictions on mobility. They also say that there has been a change in the type of guests, as before the pandemic they were mostly tourists and now they are mainly workers. Another change perceived in this sector is that most of the guests ask the staff not to engage in any cleaning tasks in the room during their stay.

Facility managers also state that people request individual rooms with private bathrooms. Whereas in the past it was frequent to see groups of two or three people staying in the same room, today these groups ask for separate rooms. Hence, hostels or inns with shared rooms are not in high demand. Pilgrims are currently being received in guesthouses, when traditionally they tended to stay at inns. Both in restaurants and accommodations, interviewees notice that people now choose quiet, more secluded places. They also state that there are no families; you do not see many groups with children or elderly people. In both cases they notice that as the clients enter the facilities, they pay attention to the signage and the first thing they do is pour some hydroalcoholic gel on.

However, despite all the changes mentioned, considering the rollout of vaccination and its evolution in other countries, they hope that things will soon return to normal. Interviewees understand that some habits incorporated in these times are here to stay, including making hydroalcoholic gel available, or going out to the restaurants earlier. They also share the perception that overall, the pandemic has made people more eager to travel, so they hope that as soon as the restrictions on mobility are lifted the sector will recover quickly. None of the people interviewed believe that there will be a change in the way people choose transportation, accommodation or even hostelry in the long term, nor that services that were not considered prior to the pandemic. They do notice that nowadays people use contactless cards more and in the case of accommodations they have also increased the use of bank transfers.

Types of tourism

The third objective of this study was to answer whether there will be changes in the type of tourism customers will choose. They answered they did not expect any changes, interviewees even comment they perceive people have an increased desire to go out and travel. However, they do understand that there have been changes in the choice of destinations, as people consider factors such as local infection rates, and pick places that include food services, are safe and not crowded.

It is to be noted that this part elicited the only comment of political nature. Interviewee I3 said: "It is a delicate matter; do you know why? Because it depends on politics, and political management is nefarious. Look, Ourense could be a top-level city and enjoy (even international) tourism year-round, because we have many thermal water sources that are being underutilized. If they invested in a good infrastructure... Unless there is work for the young, no other kind of business flourishes and tourism has no future." He was the only interviewee who held the authorities accountable for changes or possible changes in the type of tourism.

Fears

Regarding the fears that will persist once COVID-19 pandemic is over, small accommodation facilities are expected to recover before large hotels, since the latter involve contact and interaction with more people, so customers will be more reluctant to choose this type of sites. It is expected that people will continue to worry about abiding by the rules and in particular those related to cleanliness, because, at this point, it is very difficult to go back once they got accustomed. In the case of restaurants, requesting tables outdoors, which has already become customary, is likely to persist as a trend. In that regard, no interviewee expressed any customer concerns about contracting medical coverage through travel insurance.

Although no fear is perceived in general, Interviewee I5 believes that the family customers have diminished: "We see a lot of fear, especially among families; we are not seeing family trips; the only people that continue to travel are those that do it alone", although as Interviewee I7 put it, they expected things to change as vaccination progresses. "As vaccination progresses, I think everything is going to normal." We highlight the comment of Interviewee I2, who stated: "... If they make a reservation, they ask you not to charge them the booking, because of the COVID issue. That did not use to happen. You used to have 48 hours to pay". We now perceive that even if people are determined to make a trip, they are afraid the authorities may impose new measures restricting mobility.

DISCUSSION AND CONCLUSION

Based on the theoretical review, the first conclusion we can draw is that, although tourism has been affected many times, whether by pandemics, economic crises or even acts of terrorism, it is an industry that has always recovered quickly and to date it has always returned to its point of departure. None of the situations that occurred in the past caused any structural changes in the industry. Although as a result of the COVID-19 pandemic some changes are to be expected in the sector, such as the trend towards more natural and less crowded destinations, the service providers indicated that most people are concerned about the situation, but that this concern is due to compliance with and respect for the rules, and they are not driven out of fear of the disease, which would indicate that there will be no change in the consumption patterns in the long term.

The tourism sector is already fully aware of the consequences that this will have in the immediate future. In medium and long term, tourism companies wonder if the consumption habits of tourists will vary from what they were until now. Will tourists still want to travel? How Many? Under what conditions? Outside their countries? There are many unknowns that arise at this time without certain answers for now.

Companies are beginning to react and adapt to the situation, as well as planning reactivation. Faced with these expectations, companies in the sector must plan their strategy of action to attract tourists again hoping to reestablish their usual levels of occupation and income generation. The economy is not expected to recover this year 2021, but certain behaviors that may favor this sector are expected. The country would begin the stabilization phase in June, reopening gradually different activities. Here it is believed that one of the most benefited sectors would be catering and leisure, since individuals would try to forget about confinement. However, the rest of the subsectors of the tourism industry are expected to have a somewhat slower recovery. Individuals will have lost some confidence, especially after all the information received during the pandemic, such as that of tourists trapped in other countries. It is believed that, in this first phase of reopening, both flights and other tourist activities will be domestic and local. With this information, tourism companies should prepare for the first phase of attracting tourists, that is, domestic and local tourism.

In contrast to what Gössling et al. (2020) state in their work, the interviewees affirm that they do not expect any changes in the long term, although they do recognize that demand is likely to bring about some changes in the short term. On one hand those changes would be behavioral, such as going out earlier, and on the other, there will be changes in decision-making, such as evaluating that the accommodation facilities offer food service, or the rate of contagion at destination.

However, in this regard, none of the interviewees suggest making any changes, not even when announcing their services.

Although the interviewees believe that there will be no long-term changes, it is possible that some of the behaviors currently adopted - such as the preference for being able to keep more distance or the choice of accommodation with specific conditions - can persist over time, and service providers may be resisting the changes on a permanent basis. In addition, the previous health crises (SARS, MERS) do not serve as a precedent according to the interviewees, since in Galicia they have not had an impact.

It is to note that the present work focused on the supply side, and has only included facilities that continued to operate during the pandemic, that is, those that have really been able to cope with the situation. These aspects limit the scope of the conclusions. The study should be complemented by evaluating the issue from the point of view of demand and including supply actors who had to close their businesses as a result of the pandemic, either temporarily or permanently, which account for 44% of the facilities that were operational when the initial restrictions were enforced.

It is striking to see that guests shifted from shared rooms to private rooms, as people are no longer willing to share rooms. Interviewees notice this change, but fail to recognize it as permanent. The question is whether one of the possible long-term effects of the pandemic would be the end of room-sharing and even group travels. If a change of this nature is confirmed, and it is not accompanied by a reconversion of the facilities that offer shared rooms, they may risk going out of business.

The responses of the empirical part of the study also show that from the supply side, no structural change was made to adapt to the various changes perceived in the demand. They also show that service suppliers are not willing to make changes. This attitude is consistent with the interviewees' thinking that there will be no long-term changes. Somehow the service providers are managing to resist without changing their services and with the minimum adaptations required by governments. Whether with savings, subsidies, etc. or small internal reorganizations, they have been able to cover their budgets so far. However, the industry had to invest on equipment like CO_2 meters or hydroalcoholic gel dispensers. On the other hand, some changes on demand's behavior, such as requests that no cleanings be carried out in the rooms during guests' stay, have favored the cost structure of the accommodations, as human capital can be restructured. Yet, these changes are minimal and not structural.

Although not included as an objective in this study, the research answered Paisant's question (2020) about whether the costs that companies must assume will be transferred to the supply side. In that regard, the conclusion is that the drop in demand produced a dual negative effect on the companies' revenues. On one hand, it reduced the quantities sold, and on the other it caused the prices to drop, and both effects had a negative impact on yields. Unable to transfer the increased costs to demand, the toll for the decrease in profitability caused by both factors has fallen fully upon the supply.

The perception is that the sector is rather passively in the question of changes; it does not seem that changes will take place in the type of supply and in the way services are provided in Galicia, even in the absence of dramatic situations like the current pandemic. For example, even when declared that guests prefer accommodations that offer food service, places that do not offer this service are not planning to incorporate it. Having detected that resistance, the potential changes in the sector are reduced to those that could stem from the incorporation of new technologies or new investors coming from abroad with new ways of developing the industry.

The main consequences in the sector are suffered by the destinations where tourism has a greater weight in the GDP. In the case of Galicia and Spain in general, the weight of this sector in GDP (10.4% and 12% respectively) merits the existence of government guidelines that promote the industry, not only to ensure its development, but because the way the country is seen abroad depends highly on tourism, among other factors. The interviewees do not mention the absence of foreign tourists, even though this category represents almost one third of the tourists received by the Community.

Considering that people perceive that there is currently a growing interest in remote places and that people balance the health risks of destination, this is the time when Galicia should seize an opportunity for improvement. The typologies of tourism found in the Community (rural, adventure, alternative, etc.) offer a differential that should be leveraged. Right now, the efforts of the authorities and the supply side should be channeled into promoting Galicia as a safe destination that provides a solution to the current demand.

The agency responsible of tourism (Xunta de Galicia) is implementing actions in this regard. However, the supply is waiting to return to normal, ignoring that the product of this industry is a perishable good. If they achieve high levels of occupancy, even 100%, they will never make up the profits lost in this long period. Whether opportunities are seized or not is something that will be seen in the future, and could be the subject for further studies.

Focusing on the supply, after the interviews carried out, the following trends can be extracted from the demand, to which the offer must adapt. First of all, they continue to be present on the internet for the duration of the pandemic, but they should be thinking about what measures to apply as soon as it ends. To do this, they must follow the following behavioral guidelines:

- Internal tourism. As we already have mention, it is believed that individuals will remain in their countries after confinement. In Spain there is a general trend to travel within the country; only 10% of the country's population travel abroad (INE, 2019). So in the short term this trend is expected to consolidate. Even with local trips/tours, without staying far from residence. Travel with your own vehicle with or without overnight stay (staycations). The most affected destinations will be those that relied heavily on foreign tourism (mainly China and the United States), and it is precisely where the highest spending was made in the past.
- Cleaning image. This will be one of the keys after this quarantine. The tourist must perceive cleanliness and hygiene in the face of the alarm generated, greater than that perceived before this pandemic, thus feeling greater confidence. This will affect bars, restaurants, hotels, tourist apartments, transport, etc. and especially the customer service staff.
- Avoiding crowds. As long as tourists do not regain confidence, it will be difficult for them to attend concerts, fairs, theme parks, etc. and any other meeting with large number of attendees.
- Rural tourism. Given the chaos experienced in weeks after reopening in some cities, where more people are concentrated and the transmission of the virus has been greater, it is expected that individuals as soon as they can leave will move to rural and less populated areas. It will be the opportunity for inland and rural tourism.
- Private transport. In line with what was said in the first point, it is expected that individuals avoid public transport as well as crowds, resorting to their own vehicle or motorhomes for their trips.
- Price drop. An immediate measure that tourism companies will use to attract tourists will be offers and price reductions, as some companies have already done so far. Even so, experts advise that the descents should not be excessive, since tourist can get used to new prices and later the rise would be perceived as excessive.

Finally, future research will make it possible to remedy one of the limitations of this study, i.e., the number of interviews conducted. As a future line of research, the idea is to conduct a new post-pandemic analysis. The aim is to expand the number of interviews, so as get the feedback of a greater number of experts, as well as to check whether the results obtained after the pandemic are consistent with those reported in this study, collected at a time when the pandemic and certain restrictions are still in force.

REFERENCES

Baum, T., Mooney, S. K. K., Robinson, R. N. S., & Solnet, D. (2020). COVID-19's impact on the hospitality workforce – new crisis or amplification of the norm? *International Journal of Contemporary Hospitality Management, 32*(9), 2813–2829. doi:10.1108/IJCHM-04-2020-0314

Bauzá, F. J., & Melgosa, F. J. (2020, diciembre). *Turismo Post Covid-19*. Ediciones Universidad Salamanca. Available at https://www.eusal.es/index.php/eusal/catalog/view/978-84-1311-461-3/5558/6275-1

Bo, H. X., Li, W., Yang, Y., Wang, Y., Zhang, Q., Cheung, T., & Xiang, Y. T. (2020). Posttraumatic stress symptoms and attitude toward crisis mental health services among clinically stable patients with COVID-19 in China. *Psychological Medicine*, 1–2. PMID:32216863

Cadena Ser. (2020). *Habilitada la web que señala el nivel de ocupación en las playas coruñesas.* Available at https://cadenaser.com/emisora/2020/06/13/radio_coruna/1592068461_323879.html

Caínzos, Í. (2021). *Feijóo reclama que el turismo sea una prioridad política y económica.* Available at https://www.elcorreogallego.es/galicia/feijoo-reclama-que-el-turismo-sea-una-prioridad-politica-y-economica-JX7707795

Canalis, X. (2015). *El virus MERS pone en alerta a la industria turística de Asia. Hosteltur.* Available at https://www.hosteltur.com/111483_virus-mers-pone-alerta-industria-turistica-asia.html

Clúster de Turismo de Galicia. (n.d.). *CORONAVIRUS. Cronología actuaciones del Clúster Turismo de Galicia.* Available at https://clusterturismogalicia.com/gl/coronavirus-cronologia-ctg/

CNN. (2020). *What will travel look like after coronavirus?* Available on https://www.cnn.com/travel/article/coronavirus-travel-industry-changes/index.html

Consellería de Cultura e Turismo da Xunta de Galicia (2020). *Plan de reactivación dos sectores cultural e turístico fronte aos efectos derivados do COVID-10.* Author.

Cruz Torres, L., González Rodríguez, O., Placeres Hernández, J. F., & Martínez Abreu, J. (2021). La Covid-19 y los nuevos paradigmas para la gestión del turismo en la región Matanzas. *Revista Médica Electrónica, 43*(1), 2997–3002.

Deci, E. L., & Ryan, R. M. (2000). The" what" and" why" of goal pursuits: Human needs and the self-determination of behavior. *Psychological Inquiry, 11*(4), 227–268. doi:10.1207/S15327965PLI1104_01

Díaz, A. (2021). *Impacto del coronavirus en el turismo en España – Datos estadísticos*. Statista. Available at https://es.statista.com/temas/6510/impacto-del-coronavirus-en-el-sector-turistico-en-espana/#dossierSummary__chapter1

Dodds, R., & Richard, B. (2019). *Overtourism: Issues, realities and solutions* (Vol. 1). Walter de Gruyter GmbH & Co KG. doi:10.1515/9783110607369

Expansión. (2020). *El turismo restará un 4% al PIB regional*. Available at https://www.expansion.com/galicia/2020/04/21/5e9ee102468aeb79548b45c6.html

Faro de Vigo. (2020a). *Galicia bate récords históricos en turistas*. Available at https://www.farodevigo.es/galicia/2020/02/04/galicia-bate-records-historicos-turistas-15353202.html#:%7E:text=En%202019%20visitaron%20Galicia%201,con%20respecto%20al%20a%C3%B1o%20anterior

Faro de Vigo. (2020b). *Plan desescalada: Sanxenxo dividirá la playa de Silgar en 780 cuadrículas con un aforo de hasta 2.340 personas*. Available at https://www.farodevigo.es/pontevedra/2020/05/06/sanxenxo-dividira-playa-silgar-780-14782975.html

García Gaibor, J. A. (2020). *Análisis de la intención del comportamiento de los consumidores turístico de parques acuáticos post covid-19 del cantón Montalvo* (Bachelor's thesis). UTB.

Gómez Varela, J. F., Río-Rodríguez, D., & Rico-Díaz, J. (2020). Reactivación de las actividades del turismo activo español hacia la "nueva normalidad" de la COVID-19: Análisis documental sobre su regulación, recomendaciones, propuestas y protocolos. *ROTUR. Revista de Ocio y Turismo*, *14*(2), 1–22. doi:10.17979/rotur.2020.14.2.6583

Gössling, S., Scott, D., & Hall, C. M. (2020). Pandemics, tourism and global change: A rapid assessment of COVID-19. *Journal of Sustainable Tourism*, *29*(1), 1–20. doi:10.1080/09669582.2020.1758708

Hall, C. M., Scott, D., & Gössling, S. (2020). Pandemics, transformations and tourism: Be careful what you wish for. *Tourism Geographies*, *22*(3), 577–598. doi:10.1080/14616688.2020.1759131

Holmes, M., Alonzi, S., Perry, L. M., Voss, H. M., Easwar, S., & Gerhart, J. I. (2020). Impact of the COVID-19 pandemic on mental health: Real-time surveillance using Google Trends. *Psychological Trauma: Theory, Research, Practice, and Policy*, *12*(6), 567–568. doi:10.1037/tra0000872 PMID:32790441

Huertas, A., Oliveira, A., & Girotto, M. (2020). Gestión comunicativa de crisis de las oficinas nacionales de turismo de España e Italia ante la Covid-19. *El Profesional de la Información, 29*(4), e290410. doi:10.3145/epi.2020.jul.10

Khan, I., Haleem, A., & Javaid, M. (2020). Analysing COVID-19 pandemic through cases, deaths, and recoveries. *Journal of Oral Biology and Craniofacial Research, 10*(4), 450–469. doi:10.1016/j.jobcr.2020.08.003 PMID:32834980

Korstanje, M. E. (2020). El COVID-19 y El turismo rural: una perspectiva antropológica. *Dimensiones Turísticas, 4*, 179-196.

La Vanguardia. (2020). *El turismo posvirus seguirá nuevas normas de salud.* Available at https://www.lavanguardia.com/economia/20200408/48384693297/turismo-posvirus-coronavirus-catalunya.html

La Voz de Galicia. (2020). *Los dos primeros muertos en Galicia por coronavirus, de 92 y 81 años.* Available at https://www.lavozdegalicia.es/noticia/sociedad/2020/03/15/dos-primeros-muertos-galicia-92-81-anos/0003_202003G15P6992.htm

La Voz de Galicia. (2021). *Cronología de un año de coronavirus en España.* Available at https://www.lavozdegalicia.es/noticia/especiales/aniversario-pandemia/2021/03/05/cronologia-ano-coronavirus-espana/00031614956653588579113.htm

Ma, S., Kim, D. D., Cohen, J. T., & Neumann, P. J. (2020). Measuring "Fearonomic effects" in valuing therapies: An application to COVID-19 in china. *Value in Health, 23*(11), 1405–1408. doi:10.1016/j.jval.2020.06.002 PMID:33127009

Mesa, R. (2020). *Las consecuencias del coronavirus en el sector del Turismo.* Available at https://blogs.imf-formacion.com/blog/mba/consecuencias-coronavirus-en-sector-turismo/

Mooney, H., & Zegarra, M. A. (2020). *COVID-19: shock sin precedentes sobre el turismo en América Latina y el Caribe.* Publications Inter-American Development Bank. Available at https://publications.iadb.org/publications/spanish/document/COVID-19-Shock-sin-precedentes-sobre-el-turismo-en-America-Latina-y-el-Caribe.pdf

Ortega, C. (2020). *¿Qué es una entrevista estructurada, semiestructurada y no estructurada?* QuestionPro. Disponible online: https://www.questionpro.com/blog/es/entrevista-estucturada-y-no-estructurada/

Ortega, J. L. (2021). *Ingresos por turismo en España: la foto del hundimiento.* Hosteltur. Available at https://www.hosteltur.com/143168_ingresos-por-turismo-en-espana-la-foto-del-hundimiento.html

Paisant, G. (2020). El Covid-19 y la situación jurídica de los consumidores: una mirada desde Francia. *Revista de Direito do Consumidor*, 17-26.

Parady, G., Taniguchi, A., & Takami, K. (2020). Travel behavior changes during the COVID-19 pandemic in Japan: Analyzing the effects of risk perception and social influence on going-out self-restriction. *Transportation Research Interdisciplinary Perspectives*, *7*, 100181. doi:10.1016/j.trip.2020.100181

Pérez Abreu, M. R., Gómez Tejeda, J. J., & Dieguez Guach, R. A. (2020). Características clínico-epidemiológicas de la COVID-19. *Revista Habanera de Ciencias Médicas*, *19*(2).

Qiu, R. T., Park, J., Li, S., & Song, H. (2020). Social costs of tourism during the COVID-19 pandemic. *Annals of Tourism Research*, *84*, 102994. doi:10.1016/j.annals.2020.102994 PMID:32834228

Rodríguez de Luis, E. (2021). *Medidores de CO2: cómo funcionan, cómo se relacionan con la prevención de la expansión del COVID-19 y recomendaciones de compra.* Xataka. Available at https://www.xataka.com/seleccion/medidores-co2-como-funcionan-como-se-relacionan-prevencion-expansion-covid-19-recomendaciones-compra

Rogers, R. W. (1975). A protection motivation theory of fear appeals and attitude change1. *The Journal of Psychology*, *91*(1), 93–114. doi:10.1080/00223980.1975.9915803 PMID:28136248

Sánchez, E. B. (2021). (in press). Impacto de la Covid-19 en el turismo internacional. Implicaciones para el modelo turístico cubano. *Revista Temas*.

Sánchez, M. M. (2020). Flujos turísticos, geopolítica y COVID-19: Cuando los turistas internacionales son vectores de transmisión. *Geopolítica*, *11*(2), 105–114. doi:10.5209/geop.69249

Seligman, M. E. P. (2011). *Flourish: A visionary new understanding of happiness and well-being*. Free Press.

Sharfuddin, S. (2020). The world after covid-19. *Round Table (London)*, *109*(3), 247–257. doi:10.1080/00358533.2020.1760498

Turespaña. (2021). *Razones para recorrer el Camino de Santiago durante el Xacobeo 2021 - 2022.* Spain.info. https://www.spain.info/es/descubrir-espana/xacobeo-camino-santiago/

Turismo de Galicia. (2021). *Galicia destino seguro*. Available at https://www.turismo.gal/galiciadestinoseguro/portada?langId=es_ES

Wen, J., Kozak, M., Yang, S., & Liu, F. (2020). COVID-19: Potential effects on Chinese citizens' lifestyle and travel. *Tourism Review*. doi:10.1108/TR-03-2020-0110

Williams, C. C., & Kayaoglu, A. (2020). COVID-19 and undeclared work: Impacts and policy responses in Europe. *Service Industries Journal*, *40*(13-14), 914–931. doi:10.1080/02642069.2020.1757073

Wise, T., Zbozinek, T. D., Michelini, G., & Hagan, C. C. (2020). *Changes in risk perception and protective behavior during the first week of the COVID-19 pandemic in the United States*. Academic Press.

Xunta de Galicia. (2021). *El stand de Galicia registra el mayor número de actividades en Fitur y despierta el interés de los operadores presentes en la feria*. Available at https://www.xunta.gal/notas-de-prensa/-/nova/58279/stand-galicia-registra-mayor-numero-actividades-fitur-despierta-interes-los-operadores?langId=es_ES

Zaka, A., Shamloo, S. E., Fiorente, P., & Tafuri, A. (2020). *COVID-19 pandemic as a watershed moment: A call for systematic psychological health care for frontline medical staff*. Academic Press.

Zhou, J., Liu, L., Xue, P., Yang, X., & Tang, X. (2020). Mental health response to the COVID-19 outbreak in China. *The American Journal of Psychiatry*, *177*(7), 574–575. doi:10.1176/appi.ajp.2020.20030304 PMID:32375540

Zumbana Santamaria, J. A. (2021). *El marketing digital para la reactivación del turismo cultural durante el covid 19* (Bachelor's thesis). Universidad Técnica de Ambato-Facultad de Ciencias Humanas y de la Educación-Carrera de Turismo y Hotelería.

ADDITIONAL READING

Baum, T., & Hai, N. T. T. (2020). Hospitality, tourism, human rights and the impact of COVID-19. *International Journal of Contemporary Hospitality Management*.

Gretzel, U., Fuchs, M., Baggio, R., Hoepken, W., Law, R., Neidhardt, J., Pesonen, J., Zanker, M., & Xiang, Z. (2020). e-Tourism beyond COVID-19: A call for transformative research. *Information Technology & Tourism*, *22*(2), 187–203. doi:10.100740558-020-00181-3

Qiu, R. T., Park, J., Li, S., & Song, H. (2020). Social costs of tourism during the COVID-19 pandemic. *Annals of Tourism Research*, *84*, 102994. doi:10.1016/j.annals.2020.102994 PMID:32834228

Sigala, M. (2020). Tourism and COVID-19: Impact and implications for advancing and resetting industry and research. *Journal of Business Research*, *117*, 312–321. doi:10.1016/j.jbusres.2020.06.015 PMID:32546875

KEY TERMS AND DEFINITIONS

CO2 Meters: Carbon dioxide meter. Device used to check air quality (Rodríguez de Luis, 2021).

Epidemic: Disease that spreads for some time in a country, simultaneously affecting large numbers of people (Royal Spanish Academy, 2014).

IMSERSO: Institute for the elderly and social services. As one of the agencies that manage social security in Spain, IMSERSO is responsible for the complementary services provided to social security beneficiaries, including social tourism, holiday travels for the elderly, social thermalism or the stay of elderly people in spas (Institute of The Elderly and Social Services).

Pandemic: Epidemic disease that spreads to many countries or that attacks almost all individuals in a locality or region (Royal Spanish Academy, 2014).

PCR: Acronym for "Polymerase Chain Reaction". Diagnostic test that allows to detect a fragment of the genetic material of a pathogen or organism (Ministry of Health, Consumption and Social Welfare).

Xacobeo 2021: The Xacobeo, also known as the Jacobean Year, Holy Year or Jubilee Year, is celebrated when the feast of the Apostle Santiago on July 25 falls on a Sunday (TurEspaña, 2021).

Chapter 9
Innovations in Agriculture and Tourism for Tanzania's Workforce Beyond the COVID-19 Pandemic

Nyanjige Mbembela Mayala
Mwenge Catholic University, Tanzania

Ambrose Karoli Tesha
Mwenge Catholic University, Tanzania

ABSTRACT

The COVD-19 pandemic has affected most sectors of the economy around the world leaving men and women unemployed, which has necessitated the need for carrier innovations. In Tanzania, agriculture and tourism are among the very important sectors of the economy and biggest contributors to gross domestic product (GDP). Beyond the pandemic, there are opportunities to capitalize through career innovations. Findings indicate that urban agriculture, genetics editing in livestock, bees and drones, and blockchain technologies can significantly improve the agricultural sector. Market research, diversification, up-skilling, responsible tourism, new hygiene standards, and encouraging business travel will enhance the tourism sector moving forward. It is recommended that balance for innovation and development, investing in strategic collaborations, moving from single point-based interventions, and focusing on the poor in innovations are important.

DOI: 10.4018/978-1-7998-8626-6.ch009

1. INTRODUCTION

Innovation is increasingly essential for an effective response to and recovery from the COVID-19 pandemic in low and middle-income settings that are the target of official development assistance (ODA) investments. Currently, it has been more than a year since the World Health Organization (WHO) declared COVID-19 a pandemic (WHO, 2020). Hundreds of millions of people have lived through lockdowns. Many have made the abrupt shift to working from home; millions have lost jobs. The future looks uncertain. Most people around the world don't know when, or if, societies might return to normal or what kind of scars the pandemic will leave.

Amid the upheaval, employers, the labour market and graduates are talking about work-life to dozens of experts, leaders and professionals across the globe to ask: what are the greatest unknowns will they face? How will they work, live and thrive in the post-pandemic future? How is Covid-19 reshaping the world and if it is potentially forever (BBC, 2021). Looking around the issue of work in context specific, how the pandemic has normalized remote work, and what that might mean. Will people go to the offices normally again around the world and, if so, how often? What impact will a 'hybrid' way of working have on how people communicate, connect and create employments? Will work-from-home be the great leveler in terms of gender equality and diversity? What will work mean if offices are virtual and lose those day-to-day social interactions? Questions are also on what will happen to people who can't work from home as well as those whose jobs depend on a steady flow of traffic into urban hubs. Can the world learn from COVID-19 and build better safety nets for the most vulnerable workers? If the future is digital, how to make sure swathes of the global population aren't left behind especially in the developing economies (Mayala, 2021)? The whole world by now know that work will never be the same in most parts, even if people doesn't yet know all the ways in which it will be different.

The aim of this chapter is to contribute to an understanding of how Tanzania has been affected by the pandemic even though there were no total lockdowns for the country. Knowing the effects alone however is not complete in itself, but what are the relevant innovations and steps that need to be taken afterwards is important. A literature review and statistics from UNDP (2020) on the short, medium and long term effects in the key sectors of the economy are used to analyse innovations required in the agriculture and tourism sectors.

2. BACKGROUND

2.1 Agriculture

Agriculture is undoubtedly the largest and most important sector of the Tanzanian economy, with the country benefitting from a diverse production base that includes livestock, staple food crops and a variety of cash crops (FAO, 2020). The sector's contribution to GDP has more than tripled in the last 10 years, supported by rising cash crop production, an emerging agro-processing segment and strong domestic demand for processed food *(ibid)*. At the same time, farmers and other sector stakeholders face considerable challenges in modernising the industry to increase yields, exports and value-added processing. Slowing export revenues; land acquisition hurdles; and smallholder farmers struggling to access economically viable technology, adequate storage facilities, markets and credit have affected private investment (UNDP, 2020).

Agriculture accounts for 26.7 percent of Tanzania's GDP and provides employment for majority of the nation's population (URT, 2019). Opportunities exist for agriculture businesses across domestic, regional and international markets, for both traditional and new products. However, productivity is low with modest progress over the past two decades. It is dominated by smallholder farmers dependent on rain-fed production, limited use of improved seeds and fertilizers, and the low share of cultivated over arable land (UNDP, 2020).

Tanzania is also richly endowed with forest resources which cover 48.1 million hectares which is an equivalent of 55 percent of the total surface land area of Tanzania Mainland including woodlands, catchment forests, mangroves, coastal forests and government forest plantations (Mwaseba et al, 2020; Blomely, 2017). However, deforestation rate is high due to demand for firewood as a major source of energy in the majority of households, clearance of land for farming and industrial purposes etc. For instance, between 1990 and 2015 Tanzania lost an average of 17 percent of its forests a situation that is alarming (UNDP, 2020; FAO, 2020).

In the livestock sector, Tanzania has the third largest livestock population in Africa comprising 25 million cattle, 98 percent of which are indigenous breeds, complemented by 16.7 million goats, 8 million sheep, 2.4 million pigs, and 36 million chickens (Mayala et al, 2017). The country also has outstanding natural resources for livestock development including resilient livestock breeds, extensive rangelands and diverse natural vegetation. Despite these resources, the livestock sector is performing well below its potential (FAO, 2018). The sector contributes 7.4 percent to the country's GDP and the annual growth rate of the sector is low at 2.2 percent *(ibid)*. The sector is severely constrained by low livestock reproductive rates, high mortality and high disease prevalence (Mayala et al, 2019).

Fishery resources are a vital source of food and make valuable economic contributions to the local communities involved in fishery activities along the 850 km stretch of the Tanzania coastline and numerous islands (URT, 2019). Small-scale artisanal fishery accounts for the majority of fish catch produced by more than 43,000 fishermen in the country, mainly operating in shallow waters within the continental shelf, using traditional fishing vessels including small boats, dhows, canoes, outrigger canoes and dinghies. Destructive fishing methods such as drag nets and dynamite fishing pose a serious problem as they destroy important habitats for fish and other organisms, and there is a long-term trend of overharvested fishery resources (Sekadenda et al, 2020; Roberson et al, 2018).

Other development challenges include youth unemployment, climate change, addressing infrastructure bottlenecks, improving the business environment, improving service delivery to build a healthy and skilled workforce, and managing urbanization (UNDP, 2020; Mihayo and Peng, 2020).

2.2 Tourism

According to the World Travel & Tourism Council (WTTC, 2019), along with the island of Zanzibar, Tanzania's national parks and game reserves are considered its greatest tourism asset, and are important revenue earners for the government. These protected areas are vast 233,300 sq km, or 28% of Tanzania's territory which include 16 national parks, 38 game reserves, 17 game controlled areas and the Ngorongoro Conservation Area *(ibid).* Among the most famous are the Serengeti National Park, where the world's largest terrestrial mammal migration takes place, and Kilimanjaro National Park, home to Africa's highest mountain.

Tourism and travel directly accounted for 11.7% of GDP in 2020 according to the UNDP (2020). Furthermore, the WTTC (2019) estimates the sector's broader economic impact is considerably larger, taking into account indirect and induced activity (including spending by sector employees). Tourism is also a significant export earner, with visitor exports generating TSh5.46trn ($2.5bn) in 2016, or 21.4% of the total, according to the WTTC (2017), which defines exports as "spending within the country by international tourists for both business and leisure trips, including spending on transport. Meanwhile, the sector attracting a lot investment growth as new hotels and resorts open up. The tourism and travel sector employed more than 800,000 people directly in 2020 (UNDP, 2020). The sector's contribution to job creation is very important in a country with high number of youth unemployment *(ibid).*

3. MAIN ISSUES FOR TANZANIA AT A GLANCE

Following two decades of sustained growth, Tanzania reached an important milestone in July 2020, when it formally graduated to lower-middle-income country status. The report by the African Development Bank on sustainable development (AfDB, 2021) frames Tanzania's 'next leap' of development around three strategic pillars: sustaining robust medium-term growth in a challenging external environment, improving the inclusiveness of growth and its impact on poverty reduction, and fostering upward economic mobility and strengthening economic security. These three pillars reflect both the lessons of international experience and Tanzania's unique circumstances and form the basis for an actionable policy agenda to achieve the goals of the Tanzania Development Vision (TDV) - 2025. This strategic framing is also timely as the country prepares its next Five-Year Development Plan. However, the global COVID-19 pandemic has significantly slowed economic growth, adversely affecting lives and livelihoods of Tanzanians, and requiring bold policy actions to ensure that Tanzania's Low Middle Income Country (LMIC) status is maintained. Below is the current status of Tanzania politically, economically and the social context.

3.1 Political context

President Samia Suluhu Hassan was sworn in on March 19, 2021 as the United Republic of Tanzania's sixth and first woman, president, following the death of President John Pombe Magufuli on March 17, 2021 (URT, 2021). President Samia was the Vice President of the Fifth-Phase Government from October 2015. The government has prioritized efforts to clamp down corruption, improve public infrastructure systems; improve public administration and accountability, and proper management of public resources for improved social outcomes. The 2020 Worldwide Governance indicators show Tanzania has either deteriorated or has been stagnant in most governance indicators between 2012 and 2019 (except for control of corruption and political stability/absence of violence). The strongest decline has been in the rule of law, governance effectiveness, voice and accountability whereby political, media and civil society organization's freedoms have continued to shrink (WB, 2020). The changeover of the states' office may have different focus on priorities taking all other things constant.

3.2 Economic overview

Reflecting strong income growth over the past decade, on July 1, 2020 the World Bank announced that Tanzania's gross national income (GNI) per capita increased from $1,020 in 2018 to $1,080 in 2019, exceeding the threshold for lower-middle income status (WB, 2020). The country's broad vision of its development goals as a middle-income country in 2025 are set out in the Tanzania Development Vision 2025, characterized by high-quality livelihoods, peace, stability, and unity good governance, a well-educated and learning society, and a competitive economy capable of sustainable growth and shared benefits (URT, 2015). Increased GNI per capita is impressive but not enough to reach these goals. Investing in both human development and physical capital is important to achieving these broad goals and improving the quality of life for all Tanzanians.

Tanzania has fared relatively well compared to its regional peers, but economic growth has slowed significantly (WB, 2020). The real gross domestic product (GDP) growth rate fell from 5.8% in 2019 to an estimated 2.0% in 2020, and per capita growth turned negative for the first time in more than 25 years (*ibid*). The global economic slowdown has adversely affected export-oriented industries, especially tourism and traditional exports, and caused a drop in foreign investment. Gold has been the sole export to benefit from the crisis, as international gold prices rose sharply between 2019 and 2020. Although the government did not impose stringent mobility restrictions, the pandemic prompted firms and consumers to adopt precautionary behaviors, hindering domestic economic activity (WB, 2020). Meanwhile, steep declines in production, consumption, and imports have significantly reduced fiscal revenue. The pandemic has also compounded preexisting challenges in the financial sector, and the share of nonperforming loans on bank balance sheets continues to be high, while the growth of credit to the private sector has slowed (BoT, 2021).

Slowing economic activity has adversely impacted livelihoods. During June and July 2020, the World Bank conducted a COVID-19 Business Pulse Survey (COV-BPS) covering 1,000 small and medium enterprises in Tanzania. The survey data indicate that about 140,000 formal jobs were lost in June 2020, and another 2.2 million nonfarm informal workers suffered income losses (WB, 2020). Tanzanians employed in informal nonfarm microenterprises tend to be especially exposed to economic shocks, as they often have limited savings to draw on in a crisis (Marvin, 2021). Firms reported an average decline in sales of 36%, which has jeopardized the solvency of more than three-quarters of small and medium enterprises. Most affected firms have not benefited from any type of government support, and respondents suggested that tax deferrals for firms in the most severely affected sectors, including tourism and related services, could help mitigate the disruptive effect of the crisis and enable a swift recovery (BoT, 2020; Mayala, 2021).

In this part, author have directly focused on two sectors of the economy, agriculture and tourism as they are among the biggest contributor to the national economy in terms of GDP and employment especially to the vulnerable groups (women and the youth). Not only that, but the two sectors are and will be most impacted by COVID 19 in the country as projected by UNDP (2020) in the short, medium and long term.

Table 1. Significance of Sectors and Degree of Risk Associated with COVID-19 in Tanzania

SECTORS						Degree of risks from COVID-19		
	Significance and Importance to the Economy			Distributional Effect		IMMEDIATE	MEDIUM TERM	LONG TERM
	% of GDP	Employment	% Forex	Youth	Women	Mar - April	May – August	Sept-Dec
Agriculture, forestry and fishing	22.4	13,409,814	11.49%	HIGH	HIGH	LOW	MEDIUM	HIGH
Mining and quarrying	5.08	218,024	19.24%	HIGH	LOW	LOW	LOW	MEDIUM
Manufacturing	8.05	615,323	9.47	HIGH	MEDIUM	LOW	HIGH	HIGH
Construction and Real estate	13	428,411	-	HIGH	LOW	MEDIUM	HIGH	HIGH
Wholesale and retail trade	9.12	2,528,771	-	HIGH	HIGH	MEDIUM	HIGH	HIGH
Transportation and Storage	6.48	521,698	14.56%	HIGH	LOW	MEDIUM	HIGH	HIGH
Tourism and Hospitality	11.7	807,942	29.18%	HIGH	HIGH	HIGH	HIGH	HIGH
Financial & Insurance Activities	3.7	60,607	-	HIGH	MEDIUM	LOW	HIGH	HIGH
Education, Human Health & Social Work Activities	3.8	580,952	(i)	MEDIUM	HIGH	HIGH	HIGH	HIGH

Source: UNDP (2020), April: Rapid Socio-economic Impact Assessment of COVID-19 in Tanzania.

Henceforth the study analyse the innovations that are needed for the workforce to sustain jobs and move forward strongly after the pandemic.

From Table 1, it is evident that, the most significant sectors of the economy in Tanzania in terms of GDP, employment and Forex contribution will be affected in the long run. The mostly affected sectors in the long run are agriculture, followed by tourism and hospitality and manufacturing taking a third position. Education, human health and social works; transportation and storage; construction and real estate taking fourth, fifth and sixth position in that order in terms of employment levels (UNDP, 2020).

3.3 Social context

The crisis could push an additional 600,000 people below the national poverty line (WB, 2021). While the poverty headcount ratio at national poverty line (TZS 49,320 per month per adult equivalent, which is equal to $1.35 per person per day in purchasing-power-parity terms) has declined modestly over time, falling from 28.2% of population in 2012 to 26.1 in 2019. Tanzania's rapid population growth has caused the number of people living below the national poverty line to steadily increase. In 2020, the pandemic-induced economic slowdown caused the poverty rate to rise to an estimated 27.2%, compounding the effect of population growth on the absolute number of people living in poverty (AfDB, 2020). Because a large share of Tanzania's population is close to the poverty line, even a mild economic shock can push numerous households into poverty. The impact of the crisis has been especially acute among households that rely on self-employment and informal microenterprises in urban areas (Global Innovation Exchange, 2020).

3.4 COVID -19 statistics

There are no publicly available records for COVID-19 deaths in Tanzania, and no information has been released on the impact of coronavirus since May last year, when 509 cases and 21 deaths were reported up to that point (WHO, 2020). The authorities have insisted there is little to worry about, and have taken tough action against those they were accused of spreading false information by mentioning that releasing data publicly could be counterproductive as it could spread fear. Schools however were closed for three month from March to June, 2020 (Mayala, 2020); use of masks, social distancing and regular wash of hands were and are still insisted. No total lock-down though was instituted. Very few organizations especially the international ones allowed their employees to work from home. Else, life went normally.

In mid-February, 2021, the Medical Association of Tanzania issued a carefully-worded statement about an increase in patients with breathing difficulties. Although careful announcing the situation, the association pointed out that breathing difficulties could be symptoms of other conditions, such as asthma, heart disease or pneumonia, not just Covid-19. At the same time, an online survey of the public by Change Tanzania, a rights group, points to a rise in cases and deaths from late December, worsening in January and February and could be much worsening from May, June to July, 2021. Furthermore, it has been noticed that oxygen supplies were running low in hospitals like Kilimanjaro Christian Medical Centre (KCM).

As said earlier, the political regime made a turn-around in March, 2021 after the death of President John Pombe Magufuli (URT, 2021). President Samia Suluhu Hassan had come with some new ideas regarding the pandemic. She constituted a Corona Virus Special Committee chaired by Professor Said Aboud of the Department of Microbiology and Immunology at the Muhimbili National Hospital in Dar es Salaam to investigate among other issues the existence and magnitude of the pandemic and advice the government on the vaccination programme for the country. The committee submitted a report on May, 17, 2021 recommending the government to join the vaccination plan by COVAX under GAVI. The committee called on the government to report accurate information about the pandemic to both its citizens and WHO.

Furthermore, the committee also advised president Samia to strengthen COVID -19 prevention efforts, comply with the international resolutions, strengthen diagnostic capacity; finalize a covid-19 treatment guide for health workers, use traditional medicines only when they are proved by science, update disaster plans and work to establish domestic vaccine manufacturing facility. It is now a second week since the whole country is under vaccination programme (August, 2021). The vaccination program in Tanzania is under the nation vaccination program (NITA) with the responsibility of ensuring all the priority groups are well considered, to educate the citizens about the importance of the vaccination and to distribute the vaccine to the proposed places all over the country.

4. INNOVATIONS IN THE KEY SECTORS OF THE ECONOMY

Despite making millions sick and its terrible death toll, the COVID-19 pandemic has also presented opportunities (UNDP, 2020). Throughout the course of the pandemic, Africa has seen an increase in innovative solutions, including virus-testing robots, contact-tracing apps, non-invasive testing kits, foot-operated hand-washing stations, oxygen machines, drone medicine delivery service, genome sequencing, Artificial Intelligence-powered healthcare chat-bots, fabric home-made masks (*barakoa in swahili*) and much more (WHO, 2021). Many of these and other innovations were made by micro, small, and medium-sized enterprises (SMEs). The economic impact of the pandemic has been especially hard on such enterprises, many of which face potential closure or bankruptcy. As SMEs account for 90% of all businesses on the continent and 85.8% of all jobs in the informal sector, closures could lead to massive job losses and drops in consumer spending.

Throughout Africa, people are looking inward for the innovations that will move the continent and country specific forward. Governments and people are looking ahead, to anticipate the needs of the next generations and envision a better future. People are looking to each other, to build the communities, the countries and the continent that we all know is possible. The African Union was one of the first regional institutions to adopt a joint continental strategy for the outbreak (AU, 2019). Under the strategy, and in consonance with the UNDP's corporate offer to help countries prepare for, respond to, and recover from COVID-19. In this chapter study shall be looking at two sectors, Agriculture and tourism for Tanzania.

4.1 Agriculture

Tanzania, basing on the data provided in Table 1 (UNDP, 2020), it is evident that a great deal of population is going to be affected in the long run as more than 70% of the population depend on agriculture (URT, 2019). The rapid socio-economic response report established that 13,409,814 employments in agricultural, forest and fishing are at risk in the long run. It should be noticed however that, agriculture is a very good example of one of the industries that has gone through a substantial technological shift in recent years even before the COVID-19 pandemic of which can be adopted even in the post pandemic. Using the technologies may mean more farmers in the country to become more productive and enhance stability of the economy. Precision agriculture in particular, involving drones, sensors, big data, environmental controls, farm management software, smart packaging and more may have a huge leap forward into the digital age. Here the study take a look at five innovative agricultural technologies and practices that are changing agriculture across the world which Tanzania may benefit out of it in the post the pandemic.

4.1.1 Urban Agriculture and Vertical Farming

Urban centres in Tanzania as in most parts of the world were the mostly affected parts in terms of the effects and death tolls due to concentration of population and so chances of contamination (Cripps et al, 2020). The big thing about urban agriculture in particular is how to make the best use out of what is often very limited farm space for people to do the farm production. Urban farms can by nature be quite small, and could literally just be an outdoor traditional community garden. However they can still be very valuable, offering an environmentally controlled, self-contained pod. Sometimes they may even be stacked on top of each other known as vertical farming. And despite the relatively small size, yields from vertical farming can be around ten times more efficient than traditional agriculture (Andrew et al, 2021). Although vertical farming doesn't promise to turn the way we farm on its head, it can make huge strides in efficient, productive farming methods by the help of research institutions on its viability and application by expatriates from universities like the Sokoine University of Agriculture (SUA) and other agricultural developmental agencies. Traditional farmers could learn a lot from vertical farmers in their design and building structures, making the most of smart design to increase yield and reduce waste.

As the Tanzania's population continues to grow and take up more room with the big land the country have (bigger than Kenya and Uganda put together), efficiencies in space and farming practices will become all the more essential for feeding the country if used properly in terms of productivity especially after the scars of the pandemic. Unfortunately, no matter how intelligently we design and how high we build, humans are having a massive effect on the environment. Only the continuation of technical advancement in this sector can see the country having any chance of keeping up with own agricultural demands in future.

4.1.2 Artificial Intelligence, Automation and the Internet of Things

Tanzania is implementing the industrialization agenda in the Tanzania Vision 2025 (UTR, 2015). There has been a lot of discussion as to what is the focus of industrialization in the country and as to if there has been enough preparation as far as the agenda is concerned. It is no doubt that technology in the process of industrialization is something mandatory. Going wild to ask anyone what they think the future of driving might be, as most people in the developed economies will talk about driverless cars where AI takes full control. What people generally think less about however are driverless vehicles on farms? Technology is moving so fast such that companies like Smart Agriculture in USA for example, has announced its driverless tractor technology in the form of "AutoCart" software (Cripps et al, 2020). Apparently this software will fully automate a grain cart tractor, providing farmers very welcomed assistance during the busy harvest season. This innovative technological step will allow farmers to automate their existing equipment too, to maximize its capacity and efficiency.

It might sound very illusional for Tanzania in her low middle income earning state to think of such bigger technologies, but industrialization requires bigger thinking. The AutoCart software for example is actually a cloud-based platform, meaning that these automated agricultural vehicles will become part of the global internet of things (IoT). Essentially however, automated vehicles are only one small piece of IoT innovation and machine learning in agriculture. A new AI system that uses a combination of voice recognition, machine vision, and temperature sensors for example is now being trialed to keep track of the health, wellbeing and location of animals like pigs. This might be one area where the country can use the technology in livestock commercial farming. Tanzania takes 3rd position in livestock population after Ethiopia and Republic of Sudan (Mayala et al, 2017). The technology may be potentially important to commercialize livestock in Tanzania. It's all exciting stuff, but is clearly just the tip of the iceberg as other cases of AI use include highly advanced disease detection in crops using a number of similar techniques. Much of the true potential of AI has yet to even be realized with the field still being very much in its infancy.

4.1.3 Genetic editing

As explained in (ii) above, Tanzania has the third largest livestock stock in the continental after Ethiopia and the Republic of Sudan. Scientists around the world have now started to utilize CRISPR/Cas9 to carry out genetic "surgeries" (Alvi et al, 2020; Xu et al, 2016). This allows them to identify and alter an organism's genome by replacing or removing specific genetic sequencing on a strand of DNA. Now, CRISPR is being used to alter a cow's gut microbes with the aim of controlling the animal's size as well as reducing the amount of methane they produce. Adjusting the microbiomes of cows in this way could produce more meat on less food. This in turn leads to industry efficiency and increased profitability and food sufficiency. Tanzania stands a better position to improve meat, skin and hides; milk and related products using this technology to enhance production and hence exportation and food country resilience.

Scientists have also begun to engineer crops that can thrive on less water and yield more food. Of course, when messing with genetics in any ecosystem unforeseen challenges could arise there we'll have to be highly cautious that we don't create more problems than we solve. SUA is making good progress in this but more is expected to be done if Tanzania needs to keep agricultural sciences upfront.

4.1.4 Bees and drones

Tanzania has a vast and arable land suitable for agriculture and other economic activities like mining and forestry of which attracts bee settlements. It cannot also be denied with the fact that climate change is affecting most parts of the country as in the rest of the world. If climate change continues, scientists warn that food shortages could be more likely which will drive up prices of many products (Cripps et al, 2020). For this reason, public health officials have been turning their attention towards shoring up food reserves and finding alternative ways of farming.

As for Tanzania, most parts of the country is blessed with bee forests like what is seen in the Northwestern part of the country in Tabora, Kigoma and Simiyu; the Northern highlands which comprise a group of plateaus and volcanic mountains, including the Mbeya Mountains, Poroto Mountains, Kipengere Range, Mount Rungwe, Kitulo Plateau, Umalila Mountains, and Matengo Highlands; the Ufipa Plateau which extends Northwest, between Lake Tanganyika and Lake Rukwa; the eastern and western branches of the East African Rift converge in the highlands, and the Western Rift continues south as the valley of Lake Malawi; to the Northeast, the Makambako Gap separates the Southern Highlands from the Eastern Arc Mountains which all are covered by beautiful forest for bee keeping and production of other related bee products.

Drones have many uses in agriculture, but one problem that's been in the media is that a lot recently is around disappearing bees. Indeed some species are even at risk of extinction (Patel et al, 2020). This would be disastrous, as bees play a vital economic role as pollinators, helping maintain current agricultural production levels. Lucky, drones are now being used in experiments to hopefully supplement the pollination efforts that remaining bees are completing (Zheng et al, 2018). Tanzania can start using this technology to enhance the sector. Other ways that agriculture is starting to use drones includes automated crop harvesting, aerial drone photography and even potentially in future as delivery drones of which the country may start thinking about at a small scale and expand usage slowly as resources and experts are available progressively.

4.1.5 Blockchain technology

Whilst many people will have heard of blockchain within the sphere of cryptocurrency finance, the agricultural world is starting to incorporate this innovative new technology in a different way (Salah et al, 2019). Most of the earliest blockchain applications in agriculture were with regard to supply chains and traceability; the status of crops could be recorded and updated using blockchain, right from harvesting through to delivery (Demestichas et al, 2020; Kamble et al, 2020). The true benefit of this for larger operations in particular is a secure, highly accurate ledger where nothing ever goes missing in transit. All crops that belong to a specific farmer can be traced in real time.

Tanzania has been operating on a trial and error especially with exports of crops even to the nearest countries in the East African block before the pandemic. Farmers were stopped from exporting crops like maize and horticultural crops on ad-hoc. Worries were diversified from country's food sufficiency to the unknown in the market place. Slowly the government is starting to see that agricultural crops on large scale production and particularly on agribusiness requires strong environment to support farmers through the market processes. The president of the United Republic of Tanzania her excellence Samia Suluhu Hassan announced in Mwanza (May, 2021) that the country should start looking in this technology with an immediate effect so that the country is not caught in surprise while everyone have started using the blockchain technology. The technology will protect farmers by giving them the benefits they deserve. Blockchain can also be used for resource management, like tracking other sensors and equipment for example, or maintaining machinery records (Kombe et al, 2019).

4.2 Tourism and hospitality

Traveling is one of the main causes the Coronavirus has spread across the world and, consequently, government restrictions on movement and tourist traffic became a general trend (Andjela, 2021). In addition to the economic downturn, it is the reason why international tourism took a severe hit *(ibid).* Considering the fact that tourism is one of the largest and fastest-growing industries globally, a huge effort should be undertaken for tourism to reach back to its core capacities in the present situation. According to a Government of Tanzania study on the impacts of COVID-19 on the tourism sector, without the pandemic, the 2020 season would have attracted approximately 1.9 million tourists and generated US$2.9 billion of forex. Without the pandemic, it was expected that the government would have collected revenue of TZS 2.7 trillion (US$1.16 billion), and the sector would have provided direct employment to 622,000 people (URT, 2020).

The situation needs to be strategically addressed with proactive measures for tourism to regain socio-economic stability after the pandemic. This industry includes air, sea and land transportation, food supply chain, accommodation sector, entertainment, recreation, and many other changes. Consequently, there is a wide area of businesses proposing changes, and mostly because the post-COVID tourists will not be the same as pre-COVID ones. Innovative solutions regarding safety and hygiene measures, as well as the proximity of medical facilities, will be of key importance in meeting the public's expectations.

Tanzania went through a very brief period of restricted movement from March to May 2020 as well as border closures and airspace bans with barely any nationwide lockdowns. Announcements and guidance by the government to reopen airspace and restore businesses with strict adherence to WHO and other sector-specific measures from June onwards was not enough to restart and sustain the original growth trend of the tourism sector, since source markets and neighbours extended their border and air space closures, as well as their travel restrictions. This slowdown of tourism is impacting livelihoods, and has led to layoffs and unemployment.

According to the latest analysis from the World Tourism Organization (UNWTO, 2021), 40% of all destinations worldwide have now eased the restrictions they placed on international tourism in response to COVID-19. As of August 2020, tourism in Tanzania was open for business albeit with enhanced safety measures in place to protect staff and travellers, and there is no mandatory 14-day isolation or quarantine period for travellers. In the light of countries seeking to reopen their tourism sectors, the World Bank published in July an analysis, "Rebuilding Tourism Competitiveness: tourism response, recovery and resilience to the COVID-19 crisis", that provides recommendations for short- and medium-term recovery phases (WB, 2021). On top of the recommendations given by the World Bank, more innovation approaches may be undertaken as follows:

4.2.1 Market research

One innovative part of tourism for Tanzania is to make strong efforts of moving from response to recovery directed to monitor changes in traveller sentiment (Wamboye et al, 2020). It is important to understand which market segments will be the first to travel again, and what investments are required to attract more risk-adverse markets *(ibid).* For example, efforts may include improved health and hygiene at hotels and airports or permanent health screening at airports as indicated by the Global Innovation Exchange (GIE, 2020). It would be good timing now for the government, development partners and the private sector in Tanzania to better understand these responsive market segments and possible market opportunities for responsible tourism. In the short term, Tanzania should continue to re-launch her destinations through 'back in business' promotions to key source markets, and businesses should seek to understand the trade-offs of extending discount offerings.

4.2.2 Diversification

Tanzania should seek to diversify geographically from resorts to rural low-density destinations. In this area, Tanzania has long held a model of high-end low numbers. However, work can be done to diversify the tourism offering to spread opportunities for Tanzanians in other parts of the country to compliment the well-established destinations of the Serengeti, Kilimanjaro, Ngorogoro and Zanzibar. This has been the policy of the Tanzanian Ministry of Natural Resources and Tourism for many years and is reflected in the current and upcoming Tanzanian Tourism Strategy; however this may require development partner support to help catalyze the process due to the funding required (Anderson & Sanga, 2019). Tanzania is lucky to be endowed with some of the finest natural tourism assets in the world that are not going anywhere. As the world navigates its way through the global pandemic, Tanzania will remain a strong tourism destination. Promoting and expanding opportunities in domestic tourism in Tanzania will be crucial to building future resilience. This will also increase understanding and appreciation of core responsible tourism concepts of responsible community engagement and environmental protection among the national population. Furthermore, on 7th October, 2020 G20 nations committed to step up efforts to have sustainability and inclusion at the heart of tourism recovery, by placing tourism at the heart of development policies in recognition of the sector's importance for achieving the SDGs (UN, 2020). It remains to be seen how quickly this will translate into action on the ground in LDCs such as Tanzania, but it is certainly a welcome sign.

4.2.3 Responsible tourism standards

Tanzania is well placed by having the proactive Responsible Tourism Tanzania that helps audit and certify hotels and lodges to international responsible tourism criteria. The standards include items such as employee rights with regards to fair contracts and compensation, and minimising harmful social and economic impacts. With the government, the private sector and development partner support, more businesses in Tanzania could be encouraged to see the value of being certified to international responsible tourism standards. Some critics argue that the COVID-19 pandemic brought with it some fringe benefits on how much nature and ecosystems recovered following the lack of tourist activities. But it is also argued that lack of tourist movement in protected areas has increased the exploitation pressure on wildlife poaching and other illegal activities. A big lesson received during COVID-19 and that should last for a very long time is actually how to embrace principles of responsible tourism that foster environmental conservation and stakeholder awareness amid struggles to sustain the economic benefits from the tourism sector.

4.2.4 Up-skilling

There should be efforts made at training and up-skilling tourism and hospitality sector staff with a focus on stability and longer-term job opportunities (Anderson & Sanga, 2019). This will help overcome the sector's reputation for instability and sudden job losses. For example, in Tanzania the ILO with support from Norway and Swiss SECO have in the past supported the Ministry of Tourism and Natural Resources, the National College of Tourism, the Hotel Association of Tanzania and the Association of Tanzania Employers with apprenticeship and staff tourism training programmes in close partnership with hotels (URT, 2020). An area of COVID-19 impact will be the future preferences of young scholars and academicians in the field of tourism. Youth have seen first-hand the hardships caused by COVID-19 on the tourism job market. While Tanzania was not on lockdown, other business and livelihood activities were ongoing with the exception of the tourism and hospitality industry. We currently do not know for example, where the porters and hoteliers are and what are they real doing out there. Also, fresh graduates that had hoped to enter the employment market in the tourism sector after completing their studies were left stranded.

4.2.5 New hygiene standards

Tourists buy experience so every hotel must accommodate their spaces with special attention to the safety of their guests (Kaushal & Srivastava, 2021). If you are thirsty, you go to the store and buy a drink, but if you want to sit in front of a beautiful landscape on a breeze of the summer wind and drink something, you will most likely travel to some special place and pay for that experience. If this includes a potential horror disease experience, no one will be interested in buying. New standard requirements for cleaning accommodation facilities require to be highly regulated (Sigala, 2020). Elevator buttons, door handles, furniture, switches, remote controls, and other frequently touched objects must be adequately cleaned and sanitized after every use. Face masks, hand sanitizer and other hygiene equipment should always be available for guests in need. Tanzania's innovations in the front desk experience should bring a new way of welcoming guests with contact-free receptions so guests are protected from the entrance. Much as Tanzania are known for being kind and hospitable, coming up with electronic devices instead of the kind receptionist might be one of the options the country should think of.

4.2.6 Domestic Travel is a New Exotic Destination

The proximity of medical facilities will make tourists rethink the distance they are willing to travel and, in most cases, affect the rising demand for domestic tourism (Melubo, 2020). If the trend with closed international borders continues, it is possible that people will simply have no other choice. Outstanding opportunities lie in front of businesses truly listening to the customer voice and observing their behavior. It is important to send the right message to potential customers and use marketing tools to promote the value of domestic tourism (Mkwizu, & Mtae, 2018). That should be conducted in a manner of reliving nostalgic moments or the excitement of discovering hidden beauties of their country. Innovative features placed to increase health security and wellbeing will undoubtedly be based on technological solutions (Shereshava, 2021). Aiming to anticipate people's needs and make predictive models, machine learning can be very useful in marketing these destinations and targeting people who want to explore new places, or the places they have already visited a long time ago. The places already visited often evoke a feeling of serenity and confidence, and these attributes should be the most important ones communicated for travelers. As for facilities that usually host a large number of people such as museums, theme parks, theatres, and recreational centers, we've seen the use of augmented reality in practice and we are sure we will be seeing a lot of it in the future as well.

4.2.7 Encouraging business travel

There is a lot of discussion around business travel and pleasure or if the two can be branded together (Coscia, 2020). It is no wonder why a big portion of hotel industry revenues comes from the business segment, but that may be changing. Companies won't risk sending their employees on business travel because of the risk of getting sick *(ibid).* The tourism industry will suffer from this negative impact for an indefinite period, but in order to organize their team's communication and encourage collaboration in joint business projects, there are suitable technology alternatives. Re-imagining corporate travels will present quite a challenge for the tourism industry in Tanzania and elsewhere around the world. It isn't impossible though if they focus their efforts on creativity and innovation of main pain points such as major corporate events, conferences, and team-building activities (Mu et al, 2021). This is a situation where every idea counts as a contributing factor to reaching the goal of reviving business tourism. Another important aspect of future tourism is flexibility. In this industry, flexibility is what businesses are going to highlight through cancellation policies, service rates and schedule modifications. Also, new practices and policies are expected in nearly every aspect of the guest's experience.

5. RECOMMENDATIONS

It is true that most sectors of the economy in Tanzania are affected. This chapter concentrated only on two big sectors, agriculture and tourism narrating the number of labour force that will be affected post-pandemic. The innovations in the two sectors that will revive the situation and guarantee progress of the sectors are also narrated. It should be noted that a number of opportunities present themselves on the basis of the analysis above, which can be taken along in the process as recommendations. These include:

(i) Seeking to balance 'innovation for development' portfolios with more emphasis on forward looking anticipatory innovation and bottom-up adaptive innovation, including innovation from the developed economies. More should be done to encourage more collective thinking and action on adaptive and anticipatory innovations that can help to address the medium and longer term impacts of COVID-19. Doing this will involve more work to incorporate local and national efforts and voices, and 'unusual suspects', to challenge conventional thinking and approaches in a systematic and sustained fashion paving the way for more developed-developing learning and triangular partnerships.

(ii) Investing in more strategic and focused collaboration, especially with local and national actors. Currently, with large numbers of dispersed, fragmented and political decisions, the overall innovation effort risks being less than the sum of its parts. Work is already underway to share information about funded COVID-19 innovations through call for proposals by development partners all across the world. Collaboration should be expanded by building on this to ensure (1) more joined-up and collaborative investments, (2) reduce duplication and waste, and (3) strengthen collective efforts for stronger local and national innovation efforts. This will involve work to generate the political will and enabling environment for such changes, as well as tangible investments in strengthening local innovation efforts to ensure the workforce with stable employments.

(iii) Moving beyond 'single point' product-based interventions to look at processes and paradigms, using a systems-based and transformational lens. Improved decision-making would be supported by stronger and more coherent governance mechanisms that can take a big picture view of the current sector-wide effort; and identify potential gaps and areas needing more evidence or collaboration, as well as promising bright spots. COVID-19 innovation 'boards' could be established within Ministry levels i.e agriculture and tourism sectors, complemented with a sector-wide 'high level panel' to help to set overarching priorities and shared roadmaps.

(iv) Ensuring and sustaining a focus on the poorest and leaving no one behind. This means developing appropriate frameworks and processes to ensure that innovation efforts and outputs are as inclusive as possible (as indicated in Table 1 above about the youth and women effect of the pandemic on their jobs). For example, this might involve determining needs at local and national levels, analyzing how well the current portfolio is meeting these needs, and using these findings to determine innovation priorities. This may also involve examining 'big ticket' mission-driven investments such as for vaccines and tests to assess how the benefits will be realized by the poorest and most vulnerable communities in the country.

6. CONCLUSION

From the point of view, authors of this study conclude that, COVID -19 has affected people in their career and how working space are currently defined. However the situation does not mean that life has to stop. Innovations in different sectors should continue in some way so that the world economy is sustained. For Tanzania specifically, being a nation with many resource endowment stands at a better chance to rebuild and expand the two sectors (agriculture and tourism) but also the rest of the sectors if innovations continue to be adopted. Strategies for inclusive technologies adoption being in place will ensure that no one is left behind in the post-pandemic error.

7. FUTURE RESEARCH AREAS

This study has only focused on two sectors of the economy. However according to the UNDP, 2020 much more sectors of the economy are and will continue to be affected in the long run. Authors recommend that, more researches with regards to innovations and career development to ensure employment sustainability is carried out. Furthermore, research institutions and other development agencies should spearhead in advancing technologies and give hands to smallholder farmers and people working in the tourism sector at local level. This is because in one way or the other they always come late in the adoption of most technologies taking into consideration that most of the Tanzania populace are in the rural settings.

ACKNOWLEDGMENT

This research received no specific grant from any funding agency in the public, commercial, or the private sectors.

REFERENCES

G7. (2018). *The G7 Whistler Principles to Accelerate Innovation for Development Impact.* https://www.international.gc.ca/world-monde/international_relations relations_internationales/g7/documents/2018-05-31-whistler-development-developpement.aspx?lang=eng

Alvi, M. A., Ohiolei, J. A., Saqib, M., Li, L., Tayyab, M. H., Alvi, A. A., & Jia, W. Z. (2020). Echinococcus granulosus (sensu stricto)(G1, G3) and E. ortleppi (G5) in Pakistan: Phylogeny, genetic diversity and population structural analysis based on mitochondrial DNA. *Parasites & Vectors*, *13*(1), 1–10. doi:10.118613071-020-04199-8 PMID:32660553

Anderson, W., & Sanga, J. J. (2019). Academia–industry partnerships for hospitality and tourism education in Tanzania. *Journal of Hospitality & Tourism Education*, *31*(1), 34–48. doi:10.1080/10963758.2018.1480959

Andrews, E. M., Kassama, S., Smith, E. E., Brown, P. H., & Khalsa, S. D. S. (2021). A Review of Potassium-Rich Crop Residues Used as Organic Matter Amendments in Tree Crop Agroecosystems. *Agriculture, 11*(7), 580. doi:10.3390/agriculture11070580

BBC. (2021). https://www.mass.gov/news/baker-polito-administration-announces-covid-19-community-tracing-collaborative-to-further

Blomley, T., Edwards, K., Kingazi, S., Lukumbuzya, K., Mäkelä, M., & Vesa, L. (2017). When community forestry meets REDD+: Has REDD+ helped address implementation barriers to participatory forest management in Tanzania? *Journal of Eastern African Studies: the Journal of the British Institute in Eastern Africa, 11*(3), 549–570. doi:10.1080/17531055.2017.1356623

Cripps, M. G., Dowsett, C. A., Jackman, S. D., Van Koten, C., Goeke, D. F., & Houliston, G. J. (2020). Genetic variation in tolerance to defoliation in Cirsium arvense. *Weed Research, 60*(1), 78–84. doi:10.1111/wre.12391

Demestichas, K., Peppes, N., Alexakis, T., & Adamopoulou, E. (2020). Blockchain in agriculture traceability systems: A review. *Applied Sciences (Basel, Switzerland), 10*(12), 4113. doi:10.3390/app10124113

FAO. (2020). *OPSI COVID-19 Innovative Response Tracker*. https://oecd-opsi.org/covid-response/

Global Innovation Exchange. (2020). *Joint donor COVID-19 Innovation Hub*. https://covid19innovationhub.org/

InnovationO. (Ed.). (2019). *OPSI Blog*. https://oecd-opsi.org/innovation-facets-and-core-values-how-different-forms-of-innovation-can-cause-different-reactions/

Kamble, S. S., Gunasekaran, A., & Sharma, R. (2020). Modeling the blockchain enabled traceability in agriculture supply chain. *International Journal of Information Management, 52*, 101967. doi:10.1016/j.ijinfomgt.2019.05.023

Kaushal, V., & Srivastava, S. (2021). Hospitality and tourism industry amid COVID-19 pandemic: Perspectives on challenges and learnings from India. *International Journal of Hospitality Management, 92*, 102707. doi:10.1016/j.ijhm.2020.102707 PMID:33024348

Kombe, C., Sam, A., Ally, M., & Finne, A. (2019). Blockchain Technology in Sub-Saharan Africa: Where does it fit in Healthcare Systems: A case of Tanzania. *Journal of Health Informatics in Developing Countries, 13*(2).

Maker's Asylum. (2020). https://www.makersasylum.com/m19-shields/

Mayala, N. M. (2021). COVID-19's Impact on Tanzania's Economy and Key Sector Prospects. In Handbook of Research on Sustaining SMEs and Entrepreneurial Innovation in the Post-COVID-19 Era (pp. 106-121). IGI Global.

Mayala, N. M. (2021). The Role of Agriculture in Tanzania: Unpacking Industrialization Prospects and Constraints. In *Handbook of Research on Institution Development for Sustainable and Inclusive Economic Growth in Africa* (pp. 299–316). IGI Global. doi:10.4018/978-1-7998-4817-2.ch018

Mayala, N. M., Katundu, M. A., & Msuya, E. E. (2019). Socio-cultural Factors influencing livestock investment decisions among Smallholder Farmers in Mbulu and Bariadi Districts, Tanzania. *Global Business Review*, *20*(5), 1214–1230. doi:10.1177/0972150917742556

Mihayo, I. Z., & Peng, D. (2020). Role of Fishery and Forest Resources in Local Economic Performance: Evidence from the Lake Zone of Tanzania. *International Journal of Economics and Finance*, *12*(2), 1–22. doi:10.5539/ijef.v12n2p22

Mkwizu, K. H., & Mtae, H. G. (2018). Selfie and Marketing of Domestic Tourism. *International Journal of Research & Methodology in Social Science*, *4*(4), 77–87.

Mu, Y., Bossink, B., Vinig, T., & You, S. (2021). Managing service innovations at online travel agencies: Evidence from China. *Journal of Hospitality and Tourism Technology*, *12*(3), 533–547. doi:10.1108/JHTT-08-2020-0190

Mwaseba, D. L., Erkkilä, A., Friis-Hansen, E., Maro, A. H., & Maziku, J. D. (2020). Responsibilization in governance of non-industrial private forestry: Experiences from the Southern Highlands of Tanzania. *Forest Policy and Economics*, *118*, 102243. doi:10.1016/j.forpol.2020.102243

OECD. (2020). *Innovation for Development Impact*. In *Lessons from the OECD Development Assistance Committee*. OECD Publishing. doi:10.1787/62cc4634-en

Patel, V., Biggs, E., Pauli, N., & Boruff, B. (2020). Using a social-ecological system approach to enhance understanding of structural interconnectivities within the beekeeping industry for sustainable decision making. *Ecology and Society*, *25*(2), art24. doi:10.5751/ES-11639-250224

Policy Cures. (2020). *Covid-19 R&D Tracker*. https://www.policycuresresearch.org/covid-19-r-d-tracker

Robertson, M. D., Midway, S. R., West, L., Tillya, H., & Rivera-Monroy, V. H. (2018). Fishery characteristics in two districts of coastal Tanzania. *Ocean and Coastal Management*, *163*, 254–268. doi:10.1016/j.ocecoaman.2018.06.015

Salah, K., Nizamuddin, N., Jayaraman, R., & Omar, M. (2019). Blockchain-based soybean traceability in agricultural supply chain. *IEEE Access: Practical Innovations, Open Solutions*, *7*, 73295–73305. doi:10.1109/ACCESS.2019.2918000

Sekadende, B., Scott, L., Anderson, J., Aswani, S., Francis, J., Jacobs, Z., Jebri, F., Jiddawi, N., Kamukuru, A. T., Kelly, S., Kizenga, H., Kuguru, B., Kyewalyanga, M., Noyon, M., Nyandwi, N., Painter, S. C., Palmer, M., Raitsos, D. E., Roberts, M., ... Popova, E. (2020). The small pelagic fishery of the Pemba Channel, Tanzania: What we know and what we need to know for management under climate change. *Ocean and Coastal Management*, *197*, 105322. doi:10.1016/j.ocecoaman.2020.105322

Sheresheva, M., Efremova, M., Valitova, L., Polukhina, A., & Laptev, G. (2021). Russian Tourism Enterprises' Marketing Innovations to Meet the COVID-19 Challenges. *Sustainability*, *13*(7), 3756. doi:10.3390u13073756

Sigala, M. (2020). Tourism and COVID-19: Impacts and implications for advancing and resetting industry and research. *Journal of Business Research*, *117*, 312–321. doi:10.1016/j.jbusres.2020.06.015 PMID:32546875

UNDP. (2020). *Rapid Socio-economic Impact Assessment of COVID-19 in Tanzania*. UNDP.

URT. (2020). *Rapid Assessment of the Impact of Corona Virus Disease (COVID-19) on the Tanzania's Tourism Sector*. Ministry of Natural Resources and Tourism, The United Republic of Tanzania.

USAID. (2020). *Local works*. https://www.usaid.gov/localworks

Wamboye, E. F., Nyaronga, P. J., & Sergi, B. S. (2020). What are the determinants of international tourism in Tanzania? *World Development Perspectives*, *17*, 100175. doi:10.1016/j.wdp.2020.100175

World Bank. (2020). *Public Sector Innovation Facets*. https://oecd-opsi.org/projects/innovation-facets/

Xu, R., Greening, D. W., Zhu, H. J., Takahashi, N., & Simpson, R. J. (2016). Extracellular vesicle isolation and characterization: Toward clinical application. *The Journal of Clinical Investigation*, *126*(4), 1152–1162. doi:10.1172/JCI81129 PMID:27035807

Zheng, H., Cao, L., Huang, S., Neumann, P., & Hu, F. (2018). Current status of the beekeeping industry in China. In *Asian beekeeping in the 21st century* (pp. 129–158). Springer. doi:10.1007/978-981-10-8222-1_6

KEY TERMS AND DEFINITIONS

Agriculture: Is the science, art, or practice of cultivating the soil, producing crops, and raising livestock and in varying degrees the preparation and marketing of the resulting products (agribusiness). Agriculture was the key development in the rise of sedentary human civilization, whereby farming of domesticated species created food surpluses that enabled people to live in cities.

Career: An occupation undertaken for a significant period of a person's life and with opportunities for progress.

COVID-19: Is a disease caused by a new strain of coronavirus. 'CO' stands for corona, 'VI' for virus, and 'D' for disease. Formerly, this disease was referred to as '2019 novel coronavirus' or '2019-nCoV. According to the World Health Organisation, the COVID-19 virus spreads primarily through droplets of saliva or discharge from the nose when an infected person coughs or sneezes, so it's important that people also practice respiratory etiquette (for example, by coughing into a flexed elbow).

Innovation: Is the practical implementation of ideas that result in the introduction of new goods or services or improvement in offering goods or services. However, many scholars and governmental organizations have given their own definition of the concept. Some common element in the different definitions is a focus on newness, improvement and spread. It is also often viewed as taking place through the provision of more-effective products, processes, services, technologies, artworks or business models that innovators make available to markets, governments, and society. Innovation is related to, but not the same as, invention: innovation is more apt to involve the practical implementation of an invention (i.e., new / improved ability) to make a meaningful impact in a market or society, and not all innovations require a new invention.

Tanzania: Officially the United Republic of Tanzania (Swahili: *Jamhuri ya Muungano wa Tanzania*), is a country in East Africa within the African Great Lakes region. It borders Uganda to the north; Kenya to the northeast; Comoro Islands and the Indian Ocean to the east; Mozambique and Malawi to the south; Zambia to the southwest; and Rwanda, Burundi, and the Democratic Republic of the Congo to the west. Mount Kilimanjaro, Africa's highest mountain, is in northeastern Tanzania. The Tanzanian population is estimated to 60 million.

Tourism: Is the act and process of spending time away from home in pursuit of recreation, relaxation, and pleasure, while making use of the commercial provision of services. As such, tourism is a product of modern social arrangements, beginning in Western Europe in the 17th century, although it has antecedents in Classical antiquity.

Workforce: Is the total number of workers employed by a company on a specific job or a project.

Chapter 10
Sustainable Career in Agile Environment:
Cross-Sectorial Investigations

Sheikh Mohammed Rafiul Huque
https://orcid.org/0000-0001-7435-6251
Institute of Business Administration, Jahangirnagar University, Bangladesh

Mohammad Nazmul Islam
Institute of Business Administration, Jahangirnagar University, Bangladesh

Tahira Farzana
Institute of Business Administration, Jahangirnagar University, Bangladesh

Tasnima Aziza
https://orcid.org/0000-0003-3311-543X
Institute of Business Administration, Jahangirnagar University, Bangladesh

ABSTRACT

Though COVID-19 has affected all sectors, the effect varies from industry to industry, and so does their employment condition. Layoff, retrenchment, salary cut, upskilling, and reskilling for new work conditions made the work environment agile. This chapter investigated the career challenges that employees faced to maintain a sustainable career in the education, telecom, retail, restaurant, fintech industries through a qualitative research approach. The information was collected through the in-depth interviews (IDI) method with the employees across five different industries. Findings of the investigation reflected that transition from offline to the online platform was common which required new skill acquisition and execution in the job to survive in the agile environment. Adaptability with technology, self-development with skill acquisition in digital mode, regular participation in training, innovation, and so on may help the employees across the industry to make their career sustainable in an agile environment.

DOI: 10.4018/978-1-7998-8626-6.ch010

INTRODUCTION

The unprecedented COVID-19 pandemic has affected all spheres of life. Industries like education, health, financial, technology have suffered substantially due to the pandemic (Haleem et al., 2020). The agility of workers and employment to the new normal environment are the core components organizations have focused on substantially during the pandemic to stabilize their business growth (Fogarty et al., 2020). At the beginning of the pandemic, to maintain the social distance, governments across the globe have taken different initiatives like lockdown, movement restriction order, general leave, curfew, etc. All these measures have restricted the regular presence of employees in organizations (Hillier et al., 2020). To continue the operations, organizations have brought a change in their work environment. Most organizations have permitted their employees to work from home (WFH), which has required adaptability with different technology to communicate, collaborate, and considerably has affected monitoring performance. These new settings have also changed employee requirements, organizational structure, employee engagement, way of doing the job, and work-life balance (Chen, 2021). However, a large number of employees have been struggling to cope up with these sudden changes. Unemployment risk and frustration coping with the new normal environment have created high intention to leave the industry (Chen & Chen, 2021). The older, less educated, less technologically qualified employees have become a more vulnerable group in terms of job security (US Bureau of Labor Statistics, 2020). The organization has become more stringent about its employees and office space utilization (Boland et al., 2020). This pandemic has brought mixed productivity issues, work-life balance, socialization, and concentration status to their jobs (Tagliaro & Migliore, 2021). Organizations with digital capabilities have become responsive and capable of the new working behavior than their counterparts which has created a possibility to use the digital technology permanently at least partially (Chandrasekaran, 2021).

However, all these changes in the working environment have affected the career management ecosystem of employees and their surroundings. Employees' ability needs to be agile, and this ability has become the key determinant for their career success during the new normal situation. The individual may either shift from their previous career goal or need to adjust themselves to the required pathway to stay alive and remain competitive in the current job market (Agrawal et al., 2020). This chapter aims to know the changes in various sectors during the COVID-19 pandemic in Bangladesh and how these changes have affected the employees' career management in this agile environment.

METHODOLOGY

A qualitative research approach has been followed to conduct this study. A cross-sectorial investigation among the Telecommunication, Retail, Restaurant, FinTech, and Education industries in Bangladesh has been considered to explore the career management of the employees and the agility during the COVID-19 pandemic. The current industry status of the five industries has been explored by collecting primary data using the In-Depth Interview (IDI) method with a focus on career management and sustainability issues in an agile environment. In the interview process, two cases have been selected from each industry, thinking of high performing and low performing companies at the national scale (Table 1). The business cases have been selected purposively based on the performance of the business institution under the specific industry where one case has been developed to investigate the management of the leading organization and another one to investigate the management of the comparatively weak performing institution of that industry. The purposive method of selecting the sample as a business case helped explore the working environment's agility within a wider scope. Moreover, the sampling procedure was incorporated in this study to look into the cases of the industry from a qualitative perspective rather than a narrative from a quantitative aspect (Saunders et. al. 2007). In-Depth Interviews (IDI) were the primary tool to discover the underlying issues and scenarios among the sectors. A total of ten business cases have been constructed to explore the cross-sectorial business performance during the pandemic situation.

Table 1: Total Sample Coverage

Industry	No of Business Case(s)
Telecommunication	2
Retail	2
Restaurant	2
FinTech	2
Education	2
Total	10

SUSTAINABLE CAREER WITH DYNAMIC CAPABILITY: A THEORETICAL UNDERPINNINGS

The agile work environment has created interest among academics and researchers for sustainable career management. Newman (2011) opined that sustainability is conserving and improving human capital instead of diminishing it. In such a career mechanism, employees should be flexible and adaptable in response to change. Three elements are required for a sustainable career: renewability, flexibility, and integrity & integration. These elements helped the career to be responsive to the changing environment. Employees who adopt renewability characteristics remain engaged in the workplace for a long time. Organizations that employ flexibility usually enjoy more productivity and commitment from their employees. Lastly, organizations that incorporate development into their HR practices will utilize new roles of their senior employees that help knowledge transfer. The senior employees should get the opportunity to have a flexible career and unceasing learning that enables the organization to decentralize and delegate, which is a critical requirement to adapt to the frequent changes. Ultimately, a sustainable career reduces Human Resource costs as they are agile and also save the employee acquisition cost.

Career shift has been observed more both in terms of number and magnitude. Employees do not change only the employers; instead, they are changing across the industries, reflecting increased job insecurity in the global job market (Goodman & Mance, 2011). Globalization, rapid technological change, change in nature of jobs are the reasons for unstable employment (Friedman, 2005). Cappelli and Keller (2014) identified a few other reasons like taller organizational culture, change in management practice, retrenchment, offshoring the jobs to get less labor cost, contractual jobs for the frequent career shift among the individuals. On the other hand, Cullen et al. (2009) focused on demographic changes like the increased dual-earner couple, single-parent family, and aging workforce to justify the career changes.

However, to maintain their career as sustainable, employees have to develop themselves continuously. They need to be competitive enough for the current and future work and negotiate themselves in the agile environment. Continuous awareness about the skill deficiencies and overcoming them to shape up to the new environment could be possible by sufficient opportunities to develop an individual through learning and development schemes from the organizations (Lawrence et al., 2015). The continuous learning model identified three factors, i.e. social network characteristics, individual differences, and environmental characteristics that affect individuals engaging in the career-related learning management process. The participation of these learning initiatives creates opportunities for desired learning outcomes for personal benefit that are aligned with organizational performance (Molloy & Noe, 2009).

Moreover, the study of Agarwal et al. (2021) revealed that organizations are constantly discovering ways to make their employees adaptable to the changes. They found that keeping the employees involved with the new learning system rather than hiring new employees has a significant effect. Carvalho et al. (2020) emphasized sustainable operational excellence initiatives to survive in the agile environment. The organization with a culture of operational excellence may have quick adjustments to the needs of the markets. It is opined that information and communication technology is a vital requirement in the agile environment (Breu et al., 2002). Besides, proactivity, adaptability, and resilience are the behavioral dimensions that address the agility of employees. The opportunity to work in different positions and working environments in a cross-functional team fosters employee development and adaptivity in the changing environment (Ajgaonkar et al., 2021). Proactive employees take different initiatives to make a positive difference to make career progress. Proactivity is perceived as a career-related outcome and is positively related to age. As older employees have low career opportunities, they take personal initiatives to develop themselves to offset their lacking. Organizations should aim their development initiatives to attain proactive attitudes and behaviors among their employees to give them a competitive advantage in the agile environment (van Veldhoven & Dorenbosch, 2008). These initiatives may develop employability among themselves to sustain a career (Parker & Bindl, 2016).

SUSTAINABLE CAREER IN AGILE ENVIRONMENT: INDUSTRY AND WORKFORCE OVERVIEW DURING COVID-19 PANDEMIC

Context of COVID-19 Pandemic: Global to Local

The world faced several deadly pandemics at different times. The worst pandemic during the 19th century was the flu pandemic outbroke in 1889-1890. In the following century, the prominent pandemics were the cholera pandemic, the flu pandemic, the Asian Flu pandemic, HIV pandemic which outbroke in the years 1910, 1918, 1956, and 2005 respectively (MPHonline, 2021). As part of the Indian subcontinent, Bangladesh was also affected by the outbreak of pandemics in the past. During the 19th century, the most prominent pandemics were the six cholera pandemics in 1817, 1829, 1852, 1863, 1881, and 1899. In 1918-19 an Influenza pandemic widely known as the Spanish Flu hit this region deadly. H1N1 is another Flu pandemic that caused around 18,500 reported deaths in 2009 (Swetha et al., 2019).

The epicenter of the new coronavirus disease 2019 (COVID-19) was originated in China, which were reported on December 31, 2019, in Wuhan city located in Hubei province (Xu et al., 2020; Sohrabi et al., 2020; Zhu et al., 2020; Tan et al., 2020). The World Health Organization (WHO) proclaimed the virus as 2019-nCoV, which was afterward named COVID-19 (Lai et al., 2020). Meanwhile, the world had experienced 250 million confirmed cases, and total death tolled up to 5 million until November 4, 2021. Figure 1 shows the total world COVID-19 new cases and death on weekly basis from 25th April, 2020 until 16th October, 2021 (Worldometer,

Figure 1. Worldwide COVID-19 Confirmed Cases
(April 25, 2020- October 16, 2021)

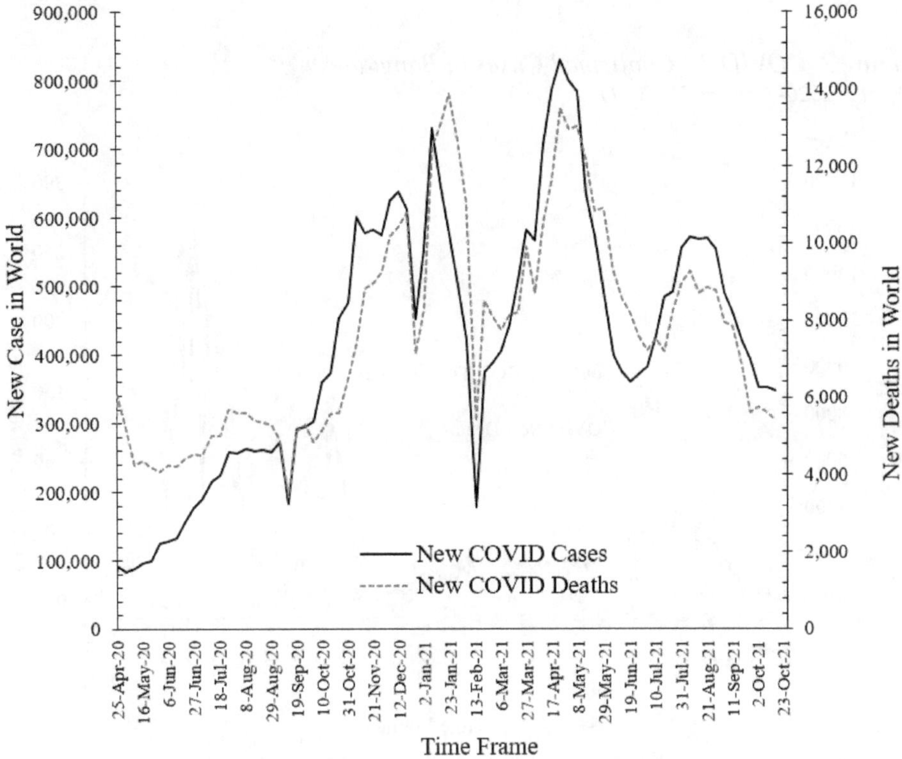

2021). However, the top five most affected countries of the COVID-19 in respect of the total number of infections and death toll were the USA, India, Brazil, UK, and Turkey, respectively, until November 4, 2021 (Reported Cases and Deaths by Country or Territory, 2021).

On March 8, 2020, the first COVID-19 case was identified in Bangladesh ("3 Bangladeshis Infected with Coronavirus", 2020). Figure 2 depicts the new cases and number of deaths due to COVID-19 in Bangladesh from 3rd April 2020, until October 15, 2021. The pattern of the 1st wave and 2nd wave shows that the 1st wave of COVID-19 was from 5th March until 7th May, 2021 and pick of 2nd wave (18th July-1st October, 2021) which was not similar to the global scale. The world has been experiencing multiple waves and until now there are three waves, 1st wave (19th September, 2020-13th February, 2021), 2nd wave (6th March 2021-19th July, 2021), and the 3rd wave from 10th July until 2nd October, 2021. The pattern of COVID-19 new cases and the number of death as well do not portray a similar fashion with world scenario (Figure 1). The figures on the other way reflect that the COVID-19 infection pattern and death scenario had a lesser impact in Bangladesh comparing the global catastrophe (Figure 1 and Figure 2).

Figure 2. COVID-19 Confirmed Cases in Bangladesh
(April 3, 2020- October 15, 2021)

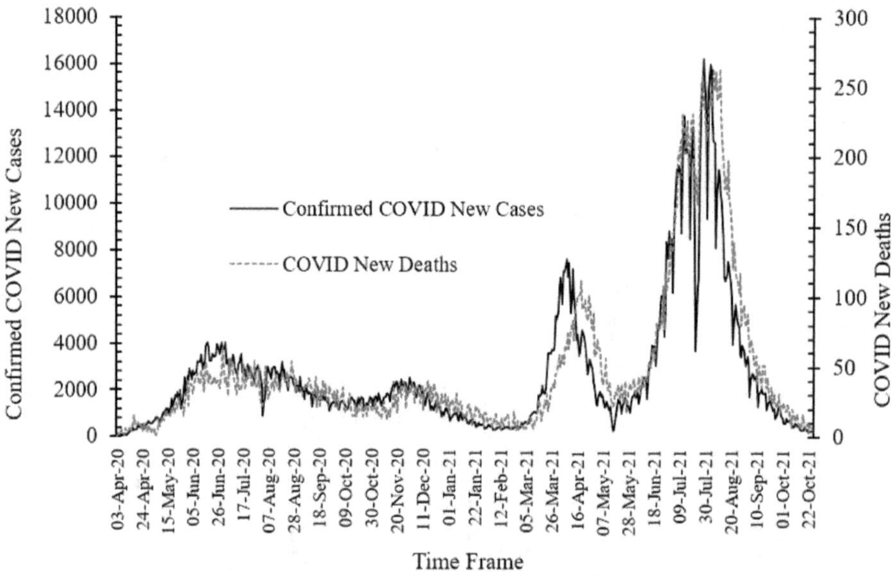

Table 2. Lockdown scenario of Bangladesh during COVID-19 pandemic

Wave	Lockdown/ General leave	Days
1st	26th March-30th May 2020	66
2nd	July 1st- 14th July July 23rd -11th August	14 20
Total		100

Source: Adopted from BetterWork, 2021

Ministry of Labor and Employment of Bangladesh issued hygiene guidelines for the employees of different sectors to prevent the spread of the virus on March 13 of 2020. The Ministry of Public Administration has declared countrywide general leave from March 26 until April 4, 2020, which was later extended until May 30, 2020 (Shawon, 2020). However, since April 26, 2020, garments factories and other industries were allowed to reopen their operations with a guideline to maintain hygiene factors with an occupancy of a limited number of workers and employees (Hillier et al. 2020). During the 1st wave of COVID-19, the closure of readymade garment factories, the primary source of the export earnings sector of Bangladesh, resulted in the unemployment of 2,138,778 workers (BetterWork, 2021). To restrict the spread of the second wave, the government imposed a strict lockdown starting from July 1, 2021, initially for seven days but later extended to July 14 ("Lockdown now from Thursday," 2021). Then the lockdown was lifted off for a week to celebrate one of the significant religious festivals, Eid-ul-Adha, from July 23, 2021. However, the government imposed another lockdown for 14 days, which extended until August 11 ("Bangladesh Reimposes Covid Lockdown for Two Weeks," 2021). However, amid the lockdown during the 2nd wave, factories resumed their operations from August 1, 2021. Table 2 and Figure 2 reflect the total lockdown status in Bangladesh and COVID-19 confirmed cases during 1st and 2nd waves. Unfortunately, the confirmed cases of the virus and policy-related outcomes concerning lockdown had a significant mismatch. It is also portrayed that lockdown was proved just a fluke rather than keeping the whole system alive. Strikingly, the educational institutions were suffered the most as the government announced the closure of all institutions from March 17 2020, and extended it in several phases until September 11 2021. After 543 days of the closure, the educational institutes were reopened at a limited scale which was a huge setback for the students and collapsing the industry, especially the privately financing institutions (BetterWork, 2021).

Career in COVID-19 Agile Environment: A Global Perspective

COVID-19 pandemic has forced many business and behavioral aspects of the society to change their business and way of life to adapt to the new normal situation (Alon et al., 2020). Hamouche (2021) opined that the pandemic has dramatically shaken the organizational structure and has created a complex and thought-provoking business environment for managers and HR practitioners. This new business environment has forced the organization to find unique solutions for the existence that also enforced their employees to cope with the unprecedented crisis. Hancock, B. & Schaninger (2020) quoted that 'we have seen HR's finest hour' in managing with the radical transformation the workforce facing, and it has helped the company to identify and reimagine their talent management practices during the recovery stages of the pandemic crisis. This massive transformation within the organization structure has required huge and intensive facilitation from the government, businesses, institutions, and people at the local and global scenario (Barneveld et al., 2020; Mahmoud Saleh & Karia, 2020)

World Bank (WB) estimated that the world economy would face a massive recession due to the pandemic outbreak and economic downturn (World Bank,

2020). A social distancing strategy has been followed widely to prevent the spread of the virus and avoid touching any surface during material handling to reduce the chance of spreading the virus (Chang et al., 2020; Eikenberry et al., 2020; Fong et al., 2020). These suggested protocols have expedited shifting to digital payment mode which had an immense effect on the business operations to cope with the new normal agile scenario (Sreelakshmi & Prathap, 2020).

Lopes et al. (2021) detected that older, unskilled workers, women, people from highly concentrated areas, and the tourism industry have faced the most adverse impact in terms of employment. Moreover, this pandemic has caused loss of jobs to those employees who had stable jobs and are motivated and committed performers. The authors suggested embracing the skills and willingness to change the occupation. This adaptability and flexibility are getting increased value in the job market as it will reduce the adverse employment impact of these employees. Proper upskilling and reskilling enables the employees to be resilient to the changing condition. Chen and Chen (2021) found that unemployed and laid-off employees of the hospitality industry are depressed, socially isolated, and traumatized due to the pandemic, which has affected their well-being negatively and has increased the intention to change their careers and leave the industry. But this impact is mediated by the individual's self-efficacy, which is present among the diversified skilled employees.

However, the jobs which cannot be performed remotely have been affected more due to the pandemic. People with lower income have also adversely affected during the lockdown. They have little scope to work in online mode due to lack of skill, nature of the job, lack of technological equipment, network facility, and suitable home conditions. On the other hand, employees who have worked from home suffer from different challenges as it negatively affects their quality of life and work-life balance. The challenges are more visible for the female employees as they have to do the majority of the household works and caring activities. Though older people who do not have updated technological skills become unemployed, the young people who are adept in information technology, robotics, and digital marketing have great potential globally in terms of employment (Almeida & Santos, 2020).

Globally, COVID-19 has created educational, training, and employment challenges that have affected socioeconomic scenarios (Autin et al., 2020). The pandemic hinders the learning of employable skills in many countries due to social distancing restrictions. This problem is severe in the less developed countries as they lack technological resources and hygiene facilities. Governments should take the necessary steps for the candidates to acquire the required skills, which will help them to start their careers. Moreover, this initiative may help the employed people to survive and grow (Segbenya et al., 2021; Mamgain, 2020). A sustainable career creates a long-term scope for individuals to be marketable in different and changing situations. Organizations have changed the training modes and methods in response to the COVID-19. Employees are also more likely to develop diverse skills to adapt to the changes. With the constrained budget, organizations initiated training addressing new required skills like remote work and communication in the dispersed team, healthy lifestyle, time management, work-life balance, stress management in new normal, etc. (Mikołajczyk, 2021).

Career Sustainability Global to Local during Pandemic: An Overview

The global COVID-19 crisis has shaken further thinking on the general concept of 'responsible management which was different in the pre-pandemic situation. The organization, university, and business schools need to reshape their concept of educating future leaders and managers. (Cornelius et al., 2007). Due to the outbreak of the deadly virus, all businesses and universities are forced to shift suddenly from the face-to-face contact environment to the online mode of operation. Many business schools, such as; London Business School, ESCP, ESSEC, Instead, and SDA Bocconi responded to a shift to a two-stage educational environment. Primarily, they have moved to the online teaching modality, and later on, they shifted to the entire teaching modality following a hybrid model (Pucciarelli & Kaplan, 2021). A similar kind of shift is also has been observed in developing countries like India. The impact of social services and digitization became evident in the education industry as well as the industry of essential household items (Sharma, 2021). During the pandemic, many retailers and e-commerce firms are facing massive disruption in the supply chain and eventually encountered huge financial losses (Mishra & Chanchani, 2020; Basu, S., 2020). Moreover, due to the government guidelines and large-scale closure of educational institutions this service industry has to move to the online teaching modality (Warrier, 2020).

In Portugal, the effect of the pandemic on the economy and employment status is incredible. More than 100,000 people have become unemployed in a short while since the beginning of March 2020, and it is expected to have a sharp fall in GDP by 6.9%, and the unemployment rate would increase to 9.6% by the end of 2020 (Almeida & Santos, 2020). The tourism industry, which is one of the significant earning sectors has affected severely due to the hindrance of mobility of people and goods that is indirectly has affected the export industry fiercely. There is intense pressure on public finance to support public and private companies in this unprecedented situation (Almeida & Santos, 2020).

However, it is a point to be mentioned that the FinTech industry, especially mobile-based payments are a medium of convenience before the global pandemic time, and it became a necessity due to the COVID-19 pandemic background. During the pandemic time, use of mobile-based payments work as an act of instrument of encouraging social distancing policy. The system has allowed people to make transactions even during the lockdown situation and even in a quarantine period. Moreover, most of the services during the pandemic have offered more incentives through online platforms, and the consumers are required to search for an option of online payments. Surprisingly, in India, the central bank has instructed bankers and has encouraged customers to use digital-based payments methods to avoid physical contact (Sreelakshmi & Prathap, 2020)

The situation is novel and unique for the entire world. Lockdown has affected employment, mode of work, reskilling, etc. As employment is the source of people's livelihood, stable employment ensures steadiness in society. Governments of different countries have offered financial support and incentives to business organizations and their employees to stabilize their employment during the COVID-19 pandemic. In most cases, the support does not include the informal sectors (Zhang, 2020; Webb et al., 2020). Ikram et al. (2021) investigated and found a negative effect of COVID-19 on the export, logistics performance, ISO 14001, and ISO 9001 certification of the most affected six Asian countries: India, Pakistan, Iran, Bangladesh, Philippines, and Indonesia. Among the six countries performance of Pakistan is comparatively better while India and Iran have faced the most losses in export.

Like in most other countries, the economy of Bangladesh is affected due to the pandemic as it hurts the agriculture, industry, and service sector. The most important export item of Bangladesh readymade garments (RMG) faced order cancellation due to the lower demand during the pandemic, disrupted supply chain, supply-demand mismatch. The most affected service sectors are health, education, banking, and other financial institutions, tourism, and hospitality (Begum et al., 2020). Alam et al. (2020) further added that the turmoil caused by the lockdown and isolation impacts the main two drivers of the Bangladesh economy: readymade garments and foreign remittance. Besides, they investigated the adverse effect of the economy on food and agriculture, trade, financial institutions to get the impact of COVID-19. Lalon (2020) emphasized the huge trade deficit, increasing non-performing loans in the banking sector, decreasing investors' confidence, and volatility of the capital market as the leading causes of the adverse impact of the economy. The tourism industry is one of the most affected industries during the pandemic. Lockdown restrictions have impacted both local and global tourism and thus have made an impact on the airlines, other transports, hotels, motels and resorts, restaurants and travel agencies, and tour operators. This industry has faced a huge economic and employment loss (Deb & Nafi, 2020). Karim et al. (2021) tried to find out the liquidity and financial health of the listed banks of Bangladesh during the pandemic. They have found all the banks have poor liquidity ratios and financial health during the second quarter of 2020. The country's electronics industry has faced different types of operational challenges. Their significant challenges are overstocks of finished goods and raw materials, order cancellations, transportation problems (Paul et el.,2021). On the other hand, the supply of beauty and personal care products is interrupted due to the limited delivery service, interruption of supplier payments, and lack of credit facilities (Chowdhury et al., 2020).

CAREER SUSTAINABILITY IN AGILITY: CASES OF CROSS-SECTORIAL INVESTIGATION IN BANGLADESH

Telecommunication (Telco) Industry

Considering the subscriber base, Bangladesh is the 8th largest mobile market globally, with a contribution of 1.8% in the overall GDP (Akhter & Jahan, 2020). The industry has four major players which are Grameenphone, Robi, Banglalink, and Teletalk. Players of the industry face hard competition because of its oligopolistic nature. The industry mainly offers internet and voice call-related services where the internet subscription growth rate is around 10%, and subscribers growth rate includes a CAGR of around 3% (LightCastle Analytics Wing, 2019). The industry has revenue growth potential considering the transformation toward 5G technological orientation in the market as the majority of the mobile data users are using 3G technology and a few 4G technologies (LightCastle Analytics Wing, 2019).

Telco 1

The organization is the largest telecommunications operator in the Telecom industry. Nearly 46% (81.54 million) of the total 175.27 million subscribers as of May 2021 are users of this mobile service provider (BTRC, 2021). This organization is also listed in the capital market of the country. They have diversified offerings for Individual and Business Consumers. Starting from voice and mobile data services, they have other offerings, including handset devices, value-added services, recharge offers, entertainment-related app solutions for individual consumers. For business organizations, they have enterprise connectivity solutions, customized business solutions, cloud solutions, OTT communication platforms, cybersecurity solutions, etc.

Working experience of a Mid-Level employee regarding career sustainability considering agile environment:

"Complete shifting of operations to an online platform has helped us to utilize proper usage of technological advancement in providing services to the stakeholders"

During pandemics, the organization has shifted its mode of internal and external operations from offline to online. Organizations working as partners for this organization also needed to be compatible to work online to make their journey sustainable with the organization. New product development or offerings to the distribution of the product have been done online considering the health safety of the employees and consumers. Device-related offerings including other tangible product offerings have been sent through home delivery service for the consumers. Organizations have become more dependent on digital platforms for their marketing activities. As a result, all the internal and external stakeholders of the organization needed to be equipped with technological knowledge to get better benefits.

Work from home (WFH) policy has been executed for the employees which were not in practice before the pandemic. Technological devices like laptops, modems have been provided by the organization to facilitate work at home. Usage of the digital platform has become mandatory for the whole organization to execute all the relevant tasks. The organization is working hard to set up a digital ecosystem for the entire organization in a way so that the effectiveness of the outcome becomes greater than earlier.

To adjust to all these changes, employees have become more concerned about demonstrating visible consistent performance to the management. Hence, employees are taking online training to increase their subject matter expertise. To increase performance, they became self-motivated to acquire knowledge from the central training portal of the organization.

"It has become very stressful to bring something new regularly by working alone at home."

Balancing work and life has become tough nowadays, considering the performance and growth expectation of the organization and ongoing uncertainties. It is not easy to perform at the level best by playing multiple roles simultaneously. For working women, it has become more challenging. Doing the diversified tasks simultaneously at the household level and organizational level has become very stressful.

Official work hours are not working upon the work from home policy, making life more miserable. Innovative tasks require isolation from others which is currently not manageable and results in poor performance in a few cases.

Sickness of the family members has become a significant concern, and dealing with this part by maintaining other regular office work has become burdensome. However, the time for giving care to adults and kids has been extended. On the other hand, me-time has been reduced to manage other tasks.

Telco 2

This case was about the only state-owned public telecom operator in the country. To provide quality services to mass subscribers the organization started its journey under the telecom industry. They have 5.82 million subscribers which are 3.32% of the total subscribers as of May, 2021(BTRC, 2021). They have both individual and corporate customers. They are working closely with the government to facilitate government support services to mass consumers. Police, RAB, Fire service, NBR, Agriculture Department, BRTA, BSTI, BTRC, Election Commission, and Health Service are the most benefited departments under their offered services. The organization mainly focuses on increasing interactivity between Government and mass people.

Working experience of a Mid-Level employee regarding career sustainability considering agile environment:

"Overall internal and external service development and its execution have become more viable under agile work environment."

The organization has started focusing on the up-gradation of the basic service offerings to cover the country's mass consumers, especially those in rural areas and are still not actively using many service offerings. To serve the internal stakeholders, new software has been developed. An employee app has been developed to monitor the internal resources. Office attendance, regular productivity under office hours, geographical location, etc. are being monitored regularly through the software-based product development.

To provide support in favor of different government initiatives, they are developing app-based solutions. Remote access to digital services is one of the significant areas of concern for the organization. In association with the Ministry of Youth and Sports, the organization has planned to provide free training to 2,500,000 rural people, which will help them overcome the fear feeling about technology and assist in obtaining available digital services.

The work-life balance scenario is better for the employees of this organization as they don't have any business targets. The organization has initiated work from home policy for its employees. As a result, employees are getting the opportunity to make a proper balance between work and life.

"Limited customer base than competitors due to lack of infrastructural capacity is frustrating"

The network quality of the telecom organization is not as strong as other competitors. As a result, their business growth is very limited. Individual consumers'

Table 3. Summary of the findings from the telecom industry

Major areas of change in the agile environment	Telco 1	Telco 2
The transition from offline to online	Yes	Yes
Availability of work from home opportunity	Yes	Yes
Execution of the work from home opportunity	Better than others	Moderate as full execution was not possible
Work-Life Balance	Not satisfactory	Satisfactory
Training availability	Yes	Yes
Survival Strategy	Ensuring consistent performance	Capacity development & creating awareness
Career sustainability requirement	Continuous performance through digital knowledge acquisition/Skill development	Capacity expansion under digital platform

response against the promotional offerings of the operator is frustrating for the internal stakeholders.

"Complete online mode of operations could not be executed during a pandemic."

Lead resources of the organization are required to make physical visits at the office based on the needs of the organization and its stakeholders. Dealing with government projects requires more physical visits than others as senior resource persons are more comfortable with the face-to-face meeting arrangements.

Service capacity expansion for the semi-urban and rural people will be a surviving strategy for the organization. The industry's potential exists in capacity development through automation, artificial intelligence-related developments, and overall skill development.

Retail industry

The market size of the retail industry of Bangladesh is approximately BDT 1,500 crore and 15% growth has been observed for the last three to four years in the sector. It is expected that the industry will grow 15 times by 2021 (Abir, 2019). The sector is also considered one of the major sectors that contribute to the employment generation and it was approximately 12% in the fiscal year 2011-2012 (Datta, 2018). Following the global trend, the retail industry of Bangladesh has scope over the online platform as online operations for the retail sector are yet to flourish at a greater scale.

Retail 1

This case was about one of the largest retail chain shops in the country. This retail brand is serving across 185+ outlets within the country. They are serving 40,000+ customers daily with their 4,300 employees. They have a partnership with thousands of suppliers. They are committed in providing quality service within affordable pricing.

Working experience of a Mid-Level employee regarding career sustainability considering agile environment:

"Loyal customer base has gone up for the brand as customers have received good service experience through the digital platform."

This brand has tried to ensure a positive service experience for its customers. They shifted to the digital platform during 2019 with the orientation of a beta version of online shopping. However, customer traffic was low in the year 2019. During the pandemic, customer traffic increased, and they introduced direct telephone calls to get the customers' order. They also declared a free home delivery service to distribute the product to the customers. In addition, they arranged a WhatsApp-based support service to provide detail about the product offerings which enabled customers to get a positive experience about the brand. They tried to incorporate feedback and complaints that they received from the customers as fast as possible i.e. they tried to be responsive toward their customers. As a result, the loyal customer base went upward for this brand.

"Serving the front line fighters of the community enabled the brand to attain a new window of opportunity."

Being the market leader, the brand showed a positive attitude toward the front line fighters of the community like doctors and police throughout the pandemic situation, which helped the brand cater to the mass consumers' positive attention. They offered a separate range of discounts for the front line fighters along with the regular discount for the mass consumers. They introduced health safety products for mass consumers. At an overall level, the brand has explored a new window of opportunity to ensure sustainability in the agile environment.

"Front end employees of the retail store had a fear of getting infected by a coronavirus and many of them got infected by the virus more than once which caused health hazards for the employees."

Employees who worked in the store had a fear of getting infected by the virus. The organization did not cut any workforce during the pandemic situation but many employees left the organization considering the probability of getting infected by the virus. Therefore, the organization needed to recruit new employees for the organization.

Retail 2

This case study is about a retail store that belongs to one of the giant organizations of Bangladesh in the FMCG sector. The core focus of this retail store is to provide competitive prices to its customers and provide ease of access to its mass consumers. They have a total of 53 outlets with more than 100,000 customers in Dhaka city. They are offering products of more than 20 categories.

Working experience of a Mid-Level employee regarding career sustainability considering agile environment:

"Employees who could cope up more with the situation could extend their working scope & could handle their work properly."

The performance got more priority for the organization in recent times. Management of the organization was more interested in skilled resource persons and subject matter experts. Those who could perform in a complex business environment could survive. Adaptability with the complex situation brought success for the performance-driven employees.

"Shifting toward the online platform brought new opportunities for retail business. Online-based new business development through the website along with the platform of online channel partners enabled the organization to increase its sales during the pandemic situation"

The organization started taking website-based direct orders from customers since the pandemic started. As a result, consumers could receive safe delivery from their store. Moreover, few established online channel partners with a strong customer base in food delivery started purchasing grocery items from the retail store online. They also shared orders with the organization. As a result, sales grew at an overall level during the pandemic situation. They also manage their suppliers online by creating different groups.

"Grocery-based business will become technology-oriented and lots of tie-ups will happen in the distribution channels including third party delivery channels of modern trade across small vendors."

Modern trade will be observing a few changes in the industry. The tech-centric focus will grow further. Many small-size vendors are showing interest to work together. App-based online stores are growing up and these stores are planning to tie up with the large established outlets for delivering their orders. So, there will be a technology-based platform where all the stakeholders will get access as per their nature of usage.

"Downsizing has been done within the organization. Employee transfer across the departments has been implemented to take on new challenges"

The organization went through downsizing and a certain percentage of employees have been shifted from one department to another. Those who could not perform were sacked from the organization. Shifting across departments has been done to ensure the good performance of the employee.

Lack of trust toward e-commerce sites has been observed in the country due to the recent failure of prominent e-commerce sites. Security and trustworthiness need to be taken care of properly for the overall benefits.

Consumers have few negative perceptions about online purchases. Sometimes organizations fail to maintain their commitment and the quality does not match with the expectation. So, to ensure trust, a proper ecosystem needs to be established in the sector.

Restaurant industry

The estimated market size of the overall restaurant business was BDT[1] 4,500 crores in the year 2019 and it was expected that the overall contribution of the sector to GDP would be 2.1% by the year 2021 (Liaquat, 2020). The total number of restaurants across the country was 60,000 and approximately 2.8 million human resources were found associated with this sector (Hossain, 2021).

The Virtual Kitchen concept is getting popular in Bangladesh under the restaurant business. It is also called cloud kitchen. A virtual or cloud kitchen is a type of commercial kitchen that does not require any physical space to serve its customers (Trehan, 2019). This type of kitchen allowed food delivery at the doorsteps of the consumers instead of availing of dine-in facilities with the help of tech-based solutions. It reduces time cost, food cost, and ensures quality food on time. Most importantly after the outbreak of coronavirus consumers have found the virtual

Table 4. Summary of the findings from the retail industry

Major areas of change in the agile environment	Retail 1	Retail 2
The transition from offline to online	Yes	Yes
Availability of work from home opportunity	Yes	Yes
Execution of the work from home opportunity	Partial execution was possible for the retail	Partial execution was possible for the retail
Work-Life Balance	Satisfactory	Moderately satisfactory
Training availability	Yes	Yes
Survival strategy	New product introduction and quality service experience offering	Growth in sales
Career sustainability requirement	Strong loyal customer base assurance	Adaptation with technology and coping up ability with the complex environment

kitchen as a good solution to avoid the risk of physical visits (Gomes, 2020). The food delivery industry is booming in Bangladesh with the assistance of technology hence the virtual kitchen has growth potential in the Bangladeshi market. Drastic changes in lifestyle since 2020 also motivated people to maintain social distance and order food online (Zaman, 2020). Crisis and change enabled cloud kitchen to distinguish themselves in the business and outperformed considering the crisis followed by change momentum has created a special place in the heart and mind of the consumers (Amit, 2020).

Restaurant 1

This case is about the country's largest restaurant service provider. They have been in the industry for the last 29 years and have enjoyed steady growth over time. At present, they have 11 branches across Dhaka city. They also offer catering and corporate services to their customers. They have taken safety measures like disinfection tunnel gate, thermal scanner, and automated hand sanitizer, etc., to protect the customers from coronavirus.

Working experience of a Mid-Level employee regarding career sustainability considering agile environment:

"Customer orders online via food delivery apps have created a new opportunity for the restaurant business."

The restaurant business was struggling from the beginning of the 1st quarter of 2020 due to the hit of the pandemic situation worldwide. Being one of the very popular restaurants in the country, this brand tried to comply with all the government guidelines. They operated with a minimum number of employees during the pandemic and were allowed to enjoy their leave for a few months with revised payment. Upon observing mass acceptance of online food delivery apps among urban consumers, this brand tied up with three major food delivery apps to get online food orders. That window of opportunity helped the brand to increase its sales.

"Introducing new offerings as per the choice of the consumers will help to sustain in the business"

This brand got popular due to its regular offering of Chinese, Thai, Indian, and Cultural cuisine items. After the lockdown of July 2021, they have started realizing that consumers' preference has changed due to the overall environment of the sector. Consumers are trying diversified things i.e. they are not confined to the traditional Chinese and Thai Items. Therefore, they think that adding new variety in the offerings will help them draw the attention of a larger customer base. So, to survive, they feel that they need to develop new offerings as per the needs of the customers.

"Restaurant owners have gone through with huge loss and it is uncertain how the loss will be recovered."

Restaurant businesses have faced great losses during the pandemic situation. As a result, they have failed to manage fixed costs like employee salary at full scale. However, the employees have accepted the reduced salary happily as they are aware of the industry situation. Their salary payment was regular during the pandemic at a discounted rate. From August 2021, they have started full-fledged operations with a fear feeling that will be required to face different challenges to recover the loss.

Restaurant 2

This case study is about a cloud kitchen that started its journey during the pandemic. The founder of the cloud kitchen was a teacher who worked in a Madrasha, a religious, academic institute. The owner of the cloud kitchen started her journey during the 2nd quarter of the pandemic to find an alternative income source as schools could not pay their salary from the 2nd quarter of 2020. During that time, many Facebook-based platforms also evolved in Bangladesh, and the owner got the motivation from those Facebook-based platforms. With that motivation, the owner created a Facebook page where she took orders about food delivery.

Working experience of the lead resource person regarding career sustainability considering agile environment:

"Serving Covid Patients and their families through the online delivery was the prime breakthrough for our cloud kitchen. Later on, customers from abroad started asking to deliver food to their old aged parents and relatives who were alone at home."

Cloud kitchen was a blessing for the covid patients. As in Bangladesh, there are many nuclear families in the urban areas where they do not have substantial support to get food if they become ill. Cloud kitchens could provide support during the pandemic. For the cloud kitchen brand, serving the covid patients was the primary source of revenue. Later on, orders from abroad were another ample opportunity for the brand. They delivered food based on the requests received from the relatives staying abroad.

"Outperformance of the Fintech organizations along with F-commerce facility made the order management easier for the new entrants of the Industry."

F-Commerce has played a positive role in organizing the business from scratch. Being the new entrants to the industry, F-Commerce helped to create brand awareness. Different delivery-based groups also have been developed through F-Commerce which was a great relief to deliver food at the customer's doorstep. People from abroad could pay easily through Fintech apps like bKash.

FinTech industry

Due to the mass acceptance of mobile technologies, digital payment has got good acceptance in the mind of the consumers of Bangladesh. At present under the FinTech industry, the value of the startup ecosystem is BDT 1.45 billion as of 2021 and it has been predicted that the valuation can reach USD 10 billion. In Asia-Pacific by 2025, the Fin-Tech market has been expected to reach over $150 billion. Bangladesh is expected to grow in terms of adopting FinTech through leveraging mobile technology. Under the FinTech industry, bKash leads the digital payments sector and they have an 80% market share in the industry. Other major players are Rocket, Nagad, SureCash, etc. ("Bangladesh – The Rising FinTech Star", 2021). The FinTech industry is an unsaturated market and it has enormous opportunities to explore (Liaquat, 2021).

Table 5. Summary of the findings from the Restaurant industry

Major areas of change in the agile environment	Case 1	Case 2
The transition from offline to online	Yes	Yes
Availability of work from home opportunity	No	Yes
Execution of the work from home opportunity	The execution was not possible	Yes
Work-Life Balance	Satisfactory	Satisfactory
Training availability	Yes	Yes
Survival strategy	Introducing new varieties & affiliation with online delivery vendors	Customized services offerings
Career sustainability requirement	Adaptability during complex situations.	Assurance of technological usage to expand customer base

FinTech 1

This case was about the market leader of the FinTech industry. This organization is operating under the approval of the central bank in Bangladesh. The organization has 240,000 agents across the country. The organization was ranked the top as the dream employer among 53 multinational and local companies across all sectors as per the Campus Track Survey of Nielsen Bangladesh ("bKash Tops Students' List", 2020).

Working Experience of a mid-level employee regarding career sustainability considering agile environment:

"Technological adaptability has facilitated more proactive and effective approach which created a positive impact on career growth."

Good time management has become more feasible after the outbreak of the pandemic situation in the year 2020. This Fintech organization allowed its employees to work from home. The organization provided all the required devices as per the needs of the employees. Due to these facilities, they could make effective use of time. They prepared extra insights to grab the market opportunities and worked on the weakness that they had.

"Customers felt the urge to use financial apps to make cash in and out from home. As a result, the volume of transactions went up and new areas of revenue could be explored for the business growth."

Social distancing created a positive impact in the mind of the consumers about using the technology at the maximum level. Online purchases and payments through financial apps went up during the pandemic situation. Moreover, other relevant stakeholders like telecom, e-commerce, and f-commerce also motivated their users to pay through financial apps as it was easy for all the stakeholders. At an overall level, financial apps were effective considering the crisis of the pandemic situation and employees were happy to serve the consumers online. Digital security-related training and development have become more crucial for the FinTech organization to make the system more structured and establish strong stakeholders' financial security. And it will ensure revenue growth in the future.

"Work from home facility helped the employee to remain mentally happy during the pandemic situation. It was easier to reduce the fear that they are not the bearer of the virus for the family. Quality time spent at home increased mental well-being as well."

Staying at home helped employees to remain safe and sound. They could utilize the time in developing their different skills and shape up the skill gap. Moreover, they could take care of the family members of the home. At an overall level, mental happiness could be ensured for the employees.

FinTech 2

This case is about a digital financial service that operates as a venture of Bangladesh Post Office. The organization has 52,000,000 customers who are doing daily transactions of BDT 700 crore (Uddin, 2021). They are offering cash in, cash out, adding money from the bank to the account or card to the account, mobile top-ups, etc. Ensuring the financial flexibility for the people of the country they are working hard and expecting to grow.

Working Experience of a mid-level employee regarding career sustainability considering agile environment:

"Overall business of mobile financial services increased during the pandemic as the usage of different app-based solutions went up for the general users. The inclusion of upper socioeconomic group consumers is a significant achievement for the organization. Stable growth has been observed for the organization."

Pandemic situation has contributed positively for the FinTech related business. They could attract consumers to use their services through app services, and their cash-in, cash-out, card-to-account transfers, etc. was much-needed support for the

Table 6. Summary of the findings from the FinTech industry

Major areas of change in the agile environment	FinTech 1	FinTech 2
The transition from offline to online	Yes	Yes
Availability of work from home policy	Yes	Yes
Execution of the work from home policy	Yes	Yes
Work-Life Balance	Very satisfactory	Satisfactory
Training availability	Yes	Yes
Survival Strategy	Focusing on the diversified offerings through innovation	Expanding business through targeting new segments of the market
Career sustainability requirement	Adaptation with technology	Consistent performance management

mass consumers during the pandemic. Moreover, the organization found that earlier major users were from the bottom tier of the economic status. Upon changing the situation during the pandemic, middle-income and higher middle-income groups started using mobile financial services, which contributed positively to the organization. They also got different government projects which added monetary value to their organization.

"Internal stakeholders of the organization are tech-savvy, which helped them to do home office smoothly. Doing work from home helped them to maintain quality family time and enabled them to stay safe at home which created healthy relationships across all the stakeholders."

Being mobile financial services providers, they had exposure to technological tools. Required devices were available at their end. So, they took good advantage of the technological application while working from home. They also maintained office hours and gave attendance regularly through their ERP system. They faced minor challenges in handling different meeting-related timelines. Sometimes they needed to attend late-night meetings which required a few adjustments in their routine.

Education (tertiary) industry

As different education levels have faced unique challenges during the pandemic, the chapter has considered only the private universities of Bangladesh to collect information on the education sector. Among the 148 universities of the country, 103 are from the private sector, which is mainly funded by the tuition fees the students pay. 16,074 people are employed in these private universities as teachers whereas, the number of students is 361,756 resulting in a teacher-student ratio of 1:23 (BANBEIS, 2019).

Education 1

Working Experience of an Academician from Higher-tier Private University:

"Students received huge authority during the pandemic time than a faculty member while attending the course"

The university was in great uncertainty of the enrollment of students during the pandemic time. The university offered a significant amount of financial discount for the students to increase their enrollment which is the only source of earning. The university did not look much at the quality of students while enrolled due to their high tuition fees and the economic uncertainty of students. The faculty during the class feels the 'students are the customers or God' that gives them a huge authority even while taking classes or examinations. It became impossible to ask all students to put their cameras on during the class environment and faculty members faces huge troubles interacting among the students. The student received huge authority to reach higher authorities of the university if something do not fit with their own will. Surprisingly, the authority addressed those complaints rather than discussing them with the faculty member of that course.

"The university is discouraging faculty members for higher study from aboard on lien without pay during the pandemic time"

There is a huge supply of faculty members during the pandemic time and they have been willing to work with lower salaries compared to industry standards. The university had a practice of encouraging faculty members to get a higher degree from abroad with lien without that would otherwise enrich the ranking of the university. The authority was in doubt to provide this facility to the faculty members which forced the faculty members to quit their job if they received an offer from aboard with financial assistance. This cannibalistic decision-making would be a great threat to career sustainability and enrichment.

"There is a huge discrimination among the faculty members from the higher authority considering the country origin they received their higher degree"

The top management of the university changes in a frequent manner that has a huge impact on the pleasure of working and working environment there too. The authority depicted discriminated gesture to the full-time faculty members and put a question on the quality of their higher degree which was obtained from some countries which are not desired to them. The faculty members were not evaluated based on their quality of publications rather evaluated the origin of their degree. This kind of mental block during the pandemic period traumatizes the existing faculty members with a scare of losing their stable job.

Education 2

Working Experience of an Academician from Lower-tier Private University:

"Initially faced trouble with the new modality however later on with the workshop based learning orientation about the usage of technology made the modality easier."

The transition from offline to online-based learning was new for academicians. Initially, they faced difficulties conducting classes online. Gradually they became used to the usage of technology. They started with zoom to conduct the classes and then shifted to Google Meet as it has convenient features and substantial time to conduct the class. The organization offered two workshops on the usage of technological tools for conducting classes and another one was about the assessment process. Workshops helped to recover the few issues associated with the online classes.

"Quality time spending with kids due to work from home policy helped a lot during the pandemic. On the other hand, job load increased due to the assessment over online, and uploading class contents regularly."

Work from home policy in the academic institutes helped academicians to give substantial time to their children and family. Covid-19 virus-related fear feeling also minimized due to home office. On the other hand, doing a regular home office and taking care of the family simultaneously created stress sometimes.

OVERALL SUMMARY FINDINGS

To explore the overall status in the five different industries, a summary table on the cross-sectors has been designed which reflect that leading organizations to the comparatively low performer in the similar sector went through a change in their workplace during pandemic situation since the beginning of 2020. Shifting the

Table 7. Summary of the findings from the education industry

Major areas of change in the agile environment	Education 1	Education 2
The transition from offline to online	Yes	Yes
Availability of work from home policy	Yes	Yes
Execution of the work from home policy	Yes	Yes
Work-Life Balance	Not satisfactory	Satisfactory
Training availability	Instruction material-based communication rather than one-to-one training.	Yes
Survival Strategy	The faculty members need to cope with the authoritarian aspect of the students in their course due to fear of losing their job	Coping up with the changing environment and learning application of the different learning tools
Career sustainability requirement	Created bar on lien without pay for higher study keeping the job as it is	Digital skill development

operations and serving online, enabled organizations and their stakeholders to be tech-savvy. Operational shifting also facilitated mid-management to top management level employees for doing work from the home office. Though work-life balance was not easy still, the satisfaction of the employees regarding work-life balance was mostly satisfactory. Digital skill application in the working environment opened up many opportunities for technology-based industries. To survive in the agile working environment, employees are focusing on their consistent performance.

CONCLUSION

Investigation on the five major industries reflects the changing environment in the business during the pandemic situation. One of the major changes that across the industries embraced was the transition of their operations from offline to online since the pandemic strike in Bangladesh during March, 2020. The operational transition has brought a change in the work environment of the industries. Work from home policy was executed for the employees except for the traditional restaurant-based industry. Mostly, management-level employees of the leading organizations and academicians could take the full opportunity of working from home. Employees of the major industries of the country could enjoy moderate to high work-life balance due to the operational change except for the high-performing organization of the

Table 8. Summary of the Cross-Sectoral Findings

Major Areas of Changes	Changes in the Industry				
	Telecom	Retail	Restaurant	FinTech	Education
The transition from offline to online	▪ There was the operational transition from offline to the online platform.	▪ There was the operational transition from offline to the online platform.	▪ There was the operational transition from offline to the online platform.	▪ There was the operational transition from offline to the online platform.	▪ There was the operational transition from offline to the online platform.
Availability of work from home policy	▪ Work from home policy was available.	▪ Work from home policy was available.	▪ Work from home policy was not available for the traditional restaurants including the leading one. ▪ The virtual kitchen was the growing concept where the nature of work is home-based.	▪ Work from home policy was available.	▪ Work from home policy was available.
Execution of the work from home policy	▪ Full-fledge work from home policy was executed in the leading organization whereas moderate execution was visible in the low-performing organization.	▪ Partial execution was feasible for the employees working at the managerial level.	▪ Execution of work from home policy was not feasible for traditional restaurants including the leading one. ▪ The virtual kitchen had the advantage of working at home due to its' type.	▪ Full-fledge work from home policy was executed for the managers across the different regions of the country under the industry.	▪ Full-fledge work from home policy was executed for the academicians.
Work-Life Balance	▪ Work-life balance was not satisfactory for the leading organization but it was better in the low-performing organization.	▪ Work-life balance was more satisfactory for the leading retail organization than low-performing one.	▪ Work-life balance was satisfactory for the employees of the industry.	▪ Work-life balance was satisfactory for the employees of the industry. Employees of the leading organization were more satisfied than others.	▪ Work-life balance was satisfactory.
Training availability	▪ Different training programs were available for the employees.	▪ Different training programs were available for the employees.	▪ Different training programs were available for the employees.	▪ Different training programs were available for the employees.	▪ Different training programs were available for the employees.
Survival Strategy	▪ The leading organization was more focused on consistent performance whereas low performing organization focused on capacity development.	▪ The leading organization introduced new products with good service experience. On the other hand, growth in sales was a major focus for the low performing one,	▪ Affiliation with online delivery vendors through apps helped traditional restaurants to survive during the complex working environment of the pandemic. ▪ Customized offerings were a major focus for the virtual kitchen.	▪ Diversified offerings through innovation facilitated to survive the leading organization. ▪ Targeting a new segment was the survival tool for the low-performing one.	▪ Adaptability and quick learning ability regarding the learning tools was the major survival strategy ▪ Need to cope with the authoritarian aspect of the students in their course due to fear of losing their job

Telecom industry. As operational changes came in the industries, training was found available for the employees of the industries. The primary orientation about the usage of various instruments for official purposes was introduced, followed by a business nature-oriented appropriate skill development program through online training.

Leading organizations of the industries focused on innovation, new product development, and affiliation with online delivery vendors through app-based solutions, consistent performance, adaptability with technology & quick learning skill development, etc. for survival against the agile work environment. Comparatively weaker organizations than the leading ones, survival strategies were crafted based on the available capacity expansion opportunity, customer number base extension, sales growth assurance, targeting new segments, and openness to learning new skills, etc.

To make the career sustainable against the agile work environment, leading organizations focused on the digital knowledge acquisition, prioritizing loyal customer base, gaining knowledge about the adaptability, technological adaptability, and digital skills development for the completion of the job responsibilities related to that specific industry. Comparatively weaker organizations are focusing on capacity development, expansion, technological orientation, and consistent performance under the digital platform. Application of the technology and improvement of the digital skills will be helping employees of different industries to grow soon which will also create a positive impact on the business growth.

REFERENCES

Abir, A. A. (2019, April 18). Retail Industry in Bangladesh: A Different Shape up Story. *LightCastle Analytics Wing*. https://databd.co/stories/organized-retail-industry-outlook-bangladesh-2077

Agarwal, V., Mathiyazhagan, K., Malhotra, S., & Saikouk, T. (2021). Analysis of challenges in sustainable human resource management due to disruptions by industry 4.0: An emerging economy perspective. *International Journal of Manpower*. Advance online publication. doi:10.1108/IJM-03-2021-0192

Agrawal, S., Smet, A. D., Lacroix, S., & Reich, A. (2020). *To emerge stronger from the COVID-19 crisis, companies should start reskilling their workforces now.* McKinsey & Company. https://www.mckinsey.com/business-functions/people-and-organizational-performance/our-insights/to-emerge-stronger-from-the-covid-19-crisis-companies-should-start-reskilling-their-workforces-now

Ajgaonkar, S., Neelam, N. G., & Wiemann, J. (2021). Drivers of workforce agility: A dynamic capability perspective. *The International Journal of Organizational Analysis*. Advance online publication. doi:10.1108/IJOA-11-2020-2507

Akhter, R. & Jahan, F. (2020). The Contribution of Telecom Industries on Bangladesh Economy. *International Journal of Humanities and Social Science Invention, 9*(9), 27-37. doi:10.35629/7722

Alam, M. S., Ali, M. J., Bhuiyan, A. B., Solaiman, M., & Rahman, M. A. (2020). The impact of covid -19 pandemic on the economic growth in Bangladesh: A conceptual review. *American Economic & Social Review*, *6*(2), 1–12. doi:10.46281/aesr.v6i2.844

Almeida, F., & Santos, J. D. (2020). The effects of COVID-19 on job security and unemployment in Portugal. *The International Journal of Sociology and Social Policy*, *40*(9/10), 995–1003. doi:10.1108/IJSSP-07-2020-0291

Alon, I., Farrell, M., & Li, S. (2020). Regime type and COVID-19 response. *FIIB Business Review*, *9*(3), 152–160. doi:10.1177/2319714520928884

Amit, S. (2020, March 10). The future of on-demand food delivery and COVID-19. *The Business Standard*. https://www.tbsnews.net/panorama/future-demand-food-delivery-and-covid-19-54274

Autin, K. L., Blustein, D. L., Ali, S. R., & Garriott, P. O. (2020). Career Development Impacts of COVID-19: Practice and Policy Recommendations. *Journal of Career Development*, *47*(5), 487–494. doi:10.1177/0894845320944486

Bangladesh - The Rising FinTech Star in South Asia. (2021, February 3). *Medici*. https://gomedici.com/bangladesh-the-rising-fintech-star-in-south-asia#

Bangladesh Bank. (2021). *Exchange rate of Taka*. https://www.bb.org.bd/econdata/exchangerate.php

Bangladesh Bureau of Educational Information and Statistics (BANBEIS). (2019). *Bangladesh Education Statistics 2019(New)*. Ministry of Education.

Bangladesh reimposes Covid lockdown for two weeks. (2021, July 23). *Aljazeera*. https://www.aljazeera.com/news/2021/7/23/bangladesh-covid-lockdown-two-weeks

Barneveld, K., Quinlan, M., Kriesler, P., Junor, A., Baum, F., & Chowdhury, A. (2020). The COVID-19 pandemic: Lessons on building more equal and sustainable societies. *Economic and Labour Relations Review*, *31*(2), 133–157. doi:10.1177/1035304620927107

Basu, S. (2020, July 10). IIM Calcutta to start online classes from August 3. *The Times of India*. https://timesofindia.indiatimes.com/city/kolkata/iim-to-start-online-classes-from-aug-3/articleshow/76882534.cms

Begum, M., Farid, M. S., Alam, M. J., & Barua, S. (2020). Covid-19 and Bangladesh: Socioeconomic analysis towards the future correspondence. *Asian Journal of Agricultural Extension. Economia e Sociologia*, 143–155. doi:10.9734/ajaees/2020/v38i930417

Better Work. (2021). *COVID-19 Timeline in Bangladesh*. https://betterwork.org/portfolio/covid-timeline-in-bangladesh/

bKash tops students' list as 'employer of choice'. (2020, December 30). *The Daily Star*. https://www.thedailystar.net/business/news/bkash-tops-students-list-employer-choice-2019241

Boland, B., Smet, A. D., Palter, R., & Sanghvi, A. (2020, June 8). *Reimagining the office and work life after COVID-19*. Mckinsey & Company. https://www.mckinsey.com/business-functions/people-and-organizational-performance/our-insights/reimagining-the-office-and-work-life-after-covid-19

Breu, K., Hemingway, C. J., Strathern, M., & Bridger, D. (2002). Workforce agility: The new employee strategy for the knowledge economy. *Journal of Information Technology*, *17*(1), 21–31. https://doi.org/10.1080/02683960110132070

BTRC. (2021). *The total number of Mobile Phone subscribers*. http://www.btrc.gov.bd/content/mobile-phone-subscribers-bangladesh-may-2021

Cappelli, P., & Keller, J. R. (2014). Talent management: Conceptual approaches and practical challenges. *Annual Review of Organizational Psychology and Organizational Behavior*, *1*(1), 305–331. https://doi.org/10.1146/annurev-orgpsych-031413-091314

Carvalho, A. M., Sampaio, P., Rebentisch, E., Carvalho, J. Á., & Saraiva, P. (2020). The influence of operational excellence on the culture and agility of organizations: Evidence from industry. *International Journal of Quality & Reliability Management*, *38*(7), 1520–1549. https://doi.org/10.1108/ijqrm-07-2020-0248

Chandrasekaran, R. (2021). The future of work: How hr drives digital transformation in the new normal. *Strategic HR Review*. Advance online publication. doi:10.1108/shr-11-2020-0094

Chang, S. L., Harding, N., Zachreson, C., Cliff, O. M., & Prokopenko, M. (2020). Modelling transmission and control of the COVID-19 pandemic in Australia. *Nature Communications*, *11*(1). https://doi.org/10.1038/s41467-020-19393-6

Chen, C. C., & Chen, M. H. (2021). Well-being and career change Intention: COVID-19's impact on unemployed and furloughed hospitality workers. *International Journal of Contemporary Hospitality Management*. Advance online publication. doi:10.1108/ijchm-07-2020-0759

Chen, Z. (2021). Influence of Working from Home during the COVID-19 Crisis and HR Practitioner Response. *Frontiers in Psychology, 12*. doi:10.3389/fpsyg.2021.710517

Chowdhury, M. T., Sarkar, A., Saha, P. K., & Anik, R. H. (2020). Enhancing supply resilience in the COVID-19 pandemic: A case study on beauty and personal care retailers. *Modern Supply Chain Research and Applications, 2*(3), 143–159. doi:10.1108/mscra-07-2020-0018

Cornelius, N., Wallace, J., & Tassabehji, R. (2007). An analysis of corporate social responsibility, corporate identity and ethics teaching in business school. *Journal of Business Ethics*, *76*(1), 117–135. https://doi.org/10.1007/s10551-006-9271-6

Cullen, J. C., Hammer, L. B., Neal, M. B., & Sinclair, R. R. (2009). Development of a typology of dual-earner couples caring for children and aging parents. *Journal of Family Issues*, *30*(4), 458–483.

Datta, P. R. (2018, February 16). The changing retail market landscape. *The Financial Express*. https://www.thefinancialexpress.com.bd/views/the-changing-retail-market-landscape-1518803754

Deb, S. K., & Nafi, S. M. (2020). Impact of covid-19 pandemic on tourism: Perceptions from Bangladesh. *SSRN Electronic Journal*. doi:10.2139/ssrn.3632798

Eikenberry, S. E., Mancuso, M., Iboi, E., Phan, T., Eikenberry, K., Kuang, Y., Kostelich, E., & Gumel, A. B. (2020). To mask or not to mask: Modeling the potential for face mask use by the general public to curtail the COVID-19 pandemic. *Infectious Disease Modelling*, *5*, 293–308. doi:10.1016/j.idm.2020.04.001

Fogarty, P., Frantiz, S., Hirschfeld, J., Keating, S., Lafont, E., Lufkin, B., Mishael, R., Ponnavolu, V., Savage, M., & Turits, M. (2020). Coronavirus: How the world of work may change forever. *BBC*. https://www.bbc.com/worklife/article/20201023-coronavirus-how-will-the-pandemic-change-the-way-we-work

Fong, M. W., Gao, H., Wong, J. Y., Xiao, J., Shiu, E. Y. C., Ryu, S., & Cowling, B. J. (2020). Nonpharmaceutical measures for pandemic influenza in nonhealthcare settings – social distancing measures. *Emerging Infectious Diseases*, *26*(5), 976–984. doi:10.3201/eid2605.190995

Friedman, T. L. (2005). *The world is flat: A brief history of the twenty-first century* (1st ed.). Macmillan.

Gomes, V. (2020, June 26). Cloud Kitchens: Future of food delivery services. *The Daily Star*. https://www.thedailystar.net/toggle/news/cloud-kitchens-future-food-delivery-services-1920413

Goodman, C. J., & Mance, S. M. (2011). Employment loss and the 2007-09 recession: An overview. *Monthly Lab. Rev., 134*(3). doi:10.1177/2319714520928884

Haleem, A., Javaid, M., & Vaishya, R. (2020). Effects of COVID-19 pandemic in daily life. *Current Medicine Research and Practice, 10*(2), 78-79. doi:10.1016/j.cmrp.2020.03.011

Hamouche, S. (2021). Human resource management and the COVID-19 crisis: Implications, challenges, opportunities, and future organizational directions. *Journal of Management & Organization*, 1–16. doi:10.1017/jmo.2021.15

Hancock, B., & Schaninger, B. (2020). *HR says talent is crucial for performance–and the pandemic proves it.* McKinsey & Company. https://www.mckinsey.com/business-functions/people-and-organizational-performance/our-insights/hr-says-talent-is-crucial-for-performance-and-the-pandemic-proves-it

Hillier, D., Newton-Lewis, T., Nair, E., & Larsen, C. (2020). Initial COVID-19 responses in Bangladesh, Kenya, Pakistan, Sierra Leone and Uganda: Documentation and learning from March to May 2020 (COVID-19 Series: Synthesis Report). *UKAID & Oxford Policy Management*. https://reliefweb.int/sites/reliefweb.int/files/resources/COVID-19-Synthesis-report-Exec-Sum-Final.pdf

Hossain, S. (2021, May 4). The restaurant industry is on the brink of collapse. *Dhaka Tribune*. https://www.dhakatribune.com/business/commerce/2021/05/04/the-restaurant-industry-is-on-the-brink-of-collapse

Ikram, M., Shen, Y., Ferasso, M., & D'Adamo, I. (2021). Intensifying effects of covid-19 on economic growth, logistics performance, environmental sustainability and Quality Management: Evidence from Asian countries. *Journal of Asia Business Studies*. Advance online publication. doi:10.1108/jabs-07-2021-0316

Karim, M. R., Shetu, S. A., & Razia, S. (2021). Covid-19, liquidity and Financial Health: Empirical Evidence from South Asian economy. *Asian Journal of Economics and Banking*, *5*(3), 307–323. https://doi.org/10.1108/ajeb-03-2021-0033

Lai, C. C., Shih, T. P., Ko, W. C., Tang, H. J., & Hsueh, P. R. (2020). Severe acute respiratory syndrome coronavirus 2 (SARS-CoV-2) and corona virus disease-2019 (COVID-19): The epidemic and the challenges. *International Journal of Antimicrobial Agents*, *55*, 105924.

Lalon, R. M. (2020). Covid-19 vs. Bangladesh: Is it possible to recover the impending economic distress amid this pandemic? *Journal of Economics and Business*, *3*(2). https://doi.org/10.31014/aior.1992.03.02.240

Lawrence, B. S., Hall, D. T., & Arthur, M. B. (2015). Sustainable careers then and now. In A. D. Vos & B. I. J. M. v. Heijden (Eds.), Handbook of research on sustainable careers (pp. 432–450). Edward Elgar Publishing. https://doi.org/10.4337/9781782547037.00033.

Liaquat, Z. B. (2020, August 11). Plea to save the restaurant industry. *The Financial Express*. https://thefinancialexpress.com.bd/views/plea-to-save-the-restaurant-industry-1597086210

Liaquat, Z. B. (2021, June 27). Bangladesh lags behind in fintech ecosystem globally. *Dhaka Tribune*. https://www.dhakatribune.com/business/2021/06/27/bangladesh-lags-behind-in-fintech-ecosystem-globally

LightCastle Analytics Wing. (2019, July 9). *Transformation in the Telecommunications Industry*. https://www.lightcastlebd.com/insights/2019/07/transformation-in-the-telecommunications-industry

Lockdown now from Thursday. (2021, June 27). *The Daily Star*. Retrieved November 7, 2021, from https://www.thedailystar.net/frontpage/news/lockdown-now-thursday-2119017

Lopes, A. S., Sargento, A., & Carreira, P. (2021). Vulnerability to COVID-19 unemployment in the Portuguese tourism and hospitality industry. *International Journal of Contemporary Hospitality Management*, *33*(5), 1850–1869. https://doi.org/10.1108/ijchm-11-2020-1345

Mahmoud Saleh, F. I., & Karia, N. (2020). Benchmarks for INGOs' effective responses during COVID-19 pandemic. *Benchmarking*, *27*(10), 2863–2886.

Mamgain, R. P. (2021). Understanding labour market disruptions and job losses amidst COVID-19. *Journal of Social and Economic Development*. doi:10.1007/s40847-020-00125-x

Mikołajczyk, K. (2021). Changes in the approach to employee development in organizations as a result of the COVID-19 pandemic. *European Journal of Training and Development*. Advance online publication. doi:10.1108/ejtd-12-2020-0171

Mishra, D., & Chanchani, M. (2020, March 24). Coronavirus scare in Bengaluru: online companies face disruption in delivery of essential goods. *The Times of India*. https://timesofindia.indiatimes.com/city/bengaluru/online-cos-face-disruption-in-delivery-of-essential-goods/articleshow/74783378.cms

Molloy, J. C., & Noe, R. A. (2009). "Learning" a Living: Continuous Learning for Survival in Today's Talent Market. In *Learning, training, and development in organizations* (pp. 352–380). Routledge.

MPHonline. (2021). *Outbreak: 10 of the Worst Pandemics in History.* https://www.mphonline.org/worst-pandemics-in-history/

Newman, K. L. (2011). Sustainable careers. *Organizational Dynamics*, *40*(2), 136–143. https://doi.org/10.1016/j.orgdyn.2011.01.008

Parker, S. K., & Bindl, U. K. (2016). *Proactivity at work: Making things happen in organizations*. Taylor & Francis.

Paul, S. K., Chowdhury, P., Chowdhury, M. T., Chakrabortty, R. K., & Moktadir, M. A. (2021). Operational challenges during a pandemic: An investigation in the electronics industry. *The International Journal of Logistics Management.* Advance online publication. doi:10.1108/ijlm-05-2021-0307

Pucciarelli, F., & Kaplan, A. (2021). Transition to a hybrid teaching model as a step forward toward responsible management education? *Journal of Global Responsibility.* Advance online publication. doi:10.1108/JGR-12-2020-0111

Saunders, M., Lewis, P., & Thornhill, A. (2007). *Research methods for business students* (4th ed.). Prentice Hall.

Segbenya, M., Baafi-Frimpong, S. A., & Oppong, N. Y. (2021). Effect of COVID-19 on acquisition of employable skills among National Service personnel in Ghana. *Journal of Work-Applied Management*, *13*(2), 215–226. https://doi.org/10.1108/jwam-12-2020-0058

Sharma, P. (2021). Customer co-creation, COVID-19 and sustainable service outcomes. *Benchmarking*, *28*(7), 2232–2258. doi:10.1108/BIJ-10-2020-0541

Shawon, A. A. (2020, May 27). Covid-19: Bangladesh likely to end general holiday on May 31. *Dhaka Tribune*. https://www.dhakatribune.com/bangladesh/2020/05/27/state-minister-update-of-lockdown-coming-soon

Sohrabi, C., Alsafi, Z., O'Neill, N., Khan, M., Kerwan, A., Al-Jabir, A., & Agha, R. (2020). World health organization declares global emergency: A review of the 2019 novel coronavirus (COVID-19). *International Journal of Surgery*, *76*, 71–76.

Sreelakshmi, C. C., & Prathap, S. K. (2020). Continuance adoption of mobile based payments in Covid-19 context: An integrated framework of health belief model and expectation confirmation model. *International Journal of Pervasive Computing and Communications*, *16*(4), 351–369. doi:10.1108/IJPCC-06-2020-0069

Tagliaro, C., & Migliore, A. (2021). "Covid-working": What to keep and what to Leave? Evidence from an Italian company. *Journal of Corporate Real Estate*. Advance online publication. doi:10.1108/jcre-10-2020-0053

Tan, W. J. Z. X., Zhao, X., Ma, X., Wang, W., Niu, P., Xu, W., & Wu, G. Z. (2020). A novel coronavirus genome identified in a cluster of pneumonia cases—Wuhan, China 2019-2020. *China CDC Weekly, 2*(4), 61-62. http://weekly.chinacdc.cn/en/article/doi/10.46234/ccdcw2020.017

Trehan, S. (2019, December 13). Virtual Kitchen – The Rise of the Delivery-Only Restaurant. *LimeTray*. https://limetray.com/blog/virtual-kitchen/

Uddin, A. K. M. Z. (2021, June 30). Who owns Nagad? *The Daily Star*. https://www.thedailystar.net/business/economy/banks/news/who-owns-nagad-2120921

US Bureau of Labor Statistics. (2020). *Employment recovery in the wake of the COVID-19 pandemic*. https://www.bls.gov/opub/mlr/2020/article/employment-recovery.htm

van Veldhoven, M., & Dorenbosch, L. (2008). Age, proactivity and career development. *Career Development International, 13*(2), 112–131. https://doi.org/10.1108/13620430810860530

Warrier, B. S. (2020, May 26). COVID-19: What next for the education sector? *The Week*. https://www.theweek.in/leisure/society/2020/05/26/covid-19-what-next-for-the-education-sector.html

Webb, A., McQuaid, R., & Rand, S. (2020). Employment in the informal economy: Implications of the COVID-19 pandemic. *The International Journal of Sociology and Social Policy, 40*(9/10), 1005–1019. https://doi.org/10.1108/ijssp-08-2020-0371

World Bank. (2020). *Global Economic Prospects*. doi:10.1596/978-1-4648-1553-9

worldometers.info. (2021). *Reported Cases and Deaths by Country or Territory*. https://www.worldometers.info/coronavirus/

Xu, Z., Shi, L., Wang, Y., Zhang, J., Huang, L., Zhang, C. & Tai, Y. (2020). Pathological findings of COVID-19 associated with acute respiratory distress syndrome. *The Lancet Respiratory Medicine, 8*(4), 420-422.

Zaman, T. (2020, August 6). Cloud Kitchens in Bangladesh: A Reality. *TRIDigital*. https://www.tridigital.com.bd/cloud-kitchens-in-bangladesh/

Zhang, H. (2020). China's employment stabilization policies in response to the impact of the COVID-19 pandemic. *International Journal of Sociology and Social Policy*. Advance online publication. doi:10.1108/ijssp-05-2020-0167

Zhu, N., Zhang, D., Wang, W., Li, X., Yang, B., Song, J., & Niu, P. (2020). A novel coronavirus from patients with pneumonia in China, 2019. *The New England Journal of Medicine*, *382*(8), 727–733.

Bangladeshis infected with coronavirus: IEDCR. (2020, March 8). *The Daily Star*. https://www.thedailystar.net/coronavirus-deadly-new-threat/news/iedcr-confirms-3-coronavirus-patients-hospitalised-bangladesh-1878022

KEY TERMS AND DEFINITIONS

Agile Environment: Companies with an Agile environment typically accept and promote change, innovation, and process improvement. People in this approach can work collaboratively with others to create an environment that is suited to their situation.

Cloud Kitchen: Cloud kitchen refers to a place where food is prepared and delivered at a customer's location by taking orders via calls and online ordering platforms. It does not offer space for people to come and dine in.

Fintech: Fintech is a business that uses technology to enhance or automate financial services and processes. The term encompasses a rapidly growing industry that serves the interests of both consumers and businesses in multiple ways. It helps consumers or financial institutions deliver financial services in newer, faster ways than traditional methods.

Lockdown: A lockdown is a requirement for people to stay where they are, usually due to specific risks to themselves or others if they can move freely.

Retail: Retail refers to the activity of selling goods or services directly to consumers or end-users. A retailer purchases goods in large quantities from manufacturers, directly or through a wholesaler, and then sells in smaller quantities to consumers for a profit.

Sustainable Career: A sustainable career can grow with the employees throughout the years, that has meaning to them, and that makes good use of their skills and experience.

Telecom Industry: The telecommunications industry consists of cable companies, internet service providers, satellite companies, and telephone companies, whereas telecommunications is defined as communicating over a distance.

ENDNOTE

1 1USD=85.80 BDT (Bangladesh Bank, 2020).

Section 4

Macro-Level Changes to Work Post-Pandemic

Chapter 11
Career Re-Invention Through Entrepreneurial Mindset and Entrepreneurial Orientation in the Post-Pandemic Era:
Multiple Cases from the Developed and Developing Countries

Lukman Raimi
https://orcid.org/0000-0002-5329-8715
School of Business and Economics, Universiti Brunei Darussalam, Brunei

Jainaba M. L. Kah
Department of Strategic Policy and Delivery, Office of the President, Gambia

ABSTRACT

The chapter explicates how career reinvention is leveraged for saving jobs and ensuring business continuity in readiness for the post-pandemic era. The employees exploited entrepreneurial mindset (EM) as a resilience strategy to save current jobs and create new jobs, while employers adopted the entrepreneurial orientation (EO) to keep their businesses afloat and meet their bottom-line. In the 20 multiple cases reviewed, some of the EM characteristics that employees manifested include determination, drive to achieve, opportunity orientation, persistent problem-solving, internal locus of control, tolerance for ambiguity, calculated risk-taking, high energy level, innovativeness, vision, passion, and team building. Comparatively, the EO dimensions that employees utilised include innovativeness, proactiveness, risk-taking, competitive aggressiveness, and autonomy. The chapter enriches the EM and EO concepts by explicating both as career re-invention strategies for saving existing jobs, creating new jobs, and ensuring business continuity in the post-pandemic era.

DOI: 10.4018/978-1-7998-8626-6.ch011

INTRODUCTION

From late 2019, the COVID-19 pandemic has continued to destroy jobs, and equally rendered several skills obsolete– a situation that calls for a pragmatic adaptation of skills and competencies to help employees and employers come to grips with the new realities (Osland et al., 2020). In most countries across the globe, proactive companies are already rethinking and reinventing their business models because of the uncertainty caused by the pandemic (Kilic, & Marin, 2020). According to the International Labour Organisation (2021a), the level of labour market disruption inflicted by the pandemic is unprecedented, as it brought working hours in the fourth quarter of 2020 down by 8.8 per cent, which corresponds to 255 million full-time jobs. Before the pandemic, the events that often trigger a career reinvention in the workplaces include corporate downsizing, increased globalization, deregulation, outsourcing, technological change, mergers, and acquisitions (Gysbers, Heppner, & Johnston, 1998; Heppner, 1998). The new norms of social distancing and travel restrictions adopted to mitigate the spread of the COVID-19 pandemic have disrupted businesses, heightened massive job losses in some sectors, and lead to a reduction of the workforce in several others (Raimi, 2021). Most of the companies laying off and downsizing operations belong to the hospitality, tourism, and leisure sectors, while the companies actively employing and expanding business operations are those in the logistics, health, medicine, retailing sectors (Lane, 2021).

In the development literature, the two views for explicating the reactions to economic recession or environmental crises are vulnerability and resilience perspectives (Kitching et al., 2009; Smallbone et al., 2012). Both perspectives are used in the field of emergency management, social psychology, and development economics among others (Martini & Vespasiano, 2015; Papathoma-Köhle, Thaler & Fuchs, 2021). The vulnerability perspective of recession posits that individuals and corporate organisations are negatively affected by exposure to external shocks because they have limited resources, limited product lines, and limited customers, which tend to restrict their ability and capacity to survive the poverty pressures and harsh economic conditions imposed on their lifestyles and livelihoods (Kitching et al., 2009; Athwal et al., 2011). In reality, employees and businesses are vulnerable to social risks, physical threats, and economic shocks imposed by the pandemic 'because they lack coping capacities' (USP, 2013). The vulnerability view, which explains the helplessness and hopelessness of the individuals and businesses in the crisis period has been challenged by the proponents of the resilience viewpoint. The resilience perspective, however, explicates that individuals and corporate organisations within the economy have the ability and capability to survive exogenous shocks resulting from crises that hit the national economy, if they can adopt proactive and innovative strategies that would make them resilient (Wedawatta & Ingirige, 2012; Kitching, et al., 2009). The salient question: How true is the assertion that the individuals and corporate organisations within the economy have the ability and capability to survive exogenous shocks resulting from the COVID-19 pandemic?

Following from the resilience argument, the pandemic presents a very good opportunity for employees and employers to leverage career reinventing as a coping strategy in readiness for the Post pandemic era. The notion of career reinvention is a complex psychosocial issue that is influenced by internal and external factors, and both factors emphasised role adjustments (Watts et al., 2015; Walker, 2019). Part of the external factors that made career reinventing (through skills development and lifelong learning) compelling before COVI-19 pandemic is the emergence of new technologies, globalization wave, demographic shifts, climate change imperatives, and migration. These factors are causing job losses during the pandemic in some sectors, while also creating new opportunities in other sectors of the economy (ILO, 2021b). To meet the fast-changing demand for highly skilled employees in the labour markets, career reinvention through reskilling, upskilling, and relearning are inevitable. Moreover, the OECD (2021) underscored the need for career reinvention, because the pandemic has reduced the demand for jobs requiring low levels of education by 40% in Australia and the United Kingdom, whereas preference for high skilled workers has increased by 25%. And that, the phenomenon of working from home (WFH) has become pervasive in Australia, Canada, New Zealand, the United Kingdom, and the United States. For the low-skilled employees and vulnerable workers, the need for retraining and upskilling interventions is critical to foster and accelerate the development of the required competencies and skills. A career reinvention programme in a period of recession requires tripartite interventions of employees, employers, and governments – an inevitable collaboration described as reskilling pathways for millions of unemployed global workforce (Chopra-McGowan and Reddy, 2021).

The role of employees in stimulating career reinvention includes creating personal career paths, undertaking self-development, and setting themselves up as "brands" for the employers (Gettler, 2003). The employees must acquire new skill sets and competencies to be able to cope and adapt effectively to radical changes in workplaces (Agrawal et al., 2020). The role of employees extends to understanding the rationale for their career reinvention, conducting skills inventory/self-assessment, investing in personal development, and removing inhibiting obstacles to career reinvention such as old age, fear, uncertainties, and cost implications (Castrillon, 2019).

The role of employers in stimulating career reinvention in the workplace includes updating the skills of their valued employers to cope with technological advances (Worthington, 2006), advancing leadership development schemes for women to aid progression to senior positions (Clarke, 2011), and introducing diversity practices, cultural and organisational change (Worthington, 2012). Also, employers must learn new ways of matching their employees' new roles made expedient by new technologies (telecommuting, automation, and AI) to strengthen their capacities to deliver new business models in the Post pandemic era (Agrawal et al., 2020).

The role of the governments in stimulating career reinvention in the economy is to initiate policy interventions that would accelerate the development of competencies and skills of the citizens to meet the changing needs of labour markets as well as foster the resilience capabilities of the people in readiness for the Post pandemic era (OECD, 2021). Besides, the government is expected to support the employees and employers with fiscal stimulus packages. In the US government activates the Coronavirus Aid, Relief, and Economic Security (CARES) Act to provide economic reliefs and stimulus packages to the small businesses to navigate the economic disruptions resulting from the pandemic. The CARES Act Paycheck Protection Program (PPP) is a loan program created to provide bail-out to businesses to ease the challenges of payroll, lease, rent mortgage, and utility payments (Bartik et al., 2020). The fiscal measures provided by developing countries such as Ghana, Kenya, Mauritius, Ivory Coast, Nigeria, Senegal, and South Africa are practically saving jobs, bailing out for small businesses, and providing social protection and welfare programs (Renzaho, 2020; Raimi, 2021).

Based on the foregoing, the employees, employers, and governments have mutually reinforcing roles with regards to career re-invention in readiness for the Post Pandemic Era. Unfortunately, career reinvention in recessionary period has not been well-researched nor contextualised as cases from which employees, employers and governments can draw lessons. To fill the knowledge gap, this chapter explicates how career reinvention is being leveraged by employees and employers for saving jobs and ensuring business continuity in readiness for the Post Pandemic Era. The intent is to contribute to an existing body of knowledge on career reinvention. The chapter is both academic and practitioner-focused, but with greater emphasis on multiple cases presentation and analysis.

METHODOLOGY

This paper adopts a qualitative research method. We find the qualitative research method useful because it allows the researchers to explain what is observed clearly and deeply (McCusker & Gunaydin, 2015; Whiffin, 2020). The non-numerical data were extracted from scholarly articles and internet resources on career reinvention, entrepreneurial mindset (EM), and entrepreneurial orientation (EO). To ensure academic rigour and objectivity in the selection of these scholarly articles a sample of 70 relevant works covering career reinvention, EM, and EO were purposively selected from the Google Scholar database and other online databases. The extracted qualitative data were analyzed using the content analysis (CA). The methodology literature describes the CA as a logical procedure for quantifying the contents of texts, writings, interviews, picture speeches, books, correspondences, and other verbal data (Denscombe, 2017). The CA functionally allows numerical and non-numerical information from texts, words, and other audio-visual and non-audiovisual materials to be compressed, classified, summarized, and tabulated into fewer sentences for meaningful interpretations and inferences in qualitative research (Horn, 2012; Saunders et al., 2016).

For more clarity, our qualitative approach follows a three-stage protocol explained below.

i. **Stage 1: Data sourcing** - This stage focuses on sourcing useful information that better provides clarity and direction to the intent of the research. For data sourcing, we previewed and explored Google Scholar and other search engines for articles from which over 70 relevant articles were selected through the purposive sampling technique.
ii. **Stage 2: Data development and conversion** – At this stage, we compiled and integrated the cases on career reinvention, EM characteristics and EO dimensions in readiness for analysis data.
iii **Stage 3: Data analysis** –The data were appraised and analysed using content analysis. This methodological approach is supported by (Jepson, 2009; Saunders et al., 2016; Williams & Shepherd, 2017).

BACKGROUND

The three concepts that underpin this chapter are sequentially discussed hereunder.

Career reinvention

Career reinvention is a phenomenon that gives employers tough times thinking about the best trade-off for saving jobs and keeping business operations afloat in the pandemic – a decision described by the Harvard Business Review as ‘a social experiment of the future of work in action’ (Jesuthasan, Malcolm & Cantrell, 2020). In the career change literature, career reinvention refers to an occupational change that requires taking up a completely new role and set of tasks (Ibarra, 2004; Walker, 2019). Scholars explained that career reinvention is one of the three distinct types of work change (occupational change), the other two are task change and position change (Heppner, 1998; Walker, 2019). Moreover, career reinvention becomes exhilarating when individuals recognised that reinventing a career is necessary to break free from unfulfilling jobs (Castrillon, 2019). Also, career reinvention decision requires professional coaching and counselling because it is a transition that involves complex psychosocial issues and role adjustments (Watts et al., 2015; Walker, 2019). The role adjustments associated with career reinvention require the readiness to manage predictable and unpredictable outcomes – a phenomenon called 'career adaptability (Savickas et al, 2009).

With particular reference to women, O'Neil and Bilimoria (2005) noted that career reinvention (the third phase in the 3-stage career development framework) requires coordinated organizational efforts through consistent coaching and mentoring, and access to organizational resources. In reality, career reinvention could be precipitated by self-induced factors and externally-induced factors. The COVID-19 pandemic is a very good example of an externally-induced career reinventing. For employees whose paid jobs have been rendered irrelevant by the pandemic, career reinvention becomes expedient and non-negotiable. A number of jobs across different sectors have been made obsolete and would no longer meet the needs of the workplaces in the Post pandemic era. Baker (2020) noted that employers are substituting full-time employees with contingent workers as a strategic cost-saving measure to save jobs and keep businesses afloat, and employees are upskilling to meet the expectations of their employers. Furthermore, there is a change in features of job advertisements across Europe and the US. The features that are mentioned in job advertisements reflected a strong preference for technical competencies and social skills. In the healthcare sector, the highly prized skills are emergency and intensive care, and basic patient care. In other sectors, transversal skills especially communication skills and teamwork are among the top mentioned skills in advertised positions (OECD, 2021). Some of the strategies for dispensing with employees that failed to reinvent their careers to match the needs of the employers include permanent lay-off, temporary layoff, voluntary temporary layoff and suspension of non-essential recruitments (University of Washington, 2021). Employers of labour in the public and private sectors must be committed to career reinvention, reskilling, and retooling by launching a talent strategy that would develop three competencies of their employees, namely: (a) critical digital and cognitive capabilities, (b) social and emotional skills, and (c) adaptability and resilience (Agrawal, et al., 2020). In readiness for the Post pandemic era, the employees must prepare for new workplace lifestyles behaviours. The four lifestyles behaviours vis-a-vis career reinvention are explained in Table 1 below.

Entrepreneurial Mindset

The concept of entrepreneurial mindset (EM) refers to a combination of traits and skills (mental attitude) that determines how an individual will interpret and respond to situations entrepreneurially. It extends to the ability to sense, act and mobilize even

Table 1. Forecasted lifestyles behaviours in workplaces

Lifestyle Mode	Back-to-normal	Wireless materialists	Gregarious simplifiers	Click rebels
Career reinvention lifestyles in workplaces	Employers and employees favour partial and conditional adoption of telework, because it provides convenience, status signaling, and profit.	Full adoption of telework, WFH and other remote technologies by employers and employees in order to maximize professional potential. This requires career reinvention.	This describes resistance by employers and employees to telework and new norms; they are relatively more comfortable with shortened workweeks.	Employers and employees welcome telework and touchless workspace because it enables self-realisation, free-lancing ethos, and open collaboration.

Source: Adapter from Echegaray (2021, p. 572).

under uncertainties (McGrath and Macmillian, 2000). The EM may also be viewed as the necessary characteristics required to be an entrepreneur or take entrepreneurial decisions in different business contexts (Zappe, Hochstedt & Kisenwether, 2013). Beyond the traditional management ideologies, the EO is required by individuals to avert the high failure rate of businesses caused by economic turbulence and harsh business environment (Morris & Kuratko, 2002). Moreover, Eno-Obong (2006) explained that people with EO are better able to perceive needs, challenges, and problems as opportunities and consequently reinvent novel ways to exploit and merge opportunities with the associated challenges. The EM is critical to the cognitive belief system of people because it exposes opportunities, and ignites a passion to pursue personal ambition, engages the faculties in ways and manners that enable people to flourish and thrive in different endeavours (The Entrepreneurial Learning Initiative, 2021). The literature identified a number of characteristics linked to EM. The EM characteristics are a combination of 7 personality traits and 6 skills (Davis, Hall & Mayer, 2016). However, this case adopted the 13 characteristics of EM identified by Kuratko (2014) that include: determination and perseverance., drive to achieve, opportunity orientation, persistent problem-solving, seeking feedback, internal locus of control, tolerance for ambiguity, calculated risk-taking, high energy level, creativity and innovativeness, vision, passion, and team building.

Entrepreneurial Orientation

The term entrepreneurial orientation (EO) is an organisational construct, which is built on three dimensions namely: innovation, proactiveness, and risk-taking (Covin & Slevin, 1989; Miller, 1983). In later years, the EO dimensions were extended with the inclusion of autonomy and competitive aggressiveness (Lumpkin & Dess,

1996). However, the EO studies have mostly used innovation, proactiveness, and risk-taking, which represent the three strategic ways entrepreneurship can best be manifested as an organizational attribute by organisations (Morris, Webb & Franklin, 2011; Wales, Covin & Monsen, 2020). The three EO dimensions are so important that the absence of any of three operationally makes an organisation to be considered less entrepreneurial (Miller, 2011).

The innovation dimension of EO refers to creating a competitive advantage in the market, by substituting, improving, renewing, and reinventing new products, services, and processes while responding to entrepreneurial opportunities (Nițu-Antonie, Feder & Munteanu, 2017). It could also be described as finding novel ways and means of delivering new, improved, better goods or services to the people and the society (Kinicki and Williams, 2010). Innovation portends a brighter future for corporate organisations in the market domain, but substantial financial implications are associated with pursuing innovation (Hornsby et al., 2009). Innovation because of the cost implications may inhibit the ability of corporate organisations to meet their short-term financial obligations (Kreiser et al., 2013), or may impose a serious drain of resources away from other value-creating activities (Dai et al., 2014).

The proactiveness dimension of EO has been defined by Covin and Miller (2014) as the way and manner (the how) organisations approach opportunities within domestic and foreign markets. The concept of proactiveness extends to being forward-looking with regards to entrepreneurial behaviour and action (Blesa, & Ripollés, 2003). To Lumpkin and Dess (1996), proactiveness is simply the extent to which corporate organisations promptly act in anticipation of future market demand that is precipitated by environmental trends. Are organisations very proactive in tapping identified market opportunities or not proactive? The risk-taking dimension of EO is defined as the propensity and willingness of an organisation to take risks in the quest to earn profit by exploiting market opportunities (Macko & Tyszka, 2009; Vereshchagina & Hopenhayn, 2009). In other words, successful corporate entrepreneurs examine the relationship between risk and return before making investment decisions, and the level of entrepreneurial risk-taking may be influenced by environmental and cultural values (Kirkman, Lowe, & Gibson, 2006; Kreiser et al., 2010). However, the profitability motive for risk-taking is at times sacrificed, because entrepreneurship is driven by different preferences or beliefs such as risk tolerance or over-optimism (Vereshchagina & Hopenhayn, 2009). In the market domain, two kinds of risky situations face organisations, namely:(a) purely chance-related risk, whose outcome depends on chance, and skill-related risk, whose outcome depends on the mastery of business skills (Macko & Tyszka, 2009).

MAIN FOCUS OF THE CHAPTER

Issues, Controversies, Problems – The EM and EO

Analysts describe the COVID-19 pandemic as the greatest public health crisis after World War II (WW2) and the most devastating economic recession after the Great Depression (Sachs, 2020). Several corporate organisations embarked on permanent or temporarily lay off of their employees because of a decline in sales and dwindling financial cashflows (Raimi, 2021; Gössling, Scott & Hall, 2020). It is predicted that the pandemic poses a greater threat to the developing countries, the majority of which hinged their development strategy on the global value chains (GVCs) that have now been disrupted (Killc & Marin, 2020). However, Holtby (2021) describes the COVID-19 pandemic as an admixture of negative and positive realities; it changes the economy and also creates new opportunities, industries, and services. People with the right entrepreneurial mindset think about the new skills to be acquired and invest in those skills through career development to harness the new opportunities, industries, and services precipitated by the pandemic. Already, proactive countries in Eastern Europe are massively investing in acquiring robots to take over reinvented roles and responsibilities of employees in workplaces. In Slovenia, the Czech Republic, and Slovakia every thousand workers are to be replaced with two robots (Killc & Marin, 2020). Based on the double-edged nature of the pandemic, this chapter explicates the EM and EO as resilience strategies for mitigating the challenges posed by the pandemic for career progression and business continuity. The predictive influence of EM characteristics on employees' behaviour in the organisational context, as well as the impact of EO dimensions on organisational behaviour, have been well-investigated and reported. But, the influence of both concepts on career, reinvention has not been well-investigated and reported.

The EO dimensions have been described as a useful tool for assessing entrepreneurial capabilities and managerial tendencies of human capital (employees and managers) for the purpose of improving the return on investment (ROI) of business organisations (Okhomina, 2010). Kusa (2016) opined that the EO is a suitable measurement for modelling entrepreneurship in both for-profit enterprises (commercial businesses) and non-profit enterprises (social enterprises). Moreover, a number of previous studies affirmed the importance of EO dimensions for organisational success. For instance, the study of Swedish family businesses found that the risk-taking dimension of EO is positively correlated with proactiveness and innovation, and the three EO dimensions have a positive relationship with performance (Naldi et al., 2007). This indicated that corporate organisations cannot dispense with the EO and its dimensions in all their day-to-day financial and operational activities.

In Malaysia, the relationships among EO, competitive advantage, and performance were examined in the women-owned SMEs. It was found that there is a significant relationship between the EO and the performance of women-owned SMEs, while competitive advantage partially mediates the EO and performance relationships (Mahmood & Hanafi, 2013). Another study conducted among 643 German and Thai companies, revealed that an adhocracy organizational culture is most effective and supportive of advancing EO in national cultures with a strong preference for individualism and low power distance. Conversely, a hierarchical organizational culture emerged as a barrier to advancing EO (Engelen et al., 2014). Besides, the study conducted among 298 enterprises revealed that organizational culture typologies such as developmental, group, and rational cultures have strong positive impacts on the three EO dimensions, but hierarchical culture has a negative impact on the EO dimensions. As influential as EO and its dimensions are, they are largely dependent on organisational culture (Kreiser et al., 2010)

SOLUTIONS AND RECOMMENDATIONS

As solutions, this section discusses multiple cases of how employees and corporate organisations manifested the EM characteristics and EO dimensions as resilience strategies to save jobs and keep businesses afloat during the pandemic. There are two sub-sections: career reinvention through EM and career reinvention through EO.

Multiple Cases of Career Reinvention through EM

This section discusses the cases on employees that leverage EM dimensions as a resilience strategy to reinvent their career and/save jobs.

The practical and tactical insights from the 10 multiple cases on how EM characteristics were unleashed to save jobs are consistent with the assertion that people with positive mindset have control over their career paths, while people who are fatalistic are less proactive, engage less and pursue unworthy career paths will less financial rewards (Holtby, 2021).

Multiple Cases of Career Re-Invention through EO

This sub-section explicates the cases on corporate organisations that leverage EO dimensions as a resilience strategy for dual benefits: reinvent the careers of their employees and keep business afloat.

The learning curves from additional 10 multiple cases of how the employers saved jobs and kept businesses afloat leveraging the EO dimensions are consistent

Table 2.

Career Re-Invention Cases 1	Context/Location
Employees managing an industrial tailoring factory in Argentina reinvented operations at the peak of COVID-19, away from sewing police uniforms to the production of surgical masks. Surgical masks prevent infection and safeguard economic operations (Duff, 2020). Career reinvention manifests in this instance because the employees up-scaled their skills and competencies to produce surgical masks.	Argentina
Takeaways on EM Characteristics To keep current jobs, save lives of fellow citizens and respond to the new economic opportunities created by scarcity of surgical masks during the pandemic, the proactive workers unleashed their EM characteristics especially opportunity orientation, persistent problem-solving, tolerance for ambiguity, calculated risk-taking, creativity and innovativeness, vision, passion, and team building to keep the economy going.	

Table 3.

Career Re-Invention Cases 2	Context/ Location
Resilient workers managing the largest printing presses in Latin America also re-tooled the machines and reinvented operations from book publishing to the production of 3D protective masks and hand sanitizer (Duff, 2020). Career reinvention manifests because the innovative workers up-scaled their skills and competencies beyond tailoring to be able to manufacture 3D protective masks and hand sanitizer products.	Argentina
Takeaways on EM Characteristics Workers in the printing companies reported leveraged EM characteristics of opportunity orientation, persistent problem-solving, tolerance for ambiguity, calculated risk-taking, creativity and innovativeness, vision, passion, and team building to save their jobs, save lives, and produce the most needed products for the society.	

Table 4.

Career Re-Invention Cases 3	Context/ Location
A specialist communication employee of the British Airways that was suddenly rendered redundant by the pandemic was forced to reinvent her career and with new skills. This tough career change decision led to the establishment of her own company. The company designs and manufactures children's plates, toy trains, tracks, and cars that are useful in homes, schools, and amusement parks (Finch, 2020).	United Kingdom
Takeaways on EM Characteristics The EM characteristics unleashed by the communication specialist that turned into a toy designer are determination, perseverance, drive to achieve, opportunity orientation, persistent problem-solving, internal locus of control, tolerance for ambiguity, high energy level, creativity and innovativeness, vision, and passion.	

Table 5.

Career Re-Invention Cases 4	Context/Location
At the peak of the pandemic, the lockdown of the economy, suspension of school activities, and restriction of international travel affected businesses and weaken social lifestyles. During the period of inactivity and business disruptions, a multi-tasking gentleman in Durham reinvented his career from a procurement officer to becoming an app creator. The affordable app allows children and Yuletide-loving adults to have exciting interactions on the app in the comfort of their homes (Finch, 2020).	United Kingdom
Takeaways on EM Characteristics The EM characteristics unleashed by the new app creator are determination, perseverance, drive to achieve, opportunity orientation, persistent problem-solving, internal locus of control, tolerance for ambiguity, high energy level, creativity and innovativeness, vision, and passion.	

Table 6.

Career Re-Invention Cases 5	Context/Location
A lady working in the care industry in Derby embraced career reinvention when her job was made redundant by lockdowns and social restrictions. She resigned from her job and started producing and selling all-alone handmade bath bombs that contain toiletries soap, shampoo, and shower gel. The patronage of the products by families, friends, and other users was massive because bath bombs and bubble baths are products people yearn to have during the lockdown. At present, she has employed seven employees that lost their jobs to the pandemic (Finch, 2020).	United Kingdom
Takeaways on EM Characteristics The most insightful EM characteristics that strengthened the lady's new career of producing handmade bath bombs are vision, passion, opportunity orientation, tolerance for ambiguity, creativity, and innovativeness. These characteristics were helpful in saving her job, provide emotional happiness to the people in lockdown, and met people's household needs.	

Table 7.

Career Re-Invention Cases 6	Context/Location
Following the closure of arts venues in line with the social distancing and COVID-19 protocols, a lady in St Albans proactively saved her job and averted redundancy by reinventing her career from fundraising consulting to a new life plan of filmmaking that had long been her passion. Her company specialises in the production of films, photography, and recording of videos to the delight of a broad spectrum of lovers of virtual entertainment (Finch, 2020).	St Albans, UK
Takeaways on EM Characteristics The most important EM characteristics that strengthened the lady's career reinvention are vision, passion, opportunity orientation, tolerance for ambiguity, creativity and innovativeness. These characteristics were helpful in saving her job and providing emotional happiness to the people in lockdown.	

Table 8.

Career Re-Invention Cases 7	Context/Location
In Reading, United Kingdom, a new mum reinvented her career twice. The first career reinvention took place in 2017 after returning from maternity leave and being relieved of her job as a planning manager with a gas company. She consequently set up an art therapy centre. Again, the lockdown and social distancing that accompanied the pandemic dealt a severe blow to the therapy centre as face-to-face sessions with trainees were halted. For the second time, she established a new company that delivers modern craft subscription boxes to prospective people at the comfort of their homes during the lockdown. Her modern craft subscription boxes are beautifully packaged and contain all the materials, tools, and step-by-step instructions on craft making and designs (Finch, 2020).	Reading, UK
Takeaways on EM Characteristics The EM characteristics that were visible in the narrated case above are vision, passion, determination, perseverance., passion, drive to achieve, opportunity orientation, persistent problem-solving, internal locus of control, tolerance for ambiguity, calculated risk-taking, high energy level, creativity and innovativeness.	

Table 9.

Career Re-Invention Cases 8	Context/Location
The devastating effect of the COVID-19 pandemic forced a lady in Harrogate, to reinvent her career from teaching to wedding event organiser. Before the lockdown, she teaches the English language to foreign students, but her job was made redundant by the pandemic, as the foreign students ceased coming to the UK for English lessons. On the advice of her sibling, she got retrained as an event planner, learning new social skills, public relations competencies, and social media strategies, and finally became a professional wedding celebrant in September 2020. As a CEO, she has the unique opportunity of interfacing with new people from all over the world	Harrogate, UK
Takeaways on EM Characteristics The EM characteristics visible in the above case are vision, passion, determination, perseverance, drive to achieve, opportunity orientation, persistent problem-solving, internal locus of control, tolerance for ambiguity, calculated risk-taking, high energy level, creativity and innovativeness.	

Table 10.

Career Re-Invention Cases 9	Context/Location
The pandemic grounded the aviation industry, leading to unprecedented redundancy and a massive sack of workers. In West Sussex, the 15-year human resources management (HRM) career of a lady in the airline industry was abruptly cut short, when her role was declared redundant and scrapped. In order to meet her social and financial obligations especially mortgage and household expenses, a career reinvention became inevitable and expedient. Consequently, she got retrained within a very short time as a certified Life/Personal Coach, working with women in need to create desirable lifestyles and emotional stability.	West Sussex, UK.
Takeaways on EM Characteristics The EM characteristics manifested by the HR specialist that became a certified Life/Personal Coach include vision, passion, determination, drive to achieve, opportunity orientation, persistent problem-solving, internal locus of control, calculated risk-taking, high energy level, creativity and innovativeness.	

Table 11.

Career Re-Invention Cases 10	Context/Location
Time is a valuable opportunity and needs to be well harnessed to create income-yielding businesses. The lockdown forced on everyone by the pandemic gave a former Senior Executive in London adequate time and idea situation, to develop his personal business model. With no plane trips, much-reduced schedule and suspension of conferences, he perfected his business model and launched an online business platform during the pandemic. The online platform is a business-to-business (B2B) that allows entrepreneurs and small businesses to provide mutually-beneficial support and advisory services to one another in the areas of marketing plans and campaigns.	London, UK
Takeaways on EM Characteristics EM characteristics that are visible in the above case include vision, passion, determination, drive to achieve, opportunity orientation, persistent problem-solving, internal locus of control, calculated risk-taking, high energy level, creativity and innovativeness.	

Table 12.

Career Re-Invention Cases 11	Context/Location
Business operations of Sri Lanka's tourism industry were terribly disrupted at the peak of the pandemic. To survive, retain employees and keep operations afloat, the tourism companies company applied the Porter Diamond model to their business operations. Diamond model was applied to their operational activities in the following ways: (a) minimizing economic leakages, (b) re-branding of destination, (c) product differentiations (d) entrepreneurship development, (e) creating domestic eco-friendly travels, (f) developing special interest tourism (SIT) and (g) exploring e-promotions (Fernando, 2021).	Sri Lanka
Takeaways on EO Dimensions The most insightful EO dimensions that strengthened Sri Lanka's tourism industry for saving jobs and continue business operations include proactiveness, innovation, risk-taking, and competitive aggressiveness.	

Table 13.

Career Re-Invention Cases 12	Context/Location
Instead of laying off workers and suspending business operations, a Portuguese company in the textile sector used a combination of strategic approaches such as co-creation, entrepreneurship, holistic thinking, and creativity to sustain businesses operations, retain workers and help the people cope with the vulnerable situation created by the COVID-19 pandemic (Santos & Dieguez, 2021).	Portugal
Takeaways on EO Dimensions The EO dimensions that helped the Portuguese company in the textile to continue business operations include proactiveness, innovation, risk-taking, and competitive aggressiveness.	

Table 14.

Career Re-Invention Cases 13	Context/Location
One of the most proactive organisations in the world with regard to workplace career reinvention is Amazon. In early 2019, many months before the COVID-19 pandemic, Amazon had committed $700 million to retrain its 100,000 employees in the US by 2025 for higher-skilled jobs in technology and software engineering to cope with the dynamism of the global economy (Bloomberg, 2019). When the pandemic struck, the leadership of Amazon expanded its career reinvention scope to support 29 million across the world upscale and upgrade their tech skills through the free cloud computing skills training and AWS-designed programmes by 2025, so that beneficiaries can fit the high-demand occupations in the Post pandemic era (Carlson, 2020).	United States
Takeaways on EO Dimensions The most insightful EO dimensions that helped Amazon in saving jobs and continue business operations include autonomy, proactiveness, innovation, risk-taking and competitive aggressiveness.	

Table 15.

Career Re-Invention Cases 14	Context/Location
Before the pandemic, JPMorgan Chase made a five-year $350 million financial commitment tagged "New Skills at Work investment' to upskill the technical skills and competencies of its workforce and non-workforce stakeholders in readiness for future work (JPMorgan Chase, 2019). When the pandemic hit the global landscape, JPMorgan Chase expanded the scope of its upskilling programme. In France alone, it injected over €4.3 million into the career reinvention and reskilling of the young people and long-term unemployed person in vulnerable communities in preparedness for stable, well-paid careers (Business Wire, 2021).	France
Takeaways on EO Dimensions The EO dimensions that are driving JPMorgan Chase's New Skills at Work investment scheme include autonomy, proactiveness, innovation, risk-taking and competitive aggressiveness.	

Table 16.

Career Re-Invention Cases 15	Context/Location
Unlike other companies in the world, Walmart invested more in wages and cross-training programs as part of its readiness for the Post pandemic era. For career reinvention and business continuity, the sum of $14 billion was budgeted. Consequently, the management retained, retrained and rewarded the employees during the pandemic, when others were firing and downsizing. The company-led career reinvention strategy extends to acquiring the capabilities to handles new leadership roles in digital workgroups including skills to work in condensed modular automated warehouses and local fulfillment centers, where Walmart stockpiles pantry items, frozen foods, consumables as well as electronics for meeting the needs of the customers in a changing world (Tyko, 2021).	United States
Takeaways on EO Dimensions The EO dimensions driving Walmart career reinvention and human capital investment to mitigate the adverse effect of the pandemic on the future of jobs and careers include autonomy, proactiveness, innovation, risk-taking, and competitive aggressiveness.	

Table 17.

Career Re-Invention Cases 16	Context/Location
Brooks Brothers and New Balance organisations implemented a career reinvention programme to save jobs and boost business continuity in the midst of the pandemic. Thinking differently about laying-off and closing down operations, both companies converted the acute shortage of personal protective equipment (PPE) into an economic opportunity. They, therefore, retool their machines and manufacturing plants, and retrain the redundant employees to handle the production of surgical masks and gowns for sale to the hospitals, clinics, and other users (Jesuthasan et al., 2020; Zavyiboroda, 2021).	United States
Takeaways on EO Dimensions The EO dimensions that are visible in the career reinvention programmes of Brooks Brothers and New Balance include autonomy, proactiveness, innovation, risk-taking and competitive aggressiveness.	

Table 18.

Career Re-Invention Cases 17	Context/Location
Tesla, Ford and General Motors are three automobile companies with enviable lessons on social experiments of the future of work in the midst of public health crisis. At the peak of the pandemic, the demand for cars dropped drastically, and the three companies shut down their plants during the lockdown. In the face of the shortage of ventilators in hospitals and clinics, both companies quickly saw economic opportunities in the situation. Consequently, they retrained their engineers and retooled their machines and plants to produce ventilators from car parts (Jesuthasan et al., 2020).	United States
Takeaways on EO Dimensions Tesla, Ford and General Motors saved jobs and lives through their social experiments because they were proactive, innovative and risk-loving. Many other automobile companies chose to lay off their redundant employees rather than reinventing their roles and responsibilities.	

Table 19.

Career Re-Invention Cases 18	Context/Location
Another lesson on career reinvention during the pandemic is the bold step by the Bank of America to temporarily convert many bankers and financial advisers into calls handlers and customer business support advisers. The new role entails handling and responding to surging calls from bank customers and as well as helping the small business owners adapt and cope with the ravaging effect of the pandemic (Jesuthasan et al., 2020; Ungarino, 2020).	United States
Takeaways on EO Dimensions The Bank of America converted redundancy to economic value because the bank leveraged the EO dimension of proactiveness, innovation, and risk-taking. Many other banks chose to lay off their redundant employees rather than reinventing their roles and responsibilities.	

Table 20.

Career Re-Invention Cases 19	Context/Location
A career reinvention was launched by a pharma company that has a sales workforce of 10,000. The company switched its operations from an offline mode to a one hundred per cent remote-working model. For the Post pandemic era, the pharmaceutical company insisted that the status quo would remain with slight modification in operations to accommodate a 30 per cent online and 70 per cent-offline in order to leverage the newly developed skills and capabilities of the sales workforce (Agrawal et al., 2020).	United States
Takeaways on EO Dimensions The career reinvention via reskilling was a success because the company leveraged the EO dimensions of proactiveness, innovation, risk-loving, autonomy and competitive aggressiveness.	

with previous scholarly findings. Liguori & Pittz (2020) noted that proactive and resilient employers are those that adopt a mindset of opportunity recognition, which helps them in identifying and exploring new opportunities in spite of the loss of profits, customers and customers, and key employees to the pandemic. Overall, the insightful lessons on career reinventing from the 20 multiple cases (EM and EO) are modelled using the Input—Process-Output framework in Figure 1 below. The career reinvention framework shows that the entire process is divided into three stages: Input, Process and Output. At the input stage 1, the pandemic made employees and employers vulnerable because jobs are lost, business operations collapsed and new norms are imposed by the different governments to manage the public health crisis. Stage 1, although harsh and undesirable, provides an opportunity for employees and employers to learn new things and norms, unlearn and relearn to cope with the imposed challenges. Process stage 2 provides an opportunity for

Table 21.

Career Re-Invention Cases 20	Context/Location
At the peak of lockdown complemented by strict enforcement of social distancing, many traditional face-to-face and online butcheries lost their face-to-face customers. However, the Online Butchery in Uganda reinvented the fortune of the company by introducing a virtual business-to-consumer (B2C) platform for meat orders. This novel approach saved jobs and stimulate business continuity. The business supplies customers with meat products through prepaid meal plans, without them leaving their homes. The business allows different types of prepaid plans ranging from weekly to monthly plans – all the plans provide customers with lunches and dinners delivered to them at home effortlessly (International Trade Centre, 2020).	Uganda
Takeaways on EO Dimensions The career reinvention by Online Butchery via virtual business-to-consumer (B2C) platform was made possible because the company leveraged the EO dimensions of proactiveness, innovation, risk-loving, autonomy and competitive aggressiveness.	

employees and corporate organisations to adapt to vulnerable situations and shocks by exploring career reinvention. At the second stage, the employees whose current jobs have been rendered irrelevant by the pandemic create personal career paths and undertake self-development programmes to make themselves indispensable brands. To keep businesses afloat, the employers support the career reinvention of their workers with career development interventions such as updating the skills of their valued employees, retooling and re-engineering of operations in order to meet set objectives. The process of transitioning from the COVID-19 pandemic era to the Post pandemic era is therefore dependent on career reinvention.

Figure 1.Career Reinvention mediated the transition from COVID-19 Pandemic Era to Post COVID Era

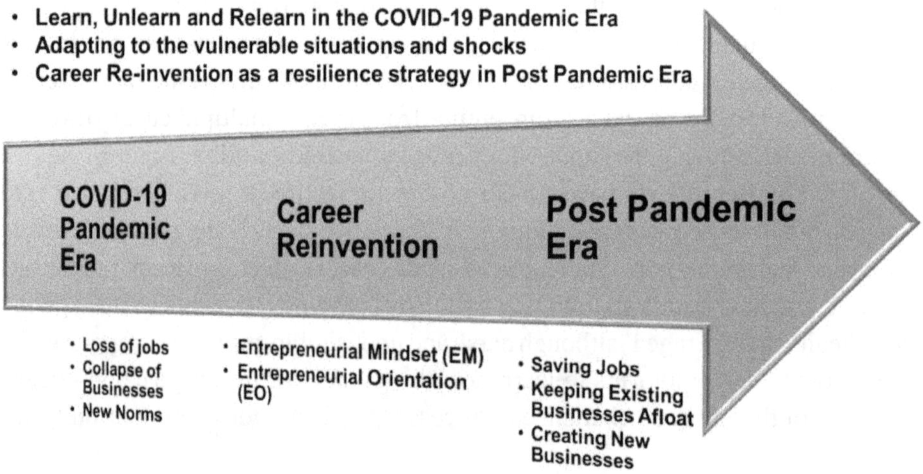

Policy Recommendations

Based on the lessons and insights from the 20 multiple cases on EM and EO explicated above, the following policy recommendations are provided.

i. For employees in the developing countries that lost their jobs to the pandemic, and who lack the financial capacity for career reinvention, it is suggested that the government and the private sector organisations assist these individuals to reform their skills through lifelong learning courses and other competencies capacity-building programmes.

ii. The governments and non-governmental organisations should provide intervention support fundings for skilling, upskilling, and reskilling for socially excluded groups such as women, disadvantaged low-skilled workers, hardest-hit businesses, and people from rural communities.
iii. In view of the fact that the pandemic caught the employees and employers unprepared, it is also recommended that career reinvention training programmes should cover various EM characteristics and EO dimensions such as action orientation, passion, need to achieve. future focus, idea generation, execution, self-confidence, optimism, persistence, proactiveness, innovation, risk-taking, autonomy, competitive aggressiveness including emotional intelligence, emerging technical skills, and social skills that enable people to cope with the socio-psychological trauma of the recessionary period.

FUTURE RESEARCH DIRECTION

Career reinvention is relevant in both the developed and developing countries, but the job competencies and skills needed in the two contexts differ in terms of sophistication, supply, demand, and monetary rewards. Therefore, more rigorous conceptual, theoretical, policy-focused and empirical studies are required in this direction.

CONCLUSION

The chapter sets out to explicate how career reinvention is being leveraged by employees and employers for saving jobs and ensuring business continuity in readiness for the Post Pandemic Era. After critical analysis and contextualising the lessons from the 20 multiple cases, it was found that the employees unleashed the EO characteristics to save their current jobs and create new jobs, while corporate organisations adopted the EO dimensions to keep their businesses afloat and meet their bottom-line. We contribute to the body of knowledge on career reinvention by validating the EM and EO as resilience strategies for career reinvention in the Post pandemic era. The chapter affirmed that the process of transitioning from the COVID-19 pandemic era to the Post-pandemic era is largely dependent on a well-planned and carefully executed career reinvention strategy.

REFERENCES

Agrawal, S., De Smet, A., Lacroix, S., & Reich, A. (2020). *To emerge stronger from the COVID-19 crisis, companies should start reskilling their workforces now.* McKinsey Insights.

Athwal, B., Brill, L., Chesters, G., & Quiggin, M. (2011). *Recession, poverty and sustainable livelihoods in Bradford.* Joseph Rowntree Foundation.

Baker, M. (2020, June). *9 Future of Work Trends Post-COVID-19.* Gartner, Inc.

Bartik, A. W., Bertrand, M., Cullen, Z. B., Glaeser, E. L., Luca, M., & Stanton, C. T. (2020). *How are small businesses adjusting to covid-19? early evidence from a survey.* Working Paper No. 26989, National Bureau of Economic Research.

Blesa, A., & Ripollés, M. (2003). The role of market orientation in the relationship between entrepreneurial proactiveness and performance. *The Journal of Entrepreneurship, 12*(1), 1–19. doi:10.1177/097135570301200101

Bloomberg. (2019, July). *Amazon Commits $700 Million to Retrain Workers - The e-commerce giant said it will retrain 100,000 workers by 2025.* Industry Week Report.

Brettel, M., Chomik, C., & Flatten, T. C. (2015). How organizational culture influences innovativeness, proactiveness, and risk-taking: Fostering entrepreneurial orientation in SMEs. *Journal of Small Business Management, 53*(4), 868–885. doi:10.1111/jsbm.12108

Business Wire. (2021). *J.P. Morgan Invests €4.3 Million in Skills Development for the Young and Long-Term Unemployed in Paris.* JPMorgan Chase & Co.

Carlson, T. (2020, December). *Amazon to help 29 million people around the world grow their tech skills with free cloud computing skills training by 2025.* Amazon.

Castrillon, C. (2019, November). How to Reinvent Your Career After 40. *Forbes.*

Chopra-McGowan, A., & Reddy, S. B. (2020, July). COVID-19: How can companies offer effective reskilling for employees? Advancing women's careers through leadership development programs. *Employee Relations.*

Covin, J. G., & Miller, D. (2014). International entrepreneurial orientation: Conceptual considerations, research themes, measurement issues, and future research directions. *Entrepreneurship Theory and Practice, 38*(1), 11–44. doi:10.1111/etap.12027

Covin, J. G., & Slevin, D. P. (1989). Strategic management of small firms in hostile and benign environments. *Strategic Management Journal, 10*(1), 75–87. doi:10.1002mj.4250100107

Dai, L., Maksimov, V., Gilbert, B. A., & Fernhaber, S. A. (2014). Entrepreneurial orientation and international scope: The differential roles of innovativeness, proactiveness, and risk-taking. *Journal of Business Venturing*, *29*(4), 511–524. doi:10.1016/j.jbusvent.2013.07.004

Davis, M. H., Hall, J. A., & Mayer, P. S. (2016). Developing a new measure of entrepreneurial mindset: Reliability, validity, and implications for practitioners. *Consulting Psychology Journal*, *68*(1), 21–48. doi:10.1037/cpb0000045

Duff, J. (2020, March). *COVID-19 Proves Workers Are Essential and Capitalists Are a Drain*. Academic Press.

Echegaray, F. (2021). What POST-COVID-19 lifestyles may look like? Identifying scenarios and their implications for sustainability. *Sustainable Production and Consumption*, *27*, 567–574. doi:10.1016/j.spc.2021.01.025 PMID:34722841

Engelen, A., Flatten, T. C., Thalmann, J., & Brettel, M. (2014). The effect of organizational culture on entrepreneurial orientation: A comparison between Germany and Thailand. *Journal of Small Business Management*, *52*(4), 732–752. doi:10.1111/jsbm.12052

Eno-Obong, H. (2006). Challenges of entrepreneurship in home economics and enhancement strategies. *Journal of Home Economic Research*, *7*, 69–75.

Finch, H. (2020, November). *16 people who switched careers during lockdown share their best advice*. Academic Press.

Gettler, L. (2003, June). Bite-size careers: It used to be jobs for life, but now managers need to give life to their jobs. *Management Today*, 20–25.

Gössling, S., Scott, D., & Hall, C. M. (2020). Pandemics, tourism and global change: A rapid assessment of COVID-19. *Journal of Sustainable Tourism*, *29*(1), 1–20. doi:10.1080/09669582.2020.1758708

Gysbers, N. C., Heppner, M. J., & Johnston, J. A. (1998). *Career Counseling: Process, Issues and Techniques*. Allyn and Bacon.

Heppner, M. J. (1998). The career transitions inventory: Measuring internal resources in adulthood. *Journal of Career Assessment*, *6*(2), 135–145. doi:10.1177/106907279800600202

Holtby, A. (2021). *How to Launch a Career During COVID-19 - Expert advice on navigating the job search without sacrificing mental health*. University of Alberta.

Hornsby, J. S., Kuratko, D. F., Shepherd, D. A., & Bott, J. P. (2009). Managers' corporate entrepreneurial actions: Examining perception and position. *Journal of Business Venturing*, *24*(3), 236–247. doi:10.1016/j.jbusvent.2008.03.002

Ibarra, H. (2004). *Working Identity: Unconventional Strategies for Reinventing Your Career*. Harvard Business School Publishing.

Ibarra, H. (2020, April). *Reinventing Your Career in the Time of Coronavirus*. Academic Press.

International Labour Organisation (2021a, January). *ILO Monitor: COVID-19 and the world of work* (7th ed.). ILO.

International Labour Organisation. (2021b). *Skilling, upskilling and reskilling of employees, apprentices and interns during the COVID-19 pandemic: Findings from a global survey of enterprises. International Labour Office*. ILO.

International Trade Centre. (2020, April). Story: Ugandan start-ups part of the solution during COVID-19 - Start-ups in Uganda are developing innovative products to help consumers and businesses survive during COVID-19. *ITC News*.

Jesuthasan, R., Malcolm, T., & Cantrell, S. (2020, April). Crisis Management - How the Coronavirus Crisis Is Redefining Jobs. *Harvard Business Review*.

Kilic, K., & Marin, D. (2020). How COVID-19 is transforming the world economy. *VoxEU. org, 10*.

Kinicki, A., & Williams, B. K. (2010). *Management: A Practical Introduction*. McGraw-Hill.

Kreiser, P. M., Marino, L. D., Dickson, P., & Weaver, K. M. (2010). Cultural influences on entrepreneurial orientation: The impact of national culture on risk taking and proactiveness in SMEs. *Entrepreneurship Theory and Practice*, *34*(5), 959–984. doi:10.1111/j.1540-6520.2010.00396.x

Kreiser, P. M., Marino, L. D., Kuratko, D. F., & Weaver, K. M. (2013). Disaggregating entrepreneurial orientation: The non-linear impact of innovativeness, proactiveness and risk-taking on SME performance. *Small Business Economics*, *40*(2), 273–291. doi:10.100711187-012-9460-x

Kuratko, D. F. (2014). *The Entrepreneurial Mind-Set in Individuals: Cognition and Ethics*. Academic Press.

Kusa, R. (2016). Measuring entrepreneurial orientation in the social context. *Entrepreneurial Business and Economics Review*, *4*(3), 117–129. doi:10.15678/EBER.2016.040309

Lane, C. (2021, April). *How Graduates Can Get Hired During The Coronavirus Pandemic*. Academic Press.

Liguori, E. W., & Pittz, T. G. (2020). Strategies for small business: Surviving and thriving in the era of COVID-19. *Journal of the International Council for Small Business*, *1*(2), 106–110. doi:10.1080/26437015.2020.1779538

Lumpkin, G. T., & Dess, G. G. (1996). Clarifying the entrepreneurial orientation construct and linking it to performance. *Academy of Management Review*, *21*(1), 135–172. doi:10.2307/258632

Macko, A., & Tyszka, T. (2009). Entrepreneurship and risk taking. *Applied Psychology*, *58*(3), 469–487. doi:10.1111/j.1464-0597.2009.00402.x

Mahmood, R., & Hanafi, N. (2013). Entrepreneurial orientation and business performance of women-owned small and medium enterprises in Malaysia: Competitive advantage as a mediator. *International Journal of Business and Social Science*, *4*(1), 82–90.

McCusker, K., & Gunaydin, S. (2015). Research using qualitative, quantitative or mixed methods and choice based on the research. *Perfusion*, *30*(7), 537–542. doi:10.1177/0267659114559116 PMID:25378417

McGrath, G. R., & MacMillan, I. C. (2000). *Entrepreneurial Mindset: Strategies for Continuously Creating Opportunity in an Age of Uncertainty*. Harvard Business School Press Books.

Miller, D. (2011). Miller (1983) revisited: A reflection on EO research and some suggestions for the future. *Entrepreneurship Theory and Practice*, *35*(5), 873–894. doi:10.1111/j.1540-6520.2011.00457.x

Morris, M. H., & Kuratko, D. F. (2002). *Corporate Entrepreneurship: Entrepreneurial development within Organisations*. Thompson South-Western.

Morris, M. H., Webb, J. W., & Franklin, R. J. (2011). Understanding the Manifestation of Entrepreneurial Orientation in the Nonprofit Context. *Entrepreneurship Theory and Practice*, *35*(5), 947–971. doi:10.1111/j.1540-6520.2011.00453.x

Naldi, L., Nordqvist, M., Sjöberg, K., & Wiklund, J. (2007). Entrepreneurial orientation, risk taking, and performance in family firms. *Family Business Review*, *20*(1), 33–47. doi:10.1111/j.1741-6248.2007.00082.x

Niţu-Antonie, R. D., Feder, E. S., & Munteanu, V. P. (2017). Macroeconomic Effects of Entrepreneurship from an International Perspective. *Sustainability*, *9*(7), 1–21. doi:10.3390u9071159

Nova, A. (2020, June). *Without the coronavirus pandemic, these jobs probably wouldn't have existed.* Academic Press.

OECD (2021, April). *OECD Policy Responses to Coronavirus (COVID-19) An assessment of the impact of COVID-19 on job and skills demand using online job vacancy data.* OECD.

Okhomina, D. (2010). Entrepreneurial orientation and psychological traits: The moderating influence of supportive environment. *Journal of Behavioral Studies in Business*, *2*, 1–16.

O'Neil, D. A., & Bilimoria, D. (2005). Women's career development phases: Idealism, endurance, and reinvention. *Career Development International*, *10*(3), 168–189. doi:10.1108/13620430510598300

Osland, J. S., Mendenhall, M. E., Reiche, B. S., Szkudlarek, B., Bolden, R., Courtice, P., Vaiman, V., Vaiman, M., Lyndgaard, D., Nielsen, K., Terrell, S., Taylor, S., Lee, Y., Stahl, G., Boyacigiller, N., Huesing, T., Miska, C., Zilinskaite, M., Ruiz, L., . . . Maznevski, M. (2020). Perspectives on Global Leadership and the COVID-19 Crisis. In Advances in Global Leadership (Vol. 13). Emerald Publishing Limited.

Raimi, L. (2021). Innovative Government-Backed Policy Measures in Nigeria for Sustaining MSMEs Post Pandemic. In N. Baporikar (Ed.), *Handbook of Research on Strategies and Interventions to Mitigate COVID-19 Impact on SMEs* (pp. 299–317). IGI Global. doi:10.4018/978-1-7998-7436-2.ch015

Renzaho, A. (2020). The Need for the Right Socio-Economic and Cultural Fit in the COVID-19 Response in Sub-Saharan Africa: Examining Demographic, Economic Political, Health, and Socio-Cultural Differentials in COVID-19 Morbidity and Mortality. *International Journal of Environmental Research and Public Health*, *17*(10), 3445. doi:10.3390/ijerph17103445 PMID:32429123

Sachs, J. D. (2020). COVID-19 and Multilateralism. Horizons. *Journal of International Relations and Sustainable Development*, (16), 30–39.

Santos, S., & Dieguez, T. (2021). Open Innovation as a Strategy to Sustainably Compete in the Textile Industry. In J. Enríquez-Díaz, L. Castro-Santos, & F. Puime-Guillén (Eds.), Financial Management and Risk Analysis Strategies for Business Sustainability (pp. 146-172). IGI Global. doi:10.4018/978-1-7998-7634-2.ch008

Sommer, S. (2020). *Sustainable Finance: An Overview. Deutsche Gesellschaft für Internationale Zusammenarbeit (GIZ)*. GmbH, Bonn and Eschborn.

The Entrepreneurial Learning Initiative. (2021). *What is Mindset?* Author.

Tyko, K. (2021). Walmart raising pay for 425,000 workers starting March 13 after strong holiday sales amid COVID-19. *USA Today*.

Ungarino, R. (2020, April). *Bank of America is pausing financial adviser training for 650 people and reassigning them to handle surging calls from consumer and small-business customers*. Academic Press.

University of Washington. (2021). *Working during COVID-19: Workforce reduction strategies*. Author.

Vereshchagina, G., & Hopenhayn, H. A. (2009). Risk taking by entrepreneurs. *The American Economic Review, 99*(5), 1808–1830. doi:10.1257/aer.99.5.1808

Wales, W. J., Covin, J. G., & Monsen, E. (2020). Entrepreneurial orientation: The necessity of a multilevel conceptualization. *Strategic Entrepreneurship Journal, 14*(4), 639–660. doi:10.1002ej.1344

Walker, L. (2019). Coaching during late career reinvention: The Discovering Model. *International Journal of Evidence Based Coaching and Mentoring*, (S13), 63–75.

Watts, J., McNair, S., & Robey, C. (2015). *Mid Life Career Review: Final Report to the Department for Business and Skills*. National Institute of Adult Continuing Education (England and Wales).

Whiffin, C. J. (2020). Choose Your Methodology: Little Quick Fix. *Sage (Atlanta, Ga.)*.

Worthington, J. (2006). Introduction: The Changing Workplace. In Reinventing the Workplace (pp. 22-29). Routledge.

Worthington, J. (2012). *Reinventing the workplace*. Routledge. doi:10.4324/9780080516035

Zappe, S. E., Hochstedt, K. S., & Kisenwether, E. C. (2013). Faculty beliefs of entrepreneurship and design education: An exploratory study comparing entrepreneurship and design faculty. *The Journal of Engineering Entrepreneurship, 4*(1), 55–79. doi:10.7814/jeen5v4p5zhk

Zavyiboroda, M. (2021, February). COVID-19: recession types, recovery scenarios, behavior change. *HR Trends*.

KEY TERMS AND DEFINITIONS

Career Reinvention: This refers to a process of re-learning, unlearning and/or skills upgrading for the purpose of taking up a completely new role and set of tasks during the period of occupational change.

Developed Countries: This refers to the high-income and industrialised nations such as the US, the UK, Japan, Canada, Germany, France, and others that set the rules, norms and standards with regards workplaces, businesses and global economic practices.

Developing Countries: This refers to the low-income and import-dependent nations in Eastern Europe, Latin America, Africa, and Asia that accept the rules, norms and standards with regards workplaces, businesses and global economic practices.

Entrepreneurial Mindset: This refers to a combination of traits and skills that enable people to identify opportunities, foresee and overcome challenges and learn from successes and setbacks in the business and non-business contexts.

Entrepreneurial Mindset Characteristics: This refers the 13 traits and skills of entrepreneurial people. They are determination and perseverance., drive to achieve, opportunity orientation, persistent problem-solving, seeking feedback, internal locus of control, tolerance for ambiguity, calculated risk taking, high energy level, creativity and innovativeness, vision, passion, and team building.

Entrepreneurial Orientation: This refers to the behaviours, processes, practices, and decision-making styles of organizations that act entrepreneurially in the business and non-business contexts.

Entrepreneurial Orientation Dimensions: This refers the 5 dimensions of entrepreneurial organisations. They include proactiveness, innovation, risk-taking, autonomy and competitive aggressiveness.

Multiple Cases: This refers to business stories with inspiring lessons from which employees and employers can acquire learning curves for coping with workplace and business challenges.

Post-Pandemic Era: This is a transitional period when the global and national economy will return to normal and full-scale business operations after the devastating disruption of workplace and businesses by the COVID-19 pandemic.

Conclusion

"You would think" are dangerous words to use to begin a sentence because what follows would be some sort of prediction or projection. This has held true with thinking about the post-pandemic era. The pandemic is not quite post even as life-saving vaccines have enabled some degree of management of the viral spread. The 1.5 billion or so doses of the U.S Food & Drug Administration-approved vaccines that are being produced monthly give hope that the world's 7 billion people will "all" get theirs in short order. Yet, there are large swaths of the population who are unvaccinated, and there are pandemic hotspots around the world still.

This book, *Career Re-Invention in the Post-Pandemic Era*, has been an endeavor of hopefulness. This was started in late January 2021 and a call for proposals going out shortly thereafter. The idea was that for those in lockdown or those working tentatively as essential workers and those around the world just trying hard to make it day-to-day that there is a benefit of anticipating a future in which each surviving self could imagine themselves forward into a new future. This book has been, in part, about worldmaking a new world and one's place in it. The projection would enable thinking about current capabilities and what else people would need to do to enhance their knowledge, their skills, and their abilities (KSAs). Perhaps a message was that we've got this, and we can handle some of the challenges of the present moment, even in the face of disease and death.

In another sense, this is about thinking of self and other as global citizens. After all, the pathogen made all vulnerable, albeit not all the world had the same resources to use to address the threat. The world was learning together what would or would not work, based on live mass-scale experiments, and with the highest of penalties for people.

In the various lockdowns, people have spent time rethinking what they value in life and how they find meaning. In many senses, people could project themselves into a future into which they are reborn from the ashes of a devastating multi-year moment.

FUTURE RESEARCH

In a way, this collection is an early work about how people can come out of a devastating pandemic and still offer economic value through their labor.

What makes this collection premature? The apparent post-pandemic era is not quite post (with a new variant of concern just recently identified in both Europe and S. Africa), and the world on the other side of the somewhat-receding pandemic is not quite what people would have predicted. Where some thought jobs would have all but disappeared, it turns out that workers are in shortage, not the work. In the U.S., due in part to the high amounts of liquidity the government has infused into the economy, inflation has been present in the five percent range. As schools meet again in person and universities ramp up studies, the various paths for learning and self-development are only just starting to form out. Likewise, those who are taking on apprenticeships and other forms of new learning are only just re-engaging in non-virtual ways. There is a lot to be learned and shared about the post-pandemic space and how people ae redefining themselves.

THANKS

As with most edited texts, the work is challenging, and it is a struggle to elicit chapters from researchers. My thanks first go to the contributors to this collection. Also, I am deeply grateful to Katie McLoughlin of IGI Global for her critical help in reaching out to potential authors, to ensure that this book would "make". As always, I am thankful to IGI Global for the opportunity to pursue an idea to see where it goes in each unique time frame. Every book is only the "art of the possible" within real-world limits.

November 2021

Shalin Hai-Jew
Kansas State University, USA

Compilation of References

Bangladeshis infected with coronavirus: IEDCR. (2020, March 8). *The Daily Star*. https://www.thedailystar.net/coronavirus-deadly-new-threat/news/iedcr-confirms-3-coronavirus-patients-hospitalised-bangladesh-1878022

Abeledo, S. (2014). Territorio, caminos y prácticas culturales de los viajes de intercambio del último siglo (departamento de Los Andes, provincia de Salta). In Espacialidades en las tierras altoandinas. Avances de investigación desde el noroeste argentino (pp. 29-62). Buenos Aires: CONICET - Instituto Interdisciplinario Tilcara, FFyL, UBA.

Abir, A. A. (2019, April 18). Retail Industry in Bangladesh: A Different Shape up Story. *LightCastle Analytics Wing*. https://databd.co/stories/organized-retail-industry-outlook-bangladesh-2077

Adedoyin, O. B. (2020). *Qualitative Research Methods*. Near East University.

Agarwal, V., Mathiyazhagan, K., Malhotra, S., & Saikouk, T. (2021). Analysis of challenges in sustainable human resource management due to disruptions by industry 4.0: An emerging economy perspective. *International Journal of Manpower*. Advance online publication. doi:10.1108/IJM-03-2021-0192

Agenor, C., Conner, N., & Aroian, K. (2017). Flourishing: An evolutionary concept analysis. *Issues in Mental Health Nursing*, *38*(11), 915–923. doi:10.1080/01612840.2017.1355945 PMID:28876964

Agrawal, S., Smet, A. D., Lacroix, S., & Reich, A. (2020). *To emerge stronger from the COVID-19 crisis, companies should start reskilling their workforces now.* McKinsey & Company. https://www.mckinsey.com/business-functions/people-and-organizational-performance/our-insights/to-emerge-stronger-from-the-covid-19-crisis-companies-should-start-reskilling-their-workforces-now

Agrawal, S., De Smet, A., Lacroix, S., & Reich, A. (2020). *To emerge stronger from the COVID-19 crisis, companies should start reskilling their workforces now.* McKinsey Insights.

Ajgaonkar, S., Neelam, N. G., & Wiemann, J. (2021). Drivers of workforce agility: A dynamic capability perspective. *The International Journal of Organizational Analysis*. Advance online publication. doi:10.1108/IJOA-11-2020-2507

Akhter, R. & Jahan, F. (2020). The Contribution of Telecom Industries on Bangladesh Economy. *International Journal of Humanities and Social Science Invention, 9*(9), 27-37. doi:10.35629/7722

Akkermans, J., Richardson, J., & Kraimer, M. (2020). The Covid-19 crisis as a career shock: Implications for careers and vocational behavior. *Journal of Vocational Behavior, 119*(1), 1–5. doi:10.1016/j.jvb.2020.103434 PMID:32390655

Alam, M. S., Ali, M. J., Bhuiyan, A. B., Solaiman, M., & Rahman, M. A. (2020). The impact of covid -19 pandemic on the economic growth in Bangladesh: A conceptual review. *American Economic & Social Review, 6*(2), 1–12. doi:10.46281/aesr.v6i2.844

Alexander, P. M., & Twinomurinzi, H. (2012). Changing career choice factors as the economic environment changes. *Proceedings of SAICSIT '12*, 295 – 305. 10.1145/2389836.2389872

Almeida, F., & Santos, J. D. (2020). The effects of COVID-19 on job security and unemployment in Portugal. *The International Journal of Sociology and Social Policy, 40*(9/10), 995–1003. doi:10.1108/IJSSP-07-2020-0291

Almeida, F., Santos, J. D., & Monteiro, J. A. (2020). The Challenges and Opportunities in the Digitalization of Companies in a Post-COVID-19 World. *IEEE Engineering Management Review, 48*(3), 97–103. doi:10.1109/EMR.2020.3013206

Alon, I., Farrell, M., & Li, S. (2020). Regime type and COVID-19 response. *FIIB Business Review, 9*(3), 152–160. doi:10.1177/2319714520928884

Alvi, M. A., Ohiolei, J. A., Saqib, M., Li, L., Tayyab, M. H., Alvi, A. A., & Jia, W. Z. (2020). Echinococcus granulosus (sensu stricto)(G1, G3) and E. ortleppi (G5) in Pakistan: Phylogeny, genetic diversity and population structural analysis based on mitochondrial DNA. *Parasites & Vectors, 13*(1), 1–10. doi:10.118613071-020-04199-8 PMID:32660553

Ames, H., Glenton, C., & Lewin, S. (2020). Purposive sampling in a qualitative evidence synthesis: A worked example from a synthesis on parental perceptions of vaccination communication. *BMC Medical Research Methodology, 19*(1), 26. Advance online publication. doi:10.118612874-019-0665-4 PMID:30704402

Amit, S. (2020, March 10). The future of on-demand food delivery and COVID-19. *The Business Standard.* https://www.tbsnews.net/panorama/future-demand-food-delivery-and-covid-19-54274

Anderson, W., & Sanga, J. J. (2019). Academia–industry partnerships for hospitality and tourism education in Tanzania. *Journal of Hospitality & Tourism Education, 31*(1), 34–48. doi:10.1080/10963758.2018.1480959

Andrews, E. M., Kassama, S., Smith, E. E., Brown, P. H., & Khalsa, S. D. S. (2021). A Review of Potassium-Rich Crop Residues Used as Organic Matter Amendments in Tree Crop Agroecosystems. *Agriculture, 11*(7), 580. doi:10.3390/agriculture11070580

Appadurai, A. (1986). *The Social Life of Things*. Cambridge University Press. doi:10.1017/CBO9780511819582

Aristovnik, A., Keržič, D., Ravšelj, D., Tomaževič, N., & Umek, L. (2020). Impacts of the Covid-19 pandemic on life of higher education students: A global perspective. *Sustainability, 12*(20), 8438. doi:10.3390u12208438

Arnink, C. L. (2020). A quantitative evaluation of shame resilience theory. *Inquiries Journal, 12*(11).

Arroyo, A. T., Kidd, A. R., Burns, S. M., Cruz, I. J., & Lawrence-Lamb, J. E. (2015). Increments of transformation from midnight to daylight: How a professor and four undergraduate students experienced an original philosophy of teaching and learning in two online courses. *Journal of Transformative Education, 13*(4), 341–365. doi:10.1177/1541344615587112

Arroyos-CalveraD.DrouvelisM.LohseJ.McDonaldR. (2021). *Improving compliance with COVID-19 guidance: a workplace field experiment.* doi:10.2139/ssrn.3760562

Ateya, M., Khalil, E., Rasheed, S., & Asokan, G. V. (2015). A protocol for literature triage in online learning for the net-generation nursing and allied health care students. *Nursing Reports, 5*(1), 22–23. doi:10.4081/nursrep.2015.5134

Athwal, B., Brill, L., Chesters, G., & Quiggin, M. (2011). *Recession, poverty and sustainable livelihoods in Bradford.* Joseph Rowntree Foundation.

Autin, K. L., Blustein, D. L., Ali, S. R., & Garriott, P. O. (2020). Career Development Impacts of COVID-19: Practice and Policy Recommendations. *Journal of Career Development, 47*(5), 487–494. doi:10.1177/0894845320944486

Baker, M. (2020, June). *9 Future of Work Trends Post-COVID-19.* Gartner, Inc.

Baker, S. R., Bloom, N., Davis, S. J., & Terry, S. J. (2020). *Covid-induced economic uncertainty* (Working Paper No. 26983). https://www.nber.org/papers/w26983

Ballou, D. J., & Huguenard, B. R. (2008). Personal and situational predictors of IS professionals' career choice satisfaction. *Proceedings of SIGMIS-CPR '08*, 50 – 57.

Bangladesh - The Rising FinTech Star in South Asia. (2021, February 3). *Medici.* https://gomedici.com/bangladesh-the-rising-fintech-star-in-south-asia#

Bangladesh Bank. (2021). *Exchange rate of Taka.* https://www.bb.org.bd/econdata/exchangerate.php

Bangladesh Bureau of Educational Information and Statistics (BANBEIS). (2019). *Bangladesh Education Statistics 2019(New).* Ministry of Education.

Bangladesh reimposes Covid lockdown for two weeks. (2021, July 23). *Aljazeera.* https://www.aljazeera.com/news/2021/7/23/bangladesh-covid-lockdown-two-weeks

Baptista Lucio, P., Almazán Zimerman, A., Loeza Altamirano, C. A., López Alcaraz, V. A. & Cárdenas Domínguez, J. L. (2020). Encuesta Nacional a Docentes ante el COVID-19. Retos para la educación a distancia [National Survey of Teachers to COVID-19. Challenges for distance education]. *Revista Latinoamericana De Estudios Educativos, 50*(ESPECIAL), 41-88. doi:10.48102/rlee.2020.50.ESPECIAL.96

Barneveld, K., Quinlan, M., Kriesler, P., Junor, A., Baum, F., & Chowdhury, A. (2020). The COVID-19 pandemic: Lessons on building more equal and sustainable societies. *Economic and Labour Relations Review, 31*(2), 133–157. doi:10.1177/1035304620927107

Bartik, A. W., Bertrand, M., Cullen, Z. B., Glaeser, E. L., Luca, M., & Stanton, C. T. (2020). *How are small businesses adjusting to covid-19? early evidence from a survey*. Working Paper No. 26989, National Bureau of Economic Research.

Baruch, Y., & Vardi, Y. (2016). A fresh look at the dark side of contemporary careers: Toward a realistic discourse. *British Journal of Management, 27*(2), 355–372. doi:10.1111/1467-8551.12107

Basu, S. (2020, July 10). IIM Calcutta to start online classes from August 3. *The Times of India*. https://timesofindia.indiatimes.com/city/kolkata/iim-to-start-online-classes-from-aug-3/articleshow/76882534.cms

Baum, T., Mooney, S. K. K., Robinson, R. N. S., & Solnet, D. (2020). COVID-19's impact on the hospitality workforce – new crisis or amplification of the norm? *International Journal of Contemporary Hospitality Management, 32*(9), 2813–2829. doi:10.1108/IJCHM-04-2020-0314

Bauzá, F. J., & Melgosa, F. J. (2020, diciembre). *Turismo Post Covid-19*. Ediciones Universidad Salamanca. Available at https://www.eusal.es/index.php/eusal/catalog/view/978-84-1311-461-3/5558/6275-1

BBC. (2021). https://www.mass.gov/news/baker-polito-administration-announces-covid-19-community-tracing-collaborative-to-further

Begum, M., Farid, M. S., Alam, M. J., & Barua, S. (2020). Covid-19 and Bangladesh: Socioeconomic analysis towards the future correspondence. *Asian Journal of Agricultural Extension. Economia e Sociologia*, 143–155. doi:10.9734/ajaees/2020/v38i930417

Bergesio, L., & González, N. (2020). Los viajes de intercambio y las ferias. Relatos y vigencia del trueque en la Puna jujeña (Argentina). *Estudios Atacameños*, (65), 407–427. doi:10.22199/issn.0718-1043-2020-0034

Better Work. (2021). *COVID-19 Timeline in Bangladesh*. https://betterwork.org/portfolio/covid-timeline-in-bangladesh/

Bieniek, M. (2021). Bartering: Price-Setting Newsvendor Problem with Barter Exchange. *Sustainability, 13*(12), 6684. doi:10.3390u13126684

bKash tops students' list as 'employer of choice'. (2020, December 30). *The Daily Star*. https://www.thedailystar.net/business/news/bkash-tops-students-list-employer-choice-2019241

Blanda, J. & Urbancikova, N. (2020). Social Entrepreneurship as a Tool of Sustainable Development. *Quality Innovation Prosperity, 24*(3). . doi:10.12776/qip.v24i3.1463

Blesa, A., & Ripollés, M. (2003). The role of market orientation in the relationship between entrepreneurial proactiveness and performance. *The Journal of Entrepreneurship, 12*(1), 1–19. doi:10.1177/097135570301200101

Blomley, T., Edwards, K., Kingazi, S., Lukumbuzya, K., Mäkelä, M., & Vesa, L. (2017). When community forestry meets REDD+: Has REDD+ helped address implementation barriers to participatory forest management in Tanzania? *Journal of Eastern African Studies: the Journal of the British Institute in Eastern Africa, 11*(3), 549–570. doi:10.1080/17531055.2017.1356623

Bloomberg. (2019, July). *Amazon Commits $700 Million to Retrain Workers - The e-commerce giant said it will retrain 100,000 workers by 2025*. Industry Week Report.

Bogna, F., Raineri, A., & Dell, G. (2020). Critical realism and constructivism: Merging research paradigms for a deeper qualitative study. *Qualitative Research in Organizations and Management, 15*(4), 461–484. doi:10.1108/QROM-06-2019-1778

Bo, H. X., Li, W., Yang, Y., Wang, Y., Zhang, Q., Cheung, T., & Xiang, Y. T. (2020). Posttraumatic stress symptoms and attitude toward crisis mental health services among clinically stable patients with COVID-19 in China. *Psychological Medicine*, 1–2. PMID:32216863

Boland, B., Smet, A. D., Palter, R., & Sanghvi, A. (2020, June 8). *Reimagining the office and work life after COVID-19*. Mckinsey & Company. https://www.mckinsey.com/business-functions/people-and-organizational-performance/our-insights/reimagining-the-office-and-work-life-after-covid-19

Bolsi, A., Longhi, F., & Paolasso, P. (2009). Pobreza y mortalidad infantil en el Norte Grande Argentino. Un aporte para la formulación de políticas públicas [Poverty and infant mortality in the Great North of Argentina. A contribution to the formulation of public policies]. Cuadernos geográficos, 45(2), 231-261.

Brändle, G. (2017). Controversias en torno al impacto social del consumo colaborativo: Algunos elementos para la discusión. Redes.com. *Revista de Estudios para el Desarrollo Social de la Comunicación, 15*, 122–143. doi:10.15213/redes.n15.p123

Braun, V., Clarke, V., Hayfield, N., & Terry, G. (2019). Thematic Analysis. In L. Liamputtong (Ed.), *Handbook of Research Methods in Health Social Sciences* (pp. 843–860). Springer. doi:10.1007/978-981-10-5251-4_103

Brettel, M., Chomik, C., & Flatten, T. C. (2015). How organizational culture influences innovativeness, proactiveness, and risk-taking: Fostering entrepreneurial orientation in SMEs. *Journal of Small Business Management, 53*(4), 868–885. doi:10.1111/jsbm.12108

Breu, K., Hemingway, C. J., Strathern, M., & Bridger, D. (2002). Workforce agility: The new employee strategy for the knowledge economy. *Journal of Information Technology, 17*(1), 21–31. https://doi.org/10.1080/02683960110132070

Bronfenbrenner, U. (2009). *The ecology of human development: Experiments by nature and design*. Harvard University Press.

Brown, B. (2006). Shame resilience theory: A grounded theory study on women and shame. *Families in Society*, *87*(1), 43–52. doi:10.1606/1044-3894.3483

Brown, B. (2012). *Daring Greatly*. Avery.

BTRC. (2021). *The total number of Mobile Phone subscribers*. http://www.btrc.gov.bd/content/mobile-phone-subscribers-bangladesh-may-2021

Budd, L., & Ison, S. (2020). Responsible Transport: A post-COVID agenda for transport policy and practice. *Transportation Research Interdisciplinary Perspectives, 6*, 1 - 5.

Buga, R., Capeneata, I., Chirasnel, C., & Popa, A. (2014). Facebook in foreign language teaching – a tool to improve communication competences. *Procedia*, *128*, 93–98. doi:10.1016/j.sbspro.2014.03.124

Buheji, M., & Buheji, A. (2020). Characteristics of 'problem-based learning' in post-COVID-19 workplace. *Human Resource Management Review*, *10*(2), 33–39.

Buschner, S., Schirru, R., Zieschang, H., & Junker, P. (2014). Providing recommendations for horizontal career change. *Proceedings of I-KNOW '14*, 1 – 4. 10.1145/2637748.2638440

Business Wire. (2021). *J.P. Morgan Invests €4.3 Million in Skills Development for the Young and Long-Term Unemployed in Paris*. JPMorgan Chase & Co.

Cadena Ser. (2020). *Habilitada la web que señala el nivel de ocupación en las playas coruñesas*. Available at https://cadenaser.com/emisora/2020/06/13/radio_coruna/1592068461_323879.html

Caínzos, Í. (2021). *Feijóo reclama que el turismo sea una prioridad política y económica*. Available at https://www.elcorreogallego.es/galicia/feijoo-reclama-que-el-turismo-sea-una-prioridad-politica-y-economica-JX7707795

Campbell, C., Shollen, S. L., Egan, C., & Neilson, B. G. (2019). The capacious model and leader identity: An integrative framework. *The Journal of Leadership Studies*, *13*(1), 6–19. doi:10.1002/jls.21622

Campos-Castillo, C., & Laestadius, L. I. (2020). Racial and ethnic digital divides in posting COVID-19 content on social media among US adults: Secondary survey analysis. *Journal of Medical Internet Research*, *22*(7), e20472. doi:10.2196/20472 PMID:32568726

Canalis, X. (2015). *El virus MERS pone en alerta a la industria turística de Asia. Hosteltur*. Available at https://www.hosteltur.com/111483_virus-mers-pone-alerta-industria-turistica-asia.html

Cappelli, P., & Keller, J. R. (2014). Talent management: Conceptual approaches and practical challenges. *Annual Review of Organizational Psychology and Organizational Behavior*, *1*(1), 305–331. https://doi.org/10.1146/annurev-orgpsych-031413-091314

Carliner, S. (1999). Industry meets academia: My year of retooling from practicing professional to tenure-track professor. In *Communication Jazz* (pp. 281–288). Improvising the New International Communication Culture. doi:10.1109/IPCC.1999.799135

Carlson, T. (2020, December). *Amazon to help 29 million people around the world grow their tech skills with free cloud computing skills training by 2025*. Amazon.

Carroll, C., Bhattacharjee, S., Chen, Y., Dubey, P., Fan, J., Gajardo, A., Zhou, X., Muller, H.-G., & Wang, J. L. (2020). Time dynamics of COVID-19. *Scientific Reports*, *10*(1), 1–14. doi:10.103841598-020-77709-4 PMID:33273598

Carvalho, A. M., Sampaio, P., Rebentisch, E., Carvalho, J. Á., & Saraiva, P. (2020). The influence of operational excellence on the culture and agility of organizations: Evidence from industry. *International Journal of Quality & Reliability Management*, *38*(7), 1520–1549. https://doi.org/10.1108/ijqrm-07-2020-0248

Cary, P. (2000). *Augustine's invention of the inner self: The legacy of a Christian Platonist*. Oxford University Press.

Castells, M. (1974). *La cuestión urbana* [The Urban Question]. Siglo XXI.

Castells, M. (2006). *La sociedad red: una visión global* [The network society: a global vision]. Alianza.

Castrillon, C. (2019, November). How to Reinvent Your Career After 40. *Forbes*.

Chandrasekaran, R. (2021). The future of work: How hr drives digital transformation in the new normal. *Strategic HR Review*. Advance online publication. doi:10.1108/shr-11-2020-0094

Chang, S. L., Harding, N., Zachreson, C., Cliff, O. M., & Prokopenko, M. (2020). Modelling transmission and control of the COVID-19 pandemic in Australia. *Nature Communications*, *11*(1). https://doi.org/10.1038/s41467-020-19393-6

Chávez, L. (2012). Implementación de tres rutas turísticas en la Zona Sierra Centro del Ecuador. Tesis de grado. Universidad Politécnica de Chimborazo. Chimborazo, Ecuador.

Chen, C. C., & Chen, M. H. (2021). Well-being and career change Intention: COVID-19's impact on unemployed and furloughed hospitality workers. *International Journal of Contemporary Hospitality Management*. Advance online publication. doi:10.1108/ijchm-07-2020-0759

Chen, Z. (2021). Influence of Working from Home during the COVID-19 Crisis and HR Practitioner Response. *Frontiers in Psychology, 12*. doi:10.3389/fpsyg.2021.710517

Cheng, H. N., Liu, Z., Sun, J., Liu, S., & Yang, Z. (2017). Unfolding online learning behavioral patterns and their temporal changes of college students in SPOCs. *Interactive Learning Environments*, *25*(2), 176–188. doi:10.1080/10494820.2016.1276082

Cheshmehzangi, A. (2021). Revisiting the built environment: 10 potential development changes and paradigm shifts due to COVID-19. *Journal of Urban Management*.

Chia, A., & Kern, M. L. (2020). Subjective wellbeing and the social responsibilities of business: An exploratory investigation of australian perspectives. *Applied Research in Quality of Life*, 1–28.

Chia, A., Kern, M. L., & Neville, B. A. (2020). Corporate social responsibility for happiness: Corporate determinants of societal happiness as social responsibility. *Business Ethics (Oxford, England), 29*(3), 422–437. doi:10.1111/beer.12274

Chinniah, B. M. N., Taylor, S., & Proches, C. G. (2020, June 25). COVID-19: The New Normal for the Workplace. *UKZNDABAonline*, *8*(21), 1–3.

Chin, T., Li, G., Jiao, H., Addo, F., & Jawahar, I. M. (2019). Career sustainability during manufacturing innovation. *Career Development International*, *24*(6), 509–528. doi:10.1108/CDI-02-2019-0034

Chopra-McGowan, A., & Reddy, S. B. (2020, July). COVID-19: How can companies offer effective reskilling for employees? Advancing women's careers through leadership development programs. *Employee Relations*.

Chowdhury, M. T., Sarkar, A., Saha, P. K., & Anik, R. H. (2020). Enhancing supply resilience in the COVID-19 pandemic: A case study on beauty and personal care retailers. *Modern Supply Chain Research and Applications, 2*(3), 143–159. doi:10.1108/mscra-07-2020-0018

Ciolan, L., Petrescu, A., Radulescu, C., & Bucur, C. (2014). Training Teachers to Use Digital Resources for the Knowledge Society. *Procedia - Social and Behavioral Sciences*, *128*(22), 415-419. doi:10.1016/j.sbspro.2014.03.180

Cirrincione, L., Plescia, F., Ledda, C., Rapisarda, V., Martorana, D., Moldovan, R. E., Theodoridou, K., & Cannizzaro, E. (2020). COVID-19 pandemic: Prevention and protection measures to be adopted at the workplace. *Sustainability, 12*(9), 1 – 18.

Clúster de Turismo de Galicia. (n.d.). *CORONAVIRUS. Cronología actuaciones del Clúster Turismo de Galicia.* Available at https://clusterturismogalicia.com/gl/coronavirus-cronologia-ctg/

CNN. (2020). *What will travel look like after coronavirus?* Available on https://www.cnn.com/travel/article/coronavirus-travel-industry-changes/index.html

Combes, B. (2008). *The Net Generation: Tech-savvy or lost in virtual space?* ASL, Berkeley, USA. research papers. doi:10.29173/iasl7966

Comisión Europea. (2016). *Una Agenda Europea para la economía*. Retrieved from https://tinyurl.com/y3y8xugv

Consellería de Cultura e Turismo da Xunta de Galicia (2020). *Plan de reactivación dos sectores cultural e turístico fronte aos efectos derivados do COVID-10.* Author.

Cornelius, N., Wallace, J., & Tassabehji, R. (2007). An analysis of corporate social responsibility, corporate identity and ethics teaching in business school. *Journal of Business Ethics*, *76*(1), 117–135. https://doi.org/10.1007/s10551-006-9271-6

Council of the European Union. (2018). *Council recommendation of 22 May 2018 on key competences for lifelong learning.* https://eur-lex.europa.eu/legal-content/EN/TXT/PDF/?uri=CELEX:32018H0604(01)&rid=7#:~:text=The%20Reference%20Framework%20sets%20out,social%20and%20learning%20to%20learn

Covin, J. G., & Miller, D. (2014). International entrepreneurial orientation: Conceptual considerations, research themes, measurement issues, and future research directions. *Entrepreneurship Theory and Practice*, *38*(1), 11–44. doi:10.1111/etap.12027

Covin, J. G., & Slevin, D. P. (1989). Strategic management of small firms in hostile and benign environments. *Strategic Management Journal*, *10*(1), 75–87. doi:10.1002mj.4250100107

Creswell, J. W. (2014). *Research design: Qualitative, quantitative, and mixed-method approaches* (4th ed.). Sage.

Cripps, M. G., Dowsett, C. A., Jackman, S. D., Van Koten, C., Goeke, D. F., & Houliston, G. J. (2020). Genetic variation in tolerance to defoliation in Cirsium arvense. *Weed Research*, *60*(1), 78–84. doi:10.1111/wre.12391

Crovi, D., & López, R. (2011). Tejiendo voces: Jóvenes universitarios opinan sobre la apropiación de internet en la vida académica [Weaving voices: young university students give their opinion on the appropriation of the internet in academic life]. *Revista Mexicana de Ciencias Politicas y Sociales*, *56*(212), 69–80.

Cruz Torres, L., González Rodríguez, O., Placeres Hernández, J. F., & Martínez Abreu, J. (2021). La Covid-19 y los nuevos paradigmas para la gestión del turismo en la región Matanzas. *Revista Médica Electrónica*, *43*(1), 2997–3002.

Csikszentmihalyi, M., & LeFevre, J. (1989). Optimal experience in work and leisure. *Journal of Personality and Social Psychology*, *56*(5), 815–822. doi:10.1037/0022-3514.56.5.815 PMID:2724069

Cullen, J. C., Hammer, L. B., Neal, M. B., & Sinclair, R. R. (2009). Development of a typology of dual-earner couples caring for children and aging parents. *Journal of Family Issues*, *30*(4), 458–483.

Cutshaw, O. (2011). First you grieve: job loss, job stagnation, and job burnout in an age of transition. In *O. Cutshaw's Surviving an information career crisis in a time of change* (pp. 45–55). Chandos Publishing. doi:10.1016/B978-1-84334-632-6.50004-2

D'Angelo, D., Sinopoli, A., Napoletano, A., Gianola, S., Castellini, G., del Monaco, A., Fauci, A. J., Latina, R., Iacorossi, L., Salomone, K., Coclite, D., & Iannone, P. (2021). Strategies to exiting the COVID-19 lockdown for workplace and school: A scoping review. *Safety Science*, *134*, 1–8. doi:10.1016/j.ssci.2020.105067 PMID:33162676

Dai, L., Maksimov, V., Gilbert, B. A., & Fernhaber, S. A. (2014). Entrepreneurial orientation and international scope: The differential roles of innovativeness, proactiveness, and risk-taking. *Journal of Business Venturing*, *29*(4), 511–524. doi:10.1016/j.jbusvent.2013.07.004

Datta, P. R. (2018, February 16). The changing retail market landscape. *The Financial Express*. https://www.thefinancialexpress.com.bd/views/the-changing-retail-market-landscape-1518803754

Davis, M. H., Hall, J. A., & Mayer, P. S. (2016). Developing a new measure of entrepreneurial mindset: Reliability, validity, and implications for practitioners. *Consulting Psychology Journal*, *68*(1), 21–48. doi:10.1037/cpb0000045

Davis, P. (2021). *Beating burnout at work*. Wharton School Press.

de Lucas Ancillo, A., del Val Núñez, M. T., & Gavrila, S. G. (2020). Workplace change within the COVID-19 context: a grounded theory approach. *Economic Research-Ekonomska Istraživanja*, 1-20.

Deb, S. K., & Nafi, S. M. (2020). Impact of covid-19 pandemic on tourism: Perceptions from Bangladesh. *SSRN Electronic Journal*. doi:10.2139/ssrn.3632798

Deci, E. L., & Ryan, R. M. (2000). The" what" and" why" of goal pursuits: Human needs and the self-determination of behavior. *Psychological Inquiry*, *11*(4), 227–268. doi:10.1207/S15327965PLI1104_01

Decree 296/2020. *Aislamiento Social Preventivo y Obligatorio* [Preventive and Compulsory Social Isolation]. https://www.boletinoficial.gob.ar/detalleAviso/primera/227042/20200320

Delgado, F., & Delgado, M. (2014). *El vivir y comer bien en los andes bolivianos. Aportes de los sistemas agroalimentarios y estrategias de vida de las naciones indígena originario campesinas a las políticas de seguridad y soberanía alimentaria*. AGRUCO -Plural Editores.

Demestichas, K., Peppes, N., Alexakis, T., & Adamopoulou, E. (2020). Blockchain in agriculture traceability systems: A review. *Applied Sciences (Basel, Switzerland)*, *10*(12), 4113. doi:10.3390/app10124113

Diab, G. M. A. E.-H., & Elgahsh, N. F. (2020). E-learning during Covid-19 pandemic: Obstacles faced nursing students and its effect on their attitudes while applying it. *American Journal of Nursing Science*, *9*(4), 295. doi:10.11648/j.ajns.20200904.33

Díaz, A. (2021). *Impacto del coronavirus en el turismo en España – Datos estadísticos*. Statista. Available at https://es.statista.com/temas/6510/impacto-del-coronavirus-en-el-sector-turistico-en-espana/#dossierSummary__chapter1

Dimas, D., & Herrera, J. (2020). La práctica del trueque en una comunidad mazahua del Estado de México. *Otra Economía*, *13*(24), 77–94.

Dodds, R., & Richard, B. (2019). *Overtourism: Issues, realities and solutions* (Vol. 1). Walter de Gruyter GmbH & Co KG. doi:10.1515/9783110607369

Doern, R. (2017). Strategies for resilience in entrepreneurship: Building resources for small business survival after a crisis. Institute of Management Studies, Goldsmiths, University of London.

Doolan, K., Barada, V., Burić, I., Krolo, K., & Tonković, Ž. (2021). *Student life during the COVID-19 pandemic lockdown: Europe-wide insights*. European Students' Union (ESU).

Duff, J. (2020, March). *COVID-19 Proves Workers Are Essential and Capitalists Are a Drain*. Academic Press.

Dzingirai, M. (2020a). Design Thinking Perspective in Entrepreneurship Education. In N. Baporikar (Ed.), *Handbook of Research on Entrepreneurship Development and Opportunities in Circular Economy* (pp. 397–416). IGI Global. doi:10.4018/978-1-7998-5116-5.ch021

Dzingirai, M. (2020b). Barriers for quality management implementation in higher education. In M. Sony, K. Karingada, & N. Baporikar (Eds.), *Quality management implementation in higher education: practices, models, and case studies* (pp. 132–151). IGI Global. doi:10.4018/978-1-5225-9829-9.ch007

Dzingirai, M., Chagwesha, M., & Mudzurandende, F. (2021). Challenges and opportunities from COVID-19 vis-à-vis informal cross-border women entrepreneurs scenario in Zimbabwe. In N. Baporikar (Ed.), *Handbook of research on sustaining SMEs and entrepreneurial innovation in the post-COVID-19 Era* (pp. 40–59). IGI Global. doi:10.4018/978-1-7998-6632-9.ch003

Dzingirai, M., Tshuma, N., & Sikomwe, S. (2021). Post-pandemic sustainability strategies for Zimbabwean SMEs. In N. Baporikar (Ed.), *Handbook of research on strategies and interventions to mitigate COVID-19 impact on SMEs* (pp. 457–476). IGI Global. doi:10.4018/978-1-7998-7436-2.ch022

Echegaray, F. (2021). What POST-COVID-19 lifestyles may look like? Identifying scenarios and their implications for sustainability. *Sustainable Production and Consumption*, *27*, 567–574. doi:10.1016/j.spc.2021.01.025 PMID:34722841

Economic Commission for Africa and International Economics Consulting. (2020). *Insights on African businesses' reactions and outlook to COVID-19*. Retrieved July 18, 2021, from https://www.uneca.org/publications/insightsafrican-businesses%E2%80%99-reactions-and-outlook-covid-19

Eikenberry, S. E., Mancuso, M., Iboi, E., Phan, T., Eikenberry, K., Kuang, Y., Kostelich, E., & Gumel, A. B. (2020). To mask or not to mask: Modeling the potential for face mask use by the general public to curtail the COVID-19 pandemic. *Infectious Disease Modelling*, *5*, 293–308. doi:10.1016/j.idm.2020.04.001

Elías, N. (1998). *La civilización de los padres y otros ensayos* [The civilisation of parents and other essays]. Editorial Universidad Nacional y Grupo Editorial Norma.

Engelen, A., Flatten, T. C., Thalmann, J., & Brettel, M. (2014). The effect of organizational culture on entrepreneurial orientation: A comparison between Germany and Thailand. *Journal of Small Business Management*, *52*(4), 732–752. doi:10.1111/jsbm.12052

Eno-Obong, H. (2006). Challenges of entrepreneurship in home economics and enhancement strategies. *Journal of Home Economic Research*, *7*, 69–75.

Estrada, M. A. R. (2021, Feb.). *From COVID-19 to COVID-21*. Preprint.

European Commission. (2006). *Recommendation of the European Parliament and of the Council*. https://eur-lex.europa.eu/LexUriServ/LexUriServ.do?uri=OJ:L:2006:394:0010:0018:en:PDF

European Commission. (2018). Competences for lifelong learning. *Official Journal of the European Union*, *189*, 1–10.

European Commission. (2020). *Digital education action plan 2021-2027*. European Commission.

European Institute of Innovation & Technology. (2020). *Public consultation: Digital education during the Covid-19 recovery period and beyond*. https://eit.europa.eu/news-events/news/consultation-digitaleducation-action-plan

European Parliamentary Research Service. (2015). *Bridging the digital divide in the EU*. https://www.europarl.europa.eu/RegData/etudes/BRIE/2015/573884/EPRS_BRI(2015)573884_EN.pdf

European University Association. (2020). *European higher education in the Covid-19 crisis*. https://eua.eu/downloads/publications/briefing_european%20higher%20education%20in%20the%20covid-19%20crisis.pdf

EUROSTAT. (2019). *Share of young people with basic or above basic digital skills*. https://ec.europa.eu/eurostat/web/products-eurostat-news/-/edn-20200715-1

Expansión. (2020). *El turismo restará un 4% al PIB regional*. Available at https://www.expansion.com/galicia/2020/04/21/5e9ee102468aeb79548b45c6.html

FAO. (2020). *OPSI COVID-19 Innovative Response Tracker*. https://oecd-opsi.org/covid-response/

Farnell, T., Skledar Matijević, A., & Šćukanec Schmidt, N. (2021). *The impact of COVID-19 on higher education: a review of emerging evidence*. NESET report. Luxembourg: Publications Office of the European Union. . doi:10.2766/069216

Faro de Vigo. (2020a). *Galicia bate récords históricos en turistas*. Available at https://www.farodevigo.es/galicia/2020/02/04/galicia-bate-records-historicos-turistas-15353202.html#:%7E:text=En%202019%20visitaron%20Galicia%201,con%20respecto%20al%20a%C3%B1o%20anterior

Faro de Vigo. (2020b). *Plan desescalada: Sanxenxo dividirá la playa de Silgar en 780 cuadrículas con un aforo de hasta 2.340 personas*. Available at https://www.farodevigo.es/pontevedra/2020/05/06/sanxenxo-dividira-playa-silgar-780-14782975.html

Fejes, A., Nylund, M., & Wallin, J. (2019). How do teachers interpret and transform entrepreneurship education? *Journal of Curriculum Studies*, *51*(4), 554–566. doi:10.1080/00220272.2018.1488998

Feldman, D. C. (1996, Summer). Managing careers in downsizing firms. *Human Resource Management*, *35*(2), 145–161. doi:10.1002/(SICI)1099-050X(199622)35:2<145::AID-HRM1>3.0.CO;2-Y

Fenwick, T. (2001). *Experiential Learning: A Theoretical Critique from Five Perspectives*. Information Series No. 385.

Fernandes, N. (2020). *Economic effects of coronavirus outbreak (COVID-19) on the world economy. 2020.* Retrieved July 15, 2021, from https://papers.ssrn.com/sol3/papers.cfm?abstract_id=3557504

Ferreira, C. C. (2020). Experiential learning theory and hybrid entrepreneurship: Factors influencing the transition to full-time entrepreneurship. *International Journal of Entrepreneurial Behaviour & Research*, *26*(8), 1845–1863. doi:10.1108/IJEBR-12-2019-0668

Finau, G., & Scobie, M. (2021). Old ways and new means: Indigenous accountings during and beyond the pandemic. *Accounting, Auditing & Accountability Journal*. https://www21.ucsg.edu.ec:2117/10.1108/AAAJ-08-2020-4753

Finch, H. (2020, November). *16 people who switched careers during lockdown share their best advice*. Academic Press.

Fogarty, P., Frantiz, S., Hirschfeld, J., Keating, S., Lafont, E., Lufkin, B., Mishael, R., Ponnavolu, V., Savage, M., & Turits, M. (2020). Coronavirus: How the world of work may change forever. *BBC*. https://www.bbc.com/worklife/article/20201023-coronavirus-how-will-the-pandemic-change-the-way-we-work

Fong, M. W., Gao, H., Wong, J. Y., Xiao, J., Shiu, E. Y. C., Ryu, S., & Cowling, B. J. (2020). Nonpharmaceutical measures for pandemic influenza in nonhealthcare settings – social distancing measures. *Emerging Infectious Diseases*, *26*(5), 976–984. doi:10.3201/eid2605.190995

França, T., & Marques, B. P. (2021). Gender and digital skills in Portuguese higher education during the Covid-19 Pandemic. In N. Tomaževič, D. Ravšelj, & A. Aristovnik (Eds.), *Higher education policies for developing digital skills to respond to the Covid-19 crisis: European and global perspectives* (pp. 59-71). European Liberal Forum.

Fredrickson, B. L., Grewen, K. M., Coffey, K. A., Algoe, S. B., Firestine, A. M., Arevalo, J., Ma, J., & Cole, S. W. (2013). A functional genomic perspective on human wellbeing. *Proceedings of the National Academy of Sciences of the United States of America*, *110*(33), 13684–13689. doi:10.1073/pnas.1305419110 PMID:23898182

Freer, L. M. (2019). Strategies for career resilience in the face of economic uncertainty. *Proceedings of SIGUCCS '19*, 20 – 22. 10.1145/3347709.3347811

Frenken, K. (2017). Political economies and environmental futures for the sharing economy en Philosophical Transactions of the Royal Societ. *Philosophical Transactions of the Royal Society A*, *375*(2095), 20160367. Advance online publication. doi:10.1098/rsta.2016.0367 PMID:28461431

Friedman, T. L. (2005). *The world is flat: A brief history of the twenty-first century* (1st ed.). Macmillan.

G7. (2018). *The G7 Whistler Principles to Accelerate Innovation for Development Impact*. https://www.international.gc.ca/world-monde/international_relations relations_internationales/g7/documents/2018-05-31-whistler-development-developpement.aspx?lang=eng

Gander, F., Gaitzsch, I., & Ruch, W. (2021). The relationships of team role and character strengths balance with individual and team-level satisfaction and performance. *Frontiers in Psychology, 11*, 566222. doi:10.3389/fpsyg.2020.566222 PMID:33329199

Gander, F., Hofmann, J., & Ruch, W. (2021). Character strengths: Person–environment fit and relationships with job and life satisfaction. *Frontiers in Psychology, 11*, 1582. doi:10.3389/fpsyg.2020.01582 PMID:32793038

García Gaibor, J. A. (2020). *Análisis de la intención del comportamiento de los consumidores turístico de parques acuáticos post covid-19 del cantón Montalvo* (Bachelor's thesis). UTB.

George, R., & George, A. (2020, April). Prevention of COVID-19 in the workplace. SAMJ. *South African Medical Journal, 110*(4), 269–270. doi:10.7196/SAMJ.2020.v110i4.14723 PMID:32657736

Gettler, L. (2003, June). Bite-size careers: It used to be jobs for life, but now managers need to give life to their jobs. *Management Today*, 20–25.

Giddens, A. (2003). *La constitución de la sociedad* [The constitution of society]. Amorrortu.

Global Innovation Exchange. (2020). *Joint donor COVID-19 Innovation Hub*. https://covid19innovationhub.org/

Gobierno Autónomo Descentralizado de la Provincia de Bolívar. (2015). *Plan de Desarrollo y Ordenamiento Territorial de Bolivar 2015- 2020*. Tomado de https://multimedia.planificacion.gob.ec/PDOT/descargas.html

Gobierno Autónomo Descentralizado de la Provincia de Chimborazo. (2020). *Plan de Desarrollo y Ordenamiento Territorial de Chimborazo 2020- 2030*. Tomado de https://multimedia.planificacion.gob.ec/PDOT/descargas.html

Gobierno Autónomo Descentralizado de la Provincia de Cotopaxi. (2015). *Actualización del Plan de Desarrollo y Ordenamiento Territorial de Cotopaxi 2025*. Tomado de http://app.sni.gob.ec/sni-link/sni/PORTAL_SNI/data_sigad_plus/sigadplusdocumentofinal/0560000110001_FINAL-PDYOT-COTOPAXI-2015_17-08-2015_18-17-17.pdf

Gobierno Autónomo Descentralizado de la Provincia de Tungurahua. (2015). *Informe Técnico para la Alineación Plan de Desarrollo y Ordenamiento Territorial PDOT Provincial - al Plan Nacional de Desarrollo 2017 - 2021*. Tomado de https://multimedia.planificacion.gob.ec/PDOT/descargas.html

Gomes, V. (2020, June 26). Cloud Kitchens: Future of food delivery services. *The Daily Star*. https://www.thedailystar.net/toggle/news/cloud-kitchens-future-food-delivery-services-1920413

Gómez Varela, J. F., Río-Rodríguez, D., & Rico-Díaz, J. (2020). Reactivación de las actividades del turismo activo español hacia la "nueva normalidad" de la COVID-19: Análisis documental sobre su regulación, recomendaciones, propuestas y protocolos. *ROTUR. Revista de Ocio y Turismo, 14*(2), 1–22. doi:10.17979/rotur.2020.14.2.6583

Gonzales, M. (2020). The Bronfenbrenner micro-and meso-systems. In M. Gonzales (Ed.), *Systems thinking for supporting students with special needs and disabilities* (pp. 81–92). Springer. doi:10.1007/978-981-33-4558-4_6

González Cabrera, I. (2018). La economía colaborativa del intercambio entre pares a una nueva economía de mercado. Revista de derecho mercantil (Madrid).

González-Sánchez, G., Olmo-Sánchez, M. I., & Maeso-González, E. (2021). Challenges and Strategies for Post-COVID-19 Gender Equity and Sustainable Mobility. *Sustainability, 13*(5), 1 - 19.

Gossenheimer, A. N., Bem, T., Carneiro, M. L. F., & De Castro, M. S. (2017). Impact of distance education on academic performance in a pharmaceutical care course. *PLoS One, 12*(4), e0175117. doi:10.1371/journal.pone.0175117 PMID:28384362

Gössling, S., Scott, D., & Hall, C. M. (2020). Pandemics, tourism and global change: A rapid assessment of COVID-19. *Journal of Sustainable Tourism, 29*(1), 1–20. doi:10.1080/09669582.2020.1758708

Government of Ireland (GoI). (2021). *Economic Recovery Plan 2021.* Department of the Taoiseach gov.ie.

Goy. (2017). *The impact of technological innovation on building a sustainable city.* https://jqualityinnovation.springeropen.com/articles/10.1186/s40887-017-0014-9

Grady, D. (2021, June 3). 'I had never faced the reality of death': A surgeon becomes a patient. *The New York Times.*

Gray, J. (2001). The end of career. *Communications of the ACM, 44*(11), 65–69. doi:10.1145/384150.384163

Gregory, A., & Halff, G. (2017). Understanding public relations in the 'sharing economy'. *Public Relations Review, 43*(1), 4–13. doi:10.1016/j.pubrev.2016.10.008

Gregory, Ch. (2012). On money debt and morality: Some reflections on the contribution of economic anthropology. *Social Anthropology, 20*(4), 380–396. doi:10.1111/j.1469-8676.2012.00225.x

Gysbers, N. C., Heppner, M. J., & Johnston, J. A. (1998). *Career Counseling: Process, Issues and Techniques*. Allyn and Bacon.

Haigh, K. Z., & Gandhi, M. (2021, April). COVID-19 Mitigation With Appropriate Safety Measures in an Essential Workplace: Lessons for Opening Work Settings in the United States During COVID-19. In Open Forum Infectious Diseases (Vol. 8, No. 4). Oxford University Press.

Haleem, A., Javaid, M., & Vaishya, R. (2020). Effects of COVID-19 pandemic in daily life. *Current Medicine Research and Practice, 10*(2), 78-79. doi:10.1016/j.cmrp.2020.03.011

Hall, C. M., Scott, D., & Gössling, S. (2020). Pandemics, transformations and tourism: Be careful what you wish for. *Tourism Geographies, 22*(3), 577–598. doi:10.1080/14616688.2020.1759131

Hämäläinena, R., De Weverb, B., Nissinen, K., & Cincinnatod, S. (2019). What makes the difference – PIAAC as a resource for understanding the problem solving skills of Europe's higher-education adults. *Computers & Education*, *129*, 27–36. doi:10.1016/j.compedu.2018.10.013

Hamari, J., Sjöklint, M., & Ukkonen, A. (2016). The sharing economy: Why people participate in collaborative consumption. *Journal of the Association for Information Science and Technology*, *67*(9), 2047–2059. doi:10.1002/asi.23552

Hamouche, S. (2020). *COVID-19 and employees' mental health: Stressors, moderators and agenda for organizational actions.* Emerald Open Research.

Hamouche, S. (2021). Human resource management and the COVID-19 crisis: Implications, challenges, opportunities, and future organizational directions. *Journal of Management & Organization*, 1–16. doi:10.1017/jmo.2021.15

Hanage, W. P., Testa, C., Chen, J. T., Davis, L., Pechter, E., Seminario, P., Santillana, M., & Krieger, N. (2020). COVID-19: US federal accountability for entry, spread, and inequities—lessons for the future. *European Journal of Epidemiology*, *35*(11), 995–1006. doi:10.100710654-020-00689-2 PMID:33136249

Hancock, B., & Schaninger, B. (2020). *HR says talent is crucial for performance–and the pandemic proves it.* McKinsey & Company. https://www.mckinsey.com/business-functions/people-and-organizational-performance/our-insights/hr-says-talent-is-crucial-for-performance-and-the-pandemic-proves-it

Hardie, B., Highfield, C., & Lee, K. (2020). Review Article Entrepreneurship education today for students' unknown futures. *Journal of Pedagogical Research*, *4*(3), 401–417. doi:10.33902/JPR.2020063022

Havaei, F., Ma, A., Staempfli, S., & MacPhee, M. (2021, January). Nurses' Workplace Conditions Impacting Their Mental Health during COVID-19: A Cross-Sectional Survey Study. *Health Care*, *9*(1), 1–14. PMID:33467080

Hegbe, S. (2016). Developing hobbies for a lifetime. *Journal of Social Welfare and Management*, *8*(2), 111–121.

Henry, M. S., Bazilian, M. D., & Markuson, C. (2020). Just transitions: Histories and futures in a post-COVID world. *Energy Research & Social Science*, *68*(101668), 1–4. doi:10.1016/j.erss.2020.101668 PMID:32839696

Heppner, M. J. (1998). The career transitions inventory: Measuring internal resources in adulthood. *Journal of Career Assessment*, *6*(2), 135–145. doi:10.1177/106907279800600202

Hernandez, X., & Valentinotti, S. (2020). On an optimal testing strategy for workplace settings operating during the COVID-19 pandemic. medRxiv. 1 - 18. doi:10.1101/2020.12.22.20248752

Hillier, D., Newton-Lewis, T., Nair, E., & Larsen, C. (2020). Initial COVID-19 responses in Bangladesh, Kenya, Pakistan, Sierra Leone and Uganda: Documentation and learning from March to May 2020 (COVID-19 Series: Synthesis Report). *UKAID & Oxford Policy Management*. https://reliefweb.int/sites/reliefweb.int/files/resources/COVID-19-Synthesis-report-Exec-Sum-Final.pdf

Holmes, M., Alonzi, S., Perry, L. M., Voss, H. M., Easwar, S., & Gerhart, J. I. (2020). Impact of the COVID-19 pandemic on mental health: Real-time surveillance using Google Trends. *Psychological Trauma: Theory, Research, Practice, and Policy*, *12*(6), 567–568. doi:10.1037/tra0000872 PMID:32790441

Holtby, A. (2021). *How to Launch a Career During COVID-19 - Expert advice on navigating the job search without sacrificing mental health*. University of Alberta.

Ho, M. H., Uy, M. A., Kang, B. N. Y., & Chan, K. Y. (2018). Impact of entrepreneurship training on entrepreneurial efficacy and alertness among adolescent youth. *Frontiers in Education*, *3*(13), 1–10. doi:10.3389/feduc.2018.00013

Honey-Rosés, J., Anguelovski, I., Bohigas, J., Chireh, V., Daher, C., Konijnendijk, C., Litt, J., Mawani, V., McCall, M., Orellana, A., Oscilowicz, E., Sánchez, U., Senbel, M., Tan, X., Villagomez, E., Zapat, O., & Nieuwenhuijsen, M. (2020, Apr. 21). *The impact of COVID-19 on public space: A review of the emerging questions*. Academic Press.

Hornsby, J. S., Kuratko, D. F., Shepherd, D. A., & Bott, J. P. (2009). Managers' corporate entrepreneurial actions: Examining perception and position. *Journal of Business Venturing*, *24*(3), 236–247. doi:10.1016/j.jbusvent.2008.03.002

Hossain, S. (2021, May 4). The restaurant industry is on the brink of collapse. *Dhaka Tribune*. https://www.dhakatribune.com/business/commerce/2021/05/04/the-restaurant-industry-is-on-the-brink-of-collapse

Hsu, L., & Hsieh, S. (2014). Factors affecting metacognition of undergraduate nursing students in a blended learning environment. *International Journal of Nursing Practice*, *20*(3), 233–241. doi:10.1111/ijn.12131 PMID:24888995

Huber, A., Strecker, C., Kachel, T., Höge, T., & Höfer, S. (2020). Character strengths profiles in medical professionals and their impact on well-being. *Frontiers in Psychology*, *11*, 11. doi:10.3389/fpsyg.2020.566728 PMID:33424679

Huertas, A., Oliveira, A., & Girotto, M. (2020). Gestión comunicativa de crisis de las oficinas nacionales de turismo de España e Italia ante la Covid-19. *El Profesional de la Información*, *29*(4), e290410. doi:10.3145/epi.2020.jul.10

Hu, R. (2020). COVID-19, smart work, and collaborative space: A crisis-opportunity perspective. *Journal of Urban Management*, *9*(3), 276–280. doi:10.1016/j.jum.2020.08.001

Ibarra, H. (2020, April). *Reinventing Your Career in the Time of Coronavirus*. Academic Press.

Ibarra, H. (2004). *Working Identity: Unconventional Strategies for Reinventing Your Career*. Harvard Business School Publishing.

Igbinakhase, I. (2021). Determinants for SMEs and entrepreneurship success post-pandemic. In N. Baporikar (Ed.), *Handbook of research on strategies and interventions to mitigate COVID-19 impact on SMEs* (pp. 168–185). IGI Global. doi:10.4018/978-1-7998-7436-2.ch008

Ikeda, R., Assilmia, F., Angelina, E., & Okawa, K. (2019). Job digital storytelling program for university students to develop career management competencies. *Proceedings of ICDTE 2019*, 127 – 131. 10.1145/3369199.3369220

Ikram, M., Shen, Y., Ferasso, M., & D'Adamo, I. (2021). Intensifying effects of covid-19 on economic growth, logistics performance, environmental sustainability and Quality Management: Evidence from Asian countries. *Journal of Asia Business Studies*. Advance online publication. doi:10.1108/jabs-07-2021-0316

ILO. (2020). *ILO Monitor: COVID-19 and the world of work* (7th ed.). Retrieved July 15, 2021, from https://www.ilo.org/global/topics/coronavirus/impacts-and-responses/WCMS_767028/lang--en/index.htm

ILO. (2020a). *ILO Monitor: COVID-19 and the world of work* (4th ed). Retrieved July 15, 2020, from https://www.ilo.org/global/topics/coronavirus/impacts-and-responses/WCMS_745963/lang--en/index.htm

ILO. (2021a). *COVID-19 and the world of work*: Seventh Edition. https://www.ilo.org/global/topics/coronavirus/impacts-and-responses/WCMS_767028/lang--en/index.htm

ILO. (2021b). *World employment and social outlook – Trends 2021*. https://www.ilo.org/global/research/global-reports/weso/trends2021/WCMS_795453/lang--en/index.htm

InnovationO. (Ed.). (2019). *OPSI Blog*. https://oecd-opsi.org/innovation-facets-and-core-values-how-different-forms-of-innovation-can-cause-different-reactions/

Instituto de Estadísticas y Censos (INEC). (2021). *Boletín Técnico N°03-2021-IPC*. Tomado de https://www.ecuadorencifras.gob.ec/documentos/web-inec/Inflacion/2021/Marzo-2021/Boletin_tecnico_03-2021-IPC.pdf

Integrative Life Center. (2021, February 22). *Shame Resilience*. https://integrativelifecenter.com/wellness-blog/shame-resilience/

International Labour Organisation (2021a, January). *ILO Monitor: COVID-19 and the world of work* (7th ed.). ILO.

International Labour Organisation. (2021b). *Skilling, upskilling and reskilling of employees, apprentices and interns during the COVID-19 pandemic: Findings from a global survey of enterprises. International Labour Office*. ILO.

International Monetary Fund. (2020). *Policy responses to COVID-19*. Retrieve July 16, 2021, from https://www.imf.org/en/Topics/ imf-and-covid19/Policy-Responses-to-COVID-19

International Trade Centre. (2020, April). Story: Ugandan start-ups part of the solution during COVID-19 - Start-ups in Uganda are developing innovative products to help consumers and businesses survive during COVID-19. *ITC News*.

Jayathilake, H. D., Daud, D., Eaw, H. C., & Annuar, N. (2021). Employee development and retention of Generation-Z employees in the post-COVID-19 workplace: A conceptual framework. *Benchmarking*, *28*(7), 2343–2364. doi:10.1108/BIJ-06-2020-0311

Jesuthasan, R., Malcolm, T., & Cantrell, S. (2020, April). Crisis Management - How the Coronavirus Crisis Is Redefining Jobs. *Harvard Business Review*.

Jimenez, J. (2021). *The burnout fix: Overcome overwhelm, beat busy, and sustain success in the new world of work*. McGraw Hill.

Joseph, B., Angeline, N. G., & Arasu, S. (2020). COVID-19—Practicing prevention in the workplace. *Indian Journal of Occupational and Environmental Medicine*, *24*(3), 133–136. doi:10.4103/ijoem.ijoem_460_20 PMID:33746423

Kamble, S. S., Gunasekaran, A., & Sharma, R. (2020). Modeling the blockchain enabled traceability in agriculture supply chain. *International Journal of Information Management*, *52*, 101967. doi:10.1016/j.ijinfomgt.2019.05.023

Kantamneni, N. (2020). The impact of the COVID-19 pandemic on marginalized populations in the United States: A research agenda. *Journal of Vocational Behavior*, *119*(103439), 1–4. doi:10.1016/j.jvb.2020.103439 PMID:32390658

Karim, M. R., Shetu, S. A., & Razia, S. (2021). Covid-19, liquidity and Financial Health: Empirical Evidence from South Asian economy. *Asian Journal of Economics and Banking*, *5*(3), 307–323. https://doi.org/10.1108/ajeb-03-2021-0033

Kaushal, V., & Srivastava, S. (2021). Hospitality and tourism industry amid COVID-19 pandemic: Perspectives on challenges and learnings from India. *International Journal of Hospitality Management*, *92*, 102707. doi:10.1016/j.ijhm.2020.102707 PMID:33024348

Kaushik, M. (2020, May-June). Post COVID-19 world: A paradigm shift at workplace. *TEST Engineering & Management*, 27675 – 27687.

Kaushik, M., & Guleria, N. (2020). The impact of pandemic COVID-19 in workplace. *European Journal of Business and Management*, *12*(15), 9–19.

Kegan, R. (1982). *The evolving self: Problem and process in human development*. Harvard University Press.

Kelly, S.M. (2021, Sept. 24). *Stop making employees turn on webcams during meetings*. CNN.

Kern, M. L., Waters, L., Adler, A., & White, M. (2014). Assessing employee wellbeing in schools using a multifaceted approach: Associations with physical health, life satisfaction, and professional thriving. *Psychology (Irvine, Calif.)*, *5*(06), 500–513. doi:10.4236/psych.2014.56060

Khan, I., Haleem, A., & Javaid, M. (2020). Analysing COVID-19 pandemic through cases, deaths, and recoveries. *Journal of Oral Biology and Craniofacial Research, 10*(4), 450–469. doi:10.1016/j.jobcr.2020.08.003 PMID:32834980

Kilic, K., & Marin, D. (2020). How COVID-19 is transforming the world economy. *VoxEU. org, 10.*

Kim, C. Y. (2002). Teachers in Digital Knowledge-Based Society: New Roles and Vision. *Asia Pacific Education Review, 3*(2), 144–148. doi:10.1007/BF03024907

Kinicki, A., & Williams, B. K. (2010). *Management: A Practical Introduction.* McGraw-Hill.

Klotz. (2021, May 30). *The Covid vaccine means a return to work. And a wave of resignations.* NBC News.

Kniffin, K. M., Narayanan, J., Anseel, F., Antonakis, J., Ashford, S. P., Bakker, A. B., Bamberger, P., Bapuji, H., Bhave, D. P., Choi, V. K., Creary, S. J., Demerouti, E., Flynn, F. J., Gelfand, M. J., Greer, L. L., Johns, G., Kesebir, S., Klein, P. G., Lee, S. Y., ... Vugt, M. (2020, August 10). COVID-19 and the Workplace: Implications, Issues, and Insights for Future Research and Action. *The American Psychologist.* Advance online publication. doi:10.1037/amp0000716 PMID:32772537

Kombe, C., Sam, A., Ally, M., & Finne, A. (2019). Blockchain Technology in Sub-Saharan Africa: Where does it fit in Healthcare Systems: A case of Tanzania. *Journal of Health Informatics in Developing Countries, 13*(2).

Korstanje, M. E. (2020). El COVID-19 y El turismo rural: una perspectiva antropológica. *Dimensiones Turísticas, 4*, 179-196.

Kowalczyk, N.K. (2014). *Perceived barriers to online education by radiologic sciences.* Academic Press.

Kreiser, P. M., Marino, L. D., Dickson, P., & Weaver, K. M. (2010). Cultural influences on entrepreneurial orientation: The impact of national culture on risk taking and proactiveness in SMEs. *Entrepreneurship Theory and Practice, 34*(5), 959–984. doi:10.1111/j.1540-6520.2010.00396.x

Kreiser, P. M., Marino, L. D., Kuratko, D. F., & Weaver, K. M. (2013). Disaggregating entrepreneurial orientation: The non-linear impact of innovativeness, proactiveness and risk-taking on SME performance. *Small Business Economics, 40*(2), 273–291. doi:10.100711187-012-9460-x

Kun, Á., Balogh, P., & Krasz, K. G. (2017). Development of the work-related wellbeing questionnaire based on Seligman's PERMA model. *Periodica Polytechnica Social and Management Sciences, 25*(1), 56–63. doi:10.3311/PPso.9326

Kuratko, D. F. (2014). *The Entrepreneurial Mind-Set in Individuals: Cognition and Ethics.* Academic Press.

Kusa, R. (2016). Measuring entrepreneurial orientation in the social context. *Entrepreneurial Business and Economics Review, 4*(3), 117–129. doi:10.15678/EBER.2016.040309

La Comisión Económica para América Latina y el Caribe (CEPAL). (2020). *Panorama Social de América Latina 2020.* CEPAL. Tomado de https://www.cepal.org/es/publicaciones/46687-panorama-social-america-latina-2020

La Vanguardia. (2020). *El turismo posvirus seguirá nuevas normas de salud.* Available at https://www.lavanguardia.com/economia/20200408/48384693297/turismo-posvirus-coronavirus-catalunya.html

La Voz de Galicia. (2020). *Los dos primeros muertos en Galicia por coronavirus, de 92 y 81 años.* Available at https://www.lavozdegalicia.es/noticia/sociedad/2020/03/15/dos-primeros-muertos-galicia-92-81-anos/0003_202003G15P6992.htm

La Voz de Galicia. (2021). *Cronología de un año de coronavirus en España.* Available at https://www.lavozdegalicia.es/noticia/especiales/aniversario-pandemia/2021/03/05/cronologia-ano-coronavirus-espana/00031614956653588579113.htm

Lackeus, M. (2019) Making enterprise education more relevant through mission creep. In Enterprising education in UK higher education: Challenges for theory and practice. Routledge Studies in Entrepreneurship.

Lackeus, M. (2015). *Entrepreneurship in education.* OECD Paris France.

Lai, C. C., Shih, T. P., Ko, W. C., Tang, H. J., & Hsueh, P. R. (2020). Severe acute respiratory syndrome coronavirus 2 (SARS-CoV-2) and corona virus disease-2019 (COVID-19): The epidemic and the challenges. *International Journal of Antimicrobial Agents*, *55*, 105924.

Lalon, R. M. (2020). Covid-19 vs. Bangladesh: Is it possible to recover the impending economic distress amid this pandemic? *Journal of Economics and Business*, *3*(2). https://doi.org/10.31014/aior.1992.03.02.240

Lane, C. (2021, April). *How Graduates Can Get Hired During The Coronavirus Pandemic.* Academic Press.

Langston, C. (2020). Entrepreneurial educators: Vital enablers to support the education sector to reimagine and respond to the challenges of COVID-19. *Entrepreneurship Education*, *3*(3), 311–338. doi:10.100741959-020-00034-4

Lauder, H., & Mayhew, K. (2020). Higher education and the labour market: An introduction. *Oxford Review of Education*, *46*(1), 1–9. doi:10.1080/03054985.2019.1699714

Lavy, S., & Benish-Weisman, M. (2021). Character strengths as "values in action": Linking character strengths with values theory–An exploratory study of the case of gratitude and self-transcendence. *Frontiers in Psychology*, *12*, 202. doi:10.3389/fpsyg.2021.576189 PMID:33613375

Law, N., Woo, D., de la Torre, J., & Wong, G. (2018). *A Global Framework ofReference on Digital Literacy Skills for Indicator 4.4.2.* UNESCO.

Lawrence, B. S., Hall, D. T., & Arthur, M. B. (2015). Sustainable careers then and now. In A. D. Vos & B. I. J. M. v. Heijden (Eds.), Handbook of research on sustainable careers (pp. 432–450). Edward Elgar Publishing. https://doi.org/10.4337/9781782547037.00033.

Lazányi, K., Vincze, A., & Szikora, P. (2021). The digital skills in the Hungarian higher education during the first wave of Covid-19. In N. Tomaževič, D. Ravšelj, & A. Aristovnik (Eds.), *Higher education policies for developing digital skills to respond to the Covid-19 crisis: European and global perspectives* (pp. 4-18). European Liberal Forum.

Lee, M. A., & Kawachi, I. (2019). The keys to happiness: Associations between personal values regarding core life domains and happiness in South Korea. *PLoS One, 14*(1), e0209821. doi:10.1371/journal.pone.0209821 PMID:30625160

Leso, V., Fontana, L., & Iavicoli, I. (2021). Susceptibility to coronavirus (COVID-19) in occupational settings: The complex interplay between individual and workplace factors. *International Journal of Environmental Research and Public Health, 18*(3), 1 - 16.

Leurent, H., & Boer, E. (2018). *The Next Economic Growth Engine Scaling Fourth Industrial Revolution Technologies in Production.* World Economic Forum.

Li, C., & Lalani, F. (2020). *The COVID-19 pandemic has changed education forever. This is how.* https://www.weforum.org/agenda/2020/04/coronavirus-education-global-covid19-online-digital-learning/

Liang, S. H., Saeedi, S., Ojagh, S., Honarparvar, S., Kiaei, S., Jahromi, M. M., & Squires, J. (2021). An Interoperable Architecture for the Internet of COVID-19 Things (IoCT) Using Open Geospatial Standards—Case Study: Workplace Reopening. *Sensors (Basel), 21*(1), 50–82. doi:10.339021010050 PMID:33374208

Liaquat, Z. B. (2020, August 11). Plea to save the restaurant industry. *The Financial Express.* https://thefinancialexpress.com.bd/views/plea-to-save-the-restaurant-industry-1597086210

Liaquat, Z. B. (2021, June 27). Bangladesh lags behind in fintech ecosystem globally. *Dhaka Tribune.* https://www.dhakatribune.com/business/2021/06/27/bangladesh-lags-behind-in-fintech-ecosystem-globally

LightCastle Analytics Wing. (2019, July 9). *Transformation in the Telecommunications Industry.* https://www.lightcastlebd.com/insights/2019/07/transformation-in-the-telecommunications-industry

Liguori, E. W., & Pittz, T. G. (2020). Strategies for small business: Surviving and thriving in the era of COVID-19. *Journal of the International Council for Small Business, 1*(2), 106–110. doi:10.1080/26437015.2020.1779538

Lindgreen, A., Di Benedetto, C. A., & Beverland, M. B. (2021). How to write up case-study methodology sections. *Industrial Marketing Management, 96*, A7–A10. doi:10.1016/j.indmarman.2020.04.012

Lindsley, W. G., Blachère, F. M., Burton, N. C., Christensen, B., Estill, C. F., Fisher, E. M., Martin, S. B., Mead, K. R., Noti, J. D., & Seaton, M. (2020). COVID-19 and the workplace: Research questions for the aerosol science community. *Aerosol Science and Technology*, *54*(10), 1117–1123. doi:10.1080/02786826.2020.1796921

Littman-Ovadia, H., Dubreuil, P., Meyers, M. C., & Freidlin, P. (2021). VIA character strengths: Theory, research and practice. *Frontiers in Psychology*, *12*, 2. doi:10.3389/fpsyg.2021.653941 PMID:33897563

Littman-Ovadia, H., Lazar-Butbul, V., & Benjamin, B. A. (2014). Strengths-based career counseling: Overview and initial evaluation. *Journal of Career Assessment*, *22*(3), 403–419. doi:10.1177/1069072713498483

Liu, T., Zheng, Z., Sha, X., Liu, H., Zheng, W., Su, H., Xu, G., Su, K.-P., So, K.-F., & Lin, K. (2021). Psychological impact in non-infectious disease specialists who had direct contact with patients with COVID-19. *BJPsych Open*, *7*(1), 1–4. doi:10.1192/bjo.2020.147 PMID:33283699

Lloyd, M. (2020). *Desigualdades educativas y la brecha digital en tiempos de COVID-19* [Educational Inequalities and Digital Gap in times of Covid 19]. Universidad Nacional Autónoma de México. Instituto de Investigaciones sobre La Universidad y la Educación

Lockdown now from Thursday. (2021, June 27). *The Daily Star*. Retrieved November 7, 2021, from https://www.thedailystar.net/frontpage/news/lockdown-now-thursday-2119017

Lopes, A. S., Sargento, A., & Carreira, P. (2021). Vulnerability to COVID-19 unemployment in the Portuguese tourism and hospitality industry. *International Journal of Contemporary Hospitality Management*, *33*(5), 1850–1869. https://doi.org/10.1108/ijchm-11-2020-1345

Lumpkin, G. T., & Dess, G. G. (1996). Clarifying the entrepreneurial orientation construct and linking it to performance. *Academy of Management Review*, *21*(1), 135–172. doi:10.2307/258632

Luna Zamora, R. (2005). *Sociología del miedo. Un estudio sobre las ánimas, diablos y elementos naturales* [Sociology of fear. A study on the souls, devils and natural elements]. Universidad de Guadalajara. formación docente en competencias digitales en clases no presenciales durante la pandemia COVID-19. doi:10.1590/SciELOPreprints.778

Lund, S., Madgavkar, A., Manyika, J., Smit, S., Ellingrud, K., Meaney, M., & Robinson, O. (2021). *The future of work after COVID-19*. McKinsey Global Institute.

Macko, A., & Tyszka, T. (2009). Entrepreneurship and risk taking. *Applied Psychology*, *58*(3), 469–487. doi:10.1111/j.1464-0597.2009.00402.x

Mahmood, R., & Hanafi, N. (2013). Entrepreneurial orientation and business performance of women-owned small and medium enterprises in Malaysia: Competitive advantage as a mediator. *International Journal of Business and Social Science*, *4*(1), 82–90.

Mahmoud Saleh, F. I., & Karia, N. (2020). Benchmarks for INGOs' effective responses during COVID-19 pandemic. *Benchmarking*, *27*(10), 2863–2886.

Maker's Asylum. (2020). https://www.makersasylum.com/m19-shields/

Makhbul, Z. K. M., & Rawshdeh, Z. A. (2021, March). Mental stress post-COVID-19. *International Journal of Public Health Science, 10*(1), 194–201.

Mamgain, R. P. (2021). Understanding labour market disruptions and job losses amidst COVID-19. *Journal of Social and Economic Development*. doi:10.1007/s40847-020-00125-x

Maritz, A., Perenyi, A., De-Waal, G., & Buck, C. (2020). Entrepreneurship as the unsung hero during the current COVID-19 economic crisis: Australian Perspectives. *Sustainability, 12*, 4612.

Martínez-Martí, M. L., Theirs, C. I., Pascual, D., & Corradi, G. (2020). Character strengths predict an increase in mental health and subjective well-being over a one-month period during the COVID-19 pandemic lockdown. *Frontiers in Psychology, 11*, 2790. doi:10.3389/fpsyg.2020.584567 PMID:33192913

Ma, S., Kim, D. D., Cohen, J. T., & Neumann, P. J. (2020). Measuring "Fearonomic effects" in valuing therapies: An application to COVID-19 in china. *Value in Health, 23*(11), 1405–1408. doi:10.1016/j.jval.2020.06.002 PMID:33127009

Mauras, S., Cohen-Addad, V., Duboc, G., la Tour, M. D., Frasca, P., Mathieu, C., Opatowski, L., & Viennot, L. (2020). Mitigating COVID-19 outbreaks in workplaces and schools by hybrid telecommuting. medRxiv. 1 - 40. doi:10.1101/2020.11.09.20228007

Mayala, N. M. (2021). COVID-19's Impact on Tanzania's Economy and Key Sector Prospects. In Handbook of Research on Sustaining SMEs and Entrepreneurial Innovation in the Post-COVID-19 Era (pp. 106-121). IGI Global.

Mayala, N. M. (2021). The Role of Agriculture in Tanzania: Unpacking Industrialization Prospects and Constraints. In *Handbook of Research on Institution Development for Sustainable and Inclusive Economic Growth in Africa* (pp. 299–316). IGI Global. doi:10.4018/978-1-7998-4817-2.ch018

Mayala, N. M., Katundu, M. A., & Msuya, E. E. (2019). Socio-cultural Factors influencing livestock investment decisions among Smallholder Farmers in Mbulu and Bariadi Districts, Tanzania. *Global Business Review, 20*(5), 1214–1230. doi:10.1177/0972150917742556

McCray, R. R., & Rawlins, J. L. (2015). Be the leader of your career: A self-centered approach to strategic career management. *Proceedings of SIGUCCs '15*, 55 – 57. 10.1145/2815546.2815575

McCusker, K., & Gunaydin, S. (2015). Research using qualitative, quantitative or mixed methods and choice based on the research. *Perfusion, 30*(7), 537–542. doi:10.1177/0267659114559116 PMID:25378417

McGrath, G. R., & MacMillan, I. C. (2000). *Entrepreneurial Mindset: Strategies for Continuously Creating Opportunity in an Age of Uncertainty*. Harvard Business School Press Books.

Mesa, R. (2020). *Las consecuencias del coronavirus en el sector del Turismo*. Available at https://blogs.imf-formacion.com/blog/mba/consecuencias-coronavirus-en-sector-turismo/

Mihayo, I. Z., & Peng, D. (2020). Role of Fishery and Forest Resources in Local Economic Performance: Evidence from the Lake Zone of Tanzania. *International Journal of Economics and Finance*, *12*(2), 1–22. doi:10.5539/ijef.v12n2p22

Mikołajczyk, K. (2021). Changes in the approach to employee development in organizations as a result of the COVID-19 pandemic. *European Journal of Training and Development*. Advance online publication. doi:10.1108/ejtd-12-2020-0171

Miller, D. (2011). Miller (1983) revisited: A reflection on EO research and some suggestions for the future. *Entrepreneurship Theory and Practice*, *35*(5), 873–894. doi:10.1111/j.1540-6520.2011.00457.x

Milne, G. J., & Xie, S. (2020). The effectiveness of social distancing in mitigating COVID-19 spread: a modelling analysis. MedRxiv. 1 - 16. doi:10.1101/2020.03.20.20040055

Mishra, D., & Chanchani, M. (2020, March 24). Coronavirus scare in Bengaluru: online companies face disruption in delivery of essential goods. *The Times of India*. https://timesofindia.indiatimes.com/city/bengaluru/online-cos-face-disruption-in-delivery-of-essential-goods/articleshow/74783378.cms

Mkwizu, K. H., & Mtae, H. G. (2018). Selfie and Marketing of Domestic Tourism. *International Journal of Research & Methodology in Social Science*, *4*(4), 77–87.

Molloy, J. C., & Noe, R. A. (2009). "Learning" a Living: Continuous Learning for Survival in Today's Talent Market. In *Learning, training, and development in organizations* (pp. 352–380). Routledge.

Montacute, R., & Holt-White, E. (2020). *COVID-19 and social mobility impact brief#2: University access & Studentfinance*. https://www.suttontrust.com/wp-content/uploads/2020/05/COVID-19-and-Social-Mobility-Impact-Brief-2.pdf

Mooney, H., & Zegarra, M. A. (2020). *COVID-19: shock sin precedentes sobre el turismo en América Latina y el Caribe*. Publications Inter-American Development Bank. Available at https://publications.iadb.org/publications/spanish/document/COVID-19-Shock-sin-precedentes-sobre-el-turismo-en-America-Latina-y-el-Caribe.pdf

Morris, M. H., & Kuratko, D. F. (2002). *Corporate Entrepreneurship: Entrepreneurial development within Organisations*. Thompson South-Western.

Morris, M. H., Webb, J. W., & Franklin, R. J. (2011). Understanding the Manifestation of Entrepreneurial Orientation in the Nonprofit Context. *Entrepreneurship Theory and Practice*, *35*(5), 947–971. doi:10.1111/j.1540-6520.2011.00453.x

MPHonline. (2021). *Outbreak: 10 of the Worst Pandemics in History*. https://www.mphonline.org/worst-pandemics-in-history/

Mukhopadhyay, B.R., & Mukhopadhyay, B.K. (2021, Jan.). *The leader's guide to new workplace culture during Covid-19*. Academic Press.

Murti, M., Achonu, C., Smith, B. T., Brown, K. A., Kim, J. H., Johnson, J., Ravindran, S., & Buchan, S. A. (2020). COVID-19 Workplace Outbreaks by Industry Sector and their Associated Household Transmission, Ontario, Canada, January to June, 2020. medRxiv. doi:10.1101/2020.11.25.20239038

Mu, Y., Bossink, B., Vinig, T., & You, S. (2021). Managing service innovations at online travel agencies: Evidence from China. *Journal of Hospitality and Tourism Technology, 12*(3), 533–547. doi:10.1108/JHTT-08-2020-0190

Mwaseba, D. L., Erkkilä, A., Friis-Hansen, E., Maro, A. H., & Maziku, J. D. (2020). Responsibilization in governance of non-industrial private forestry: Experiences from the Southern Highlands of Tanzania. *Forest Policy and Economics, 118*, 102243. doi:10.1016/j.forpol.2020.102243

Nabi, G., Walmsley, A., Liñán, F., Akhtar, I., & Neame, C. (2018). Does entrepreneurship education in the first year of higher education develop entrepreneurial intentions? The role of learning and inspiration. *Studies in Higher Education, 43*(3), 452–467. doi:10.1080/03075079.2016.1177716

Naldi, L., Nordqvist, M., Sjöberg, K., & Wiklund, J. (2007). Entrepreneurial orientation, risk taking, and performance in family firms. *Family Business Review, 20*(1), 33–47. doi:10.1111/j.1741-6248.2007.00082.x

Naude, W. (2020). *Entrepreneurial recovery from COVID-19: Decentralization, democratization, demand, distribution, and demography*. Discussion Paper Series, DP No. 13436.

Newman, K. L. (2011). Sustainable careers. *Organizational Dynamics, 40*(2), 136–143. https://doi.org/10.1016/j.orgdyn.2011.01.008

Newman, K. L. (2011). Sustainable careers: Lifecycle engagement in work. *Organizational Dynamics, 40*(2), 136–143. doi:10.1016/j.orgdyn.2011.01.008

Ng, W. T. (2020). COVID-19: Protection of workers at the workplace in Singapore. *Safety and Health at Work*, 1–3. PMID:33052261

Niemiec, R. M., & McGrath, R. E. (2019). *The power of character strengths: Appreciate and ignite your positive personality*. VIA Institute on Character.

Nițu-Antonie, R. D., Feder, E. S., & Munteanu, V. P. (2017). Macroeconomic Effects of Entrepreneurship from an International Perspective. *Sustainability, 9*(7), 1–21. doi:10.3390u9071159

Noble, C., & Billett, S. (2017). Learning to prescribe through co-working: Junior doctors, pharmacists and consultants. *Medical Education, 51*(4), 442–451. doi:10.1111/medu.13227 PMID:28164385

Nova, A. (2020, June). *Without the coronavirus pandemic, these jobs probably wouldn't have existed.* Academic Press.

Nyíri, L. (2002). Knowledge-based society and its impact on labour-market values. *Society and Economy, 24*(2), 201–218. doi:10.1556/SocEc.24.2002.2.3

O'Neil, D. A., & Bilimoria, D. (2005). Women's career development phases: Idealism, endurance, and reinvention. *Career Development International, 10*(3), 168–189. doi:10.1108/13620430510598300

Oducado, R. M., Parreño-Lachica, G. & Rabacal, J. (2021). Estrés percibido debido a la pandemia de COVID-19 entre los profesores profesionales empleados [Perceived stress due to the COVID-19 pandemic among employed professional teachers]. *Revista Internacional de Investigación e Innovación Educativas*, (15), 305–316. doi:10.46661/ijeri.5284

OECD (2021, April). *OECD Policy Responses to Coronavirus (COVID-19) An assessment of the impact of COVID-19 on job and skills demand using online job vacancy data.* OECD.

OECD. (2001). *Information and communication technologies and rural Development.* www.sourceoecd.org

OECD. (2012). *Literacy, numeracy and problem solving in technology-rich environments: Framework for the OECD survey of adult skills.* OECD Publishing. doi:10.1787/9789264128859-

OECD. (2016). *Skills matter: Further results from the survey of adult skills, OECD skills studies.* OECD Publishing.

OECD. (2018). *Transformative technologies and jobs of the future.* https://www.oecd.org/innovation/transformative-technologies-and-jobs-of-the-future.pdf

OECD. (2019a). PISA 2018 results: Vol. I. *What students know and can do?* OECD Publishing. doi:10.1787/5f07c754-

OECD. (2019b). *Skills matter: Additional results from the survey of adult skills, OECD skills studies.* OECD Publishing. doi:10.1787/1f029d8f-

OECD. (2020). *COVID-19: SME policy responses.* Retrieved 12 July, 2021, from https://read.oecd-ilibrary.org/view/?ref=119_119680di6h3qgi4x&title=Covid-19_SME_Policy_Responses

OECD. (2020). *Innovation for Development Impact.* In *Lessons from the OECD Development Assistance Committee.* OECD Publishing. doi:10.1787/62cc4634-en

OECD. (2020). *OECD digital economy outlook 2020.* OECD Publishing. doi:10.1787/bb167041-

OECD. (2021a). *OECD economic outlook 2021.* OECD Publishing. doi:10.1787/edfbca02-

OECD. (2021b). *Education at a glance 2021: OECD indicators.* OECD Publishing. doi:10.1787/b35a14e5-

OECD. (2021c). *Where: Global reach.* https://www.oecd.org/about/members-and-partners/

Office of the United States Trade Representative. (2021). *Trade Organizations: OECD.* https://ustr.gov/trade-agreements/wto-multilateral-affairs/oecd

Okhomina, D. (2010). Entrepreneurial orientation and psychological traits: The moderating influence of supportive environment. *Journal of Behavioral Studies in Business*, *2*, 1–16.

Olokundun, M., Ibidunni, S., Ogbari, M., Falola, H., & Salau, O. (2021). COVID-19 Pandemic and Antecedents for Digital Transformation in the Workplace: A Conceptual Framework. *Open Access Macedonian Journal of Medical Sciences, 9*(F), 41-46.

Ortega, C. (2020). *¿Qué es una entrevista estructurada, semiestructurada y no estructurada?* QuestionPro. Disponible online: https://www.questionpro.com/blog/es/entrevista-estucturada-y-no-estructurada/

Ortega, J. L. (2021). *Ingresos por turismo en España: la foto del hundimiento.* Hosteltur. Available at https://www.hosteltur.com/143168_ingresos-por-turismo-en-espana-la-foto-del-hundimiento.html

Osland, J. S., Mendenhall, M. E., Reiche, B. S., Szkudlarek, B., Bolden, R., Courtice, P., Vaiman, V., Vaiman, M., Lyndgaard, D., Nielsen, K., Terrell, S., Taylor, S., Lee, Y., Stahl, G., Boyacigiller, N., Huesing, T., Miska, C., Zilinskaite, M., Ruiz, L., . . . Maznevski, M. (2020). Perspectives on Global Leadership and the COVID-19 Crisis. In Advances in Global Leadership (Vol. 13). Emerald Publishing Limited.

Oszlak, O. (2017). *Merecer la Ciudad* [Deserve the City]. EDUNTREF.

Paisant, G. (2020). El Covid-19 y la situación jurídica de los consumidores: una mirada desde Francia. *Revista de Direito do Consumidor*, 17-26.

Parady, G., Taniguchi, A., & Takami, K. (2020). Travel behavior changes during the COVID-19 pandemic in Japan: Analyzing the effects of risk perception and social influence on going-out self-restriction. *Transportation Research Interdisciplinary Perspectives*, *7*, 100181. doi:10.1016/j.trip.2020.100181

Parker, S. K., & Bindl, U. K. (2016). *Proactivity at work: Making things happen in organizations.* Taylor & Francis.

Patel, V., Biggs, E., Pauli, N., & Boruff, B. (2020). Using a social-ecological system approach to enhance understanding of structural interconnectivities within the beekeeping industry for sustainable decision making. *Ecology and Society*, *25*(2), art24. doi:10.5751/ES-11639-250224

Patiño, D., Gómez-Álvarez, R., & Plaza-Angulo, J. (2017). Caracterización económica y cuantificación de la economía colaborativa. In Economía colaborativa y trabajo en plataforma: realidades y desafíos [Sharing economy and platform work: realities and challenges] (pp. 51-101). Bomarzo.

Patterson, O. (2006, December 26). Our overrated inner self. *The New York Times*.

Paul, S. K., Chowdhury, P., Chowdhury, M. T., Chakrabortty, R. K., & Moktadir, M. A. (2021). Operational challenges during a pandemic: An investigation in the electronics industry. *The International Journal of Logistics Management.* Advance online publication. doi:10.1108/ijlm-05-2021-0307

Pérez Abreu, M. R., Gómez Tejeda, J. J., & Dieguez Guach, R. A. (2020). Características clínico-epidemiológicas de la COVID-19. *Revista Habanera de Ciencias Médicas*, *19*(2).

Pérez, C. (2004). *Revoluciones tecnológicas y capital financiero* [Technological revolutions and financial capital.]. Siglo XXI.

Peterson, C., Ruch, W., Beermann, U., Park, N., & Seligman, M. E. (2007). Strengths of character, orientations to happiness, and life satisfaction. *The Journal of Positive Psychology*, *2*(3), 149–156. doi:10.1080/17439760701228938

Peterson, C., & Seligman, M. (2004). *Character strengths and virtues: A handbook and classification*. Oxford University Press.

PIAAC Expert Group in Problem Solving in Technology-Rich Environments. (2009). *PIAAC problem solving in technology rich environments: A conceptual framework*. OECD Education Working Papers, 36. Paris: OECD Publishing. doi:10.1787/19939019

Picker, R. C. (2021). *COVID 2025: How the pandemic is changing our world*. https://news.uchicago.edu/story/covid-2025-how-pandemic-changing-our-world#education

Picón, G. A., González de Caballero, G. K., & Paredes Sánchez, J. N. (2020). Desempeño y educators. *Radiologic Technology*, *85*(5), 486–493.

Pimentel, G. L. (2017). La personalización de las relaciones económicas a través de la economía colaborativa: los límites al supuesto de no-turismo: the limits to the assumption of non-turism. *Revista Académica ECO*, *17*, 107-115. Retrieved from https://tinyurl.com/y4hqvxgr

Policy Cures. (2020). *Covid-19 R&D Tracker*. https://www.policycuresresearch.org/covid-19-r-d-tracker

Poole, S. F., Gronsbell, J., Winter, D., Nickels, S., Levy, R., Fu, B., . . . Fromer, M. (2020). A holistic approach for suppression of COVID-19 spread in workplaces and universities. medRxiv. doi:10.1101/2020.12.03.20243626

Pucciarelli, F., & Kaplan, A. (2021). Transition to a hybrid teaching model as a step forward toward responsible management education? *Journal of Global Responsibility*. Advance online publication. doi:10.1108/JGR-12-2020-0111

Puzović, V., Baković, M., Bubalo, P., & Mayer, D. (2020). Accidental death from a fall from height at workplace turned out to be a COVID-19 death. *Forensic Science International: Reports*, *2*(100139), 1–4.

Qiu, R. T., Park, J., Li, S., & Song, H. (2020). Social costs of tourism during the COVID-19 pandemic. *Annals of Tourism Research*, *84*, 102994. doi:10.1016/j.annals.2020.102994 PMID:32834228

Quiña-Mera, J., Saransig-Perugachi, E., Trejo-España, D., Naranjo-Toro, M., & Guevara-Vega, C. (2019). Automation of the Barter (Exchange Management in Ecuador Applying Google V3 API for Geolocation. In Á. Rocha, C. Ferrás, & M. Paredes (Eds.), *Information Technology and Systems. ICITS 2019. Advances in Intelligent Systems and Computing* (Vol. 918). Springer. doi:10.1007/978-3-030-11890-7_21

Raimi, L. (2021). Innovative Government-Backed Policy Measures in Nigeria for Sustaining MSMEs Post Pandemic. In N. Baporikar (Ed.), *Handbook of Research on Strategies and Interventions to Mitigate COVID-19 Impact on SMEs* (pp. 299–317). IGI Global. doi:10.4018/978-1-7998-7436-2.ch015

Rastogi, P., M., Sobek, O. N., Jephson, G.. & Allison, J. (2020). *A Data-driven Indoor Air Quality Framework for Post-COVID-19 Workplace Re-entry*. Academic Press.

Ravšelj, D., & Murko, E. (2021). Higher education policies for developing digital skills in response to the Covid-19 crisis: Evidence from Slovenia. In N. Tomaževič, D. Ravšelj, & A. Aristovnik (Eds.), *Higher education policies for developing digital skills to respond to the Covid-19 crisis: European and global perspectives* (pp. 72-82). European Liberal Forum.

Reivich, K. J., Seligman, M., & McBride, S. (2011). Master resilience training in the US Army. *The American Psychologist, 66*(1), 25–34. doi:10.1037/a0021897 PMID:21219045

Renzaho, A. (2020). The Need for the Right Socio-Economic and Cultural Fit in the COVID-19 Response in Sub-Saharan Africa: Examining Demographic, Economic Political, Health, and Socio-Cultural Differentials in COVID-19 Morbidity and Mortality. *International Journal of Environmental Research and Public Health, 17*(10), 3445. doi:10.3390/ijerph17103445 PMID:32429123

Resolution 108/2020. *Ministerio de Educación* [Ministry of Education]. https://www.boletinoficial.gob.ar/detalleAviso/primera/226752/20200316

Reuschke, D., & Felstead, A. (2020). Changing workplace geographies in the COVID-19 crisis. *Dialogues in Human Geography, 10*(2), 208–212. doi:10.1177/2043820620934249

Rieckmann, M. (2020). *Innovative Learning Approaches to foster sustainable entrepreneurship competencies with regard to the SDGs in Higher Education* [Webinar]. Intrinsic project. Retrieved July 15, 2021, from https://www.intrinsic.eu/_media/rieckmann-innovative-learning-approaches-to-foster-sustainable-entrepreneurship-competencies.pdf

Robertson-Kraft, C., & Duckworth, A. L. (2014). True grit: Trait-level perseverance and passion for long-term goals predicts effectiveness and retention among novice teachers. *Teachers College Record, 116*(3).

Robertson, M. D., Midway, S. R., West, L., Tillya, H., & Rivera-Monroy, V. H. (2018). Fishery characteristics in two districts of coastal Tanzania. *Ocean and Coastal Management, 163*, 254–268. doi:10.1016/j.ocecoaman.2018.06.015

Rodríguez de Luis, E. (2021). *Medidores de CO2: cómo funcionan, cómo se relacionan con la prevención de la expansión del COVID-19 y recomendaciones de compra.* Xataka. Available at https://www.xataka.com/seleccion/medidores-co2-como-funcionan-como-se-relacionan-prevencion-expansion-covid-19-recomendaciones-compra

Rodríguez Triana, M. A., Gallón Vargas, N., & Gómez Zapata, Y. (2019). *La contabilidad en propuestas de economía solidaria y alternativa.* Academic Press.

Rogers, R. W. (1975). A protection motivation theory of fear appeals and attitude change1. *The Journal of Psychology, 91*(1), 93–114. doi:10.1080/00223980.1975.9915803 PMID:28136248

Rojas, E.F. & Poveda, L. (2018). *Estado de la Banda Ancha en América Latina y el Caribe* [Status of Broadband in Latin America and the Caribbean]. Publicación de las Naciones Unidas (CEPAL).

Rojewski, J. W., & Hill, R. B. (2014). Positioning research and practice in career and technical education: A framework for college and career preparation in the 21st century. *Career and Technical Education Research, 39*(2), 137–150. doi:10.5328/cter39.2.137

Root-Bernstein, M. (2020). *Avocations. In Encyclopedia of Creativity* (3rd ed., Vol. 1). Elsevier.

Ruseva, G. (2015). *Digital skills and youth employability.* https://all-digital.org/wp-content/uploads/2017/10/Telecentre-Europe-Youth-employability-policy-paper-Dec2015.pdf

Sachs, J. D. (2020). COVID-19 and Multilateralism. Horizons. *Journal of International Relations and Sustainable Development,* (16), 30–39.

Salah, K., Nizamuddin, N., Jayaraman, R., & Omar, M. (2019). Blockchain-based soybean traceability in agricultural supply chain. *IEEE Access: Practical Innovations, Open Solutions, 7,* 73295–73305. doi:10.1109/ACCESS.2019.2918000

Sánchez, E. B. (2021). (in press). Impacto de la Covid-19 en el turismo internacional. Implicaciones para el modelo turístico cubano. *Revista Temas.*

Sánchez, M. M. (2020). Flujos turísticos, geopolítica y COVID-19: Cuando los turistas internacionales son vectores de transmisión. *Geopolítica, 11*(2), 105–114. doi:10.5209/geop.69249

Sandle, T. (2021, Jan. 29). *International recommendations for COVID-19 workplace safety.* ISO/PAS 45005.

Santillán, K., & Lozada, V. (2013). Diseño y diagramación de una guía turística para difusión de los destinos turísticos de la Zona Sierra Centro Ecuatoriana. Tesis de grado. Universidad Politécnica Nacional. Quito, Ecuador.

Santos, S., & Dieguez, T. (2021). Open Innovation as a Strategy to Sustainably Compete in the Textile Industry. In J. Enríquez-Díaz, L. Castro-Santos, & F. Puime-Guillén (Eds.), Financial Management and Risk Analysis Strategies for Business Sustainability (pp. 146-172). IGI Global. doi:10.4018/978-1-7998-7634-2.ch008

Sartre, J.-P. (2005). *Bosquejo de una teoría de las emociones* [Sketch for a theory of emotions]. Alianza Editorial.

Saunders, M., Lewis, P., & Thornhill, A. (2007). *Research methods for business students* (4th ed.). Prentice Hall.

Schein, E.H. (1990). *Career anchors and job/role planning: The links between career pathing and career development*. Academic Press.

Schein, E. H. (1978). *Career dynamics*. Addison-Wesley.

Schleicher, A. (2020). *The impact of COVID-19 on education: Insights from education at a glance 2020*. OECD Publishing. https://www.oecd.org/education/the-impact-of-covid-19-on-education-insights-education-at-a-glance-2020.pdf

Scribano, A. (2007). *Mapeando interiores: Cuerpo, conflicto y sensaciones* [Mapping Interiors: Body, Conflict, and Sensations]. Córdoba: José Sarmiento Editor

Scribano, A. (2007a). *Policromía Corporal, cuerpos, grafías y sociedad.* [Bodily Polychrome: Bodies, spellings and Society] Córdoba: José Sarmiento Editor

Scribano, A. (2008). Sensaciones, conflicto y cuerpo en Argentina después del 2001 [Sensations, Conflict and Body in Argentina After 2001]. *Espacio Abierto, 17*(2), 205-230.

Scribano, A. (2012). Sociología de los cuerpos/emociones [Sociology of body/emotions]. *Revista Latinoamericana de Estudios sobre Cuerpos, Emociones y Sociedad, 10*(4), 93-113.

Scribano, A. (2020). La guerra de las curvas: pandemia, sensibilidades y estructuración social [The war of the curves: pandemic, sensibilities, and social structuration]. Simbiótica, 7(1).

Scribano, A., & Lisdero, P. (2019). *Digital labor, Society and Politics of Sensibilities*. Palgrave Macmillan. doi:10.1007/978-3-030-12306-2

Secretaría de Evaluación e Información Educativa. (2020). *Evaluación Nacional del Proceso de Continuidad Pedagógica. Informe preliminar de la Encuesta a Docentes* [National Evaluation of the Pedagogical Continuity Process. Preliminary report of the Teacher Survey]. https://www.argentina.gob.ar/educacion/evaluacion-e-informacion-educativa/evaluacion-nacional-del-proceso-de-continuidad-pedagogica

Segbenya, M., Baafi-Frimpong, S. A., & Oppong, N. Y. (2021). Effect of COVID-19 on acquisition of employable skills among National Service personnel in Ghana. *Journal of Work-Applied Management, 13*(2), 215–226. https://doi.org/10.1108/jwam-12-2020-0058

Sekadende, B., Scott, L., Anderson, J., Aswani, S., Francis, J., Jacobs, Z., Jebri, F., Jiddawi, N., Kamukuru, A. T., Kelly, S., Kizenga, H., Kuguru, B., Kyewalyanga, M., Noyon, M., Nyandwi, N., Painter, S. C., Palmer, M., Raitsos, D. E., Roberts, M., ... Popova, E. (2020). The small pelagic fishery of the Pemba Channel, Tanzania: What we know and what we need to know for management under climate change. *Ocean and Coastal Management, 197*, 105322. doi:10.1016/j.ocecoaman.2020.105322

Seligman, M. E. (2021, June 1). *Positive Psychology, Agency, and Human Progress* [Video]. YouTube. https://youtu.be/TjWrL1MJbj0

Seligman, M. (2018). PERMA and the building blocks of wellbeing. *The Journal of Positive Psychology, 13*(4), 333–335. doi:10.1080/17439760.2018.1437466

Seligman, M. E. (2012). *Flourish: A visionary new understanding of happiness and well-being*. Atria.

Selwyn, N. (2004). Reconsidering political and popular understandings of the digital divide. *New Media & Society, 6*(3), 341–362. doi:10.1177/1461444804042519

Seo, E., Mun, E., Kim, W., & Lee, C. (2020). Fighting the COVID-19 pandemic: Onsite mass workplace testing for COVID-19 in the Republic of Korea. *Annals of Occupational and Environmental Medicine, 32*(1), 1–4. doi:10.35371/aoem.2020.32.e22 PMID:32802338

Servicio de Rentas Internas (SRI). (2021). Recuperado de https://srienlinea.sri.gob.ec/saiku-ui/#cancel

Sharfuddin, S. (2020). The world after covid-19. *Round Table (London), 109*(3), 247–257. doi:10.1080/00358533.2020.1760498

Sharma, P. (2021). Customer co-creation, COVID-19 and sustainable service outcomes. *Benchmarking, 28*(7), 2232–2258. doi:10.1108/BIJ-10-2020-0541

Shawon, A. A. (2020, May 27). Covid-19: Bangladesh likely to end general holiday on May 31. *Dhaka Tribune*. https://www.dhakatribune.com/bangladesh/2020/05/27/state-minister-update-of-lockdown-coming-soon

Sheresheva, M., Efremova, M., Valitova, L., Polukhina, A., & Laptev, G. (2021). Russian Tourism Enterprises' Marketing Innovations to Meet the COVID-19 Challenges. *Sustainability, 13*(7), 3756. doi:10.3390u13073756

Sigala, M. (2020). Tourism and COVID-19: Impacts and implications for advancing and resetting industry and research. *Journal of Business Research, 117*, 312–321. doi:10.1016/j.jbusres.2020.06.015 PMID:32546875

Sohrabi, C., Alsafi, Z., O'Neill, N., Khan, M., Kerwan, A., Al-Jabir, A., & Agha, R. (2020). World health organization declares global emergency: A review of the 2019 novel coronavirus (COVID-19). *International Journal of Surgery, 76*, 71–76.

Sommer, S. (2020). *Sustainable Finance: An Overview. Deutsche Gesellschaft für Internationale Zusammenarbeit (GIZ)*. GmbH, Bonn and Eschborn.

Sreelakshmi, C. C., & Prathap, S. K. (2020). Continuance adoption of mobile based payments in Covid-19 context: An integrated framework of health belief model and expectation confirmation model. *International Journal of Pervasive Computing and Communications, 16*(4), 351–369. doi:10.1108/IJPCC-06-2020-0069

Stebbins, R. A. (1982). Serious leisure: A conceptual statement. *Pacific Sociological Review, 25*(2), 251–272. doi:10.2307/1388726

Stehr, N. (1994). *Knowledge societies*. Sage.

Sundararajan, A. (2016). *The sharing economy: The end of employment and the rise of crowd-based capitalism*. MIT Press.

Sunkel, G. (2006). *Las tecnologías de la información y la comunicación (tic) en la educación en América Latina: una exploración de indicadores* [Information and communication technologies (ict) in education in Latin America: an exploration of indicators]. Naciones Unidas. https://www.cepal.org/socinfo/noticias/documentosdetrabajo/9/27849/Serie126final.pdf

Sunkel, G., Trucco, D., & Espejo, A. (2013). *La integración de las tecnologías digitales en las escuelas de América Latina y el Caribe. Una mirada multidimensional* [The integration of digital technologies in schools in Latin America and the Caribbean. A multidimensional look]. Santiago de Chile: Naciones Unidas. https://repositorio.cepal.org/bitstream/handle/11362/21681/S2013023_es.pdf

Tagliaro, C., & Migliore, A. (2021). "Covid-working": What to keep and what to Leave? Evidence from an Italian company. *Journal of Corporate Real Estate*. Advance online publication. doi:10.1108/jcre-10-2020-0053

Tan, W. J. Z. X., Zhao, X., Ma, X., Wang, W., Niu, P., Xu, W., & Wu, G. Z. (2020). A novel coronavirus genome identified in a cluster of pneumonia cases—Wuhan, China 2019-2020. *China CDC Weekly, 2*(4), 61-62. http://weekly.chinacdc.cn/en/article/doi/10.46234/ccdcw2020.017

Tellis, W. (1997). Application of a case study methodology. *Qualitative Report, 3*(3), 1–19.

Terras, M. M., & Ramsay, J. (2015). Massive open online courses (MOOCs): Insights and challenges from a psychological perspective. *British Journal of Educational Technology, 46*(3), 472–487. doi:10.1111/bjet.12274

Teti, M., Schatz, E., & Liebenberg, L. (2020). Methods in the time of COVID-19: The vital role of qualitative inquiries. *International Journal of Qualitative Methods, 19*, 1609406920920962. doi:10.1177/1609406920920962

The Entrepreneurial Learning Initiative. (2021). *What is Mindset?* Author.

Tomprou, M., Dabbish, L., Kraut, R. E., & Liu, F. (2019). Career mentoring in online communities: Seeking and receiving advice from an online community. Proceedings of CHI 2019, 1 – 12.

Trehan, S. (2019, December 13). Virtual Kitchen – The Rise of the Delivery-Only Restaurant. *LimeTray*. https://limetray.com/blog/virtual-kitchen/

Tsekeris, C. (2019). Surviving and thriving in the Fourth Industrial Revolution: Digital skills for education and society. *Homo Virtualis, 2*(1), 34–42. doi:10.12681/homvir.20192

Tugade, M. M., & Fredrickson, B. L. (2004). Resilient individuals use positive emotions to bounce back from negative emotional experiences. *Journal of Personality and Social Psychology*, *86*(2), 320–333. doi:10.1037/0022-3514.86.2.320 PMID:14769087

Turespaña. (2021). *Razones para recorrer el Camino de Santiago durante el Xacobeo 2021 - 2022.* Spain.info. https://www.spain.info/es/descubrir-espana/xacobeo-camino-santiago/

Turismo de Galicia. (2021). *Galicia destino seguro.* Available at https://www.turismo.gal/galiciadestinoseguro/portada?langId=es_ES

Tyko, K. (2021). Walmart raising pay for 425,000 workers starting March 13 after strong holiday sales amid COVID-19. *USA Today*.

Uddin, A. K. M. Z. (2021, June 30). Who owns Nagad? *The Daily Star*. https://www.thedailystar.net/business/economy/banks/news/who-owns-nagad-2120921

Uleanya, C., & Alex, J. (2021). Higher education policies for developing digital skills: Lessons learnt from the Covid-19 crisis in South Africa. In N. Tomaževič, D. Ravšelj, & A. Aristovnik (Eds.), *Higher education policies for developing digital skills to respond to the Covid-19 crisis: European and global perspectives* (pp. 110-119). European Liberal Forum.

UN. (2020). *Policy brief: Education during COVID-19 and beyond.* https://www.un.org/development/desa/dspd/wp-content/uploads/sites/22/2020/08/sg_policy_brief_covid-19_and_education_august_2020.pdf

UN. (2021). *COVID-19 and higher education: Education and science as a vaccine for the pandemic.* https://www.un.org/en/academic-impact/covid-19-and-higher-education-education-and-science-vaccine-pandemic

UNCTAD. (2020b). *The need to protect science, technology and innovation funding during and after the COVID-19 crisis.* Policy Brief No. 80. Retrieved July 10, 2021, from https://unctad.org/webflyer/need-protect-science-technology-and-innovation-funding-during-and-after-covid-19-crisis

UNDP. (2020). *Rapid Socio-economic Impact Assessment of COVID-19 in Tanzania.* UNDP.

UNESCO. (2018). *Digital skills critical for jobs and social inclusion.* https://en.unesco.org/news/digital-skills-critical-jobs-and-social-inclusion#:~:text=Digital%20skills%20are%20defined%20as,to%20access%20and%20manage%20information

UNESCO. (2021). *Institute of statistics: Education statistics.* http://data.uis.unesco.org/

Ungarino, R. (2020, April). *Bank of America is pausing financial adviser training for 650 people and reassigning them to handle surging calls from consumer and small-business customers.* Academic Press.

United Nations. (2020a). *Impact of the Pandemic on Trade and Development. Transitioning to a New Normal.* United Nations Conference on Trade and Development. Retrieved July 2, 2021, from https://unctad.org/webflyer/impact-covid-19-pandemic-trade-and-development-transitioning-new-normal

United Nations. (2020b*). Entrepreneurship for sustainable development.* United Nations General Assembly, Seventy-fifth session, A/75/257. Retrieved July 3, 2021, from https://digitallibrary.un.org/record/1639377

United Nations. (2020c). *External debt sustainability and development.* A/75/281. Retrieved July 16, 2021, from https://unctad.org/system/files/official-document/tc2015d1rev2_S04_P02.pdf

University of Washington. (2021). *Working during COVID-19: Workforce reduction strategies.* Author.

URT. (2020). *Rapid Assessment of the Impact of Corona Virus Disease (COVID-19) on the Tanzania's Tourism Sector.* Ministry of Natural Resources and Tourism, The United Republic of Tanzania.

US Bureau of Labor Statistics. (2020). *Employment recovery in the wake of the COVID-19 pandemic.* https://www.bls.gov/opub/mlr/2020/article/employment-recovery.htm

USAID. (2020). *Local works.* https://www.usaid.gov/localworks

van Veldhoven, M., & Dorenbosch, L. (2008). Age, proactivity and career development. *Career Development International, 13*(2), 112–131. https://doi.org/10.1108/13620430810860530

Vapñarsky, C., & Gorojovsky, N. (1990). El crecimiento urbano en la Argentina [Urban Growth in Argentine]. IIED.

Vereshchagina, G., & Hopenhayn, H. A. (2009). Risk taking by entrepreneurs. *The American Economic Review, 99*(5), 1808–1830. doi:10.1257/aer.99.5.1808

Viramgami, A., Pagdhune, A., Sarkar, K., & Balachandar, R. (2020). Occupational Health and Safety Practices at workplace during COVID-19 Pandemic. *Journal of Comprehensive Health, 8*(2), 77–82.

Volpone, S. D., Perry, S. J., & Rubino, C. (2013). An exploratory study of factors that relate to burnout in hobby-jobs. *Applied Psychology, 62*(4), 655–677. doi:10.1111/j.1464-0597.2012.00502.x

Wales, W. J., Covin, J. G., & Monsen, E. (2020). Entrepreneurial orientation: The necessity of a multilevel conceptualization. *Strategic Entrepreneurship Journal, 14*(4), 639–660. doi:10.1002ej.1344

Walker, L. (2019). Coaching during late career reinvention: The Discovering Model. *International Journal of Evidence Based Coaching and Mentoring*, (S13), 63–75.

Wamboye, E. F., Nyaronga, P. J., & Sergi, B. S. (2020). What are the determinants of international tourism in Tanzania? *World Development Perspectives, 17*, 100175. doi:10.1016/j.wdp.2020.100175

Warrier, B. S. (2020, May 26). COVID-19: What next for the education sector? *The Week*. https://www.theweek.in/leisure/society/2020/05/26/covid-19-what-next-for-the-education-sector.html

Watts, J., McNair, S., & Robey, C. (2015). *Mid Life Career Review: Final Report to the Department for Business and Skills*. National Institute of Adult Continuing Education (England and Wales).

Webb, A., McQuaid, R., & Rand, S. (2020). Employment in the informal economy: Implications of the COVID-19 pandemic. *The International Journal of Sociology and Social Policy*, *40*(9/10), 1005–1019. https://doi.org/10.1108/ijssp-08-2020-0371

WEF. (2016). *The future of jobs employment, skills and workforce strategy for the fourth industrial revolution*. Geneva: World Economic Forum. https://www3.weforum.org/docs/WEF_Future_of_Jobs.pdf

WEF. (2019). *The global competitiveness report 2019*. Geneva: World Economic Forum. https://www3.weforum.org/docs/WEF_TheGlobalCompetitivenessReport2019.pdf

WEF. (2020a). *Challenges and opportunities in the post-COVID-19 world*. Retrieved July 15, 2021, from https://www.weforum.org/reports/post-covid-19-challenges-and-opportunities

WEF. (2020a). The global competitiveness report 2020. Geneva: World Economic Forum. https://www.weforum.org/reports/the-global-competitiveness-report-2020

WEF. (2020b). *Great Reset: What university entrepreneurship can bring to the post-COVID world?* Retrieved July 10, 202, from https://www.weforum.org/agenda/2020/07/university-entrepreneurship-post-covid-19-world/

WEF. (2020b). *The future of jobs report 2020*. Geneva: World Economic Forum. https://www.weforum.org/reports/the-future-of-jobs-report-2020

Wen, J., Kozak, M., Yang, S., & Liu, F. (2020). COVID-19: Potential effects on Chinese citizens' lifestyle and travel. *Tourism Review*. doi:10.1108/TR-03-2020-0110

West, M., Kraut, R., & Wi Chew, H. (2019). *I'd blush if I could. Closing gender divides in digital skills through education*. UNESCO.

Wetherill, K., Burton, G., Calhoun, D., & Thomas, C. C. (2002, January). Redefining professional career development in the twenty-first century: A systemic approach. *High School Journal*, *85*(2), 54–66. doi:10.1353/hsj.2001.0026

Whiffin, C. J. (2020). Choose Your Methodology: Little Quick Fix. *Sage (Atlanta, Ga.)*.

WHO. (2021). *WHO coronavirus (COVID-19) dashboard*. https://covid19.who.int/

Williams, C. C., & Kayaoglu, A. (2020). COVID-19 and undeclared work: Impacts and policy responses in Europe. *Service Industries Journal*, *40*(13-14), 914–931. doi:10.1080/02642069.2020.1757073

Winocur, R. (2006). Internet en la vida cotidiana de los jóvenes [Internet in the daily life of young people]. *Revista Mexicana de Sociología, 68*(3), 551-580. http://www.scielo.org.mx/scielo.php?script=sci_arttext&pid=S0188-25032006000300005&lng=es&nrm=iso

Wise, T., Zbozinek, T. D., Michelini, G., & Hagan, C. C. (2020). *Changes in risk perception and protective behavior during the first week of the COVID-19 pandemic in the United States.* Academic Press.

Wong, E., Ho, K. F., Wong, S. Y., Cheung, A. W., & Yeoh, E. (2020). Workplace safety and coronavirus disease (COVID-19) pandemic: survey of employees. Bulletin of the World Health Organization. doi:10.2471/BLT.20.255893

World Bank. (2020). *Global Economic Prospects.* doi:10.1596/978-1-4648-1553-9

World Bank. (2020). *Map of SME support measures in response to COVID-19.* Retrieved July 4, 2021, from https://www.worldbank.org/en/data/interactive/2020/04/14/map-of-sme-support-measures-in-response-to-covid-19

World Bank. (2020). *Public Sector Innovation Facets.* https://oecd-opsi.org/projects/innovation-facets/

World Bank. (2020). *The COVID-19 crisis response: Supporting tertiary education for continuity, adaptation, and innovation.* World Bank. https://documents1.worldbank.org/curated/en/621991586463915490/The-COVID-19-

worldometers.info. (2021). *Reported Cases and Deaths by Country or Territory.* https://www.worldometers.info/coronavirus/

Worthington, J. (2006). Introduction: The Changing Workplace. In Reinventing the Workplace (pp. 22-29). Routledge.

Worthington, J. (2012). *Reinventing the workplace.* Routledge. doi:10.4324/9780080516035

WTO. (2020). *E-commerce, trade and the COVID-19 pandemic.* Retrieved July 18, 2021, from https://www.wto.org/english/tratop_e/covid19_e/ecommerce_report_e.pdf

Xiao, F., Barnard-Brak, L., Lan, W., & Burley, H. (2019). Examining problem solving skills in technology-rich environments as related to numeracy and literacy. *International Journal of Lifelong Education, 38*(3), 327–338.

Xu, Z., Shi, L., Wang, Y., Zhang, J., Huang, L., Zhang, C. & Tai, Y. (2020). Pathological findings of COVID-19 associated with acute respiratory distress syndrome. *The Lancet Respiratory Medicine, 8*(4), 420-422.

Xunta de Galicia. (2021). *El stand de Galicia registra el mayor número de actividades en Fitur y despierta el interés de los operadores presentes en la feria.* Available at https://www.xunta.gal/notas-de-prensa/-/nova/58279/stand-galicia-registra-mayor-numero-actividades-fitur-despierta-interes-los-operadores?langId=es_ES

Xu, R., Greening, D. W., Zhu, H. J., Takahashi, N., & Simpson, R. J. (2016). Extracellular vesicle isolation and characterization: Toward clinical application. *The Journal of Clinical Investigation*, *126*(4), 1152–1162. doi:10.1172/JCI81129 PMID:27035807

Yearby, R., & Mohapatra, S. (2020). *Structural discrimination in COVID-19 workplace protections.* Health Affairs Blog.

Youn, S. (2021, June 29). America's workers are exhausted and burned out and some employers are taking notice. *The Washington Post.*

Zahra, S. A. (2021). International entrepreneurship in the post-Covid world. *Journal of World Business*, *56*(1), 101143. doi:10.1016/j.jwb.2020.101143

Zaka, A., Shamloo, S. E., Fiorente, P., & Tafuri, A. (2020). *COVID-19 pandemic as a watershed moment: A call for systematic psychological health care for frontline medical staff.* Academic Press.

Zaman, T. (2020, August 6). Cloud Kitchens in Bangladesh: A Reality. *TRIDigital.* https://www.tridigital.com.bd/cloud-kitchens-in-bangladesh/

Zappe, S. E., Hochstedt, K. S., & Kisenwether, E. C. (2013). Faculty beliefs of entrepreneurship and design education: An exploratory study comparing entrepreneurship and design faculty. *The Journal of Engineering Entrepreneurship*, *4*(1), 55–79. doi:10.7814/jeen5v4p5zhk

Zarzour, H., Bendjaballah, S., & Harirche, H. (2020). Exploring the behavioral patterns of students learning with a Facebook-based e-book approach. *Computers & Education*, *156*, 103957. https://doi.org/10.1016/j.compedu.2020.103957

Zavyiboroda, M. (2021, February). COVID-19: recession types, recovery scenarios, behavior change. *HR Trends.*

Zhang, H. (2020). China's employment stabilization policies in response to the impact of the COVID-19 pandemic. *International Journal of Sociology and Social Policy.* Advance online publication. doi:10.1108/ijssp-05-2020-0167

Zhang, J., & Huang, J. (2021). Entrepreneurial self-efficacy mediates the impact of the post-pandemic entrepreneurship environment on college students' entrepreneurial intention. *Frontiers in Psychology*, *12*, 643184. doi:10.3389/fpsyg.2021.643184 PMID:33995198

Zhang, W. B., Ge, Y., Liu, M., Atkinson, P. M., Wang, J., Zhang, X., & Tian, Z. (2021). Risk assessment of the step-by-step return-to-work policy in Beijing following the COVID-19 epidemic peak. *Stochastic Environmental Research and Risk Assessment*, *35*(2), 481–498. doi:10.100700477-020-01929-3 PMID:33223954

Zheng, H., Cao, L., Huang, S., Neumann, P., & Hu, F. (2018). Current status of the beekeeping industry in China. In *Asian beekeeping in the 21st century* (pp. 129–158). Springer. doi:10.1007/978-981-10-8222-1_6

Zhou, J., Liu, L., Xue, P., Yang, X., & Tang, X. (2020). Mental health response to the COVID-19 outbreak in China. *The American Journal of Psychiatry*, *177*(7), 574–575. doi:10.1176/appi.ajp.2020.20030304 PMID:32375540

Zhu, Q., Tan, R., & Li, L. (2020). Relationship between practice of work values and career success: based on the regulating of career adaptability. *Proceedings of ICCMB 2020*, 266 – 270. 10.1145/3383845.3383854

Zhu, N., Zhang, D., Wang, W., Li, X., Yang, B., Song, J., & Niu, P. (2020). A novel coronavirus from patients with pneumonia in China, 2019. *The New England Journal of Medicine*, *382*(8), 727–733.

Zumbana Santamaria, J. A. (2021). *El marketing digital para la reactivación del turismo cultural durante el covid 19* (Bachelor's thesis). Universidad Técnica de Ambato-Facultad de Ciencias Humanas y de la Educación-Carrera de Turismo y Hotelería.

About the Contributors

Shalin Hai-Jew works as an instructional designer at Kansas State University (K-State). She has taught at the university and college levels for many years (including four years in the People's Republic of China) and was tenured at Shoreline Community College but left tenure to pursue instructional design work. She has Bachelor's degrees in English and psychology, a Master's degree in Creative Writing from the University of Washington (Hugh Paradise Scholar), and an Ed.D in Educational Leadership with a focus on public administration from Seattle University (where she was a Morford Scholar). She tested into the University of Washington at 14. She reviews for several publishers and publications. She has worked on a number of instructional design projects, including public health, biosecurity, one health, mental health, PTSD, grain science, turfgrass management, social justice, and others. She has authored and edited a number of books. Hai-Jew was born in Huntsville, Alabama, in the U.S. Currently, she is working on multiple projects. She returned to work in the office in late April 2021 and has been masking and practicing hand hygiene to try to be as safe as possible. She is grateful to have also recently received her booster shot of the Moderna vaccine against SARS-CoV-2.

* * *

Noelia Araújo Vila is PhD in Tourism Management and Planning (2013) and Bachelor in Business Administration and Management (2006). Since 2007 she collaborates in the coordination tasks of the University Master in Tourism Management and Planning and teaches as professor in the Departments of Business Organization and Marketing and Financial Economics and Accounting (University of Vigo). She participates in various research projects linked to the tourism and business sector. She is a member of the research group of the University of Vigo Emitur (Marketing and Tourism). She holds a Master in Management and Management of SMEs with a prize for the best business project. She has numerous publications (articles and book's chapters) in the fields of tourism, marketing and business management.

Andrea Areán-Magnou was born in 1987 in Montevideo, Uruguay. There she received her Bachelor's degree in Business Administration and Management (2011). After working for several years in a steel trading company, she decided to focus on tourism. She moved to Santa Marta, Colombia, where she established her own hostel. In Spain, she received her Master's degree in Interior and Health Tourism (University of Vigo, 2021).

Tasnima Aziza serves as an Associate Professor at the Institute of Business Administration (IBA), Jahangirnagar University, a public university located in Dhaka, Bangladesh. Before that, she started her career at a private university. In her more than twenty years of experience, she enjoys teaching mainly finance and human resource management courses. Her areas of interest are work-life balance, job satisfaction, employee motivation, bank management, corporate finance, working capital management, strategic management, etc. She works as a volunteer for Moral Parenting Trust. This charity organization supports the invincible students of different educational institutes all over Bangladesh who are struggling against poverty to save their dream of life.

Uriel Castillo is an Economist, Master in International Business Creation and Ph.D. in Economic Development. Professor in the field of business and economics in the Master of Finance and Business Economics and in the Master of International Business at the Catholic University of Santiago de Guayaquil. Important experience as a researcher on development issues in poor societies. Registered in the database of researchers of the National Secretariat of Sciences and Technology of Ecuador (SENESCYT).

Katie Drescher, J.D., PCC, is a certified professional coach and consultant. She works with professionals in multinational and governmental organizations across the fields of tech, finance, hospitality, and creative arts. Using evidence-based coaching tools rooted in neuroscience, conscious leadership, and whole-person approaches, she helps clients thrive in a rapidly changing world. Katie holds a B.A. from Lawrence University, a J.D. from Washington University in St. Louis, a Professional Coaching Certificate from the University of Wisconsin-Madison, and a Certificate in Positive Psychology from the University of Pennsylvania.

Mufaro Dzingirai is a PhD candidate in Business Management at Midlands State University and a lecturer in the Department of Business Management, Midlands State University. He received his Master of Commerce in Strategic Management and Corporate Governance degree from Midlands State University in 2016. He was hired as a teacher by the Ministry of Education from 2014 to 2016. In 2013, he received the MSU Book Prize. His research interests include Higher Education, Strategy, Management, Finance, and Entrepreneurship.

Maureen Ebben, Ph.D., is an Associate Professor in the Department of Communication and Media Studies at the University of Southern Maine in Portland, Maine. An awarding-winning teacher and scholar, her research focuses on human communication in the context of work, technology, and media and has been published in the volumes, Maintaining Social Well-Being and Meaningful Work in a Highly Automated Job Market, Post-Pandemic Pedagogy: Predicting the Change to Come, Privacy Concerns Surrounding Personal Information Sharing on Health and Fitness Mobile Apps, as well as journals such as Learning, Media, and Technology and Women and Language. She is a member of the National Communication Association, and the Organization for the Study of Communication, Language, and Gender.

Constanza Faracce Macia is a Sociologist (UBA). Candidate for a Master's Degree in Research in Social Sciences (FSOC-UBA). Member of the Center for Research on Consumption, Sensibilities and Creativity (CICSEC) of the University of Palermo and of the Study Group of Social Policies and Emotions, of the Center for Sociological Studies and Research (CIES). Member of the Editorial Team of the Latin American Journal of Bodies, Emotions and Society (RELACES). She is currently investigating emotions and food interventions.

Tahira Farzana obtained her MBA degree from the Institute of Business Administration, Jahangirnagar University, Bangladesh. Currently, she is working as Assistant Professor at the Institute of Business Administration, Jahangirnagar University, Bangladesh. She has experience of 10 years of in the market and social research. She has experience of working with the prominent research organizations of Bangladesh. Her major area of interest includes Social Entrepreneurship, Entrepreneurship development for physically challenged people, Innovation, and Marketing. She has an affiliation with the Physically Development Foundation (PDF) and the Social Welfare Club of the Institute of Business Administration, Jahangirnagar University, Bangladesh.

Sheikh Mohammed Rafiul Huque is the professor of the Institute of Business Administration (IBA), Jahangirnagar University, Dhaka, Bangladesh. He has been involved in teaching and research activities for around 20 years in Bangladesh, Malaysia, and Japan. His research interest is organic agriculture, agriculture value chain and supply chain management, and strategic and entrepreneurial issues in educational sectors. Meanwhile, he publishes ed more than 24 publications that include three book chapters on higher education, innovation in management in education, and entrepreneurship education in Bangladesh published from IGI Global. Moreover, he has been involved as a project leader and member of different projects related or organic movement, rural sustainability, community participation, and livelihood management and strategic issues of agribusiness funded by international organizations. He has been serving as a resource person of the Asian Productivity Organization (APO), Japan and he is an editorial member of the Journal of Business Management and Accounting and Issues in Social and Environmental Accounting and reviewer of SCOPUS and ISI indexed journals.

Mohammad Nazmul Islam is currently working as an Associate Professor at the Institute of Business Administration, Jahangirnagar University situated in Dhaka, Bangladesh. He has about twenty years of teaching experience. His area of interest is Management Accounting, Management Science, Finance, and Strategic Management-related issues in the education sector in Bangladesh. He has several journal publications in reputed journals in-home and abroad. He has been working as a member of the Finance committee at Jahangirnagar University for more than five years. Moreover, he has been deeply involved in making online examination-related policy issues for public universities especially at Jahangirnagar University in Bangladesh.

Jainaba M. L. Kah has a Ph.D. in Urban Planning and Policy Development from the Edward J. Bloustein School, Rutgers – The State University of New Jersey, USA. She also earned a Masters in Development Economics (M.D.E.) from Dalhousie University, Canada, and a Bachelor of Commerce (Cum Laude) from St. Mary's University in Halifax, Canada. Prof. Jainaba M.L. Kah (née: Saho) is the Director General of the Department of Strategic Policy & Delivery (DSPD) at Office of The President in The Gambia. DSPD is the technical arm of the Office of The President, functioning to assist and enable the President to develop, implement and monitor the vision of the government and to provide strategic leadership for cross-sectoral policies or programmes. As the Director General of DSPD, Professor Jainaba M.L. Kah is responsible for leadership, strategic management, innovations, talent management and functionality of the Department in liaison with the Office of the Secretary General, the Cabinet Office and other Ministries, Departments and Agencies (MDAs) and other stakeholders. Prof. Kah has extensive practitioner experience having worked for the World Bank as an Urban/Transport Specialist and also served as a consultant for the USA Federal Transit Administration; Financial Analyst for Amnesty International; and Audit Senior at KPMG. Prof. Kah served for four years as the Chairperson of the Adjudication Committee of the All Africa Public Sector Innovation Awards (AAPSIA), which is the first Africa wide ministerial initiative celebrating innovation in the Public Sector.

Nyanjige M. Mayala is a Lecturer in the department of Economics and Business Studies (DEBS) of the Mwenge Catholic University (MWECAU). She holds a PhD in Investment Analysis from Moshi Co-operative University (MoCU), MBA and BCom from the University of Dar Es Slaam; and PFCMP from MoCU. Mayala worked with (MoCU), Water Utility Partnership Africa (WUP) by the AfDB, Branch Manager with Barclays Bank (T) and a Sales Coordinator with Bonitte Bottlers. She has published in areas of marketing, water utility management, investment decisions, tourism, cross-cutting issues like COVID-19 in areas related to industrialisation, business development and agriculture in rural Tanzania.

Rodgers Ndava holds a Master of Commerce in Strategic Management and Corporate Governance degree from Midlands State University (MSU) and a Bachelor of Commerce in Business Management (Honours) majoring in Finance from the same institution. He is a former Zimbabwe Revenue Authority (ZIMRA) employee hired on a seasonal basis. He is a keen scholar on Tax Compliance, Small Business Management, Entrepreneurship, Finance, and Strategic Management.

Lukman Raimi is an Assistant Professor of Entrepreneurship in the School of Business and Economics (SBE), Universiti Brunei Darussalam (UBD). Prior to joining the UBD, he was an Assistant Professor and the Chair of Entrepreneurship at the American University of Nigeria (AUN). Also, he was formerly the Coordinator of the Graduate Program in the School of Business & Entrepreneurship and the Director Centre for Entrepreneurship in AUN. Besides, he was a former Coordinator of Training and Part-Time Programme at the Centre for Entrepreneurship Development, Yaba College of Technology, Nigeria. He is an Entrepreneurship Educator trained at the Entrepreneurship Development Institute (EDI), Ahmedabad, India under the World Bank-Step B Project. He had specialized training in Enterprise Education for Employability (EEE) at the Pan-Atlantic University Nigeria under the British Council's sponsorship. He was an alumnus of the Cumberland Lodge Residential Mentoring (2014), Windsor, United Kingdom. He attended 2019 Experiential Classroom XX organised for Entrepreneurship Educators at the University of Tampa, Tampa, Florida, United States. He has attended/delivered conferences/seminar papers in Turkey, Malaysia, Ghana, Togo, India, Belfast, Leicester, the United States. His publications are listed in Scopus, Researchgate, Publons, and Google Scholar. He was honored with the Best Ph.D. Thesis Award for Faculty of Business and Law (2016), De Montfort University, Leicester UK. His paper titled "Corporate social responsibility, waqf system, and zakat system as a faith-based model for poverty reduction", was awarded Highly Commendable Academic Paper by World Journal of Entrepreneurship, Management, and Sustainable Development, Emerald Group Publishing Limited, UK. His research interests include Entrepreneurship: Social

Entrepreneurship, Entrepreneurial/Digital Innovation, Medical Entrepreneurship, Development Economics, CSR & Sustainability, SDGs, and Family Business.

Ambrose K. Tesha (MSc) is Assistant lecturer Procurement and Supply Chain Management. Field of expertise: Public procurement; supply chain management, sustainable developments logistics & transportations, Production management, Procurement audit and assurance inventory control management. Mwenge Catholic University (MWECAU), Department of Economic and Business Studies.

Gabriela Vergara is a Sociologist (UNVM). Master's Degree in Social Sciences (ETS-UNC). Phd in Social Sciences (UBA). Researcher in the Nacional Scientific and Technical Research Council (Cconfines-CONICET). Researcher in the Center for Sociological Studies and Research (CIES). Coordinator of Studies Social Group of Subjectivities and Conflic (GESSYCO). Regular Associate Proffesor in the National University of Rafaela. She is currently investigating about women, work, sensibilities, and structuration process.

Index

D

E

F

G

H

I

L

M

O

P

R

S

T

U

V

W

X

www.ingramcontent.com/pod-product-compliance
Lightning Source LLC
LaVergne TN
LVHW081341300926
849161LV00008B/2044